Change
and
Tradition

Cultural and Historical Perspectives

Change and Tradition Faculty
Butler University

KENDALL/HUNT PUBLISHING COMPANY
4050 Westmark Drive   Dubuque, Iowa 52002

All readings have been selected by the Change and Tradition faculty, John Cornell, coordinator. Introductions written by Change and Tradition staff members are followed by the writer's names. Introductions that appear without attributions are taken from the publications in which the selections originally appeared.

Butler University
4600 Sunset Avenue
Indianapolis, Indiana 46208

Printed in the United States of America
10 9 8 7 6 5 4 3 2

Contents

Revolutionary France

Victorian England

Fifth Century Athens

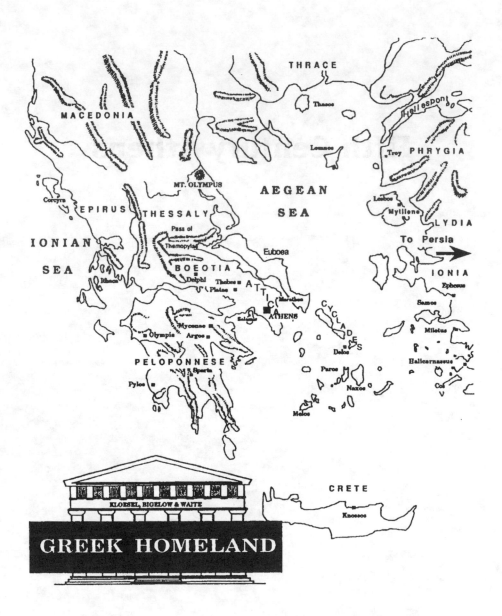

THRACE

MACEDONIA

MT. OLYMPUS

Corcyra

EPIRUS

THESSALY

IONIAN

SEA

Pass of
Thermopylae

BOEOTIA

Delphi   Thebes

Plataea

Ithaca

Mycenae

Olympia   Argos

PELOPONNESE

Sparta

Pylos

AEGEAN

SEA

Thasos

Lemnos

Troy   PHRYGIA

Lesbos

Mytilene

LYDIA

To Persia

IONIA

Ephesus

Samos

Miletus

Halicarnassus

Cos

Euboea

ATTICA

Marathon

Salamis   ATHENS

C
Y
C
L
A
D
E
S

Delos

Paros

Naxos

Melos

Hellespont

CRETE

Knossos

KLOESEL, BIGELOW & WAITE

GREEK HOMELAND

From The Iliad

Homer

Homer is thought to have been a singer of awesome talent who composed the *Iliad* and the *Odyssey* more or less as we have them today, bringing to culmination a tradition of singing which must have stretched from the time of the Trojan War (c. 1200 B.C.) to his own time (c. 700 B.C.). It seems that Homer's gifts brought about the downfall of his own tradition, for after the *Iliad* and *Odyssey* were written down, memorization became the rule, and singers lost the ability to improvise a fresh song with each performance.

The first three words of the *Iliad* are "wrath, sing, goddess," which give us a lot of information.

Wrath. This is a story not about the life of Achilles nor about the Trojan War, but about the wrath of Achilles. In fact, the *Iliad* is a perfectly told tale of wrath. We see the birth of the wrath in Book I. After that there is the maintenance of the wrath, when Agamemnon offers Briseis back along with other gifts, but Achilles refuses. Then we see the false death of the wrath, when Achilles' wrath against Agamemnon is dropped, swallowed by the enormous wrath he feels at the death of his friend Patroclus and his desire to "get back" by killing Trojans. Finally we see the true death of wrath, when Priam, king of Troy, sneaks into Achilles' tent to buy back the dead body of his son, and Achilles treats him with compassion.

Sing. The *Iliad* is a song, not a book. It was originally developed as part of an oral tradition.

Goddess. Homer did not conceive of himself as author. As the gods stand behind human action in the *Iliad,* so Homer felt the Muse inspiring his song.

A note about the translation:

Homer's Greek is, as Matthew Arnold noted: (1) rapid, (2) plain and direct in thought and expression, (3) plain and direct in substance, and (4) noble. In this translation some simplifications preserve Homer's rapidity.

- Omission of some obscure names and places.

- Use of common words for obscure ones, for example, "The Greeks" for "the Achaeans," "the Danaans," and "the Argives"—Homer's three words for the Greeks. There was no country called Greece in ancient times. The identity of the Greeks came from their speaking a common language.
- Identification of the person or god when it seems helpful. For example, "Agamemnon, son of Atreus" where the Greek has merely "son of Atreus" or "the maiden Chryseis" rather than "Chryseis" to remind you who she is. This is faithful to the spirit if not the letter of the Greek. The Greeks always knew instantly who was being mentioned, and so should you. This material was not *hard* for them.
- Identification of the doer or speaker, where a bare translation of the Greek might leave you wondering. (For example, "So Zeus spoke," rather than "so he spoke.')
- Omission of connectives. It came naturally to the Greeks always to use connecting words (especially de = and/but); it comes just as naturally to us to omit them.
- Paragraphing and titling, done for clarity and ease of remembrance.
- For help with names of people or gods who appear in the text, refer to the glossary at the end of this excerpt.

Paula Saffire

Book I

Opening

Wrath, goddess—sing me the wrath of Achilles,
the murderous wrath, which heaped ten thousand pains on the Greeks,
and sent many mighty souls to Hades, souls of heroes—
but the men themselves were left for dogs to scavenge,
for vultures to feast on. And the will of Zeus was accomplished.   5
This it was that first began the quarrel,
when Agamemnon and Achilles stood apart in strife.

Agamemnon and Chryses

Who of the gods set the two to fight? It was Apollo,
son of Zeus and Leto. Angered at Agamemnon, he sent plague
to rage among the Greeks. And soldiers were dying—   10
all because Agamemnon treated Chryses without honor.
This man, priest of Apollo, came to the Greeks' swift ships
to ransom his daughter. He brought countless gifts,
carrying woollen strips sacred to Far-Shooting Apollo,
wound round a golden staff. He begged the Greeks,   15
especially the two generals, Agamemnon and Menelaus:
"You two, sons of Atreus, and you other well-armored Greeks,

4

may the gods who dwell in Olympus grant you
the sack of Priam's city, Troy, and a safe return home.
Release my dear daughter, and take these gifts in return,   20
honoring Apollo the Far Shooter, the son of Zeus."

Then the other Greeks voiced agreement—
to honor the priest and take the shining gifts.
But this did not please the spirit of Agamemnon,
who dismissed the man brusquely with harsh words: 25
"Old man, don't let me find you by the ships—
don't linger now and don't come back later—
or you may find your wool and staff cannot protect you.
I'll not give her back. Sooner will she grow old
in my house in Argos far from her homeland,   30
working at the loom and coming to my bed.
Go—don't make me angry—if you want to be safe."

Thus he spoke. And the old man was frightened and obeyed.
Silently he went to the shore of the foam-furling sea,
Then, moving far off, the old man Chryses prayed   35
to Lord Apollo, born of Fair-Haired Leto.
"Hear me, Lord of the Silver Bow, you who guard my town,
who rule with power over the holy precincts of my land,
if what I sacrificed in your temple was pleasing to you,
if ever I burned for you the rich fat of thigh bones   40
of bulls or of goats, grant my deep desire:
make the Greeks pay for my tears with your arrows."

Thus he spoke in prayer. And Bright-Shining Apollo heard him.
Down he came from the peaks of Olympus, angry at heart,
with a bow on his shoulders and a quiver full of arrows.   45
And the arrows whirred as he shot from the shoulder
in anger. He went unseen, like the night.
He was far from the ships, but his arrows went near.
And a fearful whirring sound came from his silver bow.
First he struck the mules and the sleek dogs.   50
Then he hit them, the men, hurling his sharp-tipped arrows.
And funeral pyres were burning day and night.

Achilles and Agamemnon
For nine days Apollo ranged with his arrows.
On the tenth Achilles called the army to assembly.

(It was Hera, White-Armed goddess, who gave him the idea.   55
She cared about the Greeks, and saw they were dying.)
When they were gathered and called to order
swift-footed Achilles stood up and addressed them:
"Generals, sons of Atreus, it seems we're cut off
from our homecoming. We'll be lucky just to avoid death.   60
For war and plague together are our downfall.
Come now, let us consult a seer or priest
or even a dream-interpreter, since Zeus sends waking dreams,
someone to tell us why Bright-Shining Apollo so rages.
Does he find fault with our vows, or with our hecatombs?[1]   65
Does someone need to gather sheep or unblemished goats
and offer them on the altar to ward off this plague?"

Thus Achilles spoke, and sat down. Then Calchas stood up,
by far the best of those who understand bird signs.
He knew what is and what will be and what has been before.   70
And he it was who led the ships of the Greeks to Troy,
through his own skill in prophecy, gift of Bright-Shining Apollo.
With good intentions toward them all he spoke in assembly:
"Oh Achilles, you ask me to tell the tale
of the wrath of Apollo, Lord of Hundredfold Arrows.   75
Very well, I shall speak. But you take heed and promise,
on your oath, to be my champion and protect me.
For I think a certain man will be enraged, a man who has
the greatest power among the Greeks, a man whom all obey.
For a king has power when angry with a man of lower rank.   80
Even if he swallows down his anger for the day,
yet he will keep it for later times, until he fulfills
what is in his spirit. Promise you will keep me safe."

Then in response swift-footed Achilles spoke:
"Take courage, Calchas. Say any prophecy you know.   85
For by Apollo—who is dear to Zeus, and to whom you pray
when you reveal divine messages to the Greeks—
no one, while I am alive and see the light of day on earth,
will bear a heavy hand against you near the hollow ships,
when you reveal divine messages to the Greeks—
no one of all our men, not even if you mean Agamemnon,   90
who now can boast to be the greatest of the Greeks.

---

1   A hecatomb is a large sacrifice, originally of 100 oxen.

Then the skilled prophet took courage and spoke up:
"Apollo finds no fault with our vows or hecatombs.
It is because of the priest whom Agamemnon dishonored,
not releasing his daughter and taking his gifts. This is why   95
Far-Shooting Apollo has given us pains, and will go on giving.
Never will he ward off grievous plague from the Greeks,
not until the ox-eyed maiden is given back to her father,
with no gifts in return, and Chryses, in his mighty force,
has made a holy hecatomb. Only that will appease the god."   100

Having spoken, he sat down. Then another stood up—
the hero Agamemnon, son of Atreus, who ruled over many.
He was upset, in black spirits, filled with energy,
and his two eyes gleamed like fire.
With an evil look he spoke to Calchas first of all: 105
"Seer of evils, your message has yet to be good.
Always you hold it dear in your spirit to prophesy evils.
The good you never speak nor bring to achievement.

And now you speak in public, prophesying to the Greeks
that Far-Shooting Apollo works out pains for us because of this: 110
because I would not accept the shining gifts
which Chryses offered for his daughter, since my wish
is to have her in my home. I *do* prefer her to Clytamnestra, _Agamemnon's wife_
my lawful wife; for the girl is not inferior to her,
not in body or features, nor in wits or skill.   115
Still, I am willing to give her back, if this is better.
I would rather that my men be saved than that they perish.
But let some honor-gift be straightway made ready for me,
lest I be the only Greek without one—which is not fitting.
All of you, see to it. Find me an honor-gift from elsewhere."   120

Then swift-footed Achilles spoke in reply:
"Renowned son of Atreus, greediest for gain of all,
how can the great-hearted Greeks give you an honor-gift?
We don't have great stores of gifts lying around.
What we won by sacking cities has been divided up.   125
It is not fitting to collect the gifts again and redistribute.
But you now, let the girl go for the sake of the god.
The Greeks will pay you back tripled, quadrupled,
if ever Zeus grants us the capture of fair-walled Troy."

7

Then in response spoke powerful Agamemnon: 130
"Not like this, godlike Achilles, don't try to cloud my wits,
great as you are. You'll not outdo me, you'll not persuade me.
Do you want to see me lacking, while you yourself still have
an honor-gift, and so you bid me give her back?
If the great-hearted Greeks will give me an honor-gift, 135
choosing one that suits me, then there will be a balance.
But if they will not, then I myself will take one.
Maybe it will be yours, or maybe Ajax's honor-gift,
or maybe Odysseus'. Whoever's I take, he will be angry.
But come, let us consider these things some other time. 140
As for now, let us pull the black ship into the bright salt sea
and gather rowers as needed, and let us make a hecatomb,
bringing on board the fair-cheeked daughter of Chryses.
And let one man lead and be in charge,
either Ajax or Idomeneus or bright Odysseus, 145
or you, Achilles, who strike all men with awe—
a man who will make sacrifice and appease Far-Working Apollo."

Swift-footed Achilles looked up from under his eyebrows and spoke:
"You greedy-hearted man, cloaked in shamelessness,
how could you persuade any Greek with spirit 150
to go on a journey or to fight men by force in battle?
It was not on account of the Trojan spearmen that I came here
to do battle, for they never gave me any cause for blame.
They never drove away my horses or my cattle;
they never came to my land, fertile Phthia, nurse of heroes, 155
and ravaged my crops. For between their land and mine
are shady mountains and a sounding sea. It was for you,
shameless man, that we followed, so you could rejoice
and win honor; for you, dog-face, and your brother Menelaus,
we came to Troy. But you don't value this or care. 160
And now you threaten me, you'd dare to take my honor-gift,
for which I worked hard, and which the Greeks gave me.
My honor-gift cannot equal yours when in time
the Greeks sack Troy, city of fair dwellings.
The greater part of the rush of warfare is done by *my* hands. 165
But when it comes to distribution, it's *you* who'll get
the greater honor-gift. Little as it is, mine's dear to me.
I'll keep it. I'm going to my ships. I'm sick of making war.
I'm going home, to Phthia; that's the better course— 170
to go back with my beak-prowed ships. I won't stay here

dishonored, amassing property and wealth for you."

Then Agamemnon, king of men, spoke in response:
"Run away then, if that's what your spirit urges, I'll not
beg you to stay here on account of me. I've got others
who will honor me, especially Zeus, skilled in planning.   175
You are most hateful to me of god-nourished kings.
For always strife is dear to you, wars and battles.
If you are the stronger, the god has given you this gift.
Go home, with your ships and your comrades,
rule over the locals. I won't waste any grief on you,   180
nor do I take heed of your anger. This is my threat:
just as Bright-Shining Apollo has stripped the girl from me—
and I *will* send her, in my ship with my comrades—so I will take
your fair-cheeked girl, Briseis. I'll come myself
to your ship and take your honor-gift, so you will know   185
how much more powerful I am than you. And others will learn
not to dare to make themselves my equal face-to-face."

He spoke, and a burden came on Achilles. His heart was divided
in his thick-haired chest as he pondered these things:
whether he should draw the sharp sword from his thigh   190
and drive the others away, then kill Agamemnon,
or whether he should stop his anger, hold his spirit in check.

Athena Appears
While he was pondering these things in his spirit and his heart,
and while he was drawing the great sword from its sheath,
Athena came down from heaven, sent by White-Armed Hera,   195
who in her spirit loved and cared for both men.
Athena stood behind and took hold of Achilles by his blond hair,
appearing to him only, for the others did not see.
Achilles was dumbfounded. He turned around and knew at once:
this was Pallas Athena. And her two eyes gleamed fearfully.   200

Addressing her, he spoke forth winged words.
"Why now, child of Zeus, Aegis-Holder,[2] why have you come?
So that you may see the insult of Agamemnon, son of Atreus?

---

2 Aegis: a scary object, perhaps a normal shield with a scary image, perhaps a
   lightning bolt. (Zeus held it but often let Athena carry it.)

9

But to you I shall say this, and I think it will be accomplished:
for his acts of insolence he will soon lose his life."   205

Then again Athena, owl-eyed goddess, spoke:
"I came to stop your energy, if you will listen.
From heaven I came, sent by White-Armed Hera,
who in her spirit loves and cares for you both.
Come, leave off your strife, take your hand off your sword.   210
Insult him as you wish in words, and it will come to pass.
I shall say this, and it will be a thing accomplished:
Someday you will receive three times as many shining gifts
on account of this insult. But hold off, and listen to me."

Then swift-footed Achilles spoke in response.   215
"I must obey the word, goddess, which comes from the two of you,
though my spirit is enraged. This way is better.
Whoever listens to the gods, the gods also hear him."
He spoke and with his strong hand on the silver handle
put back the mighty sword into its sheath. He paid heed   220
to Athena's words. And she went back to Olympus,
to be with the other gods in the home of Aegis-Holding Zeus.

Achilles, Nestor, and Agamemnon
And Achilles once again with harsh words
addressed Agamemnon, and did not cease from his rage:
"You drunkard, with the face of a dog and the heart of a deer,   225
you've never dared to gird yourself for battle
with the rest, nor to lay an ambush with the Greek chiefs.
Your heart knows only this: to range up and down
the ranks of the Greeks, stripping others of their gifts
if anyone should speak face-to-face with you.   230

"You devourer of the people, you must rule over nobodies,
or else, I swear, this would have been your last outrage.
But I shall speak out and take a great oath. By this staff—
which never again can bear leaves or branches
since it was first cut from its stump in the mountains;   235
nor will it bloom again, once the copper axe has peeled
its bark and its leaves; and now in turn the Greeks carry it
in their hands, administering justice, as they uphold
the decrees of Zeus—this shall be my great oath: I swear,
one day longing for Achilles will come to the Greeks,   240

10

to all of them. And you won't be able to ward off the Trojans,
for all your grief, while many fall dying, under the stroke
of man-slaughtering Hector. And anger will tear your heart,
because you did no honor to the best of the Greeks."

So spoke Achilles, and threw to the ground the staff   245
studded with nails of gold. And he himself sat down.
Now Agamemnon, too, was filled with wrath. So Nestor sprang up,
a gifted speaker, well-versed in pleasing words,
and from his tongue flowed a voice sweeter than honey.
Already two generations of mortal men had taken birth   250
in his time in holy Pylos, had grown up there,
and perished; and now over the third he was ruling.
Meaning well he spoke to them and said these words:

"Oh my, surely a great grief comes to the land of the Greeks.
Surely Priam and the children of Priam may be glad   255
and the other Trojans may greatly rejoice in their spirit
if they were to learn how you are wrangling, the two of you,
superb among the Greeks at planning, superb at fighting.
Listen to what I say. For you are both younger than me.

"Once I contended with men who were better than you,   260
and they never treated me with disrespect.
Never have I seen such men nor will I see them—
men like Peirithous and Dryas, shepherd of the people,
men like Kaineus, Exadius, and godlike Polyphemus,
and Aegeus' son Theseus, who resembled the gods.   265
Those men grew up as the strongest men on earth.
Strongest they were, and with the strongest they fought,
with wild mountain creatures, and dealt them awesome destruction.
And I contended alongside these men, having left Pylos,
far away from my far-off land—for they themselves had summoned
    me.   270
And I fought by myself, single-handed. And with those men
not one of the mortal men who are now on earth could fight.
And they took heed of my advice and listened to what I said.
So you, too, listen to my words; it is better to listen.

"Good man that you are, don't take away his maiden,   275
but let things be, as the Greeks first gave the honor-gift.
As for you, Achilles, do not wish to compete with a king,

11

force against force. For never did a scepter-holding king,
to whom Zeus has given glory, have the same honor for his share.
If you are stronger, then your goddess mother bore you to be so,   280
but he is more powerful, since he rules over more men.
Agamemnon, son of Atreus, you, too, stop exercising your might.
But I implore Achilles to let go of his anger. He is our barrier,
the one who keeps back evil war from all the Greeks."

Then in response spoke powerful Agamemnon.   285
"Yes, old man, what you said has its share of what is proper.
But this one here wants to be above all the others.
He wants to have power over all, to be king over all,
and to call the signals for all; but I think none will listen.
And if the gods who are forever have made him a spearsman   290
does that mean they gave him the right to speak words of blame?"

Then bright Achilles interrupted to reply:
"Well then, I would be called a coward and a nobody
if I were to give in to you: *whatever you say, sir.*
Give your orders to others, don't call the signals   295
for me. For I think I will never listen to you.
And I'll say something else, take this into your heart:
I'll not raise my hand to fight you over the maiden—not you
nor the rest of you, since all who gave her have taken her away.
But as for anything else with me on my black ship,   300
not one thing could you take from me against my will.
And if you try it—let everyone here know this—
in no time your black blood will gush around my spear."

Thus the two did battle of words, force against force,
then stood up, releasing the assembly near the Greek ships.   305

Chyrseis Is Sent/The Army Is Purified/Messengers Are Sent
Achilles went toward his shelters and well-balanced ships,
in the company of Patroclus and his other comrades.
But Agamemnon drew his swift ship forth into the sea,
He picked twenty rowers to put on board, and animals for a hecatomb
to the god. And leading fair-cheeked Chryseis, he let her go.   310
Along with them as leader went quick-thinking Odysseus.
They went on board and sailed the watery ways,
while Agamemnon ordered the people to wash off all pollution.

12

They washed off, throwing all pollution into the salt sea,
then performed for Apollo perfect hecatombs   315
of bulls and goats, on the shore of the barren salt sea.
And the smell of fat rose heavenward in curls of smoke.
The army busied itself with these things.

As for Agamemnon,
he did not forget his hostility and threats to Achilles.
He spoke to both Talthybius and Eurubates,   320
the two of them heralds, nimble in service:
"Go to the shelter of Achilles, son of Peleus,
take fair-cheeked Briseis by the hand, and lead her out.
And if he refuses to give her, I myself will come with more men
and take her—which should just make him shudder more."   325
He spoke and sent them forth, laying on them words of power.

Briseis Is Taken

Against their will they went along the shore of the barren salt sea
and arrived at the ships and shelters of Achilles' men.
They found him sitting near his shelter and black ship,
and Achilles was not glad to see the two of them.   330
They were frightened and felt a sense of shame before a king.
They stood there, saying nothing, asking nothing.
But he understood in his heart and he spoke:

"I greet you, heralds, messengers of Zeus and men.
Come closer. It's not you I blame, but Agamemnon,   335
who has sent you forth for the maiden Briseis.
Well then, god-born Patroclus, lead the maiden out
and give her to them to lead away. These two are my witnesses.
In the name of the blessed gods and mortal men,
in the name of our ruthless king, if ever he needs me   340
to ward off the shameful plague of war from the others,
I swear this is so: His heart boils with destruction,
he knows nothing, he cannot see before him or behind him,
so that the Greeks may fight in safety near their ships."

So he spoke. Patroclus listened to his dear companion,   345
and led out fair-cheeked Briseis from the shelter and gave her
to them to lead away. And the two went back to the Greek ships.
And she, a woman, went with them against her will.

Achilles and Thetis

But Achilles
wept and sat withdrawn, apart from his comrades,
by the shore of the gray salt sea, looking at the endless water.   350
Many times he called on his mother, stretching forth his hands:
"Mother, since you bore me to be short lived, loud-thundering Zeus
of Olympus should grant me honor at least. But not even a little
has he given me. I am dishonored by the wide-ruling son of Atreus,   355
by Agamemnon—who snatched my honor-gift and keeps it for
    himself."

He spoke pouring out tears, and the lady his mother heard him.
Sitting in the depths of the salty water beside her aged father,
quickly she rose from the gray salt sea, like a mist,
and she sat before him as he poured out tears. With her hand   360
she caressed him, and spoke to him, calling out his name:
"Oh child, why do you cry? What suffering has come to your heart?
Tell me—don't keep it hidden in your mind—so we may both know."

And swift-footed Achilles answered her, with deep sighs:
"You know. Why must I tell you, since you know all?   365
We went to the Thebe, sacred city of Eetion,
and sacked it, took everything away,
and the sons of the Greeks made a division of most things.
But Agamemnon chose for himself fair-cheeked Chryseis,
whose father was priest of Far-Shooting Apollo.   370
And Chryses came to the swift ships of the bronze-clad Greeks
to ransom his daughter. He brought countless gifts,
carrying woollen strips sacred to Far-Shooting Apollo,
wound round a golden staff. He begged the Greeks,
especially the two generals, Agamemnon and his brother Menelaus: 375
Then the other Greeks voiced agreement—
to honor the priest and take the shining gifts.
But this did not please the spirit of Agamemnon,
who dismissed the man brusquely with harsh words.
The old man went back in anger, and Apollo heard his prayers;   380
for the man was dear to him. Apollo threw an evil arrow
among the Greeks, and the people were dying, one after another.
In every direction the god's arrows struck,
hitting the great army of the Greeks. And our seer,

14

full of knowledge, told us the meaning of Far-Shooter's signs.   385
And right away I, first of everyone, urged that we appease the god.
Then anger took hold of Agamemnon and standing up at once
he made a threatening speech—now brought to fulfillment.
The one girl is being led to Chryses in a swift ship
by the ever-alert Greeks, along with gifts for the king.   390
As for the other, messengers have just left my shelter
leading away Briseis, whom the sons of the Greeks gave to me.

"But you, if you are able, give your own son protection.
Go to Olympus and beg Zeus, if ever the help you gave him,
in word or in deed, pleased his heart. For many times   395
in the halls of my father I have heard you say in boast
that you warded off the shameful plague of destruction,
from Zeus of the Black Clouds, you alone of the immortal gods,
that time when the other Olympians wanted to tie him up—
Hera and Poseidon and Pallas Athena.   400
But you, goddess, came to him and got him untied,
quickly calling to high Olympus the Hundred-Handed one,
whom gods name Briareus, but men name after his father;
and Briareus was in turn stronger than his father,
and used to sit at Zeus' side, exulting in honor.   405
And the blessed gods, in fear of him, left off tying Zeus.

"So now, sit near him, take his knees, remind him of these things.
See if somehow he might be willing to help the Trojan side,
and hem the Greeks in, between their ships' edge and the salt sea—
as they are being killed. Let them see their profit from this king,   410
and let wide-ruling Agamemnon, son of Atreus, recognize
his own madness—that he did no honor to the best of the Greeks."

Then Thetis spoke in answer, pouring down tears:
"Oh my child, why did I rear you? What an unhappy birth!
If only you could sit beside the ships without weeping and sorrow,   415
since your fate is to be short-lived, and not to last long.
But you have both: misery beyond others, and a life soon to end.[3]
What an evil destiny awaited you when I gave birth in my palace.
I will go myself to snow-capped Olympus, and pass the word to Zeus,
who Delights in Thunder, to see if he might listen.   420

---

3   Apparently Achilles was offered the choice of a long, ordinary life or a short,
    glorious one. Being Achilles, the ultimate hero, he chose the latter.

"As for you, sit near your swift ships and keep your wrath
against the Greeks. Abstain from all fighting.
Yesterday Zeus went to the ocean to feast with the Ethiopians,
excellent men, and the gods all followed along.
On the twelfth day they will come again to Mount Olympus.   425
Then I will cross the bronze threshold of the home of Zeus
and take hold of his knees, and I think he will listen."
Saying this she went off, and left him there
angered in his spirit over the amply-clothed woman,
whom they had taken from him by force, against his will.

Return of Chyrseis/Sacrifice of the Greeks

But Odysseus   430
went to Chryses bringing animals for the holy hecatomb.
And when they came within the very deep harbor,
they took down the sails and stowed them in the black ship,
and took down the mast-ropes and mast, setting them quickly
in place, then rowed the ship in with their oars.   435
They threw out anchor-stones and tied up the ship with a cable.
And out they stepped themselves into the surf of the sea,
and out they brought animals for a hecatomb to Far-Shooting Apollo.
And out came the maiden Chryseis, from the sea-crossing ship.

Then quick-thinking Odysseus led her to the altar   440
and placed her in the arms of her dear father, and spoke:
"Oh Chryses, Agamemnon, king of men, sent me forth
to bring you your child, and perform a holy hecatomb for the Greeks
to Phoebus Apollo, so that we may appease our lordly king,
who has laid many cares on us to make us groan."   445
He said this and put her in his arms. And Chryses in joy
took his dear daughter.

Quickly they set about the holy hecatomb
of animals, one after the other, on the well-built altar.
Then they washed themselves and scattered barley. And among them
Chryses made a mighty prayer, holding up his hands: 450
"Hear me, Lord of the Silver Bow, you who guard my town,
who rule with power over the holy precincts of my land,
Once before it happened that you heard my prayers
and honored me, smiting the great Greek army.
So now, this time too, grant my deep desire: 455
ward off the shameful plague from the Greeks."

16

So he spoke in prayer, and Phoebus Apollo heard.
But when they had prayed and scattered the barley,
they drew back the animals' heads and slaughtered them,
then skinned them and cut off the thigh bones, wrapping them   460
in a double fold of fat, with raw pieces of meat on top.
The old man burned these on a wood skewer, and over the whole
poured fiery wine. And the young men held out five-tined forks.

When they had burned the thigh bones and shared the innards,
they cut the rest into pieces and set them on spits,   465
and roasted them carefully, then took them off
and feasted; and no one's spirit lacked a fair share of food.

When they had put away their desire for eating and drinking,
the young men filled mixing bowls to the brim with wine,   470
then poured wine in every cup, with the first few drops as offering.
The young men appeased the god with music all day long,
singing the Greeks' beautiful Apollo-hymn, chanting
for the Far-Worker. And he heard it, delighted in his heart.

And when the sun went down and twilight came,   475
the men went to sleep next to the cables of their ship.

When the newborn Dawn appeared with rosy fingertips,
they set out to sea, to rejoin the great army of the Greeks.
And Apollo Far-Worker sent them a favoring wind as escort.
They set up the mast and hoisted the white sails,   480
and the wind blew into mid-sail. At the rear a surging wave
roared loudly as the ship cut her way through,
breasting the waves, pressing forward on the journey.

When they got to the great army of the Greeks,
the men drew the black ship up on shore,   485
on mounds of sand, with long timbers as support.
And they themselves scattered to their shelters and their ships.

As for swift-footed Achilles, god-born son of Peleus,
he sat raging, near his swift-sailing ships.
He would not go to assembly where men win glory,   490
he would not go to battle. His heart was wasting away
as he stayed back, longing for war cries and battle.

Zeus and Thetis

But when there came the twelfth dawn after this,
the everlasting gods returned to Olympus in a group,
Zeus leading. Thetis did not forget her own son's request.   495
Up she went, early in the morn, from the swelling sea
and came to great heaven and Mount Olympus.
She found Far-Seeing Zeus, Son of Cronus, apart from others,
sitting on the highest peak of many-ridged Olympus.
She sat down before him and took hold of his knees[4]   500
with her left hand; with her right, she touched his chin,
and in entreaty spoke to Zeus the King, Son of Cronus.
"Father Zeus, if ever I helped you among the immortal gods,
either in word or deed, grant me my desire:
Honor my son, who is the shortest-lived of all.   505
As it is, Agamemnon, the king of men, has dishonored him.
He took his honor-gift, keeps it himself. He stripped him.
But you, Olympian Zeus, Counselor, honor him.
Give the power to the Trojans for however long it takes
to make the Greeks honor my son and magnify his claims."   510

Thus she spoke. But Cloud-Gathering Zeus did not answer.
He sat in silence. Thetis, once she had taken his knees,
held on as if grafted to them, and spoke a second time:
"Promise me truly, and give it your nod,
or say no—you've nothing to fear—so that I may learn   515
just how dishonored I am among the gods."

Then Cloud-Gathering Zeus responded in distress:
"These are deadly doings when you urge what will bring conflict
between Hera and me. As it is, she lashes me with blaming words,
and among the immortal gods, always quarrels with me.   520
Her complaint is that I help the Trojans in their battle.
Be going now, lest Hera notice anything.
I will take care that these things come to pass.
Come! I'll nod my head, so you will be persuaded.
This is my greatest pledge among the immortals.   525
It can't be taken back, it can't be false,
it can't go unfulfilled, if ever I should nod my head."

---

4   This was the official posture for making a prayerful request, both of a person and
     a god.

18

The Son of Cronus spoke, and nodded with blue-black eyebrows.
And from the head of the immortal king an ambrosial mane
showered all around, which made Olympus tremble.   530

So the two made their plans, then separated. Thetis leapt
into the deep salt sea from shining Olympus,
while Zeus went to his home.

Zeus, Hera, and Hephaestus
And all the gods stood up
from their seats to face their father. No one dared
to stay in place as Zeus approached, but all stood facing him.   535
Then Zeus sat down on his throne. But Hera did not fail
to notice how he had been in a joint planning session
with Silver-Sandaled Thetis, born of the Old Man of the Sea.
At once she spoke to Zeus, son of Cronus, with heartbiting words:

"Which of the gods, you crafty schemer, was making plans with you?   540
Whenever you're away from me, you always like to think up secrets
and decide on them. But never have you had the heart
to come forth and tell me openly what you intend."

Then the Father of Gods and Men answered her:
"Hera, don't think you can know all the things I say.   545
Some of them will be hard for you, wife though you are.
Whatever is right and fit for you to hear,
no other god or man will know before you.
But when I want to make some plan apart from the gods,
stop investigating, don't inquire over every little thing."   550

Then Ox-Eyed mistress Hera spoke in response:
"Most terrible one, son of Cronus, what are you talking about?
I have not investigated before, nor made too many inquiries.
But suit yourself, think anything you want. Right now
a terrible fear has come upon me: you've been won over   555
by Silver-Sandaled Thetis, born of the Old Man of the Sea.
Early in the morn she sat near you and took hold of your knees.
And I think you gave her the nod, that truly you would honor
Achilles, and you would kill many Greeks near their ships."

Then Cloud-Gathering Zeus spoke in response: 560
"Dear goddess, you always suspect, I can do nothing unnoticed.
Still, you won't get your way, unless it is to fall

19

from my favor—which should just make you shudder more.
Suppose you're right: then that's the way I want it.
So sit quietly, and listen to what I say. 565
For all the gods in Olympus won't be able to help you
if I come near and lay my unconquerable hands on you."

Thus he spoke, and ox-eyed mistress Hera was afraid.
She sat quietly, forcing her heart to bend in submission.
And throughout Zeus' home, the gods were in distress. 570
Hephaestus, the Famed Craftsman, began to speak among them,
wishing to do kind service to White-Armed Hera,
his dear mother: "These will be deadly deeds, unbearable,
if on account of mortals the two of you quarrel so,
and start a brawl among the gods. We'll lose our pleasure 575
in the feast, since worse matters will prevail.
Mother, I'll give some advice you already understand:
do kind service to dear Father Zeus, so that not again
will he quarrel and cause upheaval at our feast.
For what if the Olympian Sender of Lightning should wish 580
to hurl us from our seats? He is by far the strongest.
Address him, then, with soothing words, and right away
Zeus the Olympian will be gracious to us."

Thus he spoke, and rushed up with a two-handled cup
to his dear mother. He handed it to her and spoke: 585
"Take heart, mother, and bear up amid your troubles.
I would not want these eyes of mine to see you struck,
for you are dear to me. I could not help, for all my grief.
For no one is able to oppose Olympian Zeus. One other time
I hoped to ward him off from you: he seized me 590
by the foot and threw me from the divine threshold.
All the day I dropped. Then, when the sun was setting,
I fell onto the isle of Lemnos, with little life left in me.
There some Lemnians took care of me after my fall."

Thus he spoke, and White-Armed Hera smiled, 595
and with that smile reached to take the cup from her son.
But Hephaestus went among the gods, beginning from the left,
drawing sweet nectar from a mixing bowl and pouring it like wine.
Then laughter unquenchable arose among the immortal gods,
when they saw him hustling and bustling around the palace. 600

20

Thus then the whole day long, right up to sunset,
they feasted; and no one's spirit lacked a fair share of food,
nor was there lack of beauteous lyre, which Apollo held,
nor of the Muses, who took turns singing in a beautiful voice.

But when the shining light of the sun went down   605
then they went home to lie down, each one to the place
where Famous Hephaestus, Lame in both Limbs,
had made a dwelling with his ready skills.
And Olympian Zeus, the Sender of Lightning, went to his own bed,
where he used to lie when sweet sleep came upon him.   610
Going up, he went to sleep, with Gold-Throned Hera at his side.

Book VI

Greeks and Trojans are battling. Hector, commander of the Trojans and son of the King and Queen of Troy, has gone back to the city to have his mother offer a sacrifice. He then speaks with his brother Paris (whom Homer calls Alexandros) and Helen. Then he goes on to look for his wife, Andromache.

Hector and Andromache = man ⫶ wife

Not finding his faultless wife inside,
Hector stood on the threshold and spoke to the maids: 375
"Where did white-armed Andromache go when she left the halls?
Tell me truly, maids, without error. Did she to go
to meet my brothers or well-clothed sisters?
Or did she go with the other long-haired Trojan women,
to Athena's temple, to appease the grim goddess?"   380

Then in turn a trusty housekeeper spoke to him:
"Hector, since you have asked for the truth, she did not go
to meet your brothers or well-clothed sisters,
nor did she go with the other long-haired Trojan women,
to Athena's temple, to appease the grim goddess.   385
But she went to the great tower of Troy when she heard
that the Trojans were worn out, while Greek strength was great.
Hurrying, she went toward the wall like one raving,
while a nurse went along carrying the child."

So spoke the trusty housekeeper. Hector rushed from his home   390
and retraced his steps over the well-built streets.
He went through the great city and came to the western gates,

the exit which led out to the plains.
There Andromache came running to meet him,
his well-dowered wife, daughter of great-hearted Eetion,   395
Eetion, who dwelt in a woodland area near Thebe,
and who was king over the Cilician men. It was his daughter,
Andromache, who belonged to bronze-helmeted Hector.

She stood across from him; and a maidservant went with her,
holding to her bosom the child, still an innocent baby,   400
Hector's dear son, like a beautiful star in his shining.
Hector called him Scamander, after the river; others Astyanax,
meaning City-King—since Hector alone was protector of Troy.
Seeing his son, Hector gave a silent smile,
while Andromache stood nearby pouring out tears.   405

She clung to Hector as if grafted, called out and spoke to him:
"Amazing man, your strength will kill you. You have no pity
for your little infant, nor for ill-fated me, who will soon
be your widow. For soon all the Greeks will kill you
in their onslaught. And it would be better for me,   410
once I have lost you, to enter the earth. For there will be
no more comfort, once you have met your doom—
only pains.
          I do not have a father or mistress mother
For bright Achilles killed my father and sacked
the Cilicians' city of fair dwellings, high-towered Thebe.   415
He killed Eetion. He did not strip him
of his armor, but keeping some reverence in his spirit,
he cremated him along with his intricate armor
and heaped up a tomb over him. And around that tomb
the mountain nymphs, maidens of aegis-holding Zeus,   420
caused elm trees to grow. I had seven brothers
in the palace. They all went down to Hades in a single day.
Swift-footed, bright Achilles slew them all
as they tended their shambling oxen and shining sheep.
As for my mother, once queen of her woodland kingdom,   425
after bringing her here along with the rest of his booty,
Achilles let her go, for a ransom of countless gifts.
In her father's halls Artemis dealt her a death-arrow.

Hector, you are my father and mistress mother,
you are also my brother, and my flourishing husband.   430

Come now, take pity, and stay here at the tower.
Don't make your child an orphan, your wife a widow.
Station the people near the wild fig tree, where the city
is most easily entered and the walls may be scaled.
Three times the best Greeks have attacked at this spot,   435
with both Ajaxes in the lead and far-famed Idomeneus,
or with Agamemnon and Menelaus, and Diomedes, Tydeus' mighty son.
Perhaps someone who knew oracles gave them this advice,
or perhaps their spirit commands this and urges them on."

Then in turn great Hector of the flashing helmet spoke to her: 440
"These things mean much to me, lady. But I am ashamed,
most terribly, before Troy's men and long-robed women
if I shrink back, far from battle, like a coward. My spirit
does not allow me to do this, for I've learned to be valiant
always and to fight in the forefront of the Trojans,   445
winning great glory for my father and also for myself.
For I know this well in my heart and my spirit:
the day will come when sacred Troy will perish,
and Priam, and the people of Priam of the great ash spear.

"But I do not care as much about the grief that will come   450
to the Trojans, nor to Hecuba herself nor to king Priam,
nor to my brothers, many and valiant, who will fall
in the dust at their enemies' hands, as I care about the grief
that will come to you, when one of the bronze-clad Greeks
will lead you off in tears, taking away the day of your freedom.   455
Perhaps you will be in Argos drawing water from a spring
or weaving at someone else's loom, greatly against your will,
as strong necessity bears down on you.

"And someone someday, seeing you pour down a tear, might say:
'This was the wife of Hector, who was best in battle   460
of the horse-taming Trojans when they fought for Troy.'
Someone someday will say this. And fresh grief will come to you
to feel the loss of such a man, one to ward off your day of slavery.
As for me, may a heaped-up mound of earth hide me, dead,
before I hear your shouts and learn they've dragged you away."   465

Thus he spoke. And radiant Hector reached out for his child.
But the child shrank back, with screams, to the breast
of his amply-clothed nurse, upset by the sight of his father,

terrified at the bronze and at the horse-haired crest
which he perceived at the top of the helmet, nodding dreadfully.   470
Then his dear father gave a laugh, and also his mistress mother.
And at once radiant Hector took the helmet off his head
and put it down, all gleaming, on the ground.
Then, when he had kissed his dear son and tossed him in his arms,
he spoke in prayer to Zeus and all the other gods: 475
"Zeus and all the other gods, grant that this child, my son,
may be as I am—highly visible among the Trojans,
good in fighting force, and ruling with vigor over Troy.
And may someone someday say, as he comes back from war,
'This one is far better than his father.' May he kill the enemy   480
and win bloody spoils, bringing joy to the heart of his mother."

Thus he spoke. And he put his child in the arms of his wedded wife.
She took him to her fragrant breast and gave a tearful laugh.
And her husband felt pity perceiving this,
and stroked her with his hand and called out and spoke to her: 485
"Amazing woman, do not grieve for me overmuch in your spirit.
No one will hurl me to Hades before my destined decree.
As for fate, I say that no one yet has fled it,
not the coward, not the valiant, once it begins to unwind.
But go home and take care of your own work,   490
the loom and the spindle, and tell the serving women
to tend to their work. War is for the men,
for me especially, and for all who were born in Troy."

So speaking radiant Hector took up up his helmet
with its horse-hair plume. His dear wife turned homeward,   495
but kept looking back, and her cheeks bloomed with tears.
Swiftly she came to the fair dwellings which were the home
of manslaughtering Hector, and there she came upon
many serving women, and she led them in the mourning wail.
In his own house they wailed for Hector while he was yet alive.   500
For they did not expect to see him return,
escaping the strength and hands of the Greeks.

Glossary to The Iliad

THE GREEKS

Achilles—Son of Peleus and Thetis, Achilles is half-divine and the greatest fighter on the Greek side. Near the end of the epic, he kills Hector, the greatest Trojan fighter.

Agamemnon—Chief leader of the Greeks, King of Mycene, brother of Menelaus, from whom Paris stole Helen.

Ajax—There were two Ajaxes among the Greeks. Ajax the Greater was King of Salamis, a big man who was second only to Achilles in strength and bravery. He later fought Hector and rescued the body of Achilles from the Trojans. Ajax the Lesser was a small man who was King of Locris. He held his own among the other heroes but was boastful, arrogant, and quarrelsome.

Briseis—After battle, the victorious side would take everything of value—including women—from the enemy and distribute the spoils among the fighters, the best spoils going to the bravest and most successful warriors. Achilles had been awarded the lovely Briseis as a battle prize.

Calchas—Soothsayer who could foretell the future and interpret the reason for events.

Clytamnestra—Wife of Agamemnon and sister of Helen. Greeks listening to the *Iliad* would have been aware of the bloody tale of Clytamnestra who was overcome with jealousy and anger when her husband brought captive women home from the war with Troy.

Idomeneus—Lord of Crete, Greek warrior.

Menelaus—King of Sparta, brother of Agamemnon, first husband of Helen. By the fifth century B.C. Sparta and Athens are great rivals, but in the *Iliad* Athens is only a small city, of no particular importance.

Nestor—King of Pylos, Nestor had been a great warrior in his youth. He is most important in the *Iliad* as a counselor who remembers the past and its traditions.

Odysseus—King of Ithaca and a Greek leader noted for his intelligence and cunning. The ruse of the Trojan Horse is Odysseus' idea, and he is the central figure in Homer's *Odyssey,* the story of a ten-year homeward journey following the Trojan War.

Patroclus—Greek warrior, cousin and closest companion of Achilles.

THE TROJANS

Andromache—wife of Hector who pleads with him to stay away from the fighting.

Astyanax—infant son of Hector and Andromache.

Chryseis—From a town south of the Trojan region, this daughter of Chryses was awarded by the Greeks to Agamemnon as a battle prize ("honor gift"), an action which angered Apollo.

Chryses—Priest of Apollo and father of Chryseis who pleaded with the Greeks for her return.

Hecuba—Priam's wife, who leads the Trojan women in their sacrifice to Athena.

Hector—Son of Priam, field commander of the Trojans and their greatest fighter, he is killed by Achilleus in Book XXII.

Helen—So beautiful is Helen that her father, Tyndareus, requires from all the princes of Greece an oath of mutual assistance should anyone steal her from Menelaus. That is why the theft of Helen involves all of Greece. Helen is sister of Clytemnestra, Agamemnon's wife.

Paris (Alexandros)—Younger son of Priam, second husband of Helen. The story known as "The Judgment of Paris" helps explain the Trojan War: on Mount Olympus the goddesses Hera, Athena, and Aphrodite all claim the title of most beautiful. Forced to choose among them, Paris takes the most tempting bribe, Aphrodite's offer to give him as his wife the most beautiful of mortal women—Helen. Thus, Athena and Hera support the Greeks, while Aphrodite supports the Trojans.

Priam—King of Troy, father of Hector, Paris, and others (50 sons and 12 daughters). Priam is old at the time of the *Iliad* and he does not join in the fighting.

GODS & GODDESSES

Apollo—God of healing, archery, music, and prophecy. Chryses was his priest.

Athena—Goddess of wisdom, she is on the side of the Greeks.

Hephaestus—Blacksmith to the gods, only he among the Olympians is physically defective. Thetis saved his life when Hera cast him from Mount Olympus.

Hera—Wife of Zeus and supporter of the Greeks.

Thetis—a nereid (sea nymph), given by the gods in marriage to the mortal Peleus, and by him mother of Achilles.

Zeus—Son of Cronos, King of the Olympian gods. Zeus' job is to keep peace among the gods who quarrel about the Trojan War, but even he must bow to Fate or Destiny, which has decreed that Troy must fall.

Poetry of Sappho

Sappho sang her poems on the island of Lesbos in the 600s B.C. She is said to have been the first poet to make love her main theme. The Greeks admired her poetry greatly; Plato called her "the Tenth Muse." As an ancient comment goes, her poems are "few, but roses."

Only a small fraction of Sappho's poetry survives. (There is always hope that new poems will turn up in the sands of Egypt.) No long poem survives whole, except for "Prayer to Aphrodite." Dots in a poem show where words are missing. There are no titles in the Greek.

Paula Saffire

1. Prayer to Aphrodite

Immortal Aphrodite of the rich-wrought throne,   1
child of Zeus, trap-weaver, I implore you—
not with sorrows, not with your frenzies, mistress,
                break not my spirit.

But come here, if ever in times before,   4
marking my voice from far off,
you heard; and leaving your father's home
                of gold[1], you came

with chariot yoked. Sparrows, swift and beautiful,   7
drew you over the dark earth
with a thick wing-beat, down from heaven
                through mid-air.

Translated by Paula Saffire. Copyright © 1993 by Paula Saffire. Reprinted by permission.

1   The Greek is ambiguous. "Of gold" could describe the father's home on Olympus, or the chariot. And, of course, Aphrodite was known as "the golden goddess." There is just the possibility that gold refers neither to home nor chariot, but to the coming—"you came a golden coming."

Suddenly they came and you, blessed one,   10
with a smile on your immortal face,
you asked *what now* I was suffering and *what now*[2]
                    I was calling for,

and *what* it was I most wanted to have   13
in my raving heart. "Whom *now* shall I persuade
to join you in friendship? Who is it, Sappho,
                    who does you wrong?"

"For the one who flees, soon will pursue.   16
And the one who refuses gifts soon will give them.
And the one who doesn't love soon will love,
                    even against her[3] will."

Now, too, come to me, and release me   19
from hard cares, and bring to pass
whatever my heart desires. And you yourself,
                    be my ally in battle.[4]

2. Invitation to the Goddess[5]

Come to me from the isle of Crete.   1
Here is your sacred temple,
here your lovely apple groves, where your altars
                    are smoking with frankincense.

---

2   Italics show the repetition, unmistakable in Greek, of *hoti* = "what" or "why" and
    deute = "again." Aphrodite's tone seems to be one of amused, even affectionate,
    exasperation.

3   Notice how the gender is ambiguous until the very end. Only with the feminine
    participle ("not willing") do we realize this is a female pursuing a female.

4   "Ally in battle," a Homeric term, showing that women, too, have their heroic
    exploits—but on the battlefield of love. Though Sappho has been imploring, the
    term "ally in battle" introduces a note of equality.

5   This is a most mysterious, and probably mystical, poem. What are the women
    doing? To whose festivities is Aphrodite invited? Are the women lying on the
    grass? Are there spring showers? Or is there a brook nearby which sounds as if it is
    washing through the trees? What makes the sleep magic? (*Koma* in Greek, an
    especially deep sleep, from which our word "coma" comes.) Is there really a
    meadow, or is this possibly an erotic landscape of the human body? One thing is
    certain: Aphrodite is asked to provide a transformative experience. In Sappho the
    sacred and the sexual are mingled.

Cool water splashing sounds through branches   4
of apple trees, and roses all around
cast their shadow, while down through quivering leaves
             drips a magic sleep.

Here is a meadow where horses may graze,   7
all abloom with the flowers of spring.
And breezes are blowing a gentle breath of honey
. . .

Come now and pour your luxurious mixture   10
in our golden cups. Add your nectar
to our festivities. Oh, Lady of Cyprus,
             be our pourer of wine.

3. Some Say[6]

Some say a troop of cavalry, some say the infantry,   1
some say a fleet of ships is the fairest sight
on this black earth, but I say
             it's whatever you love.

It is utterly simple to make this understood   4
by anyone. For she who surpassed all in beauty,
Helen, though she had a husband who was
             best of all,

left him and went sailing off to Troy   7
utterly forgetful of her daughter
and her dear parents. For it was . . .
            that led her on.[7]

. . .
. . . lightly   10

---

6   This short, lighthearted poem offers a complex and profound line of thought. Sappho manages to champion personal valuation over the group values of her day and to show women (both Helen and herself) as active lovers, even suggesting the inner qualities (expressed in walk and sparkle) which elicit love.—all in the space of a few lines which go full circle, from the military, through love, and back to the military.

7   The Greek verb is *parago,* which may be "lead onward" (neutral) or "lead astray" (negative). The English "led her on" is meant to be ambiguous as well.

. . . which puts me in mind of Anaktoria[8]
                                    who is no longer here.

I would rather see her lovely walk   13
and the bright sparkle of her face
than all the chariots of Lydia or a parade
                                    of armored infantry.

4. Remembrance[9]

. . .
"I wish I were dead. I mean it."   1
With tears streaming down
                          she was leaving me.

And this is what she said: "Oh Sappho,   4
what terrible things we've been through.
I swear, it's against my will
                          that I'm leaving you."

This then to her was my reply: 7
"Go now, faring well,
and remember me. For you know
                          how we cared for you.

"Or maybe you've forgotten.   10
Well then, let me remind you . . .
of the beautiful things
                          we've been through.

"How many times you made yourself a crown   13
of violets and roses, of crocuses
and . . . to wear
                          at my side.

"How many times you fashioned garlands,   16
made a necklace to hang

---

8   Anaktoria may be someone who left Sappho's circle of friends and went off to
    Lydia to be married.
9   This poem is about leave-taking and remembrance. In taking leave Sappho gives
    the sort of benediction from the heart which we must always give when parting
    from a loved one. She also corrects her friend and advises her to make a stand
    against sorrow by affirming her beautiful memories. And in these memories we
    see, once again, the mingling of the sacred and the sexual.

around your soft throat
                  woven from flowers.

"And many times you oiled yourself   19
with myrrh, scented with blooms,
. . .
                  ointment of kings

"And on soft bedding   22
very tender . . .
you satisfied desire
                  with your letting go.

"There wasn't any . . .   25
nor any . . .
there wasn't any holy place . . .
                  from which we stayed away.

"There wasn't any grove . . .   28
. . . dancing . . .
. . . sound . . ."

5. Once again[10]

Once again I am shaken
by Love,
the limb-loosener,
the bittersweet,
the irresistible creeping thing.

---

10 This little poem (eight words in Greek) shows the impossibility of ever hitting the target perfectly in translation. The key words describing love are:
    "limb loosener," used by Homer for sleep, by others for love;
    "bittersweet," a word perhaps created by Sappho;
    "irresistible," literally that against which there is no means or device—*mechane,* related to "machine"
    "creeping thing," *orpeton,* related to our word "reptile."
    The last word expresses the feeling that love is a "creepy crawly" or it may possibly mean "flying thing," and express the feeling that love is like a bat, or like one of the destructive spirits that flew out of Pandora's jar.
    There are English translations which would represent the meaning of the Greek, but their tone is wrong—"creepy-crawly" (inelegant); "creeps/gets/crawls under my skin" (too suggestive, and lacks the idea of locomotion); "comes creeping like a snake," (perfect except for Freudian associations).

6. Lovestruck

That man[11] seems to me equal to the gods   1
who has the fortune to sit facing you
and from nearby to catch the sound
                              of your sweet voice

and your delicious laughter. I swear,   4
this sets the heart inside me palpitating.
For the moment I see you, that very moment,
                              I can no longer speak.

My tongue is shattered, and thin streams of fire   7
start to race beneath my skin.
My eyes see not a thing, and in my ears
                              is one great buzz.

Sweat pours down, and a trembling   10
seizes me. I turn greener[12]
than grass, and am all but dead,
                              it seems to me.

But there is nothing that cannot be endured.   13
Even a poor man . . .[13]

---

11 The man, whoever he is, is peripheral. What Sappho describes is not a bout of
    jealousy, as some have thought; but the earthquake she experiences whenever she
    sees her beloved. The language is plain, almost clinical, yet the poem has a rare
    grace. Sappho describes the state of being lovestruck so well that we can identify
    with her, some twenty-six hundred years later.
12 We would expect a person to blush pink or turn white, but people with
    Mediterranean complexions are said to turn a greenish hue.
13 The continuation [if it is one—there were no spaces to divide separate poems in
    the original] is unclear. What might Sappho have gone on to say? Even a poor
    man dares to hope for riches (as I dare to hope for you)?

From The History

———◆———

Herodotus

Herodotus completed *The History* in 425 b.c.e., when the city of Athens was in the early years of its long, difficult and costly war with Sparta. Although *The History* offers a glimpse of all civilizations known to the Greeks, it is primarily about the conflicts between Greeks and Persians. These conflicts between very different kinds of societies—the small, independent Greek polises and the enormous Persian empire—had most recently erupted early in the fifth century, during Herodotus' childhood, when Greek city states on the coast of Asia Minor and throughout the Aegean had revolted from the Persians. Cities from the Greek mainland—most notably Athens—supported these rebellions and incurred the wrath of successive Persian emperors. Herodotus tells the dramatic story of how Persia sought to punish Athens, and failed, first with an expeditionary force defeated at the battle of Marathon (490 b.c.e.) and then with an enormous army and navy sent across the Hellespont ten years later. The following passages describe the Athenians' preparations for the battle of Salamis (480 b.c.e.) in which the Athenians lost their city to the invading Persians, only to regain it—together with a new sense of themselves as leaders among the Greeks. The confidence, daring, and sense of purpose which the Athenians acquired in their stunning victories in the Persian Wars were the driving force behind their accomplishments later in the fifth century. Herodotus is perhaps reminding his Athenian audience, weary and struggling in their war with Sparta, *why* their city is worth defending.

John Cornell

From Book 7

I. The Oracle

138. The King's expedition was in name directed against Athens, but it was sent against all Greece. Though the Greeks knew this far in advance, they did not all take it in the same way. Some of them gave earth and water to the Persians and were confident that they would suffer nothing unpleasant at the hand of the barbarian; but others, who had not given these symbols, were reduced to great fear, inasmuch as there were not enough ships in Greece to meet the invader, nor were many of these people willing to prosecute the war seriously but were turning eagerly to the Persian interest.

139. At this point I am forced to declare an opinion that most people will find offensive; yet, because I think it true, I will not hold back. If the Athenians had taken fright at the approaching danger and had left their own country, or even if they had not left it but had remained and surrendered to Xerxes, no one would have tried to oppose the King at sea. If there had been no opposition to Xerxes at sea, what happened on land would have been this: even if the Peloponnesians had drawn many walls across the Isthmus for their defense, the Lacedaemonians would have been betrayed by their allies, not because the allies chose so to do but out of necessity as they were taken, city by city, by the fleet of the barbarian; thus the Lacedaemonians would have been isolated and, though isolated, would have done deeds of the greatest valor and died nobly. That would have been what happened; or else they would, before this end, have seen that all the other Greeks had Medized and so themselves would have come to an agreement with Xerxes. In both these cases, all of Greece would have been subdued by the Persians. For I cannot see what value those walls drawn across the Isthmus would be, once the King was master by sea. So, as it stands now, a man who declares that the Athenians were the saviors of Greece would hit the very truth. For to whichever side they inclined, that was where the scale would come down. They chose that Greece should survive free, and it was they who awakened all the part of Greece that had not Medized, and it was they who, under Heaven, routed the King. Not even the dreadful oracles that came from Delphi, terrifying though they were, persuaded them to desert Greece; they stood their ground and withstood the invader when he came against their own country.

140. For the Athenians had sent envoys to Delphi and stood ready to consult the god; and when they had performed the usual rites about the shrine and had entered the inner hall and sat down there, the Pythia, whose name was Aristonice, gave utterance as follows:

> Wretched ones, why sit you here? Flee and begone to remotest
> Ends of earth, leaving your homes, high places in circular city;
> For neither the head abides sound, no more than the feet or the body;
> Fire pulls all down, and sharp Ares, driving his Syrian-bred horses.
> Many a fortress besides, and not yours alone shall he ruin.

Many the temples of God to devouring flames he shall give them.
There they stand now, the sweat of terror streaming down from them.
They shake with fear; from the rooftops black blood in deluging torrents.
They have seen the forthcoming destruction, and evil sheerly constraining.
Get you gone out of the shrine! Blanket your soul with your sorrows.

141. When the Athenian envoys heard this, they were in extreme distress. They were prostrated by their calamity, foretold by the oracle; but Timon, son of Androbulus, who was as notable a Delphian as any, counseled them to take suppliant boughs and consult the oracle a second time, as suppliants. The Athenians followed his advice and said to the god: "My Lord, give us a better oracle about our fatherland; be moved to pity the suppliant boughs with which we come before you, or we will never go away from your shrine but remain right here till we die." When they said this, the priestess gave them this second answer:

No: Athena cannot appease great Zeus of Olympus
With many eloquent words and all her cunning counsel.
To you I declare again this word, and make it as iron:
All shall be taken by foemen, whatever within his border
Cecrops contains, and whatever the glades of sacred Cithaeron.
Yet to Tritogeneia shall Zeus, loud-voiced, give a present,
A wall of wood, which alone shall abide unsacked by the foemen;
Well shall it serve yourselves and your children in days that shall be.
Do not abide the charge of horse and foot that come on you,
A mighty host from the landward side, but withdraw before it.
Turn your back in retreat; on another day you shall face them.
Salamis, isle divine, you shall slay many children of women,
Either when seed is sown or again when the harvest is gathered.

142. This oracle seemed to be kinder than the earlier, and indeed it was so. So the envoys wrote it down and went home to Athens. When they had left Delphi and made their report to the people at home, there were many judgments on the part of those who sought what the meaning of the oracle might be, but there were two that clashed more than all the others. Some of the elder men said that they thought that the god predicted that the Acropolis would be saved. For in the old days the Acropolis of Athens had been fenced in with a thorn hedge. Some, therefore, construed this thorn hedge to be the wooden wall. But there were others who said that the god signified the ships, and they urged the abandonment of all else and the preparation of the fleet. But these who claimed that the wooden wall was the ships were baffled by the last two verses of the Pythia's oracle, "Salamis, isle divine, you shall slay many children of women, Either when seed is sown or again when the harvest is gathered." In respect of these lines of verse, the opinion of those who construed the ships as the wooden wall was confounded. For the interpreters of the oracles took the verses in this sense: that the Athenians

35

must prepare themselves for a sea battle at Salamis, which they would certainly lose.

143. Now there was a man among the Athenians who at this moment was but lately come into their front ranks. His name was Themistocles, and he was called the son of Neocles. This man said that the oracle interpreters construed the whole matter wrongly. For if the verses had been really directed against the Athenians, then the oracle would have been given much less mildly; it would have run "O cruel Salamis" instead of "Salamis, isle divine," if its inhabitants were going to die there. No, he said, to anyone who interpreted the oracle of the god rightly, it was given against the enemy and not the Athenians. So he counseled them to prepare for a fight at sea, since the ships were their wooden wall. This was Themistocles' explanation, and the Athenians decided that it was preferable to that of the oracle-interpreters; for the latter would not have them prepare for a sea fight or indeed, to tell the truth, put up a handsworth of resistance at all; they should just leave Attica and settle in some other country.

From Book 8

II. The Abandonment of Athens

40. The Greek navy, leaving Artemisium, put in at Salamis at the request of the Athenians. The Athenians asked this so that they might themselves get their women and children safely out of Attica and, furthermore, make up their minds as to what to do. For as things were, they had to lay their plans as men who had been deceived in their judgment. For they had thought that they would find the Peloponnesians, in full force, awaiting the onset of the barbarians in Boeotia, but not a particle of this was true; instead, they learned that the Peloponnesians were fortifying the Isthmus, which showed that what they were really concerned with was the survival of the Peloponnese; this was what they were going to guard and let everything else go. That was the knowledge the Athenians had when they asked the Greeks to put the fleet into Salamis.

41. The rest of the Greeks made for Salamis, but the Athenians for their own country. After arriving there, they made a proclamation that every Athenian should save his children and household in any way he could. Then most sent them off to Troezen, and some to Aegina, and some to Salamis. They hurried to bring what belonged to them into safety, because they wished to comply with the oracle, and also for this reason, particularly: the Athenians say that there is a large snake that inhabits the shrine, as a guard of the Acropolis. They say, besides, that they make him a monthly provision of "food," as for a real creature—the monthly food being a honey cake. This honey cake in all time past had been eaten up, but, now only, it was left untouched. When the priestess told them this, the Athenians were even more bent on leaving the city, thinking that Athena herself had deserted the Acropolis. So when all was conveyed away, they themselves returned to the fleet.

36

III. Siege and Destruction of Athens; The Decision to Fight at Salamis

49. When the commanders from these aforementioned cities met at Salamis, they held a debate. Eurybiades presented the proposition that anyone who pleased should declare where, among the territories of which the Greeks were master, would be most suitable place to fight their sea battle; for Attica was at this point already given over for lost; it was about the rest that he inquired. The most of the opinions of those who spoke agreed that they should sail to the Isthmus and fight for the Peloponnese; the reason they produced for this was that, if they were beaten in the sea fight and were at Salamis, they would be beleaguered in an island where no help could show up for their rescue; but if they fought off the Isthmus, they could put into a coastline that was their own.

50. At the moment when the Peloponnesian commanders were arguing like this, there came a man of Athens with the news that the barbarian had arrived in Attica and was giving it to fire and sword. For the army that was with Xerxes had come through Boeotia and, having burned the city of the Thespians (the inhabitants of which had themselves gone away to the Peloponnese) and likewise the city of the Plataeans, had now come to Athens and there was ravaging everything entirely. They had burned Thespia and Plataea when they learned from the Thebans that these cities had not espoused the Persian cause.

51. From the crossing of the Hellespont, from which the barbarians began their march, they had spent one month in their passage into Europe, and then, in three more months, they were in Attica, during the archonship of Calliades at Athens. The city they captured was empty; in it there were only a few Athenians, whom they found in the temple; these were temple stewards and poor men, and they had barricaded the Acropolis with doors and planks to defend themselves from the attackers. These men had not gone away with the rest to Salamis because of lack of means and, besides, because they had their own conviction of having found out the meaning of the oracle that the Pythia had given about the wooden wall that would be impregnable. This,[1] they decided, was that very refuge according to the prophecy, and not the ships.

52. The Persians established themselves on the hill opposite the Acropolis that is called by the Athenians the Areopagus, and they besieged the Acropolis in this way: they wrapped tow around their arrows and set them alight and shot them into the barrier. There the Athenians who were besieged still defended themselves, all the same, although they were reduced to the extremity of ill, and their barrier had betrayed them. They refused to receive any propositions of the Pisistratids about surrender, but they staunchly defended themselves by various means and especially by launching down great stones on the barbarians as they approached the gates, so that for a great time Xerxes was at a loss, being unable to beat them.

53. But at last the barbarians found a way out of their difficulties. For according to the prophecy, all of Attica on the mainland must be overcome by the Persians. In front of the Acropolis, but behind the gates and the road up, there

---

1   The barricade of doors and planks.

was a place where no one was on guard, for no one had thought that any man could ascend there; it was near the shrine of Aglaurus, the daughter of Cecrops, and at it, though it was a very precipitous place, some men managed to climb up. When the Athenians saw that these had got to the top, to the Acropolis itself, some of them threw themselves down headlong from the wall and so found their deaths, but others fled to the inner chamber. Those of the Persians who had climbed up turned to the gates and opened these up and butchered the suppliants there. When these had all been laid low, the barbarians plundered the shrine and set the whole Acropolis afire.

54. Having taken Athens absolutely, Xerxes sent a horseman to Susa to tell Artabanus of his present good fortune. On the day after the sending of the messenger, he summoned such exiles of the Athenians as were in his train and bade them go up to the Acropolis and in their own fashion perform the sacrifices. He did this either because he had seen some vision in his sleep or because he began to have scruples about having burned the temple. The exiles did as he bade them.

55. I will tell you why I have mentioned this. There is on the Acropolis a temple that is called the shrine of Erechtheus Earthborn, and there is in the shrine an olive tree and a salt pool, about which the story goes among the Athenians that, when Poseidon and Athena had their contest for the possession of the land, the two gods made these two objects their witnesses.[2] Now it happened that the olive was burned, with all the rest of the shrine, by the barbarians; but on the day after the burning, when those Athenians by the King's instructions came up to the shrine to sacrifice, they saw the olive had put forth from its stump a shoot of about a cubit's length. They reported this.

56. The Greeks in Salamis, when they had word of what had happened to the Acropolis of Athens, were in such turmoil of mind that some of the generals did not even wait for the formal settlement of the proposition that they were debating but fell into their ships and hoisted the sails to run away. Those of them who were left decided formally to fight at sea for the Isthmus. So night came on, and the conference broke up and the people went to their ships.

57. At this moment, when Themistocles got to his ship, one Mnesiphilus, an Athenian, asked him what decision had been reached. This man was then told by Themistocles that it was resolved to draw off the ships to the Isthmus and fight for the Peloponnese. Mnesiphilus said, "If once they draw off the ships from Salamis, you will never again fight for any fatherland at all; everyone will run off, each one to his own city, and neither Eurybiades nor any other man will be able to keep the army from scattering. Greece will be lost, and all through sheer folly. If there is any means at all by which you can undo this decision, if by any means you can persuade Eurybiades to change his mind and stay here, do so."

---

2   "Witnesses," a literal rendering of the Greek, perhaps leaves something obscure in the English. Poseidon created the salt pool, Athena the olive, and Cecrops gave his judgment in favor of the goddess. These objects were made as evidence of the power of each god.

58. What Mnesiphilus suggested pleased Themistocles extremely, but he made the man no answer and went off to Eurybiades' ship. When he came there, he said that he wanted to consult the commander on a matter of common interest. So Eurybiades told him to come aboard and talk, if he pleased. Then Themistocles sat down and spelled out all that he had heard from Mnesiphilus, but he recounted it as though it were his own idea, and he added much besides until, in his urgency, he persuaded the commander to disembark and to summon the generals to a conference.

59. When they had all collected, but before Eurybiades put before them the reason for which he had summoned them, Themistocles was most vehement in the words of entreaty that he used. While he was talking, the Corinthian general Adimantus, son of Ocytus, said, "Themistocles, in the games, those who get off the mark too soon are whipped." Themistocles, in his defense, said, "But those who get left behind never get crowned."

60. So he made a soft answer to the Corinthian; but to Eurybiades he said not a word of what had passed between them before—to the effect that, if they once left Salamis, they would break up and run away—for in the presence of the allies it would not have been suitable for him to make accusations against anyone. But he held to quite another tack in his argument and said to Eurybiades: "It is in your hands to save Greece if you will be persuaded by me and stand and fight at sea here rather than yield to the arguments of these others and draw away your ships to the Isthmus. Just listen and compare the two cases. If you engage off the Isthmus, you will be fighting in the open sea, which suits us least, since our ships are the heavier and fewer in number. Besides, you will lose Salamis, Megara, and Aegina, even if we win a general victory. And the enemy's land army will follow his fleet, and so you will bring them down into the Peloponnese and endanger the safety of all Greece. If you do what I say, you will find corresponding advantages: first, we will be engaging their many ships with our few in a confined space, and, if the probable chances of war occur, we shall win a great victory. For to fight in a confined space is to our advantage, as to fight in the open sea is to theirs. Again, there is the survival of Salamis, to which we have conveyed for safety our wives and children. Finally, there is this matter, too, in my plan, which is exactly what you set most store by: if you stay here and fight your sea battle here, you will be defending the Peloponnese exactly as though you were fighting near the Isthmus, and you will not be bringing the enemy down to the Peloponnese—if you are wise. If what I expect happens and we win with the fleet, the barbarians will never get to the Isthmus at all; they will never move a foot beyond Attica, and they will depart in disorder. Besides, we will profit by the survival of Megara and Aegina and Salamis; about the last there is an oracle among us that at that place we shall have the upper hand of our enemies. It is when men make probable designs that success oftenest attends them; if their designs are improbable, not even the god is willing to lend his help to the plans of men."

61. While Themistocles spoke like this, the Corinthian, Adimantus, again inveighed against him: "Hold your tongue," said he; "you have no country." And he was for not letting Eurybiades put the question to the vote on the motion of a

"cityless man"; Themistocles should contribute an opinion only when he had a city behind him. The taunts of the Corinthian were directed at Themistocles because Athens had been captured and was now occupied by the enemy. At this moment Themistocles abused Adimantus and the Corinthians both; he made it clear to them in his speech that Athens had a city and land greater than theirs—the Corinthians'—so long as they had two hundred fully manned ships; "for," said he, "there are no Greeks able to withstand an attack by us."

62. Having made this point, he went on in his speech to Eurybiades, speaking ever more vehemently: "Eurybiades, if you stand your ground here, by such standing you will be a good man; if you go away, you will utterly destroy Greece; for the whole power of this war is carried in our ships. Do what I say. If you refuse, we will straightaway gather all our households and take them away to Siris in Italy. It is ours of old, and there are oracles that say that it is by us that it must be colonized. When you people are deprived of such allies as we are, you will remember my words."

63. At these words of Themistocles, Eurybiades was forced to change his mind. In my opinion, this change was because he especially dreaded that the Athenians would desert them if he drew off the fleet to the Isthmus; for if the Athenians quit, the rest of the alliance was not capable of sustaining the fight. So he chose the plan that they should stay where they were and fight the sea fight through.

IV. Victory

83. When the Greeks were finally convinced by what the Tenians said, they made their preparations to fight. The daylight was coming, and they called a meeting of those who were serving on board. Themistocles spoke well, better than all the others; for all his words were a contrast of the worse and the better side in man's nature and position in the world, and he bade them ever choose the better, and wound up his oration by urging them to board their ships. So on board they went, and at this moment there came from Aegina the trireme that had been sent for the sons of Aeacus.

84. Then the Greeks launched all their ships to sea, and, as they did so, the barbarians attacked them. Under the attack, the rest of the Greeks began to back water and were beaching their ships; but Aminias of Pallene, an Athenian, pushed ahead and rammed an enemy ship. The two were thoroughly entangled and could not be separated, and so the rest of the Greeks came to Aminias' help and joined the fight. That is how the Athenians say the battle began; but the Aeginetans say that it was the ship that had been sent to Aegina to bring the Aeacidae, that she it was who began it. It is said, too, that a phantom of a woman appeared and shouted her commands loud enough for all the Greek camp to hear, taunting them first with the words, "You crazy Greeks, how long will you continue backing water?"

86. That is the story of those men. But the majority of the ships at Salamis were crippled, some being destroyed by the Athenians and some by the Aeginetans. For since the Greeks fought with proper discipline and in ordered ranks, and the barbarians with no order and no longer doing anything with a sense of purpose, what was bound to happen to them was what happened.

40

From History of the Peloponnesian War

━━◆◆◆━━

Thucydides

Unlike Herodotus who wrote about the Persian wars of the previous generation and about cultures in the distant past, his younger contemporary Thucydides (471–400 b.c.e.) wrote a history of current events. In *The Peloponnesian War,* Thucydides attempts to explain this decades-long conflict between Athens and Sparta while it was still going on. Thucydides himself served as an Athenian commander during the first years of the war and was banished from the city for failing to defend the strategic city of Amphipolis. He spent the rest of his life collecting information, weighing different accounts, and writing *The Peloponnesian War,* which remained uncompleted at his death.

In contrast to most ancient authorities, Thucydides did not blame the outbreak and outcome of the war upon the leading Athenian statesman Pericles. Instead, he thought that the war was made inevitable by "the growth of the power of Athens, and the alarm which this inspired in Lacedæmon [Sparta]." Thucydides attributed Athens' losses to a democracy bereft of Pericles' firm leadership and to the subsequent rise of demagogues who swayed the citizens in assembly. Having himself been reprimanded by the demos of Athens, Thucydides does not present a kind picture of democracy in his history of the war.

The following three selections suggest Thucydides' portrayal of the degeneration of Athens during the course of the Peloponnesian War. In his "Funeral Oration" (431 b.c.e.) honoring Athenian soldiers slain during the first year of fighting, Pericles articulates his vision of democratic Athens. He reminds fellow Athenians of the unique attributes and accomplishments of their city which make it worth continuing the war with Sparta to save.

John Cornell

From *The Peloponnesian War* by Thucydides, translated by Rex Warner. Copyright 1954. Reprinted by permission of Penguin Books, Ltd.

Pericles' Funeral Oration

In the same winter the Athenians, following their annual custom, gave a public funeral for those who had been the first to die in the war. These funerals are held in the following way: two days before the ceremony the bones of the fallen are brought and put in a tent which has been erected, and people make whatever offerings they wish to their own dead. Then there is a funeral procession in which coffins of cypress wood are carried on wagons. There is one coffin for each tribe, which contains the bones of members of that tribe. One empty bier is decorated and carried in the procession: this is for the missing, whose bodies could not be recovered. Everyone who wishes to, both citizens and foreigners, can join in the procession, and the women who are related to the dead are there to make their laments at the tomb. The bones are laid in the public burial-place, which is in the most beautiful quarter outside the city walls. Here the Athenians always bury those who have fallen in war. The only exception is those who died at Marathon, who, because their achievement was considered absolutely outstanding, were buried on the battlefield itself.

When the bones have been laid in the earth, a man chosen by the city for his intellectual gifts and for his general reputation makes an appropriate speech in praise of the dead, and after the speech all depart. This is the procedure at these burials, and all through the war, when the time came to do so, the Athenians followed this ancient custom. Now, at the burial of those who were the first to fall in the war Pericles, the son of Xanthippus, was chosen to make the speech. When the moment arrived, he came forward from the tomb and, standing on a high platform, so that he might be heard by as many people as possible in the crowd, he spoke as follows:

"Many of those who have spoken here in the past have praised the institution of this speech at the close of our ceremony. It seemed to them a mark of honour to our soldiers who have fallen in war that a speech should be made over them. I do not agree. These men have shown themselves valiant in action, and it would be enough, I think, for their glories to be proclaimed in action, as you have just seen it done at this funeral organized by the state. Our belief in the courage and manliness of so many should not be hazarded on the goodness or badness of one man's speech. Then it is not easy to speak with a proper sense of balance, when a man's listeners find it difficult to believe in the truth of what one is saying. The man who knows the facts and loves the dead may well think that an oration tells less than what he knows and what he would like to hear: others who do not know so much may feel envy for the dead, and think the orator over-praises them, when he speaks of exploits that are beyond their own capacities. Praise of other people is tolerable only up to a certain point, the point where one still believes that one could do oneself some of the things one is hearing about. Once you get beyond this point, you will find people becoming jealous and incredulous. However, the fact is that this institution was set up and approved by our forefathers, and it is my duty to follow the tradition and do my best to meet the wishes and the expectations of every one of you.

"I shall begin by speaking about our ancestors, since it is only right and proper on such an occasion to pay them the honour of recalling what they did. In this land of ours there have always been the same people living from generation to generation up till now, and they, by their courage and their virtues, have handed it on to us, a free country. They certainly deserve our praise. Even more so do our fathers deserve it. For to the inheritance they had received they added the empire we have now, and it was not without blood and toil that they handed it down to us of the present generation. And then we ourselves, assembled here today, who are mostly in the prime of life, have, in most directions, added to the power of our empire and have organized our State in such a way that it is perfectly well able to look after itself both in peace and in war.

"I have no wish to make a long speech on subjects familiar to you all: so I shall say nothing about the warlike deeds by which we acquired our power or the battles in which we or our fathers gallantly resisted our enemies, Greek or foreign. What I want to do is, in the first place, to discuss the spirit in which we faced our trials and also our constitution and the way of life which has made us great. After that I shall speak in praise of the dead, believing that this kind of speech is not inappropriate to the present occasion and that this whole assembly, of citizens and foreigners, may listen to it with advantage.

"Let me say that our system of government does not copy the institutions of our neighbours. It is more the case of our being a model to others, than of our imitating anyone else. Our constitution is called a democracy because power is in the hands not of a minority but of the whole people. When it is a question of settling private disputes, everyone is equal before the law; when it is a question of putting one person before another in positions of public responsibility, what counts is not membership of a particular class, but the actual ability which the man possesses. No one, so long as he has it in him to be of service to the state, is kept in political obscurity because of poverty. And, just as our political life is free and open, so is our day-to-day life in our relations with each other. We do not get into a state with our next-door neighbour if he enjoys himself in his own way, nor do we give him the kind of black looks which, though they do no real harm, still do hurt people's feelings. We are free and tolerant in our private lives; but in public affairs we keep to the law. This is because it commands our deep respect.

"We give our obedience to those whom we put in positions of authority, and we obey the laws themselves, especially those which are for the protection of the oppressed, and those unwritten laws which it is an acknowledged shame to break.

"And here is another point. When our work is over, we are in a position to enjoy all kinds of recreation for our spirits. There are various kinds of contests and sacrifices regularly throughout the year; in our own homes we find a beauty and a good taste which delight us every day and which drive away our cares. Then the greatness of our city brings it about that all the good things from all over the world flow in to us, so that to us it seems just as natural to enjoy foreign goods as our own local products.

43

"Then there is a great difference between us and our opponents, in our attitude towards military security. Here are some examples: Our city is open to the world, and we have no periodical deportations in order to prevent people observing or finding out secrets which might be of military advantage to the enemy. This is because we rely, not on secret weapons, but on our own real courage and loyalty. There is a difference, too, in our educational systems. The Spartans, from their earliest boyhood, are submitted to the most laborious training in courage; we pass our lives without all these restrictions, and yet are just as ready to face the same dangers as they are. Here is a proof of this: When the Spartans invade our land, they do not come by themselves, but bring all their allies with them; whereas we, when we launch an attack abroad, do the job by ourselves, and, though fighting on foreign soil, do not often fail to defeat opponents who are fighting for their own hearths and homes. As a matter of fact none of our enemies has ever yet been confronted with our total strength, because we have to divide our attention between our navy and the many missions on which our troops are sent on land. Yet, if our enemies engage a detachment of our forces and defeat it, they give themselves credit for having thrown back our entire army; or, if they lose, they claim that they were beaten by us in full strength. There are certain advantages, I think, in our way of meeting danger voluntarily, with an easy mind, instead of with a laborious training, with natural rather than with state-induced courage. We do not have to spend our time practising to meet sufferings which are still in the future; and when they are actually upon us we show ourselves just as brave as these others who are always in strict training. This is one point in which, I think, our city deserves to be admired. There are also others:

"Our love of what is beautiful does not lead to extravagance; our love of the things of the mind does not make us soft. We regard wealth as something to be properly used, rather than as something to boast about. As for poverty, no one need be ashamed to admit it: the real shame is in not taking practical measures to escape from it. Here each individual is interested not only in his own affairs but in the affairs of the state as well: even those who are mostly occupied with their own business are extremely well-informed on general politics—this is a peculiarity of ours: we do not say that a man who takes no interest in politics is a man who minds his own business; we say that he has no business here at all. We Athenians, in our own persons, take our decisions on policy or submit them to proper discussions: for we do not think that there is an incompatibility between words and deeds; the worst thing is to rush into action before the consequences have been properly debated. And this is another point where we differ from other people. We are capable at the same time of taking risks and of estimating them beforehand. Others are brave out of ignorance and, when they stop to think, they begin to fear. But the man who can most truly be accounted brave is he who best knows the meaning of what is sweet in life and of what is terrible, and then goes out undeterred to meet what is to come.

"Again, in questions of general good feeling there is a great contrast between us and most other people. We make friends by doing good to others, not by receiving good from them. This makes our friendship all the more reliable, since

44

we want to keep alive the gratitude of those who are in our debt by showing continued goodwill to them: whereas the feelings of one who owes us something lack the same enthusiasm, since he knows that, when he repays our kindness, it will be more like paying back a debt than giving something spontaneously. We are unique in this. When we do kindnesses to others, we do not do them out of any calculations of profit or loss: we do them without afterthought, relying on our free liberality. Taking everything together then, I declare that our city is an education to Greece, and I declare that in my opinion each single one of our citizens, in all the manifold aspects of life, is able to show himself the rightful lord and owner of his own person, and do this, moreover, with exceptional grace and exceptional versatility. And to show that this is no empty boasting for the present occasion, but real tangible fact, you have only to consider the power which our city possesses and which has been won by those very qualities which I have mentioned. Athens, alone of the states we know, comes to her testing time in a greatness that surpasses what was imagined of her. In her case, and in her case alone, no invading enemy is ashamed at being defeated, and no subject can complain of being governed by people unfit for their responsibilities. Mighty indeed are the marks and monuments of our empire which we have left. Future ages will wonder at us, as the present age wonders at us now. We do not need the praises of a Homer, or of anyone else whose words may delight us for the moment, but whose estimation of facts will fall short of what is really true. For our adventurous spirit has forced an entry into every sea and into every land; and everywhere we have left behind us everlasting memorials of good done to our friends or suffering inflicted on our enemies.

"This, then, is the kind of city for which these men, who could not bear the thought of losing her, nobly fought and nobly died. It is only natural that every one of us who survive them should be willing to undergo hardships in her service. And it was for this reason that I have spoken at such length about our city, because I wanted to make it clear that for us there is more at stake than there is for others who lack our advantages; also I wanted my words of praise for the dead to be set in the bright light of evidence. And now the most important of these words has been spoken. I have sung the praises of our city; but it was the courage and gallantry of these men, and of people like them, which made her splendid. Nor would you find it true in the case of many of the Greeks, as it is true of them, that no words can do more than justice to their deeds.

"To me it seems that the consummation which has overtaken these men shows us the meaning of manliness in its first revelation and in its final proof. Some of them, no doubt, had their faults; but what we ought to remember first is their gallant conduct against the enemy in defence of their native land. They have blotted out evil with good, and done more service to the commonwealth than they ever did harm in their private lives. No one of these men weakened because he wanted to go on enjoying his wealth: no one put off the awful day in the hope that he might live to escape his poverty and grow rich. More to be desired than such things, they chose to check the enemy's pride. This, to them, was a risk most glorious, and they accepted it, willing to strike down the enemy and relinquish everything else. As for success or failure, they left that in the doubtful

45

hands of Hope, and when the reality of battle was before their faces, they put their trust in their own selves. In the fighting, they thought it more honourable to stand their ground and suffer death than to give in and save their lives. So they fled from the reproaches of men, abiding with life and limb the brunt of battle; and, in a small moment of time, the climax of their lives, a culmination of glory, not of fear, were swept away from us.

"So and such they were, these men—worthy of their city. We who remain behind may hope to be spared their fate, but must resolve to keep the same daring spirit against the foe. It is not simply a question of estimating the advantages in theory. I could tell you a long story (and you know it as well as I do) about what is to be gained by beating the enemy back. What I would prefer is that you should fix your eyes every day on the greatness of Athens as she really is, and should fall in love with her. When you realize her greatness, then reflect that what made her great was men with a spirit of adventure, men who knew their duty, men who were ashamed to fall below a certain standard. If they ever failed in an enterprise, they made up their minds that at any rate the city should not find their courage lacking to her, and they gave to her the best contribution that they could. They gave her their lives, to her and to all of us, and for their own selves they won praises that never grow old, the most splendid of sepulchres—not the sepulchre in which their bodies are laid, but where their glory remains eternal in men's minds, always there on the right occasion to stir others to speech or to action. For famous men have the whole earth as their memorial: it is not only the inscriptions on their graves in their own country that mark them out; no, in foreign lands also, not in any visible form but in people's hearts, their memory abides and grows. It is for you to try to be like them. Make up your minds that happiness depends on being free, and freedom depends on being courageous. Let there be no relaxation in face of the perils of the war. The people who have most excuse for despising death are not the wretched and unfortunate, who have no hope of doing well for themselves, but those who run the risk of a complete reversal in their lives, and who would feel the difference most intensely, if things went wrong for them. Any intelligent man would find a humiliation caused by his own slackness more painful to bear than death, when death comes to him unperceived, in battle, and in the confidence of his patriotism.

"For these reasons I shall not commiserate with those parents of the dead, who are present here. Instead I shall try to comfort them. They are well aware that they have grown up in a world where there are many changes and chances. But this is good fortune for men to end their lives with honour, as these have done, and for you honourably to lament them: their life was set to a measure where death and happiness went hand in hand. I know that it is difficult to convince you of this. When you see other people happy you will often be reminded of what used to make you happy too. One does not feel sad at not having some good thing which is outside one's experience: real grief is felt at the loss of something which one is used to. All the same, those of you who are of the right age must bear up and take comfort in the thought of having more children. In your own homes these new children will prevent you from brooding over those who are no more, and they will be a help to the city, too, both in filling the empty

46

places, and in assuring her security. For it is impossible for a man to put forward fair and honest views about our affairs if he has not, like everyone else, children whose lives may be at stake. As for those of you who are now too old to have children, I would ask you to count as gain the greater part of your life, in which you have been happy, and remember that what remains is not long, and let your hearts be lifted up at the thought of the fair fame of the dead. One's sense of honour is the only thing that does not grow old, and the last pleasure, when one is worn out with age, is not, as the poet said, making money, but having the respect of one's fellow men.

"As for those of you here who are sons or brothers of the dead, I can see a hard struggle in front of you. Everyone always speaks well of the dead, and even if you rise to the greatest heights of heroism, it will be a hard thing for you to get the reputation of having come near, let alone equalled, their standard. When one is alive, one is always liable to the jealousy of one's competitors, but when one is out of the way, the honour one receives is sincere and unchallenged.

"Perhaps I should say a word or two on the duties of women to those among you who are now widowed. I can say all I have to say in a short word of advice. Your great glory is not to be inferior to what God has made you, and the greatest glory of a woman is to be least talked about by men, whether they are praising you or criticizing you. I have now, as the law demanded, said what I had to say. For the time being our offerings to the dead have been made, and for the future their children will be supported at the public expense by the city, until they come of age. This is the crown and prize which she offers, both to the dead and to their children, for the ordeals which they have faced. Where the rewards of valour are the greatest, there you will find also the best and bravest spirits among the people. And now, when you have mourned for your dear ones, you must depart."

The Mytilenian Debate

In the "Mytilenian Debate" (427 b.c.e.), we witness a decision by the Athenian assembly directed towards a rebellious ally. Throughout the fifth century, the powerful city of Mytilene (on the island of Lesbos) had been a greatly valued, independent, and democratic member of the Athenian alliance. But in the fourth year of the war, anti-Athenian aristocrats took control of the city and severed all ties with Athens. Unwilling to allow such a major defection from their coalition, the Athenians spent a whole year, a lot of money, and a large contingent of ships and soldiers besieging Mytilene. With the help of democratic sympathizers from inside the city walls, the Athenians finally captured the town. The revolt of Mytilene had been a severe blow to the Athenian alliance and a real danger in their war with Sparta. In a first debate (unrecorded by Thucydides), the Athenians angrily decided to punish all the citizens of Mytilene alike. What Thucydides records here is the second day of debate, in which the Athenian assembly reconsiders its decision.

John Cornell

47

When Salaethus and the other prisoners reached Athens, the Athenians immediately put Salaethus to death in spite of the fact that he undertook, among other things, to have the Peloponnesians withdrawn from Plataea, which was still being besieged. They then discussed what was to be done with the other prisoners and, in their angry mood, decided to put to death not only those now in their hands but also the entire adult male population of Mytilene, and to make slaves of the women and children. What they held against Mytilene was the fact that it had revolted even though it was not a subject state, like the others, and the bitterness of their feelings was considerably increased by the fact that the Peloponnesian fleet had actually dared to cross over to Ionia to support the revolt. This, it was thought, could never have happened unless the revolt had been long premeditated. So they sent a trireme to Paches to inform him of what had been decided, with orders to put the Mytilenians to death immediately.

Next day, however, there was a sudden change of feeling and people began to think how cruel and how unprecedented such a decision was—to destroy not only the guilty, but the entire population of a state. Observing this, the deputation from Mytilene which was in Athens and the Athenians who were supporting them approached the authorities with a view to having the question debated again. They won their point the more easily because the authorities themselves saw clearly that most of the citizens were wanting someone to give them a chance of reconsidering the matter. So an assembly was called at once. Various opinions were expressed on both sides, and Cleon, the son of Cleaenetus, spoke again. It was he who had been responsible for passing the original motion for putting the Mytilenians to death. He was remarkable among the Athenians for the violence of his character, and at this time he exercised far the greatest influence over the people.[1] He spoke as follows:

"Personally I have had occasion often enough already to observe that a democracy is incapable of governing others, and I am all the more convinced of this when I see how you are now changing your minds about the Mytilenians. Because fear and conspiracy play no part in your daily relations with each other, you imagine that the same thing is true of your allies, and you fail to see that when you allow them to persuade you to make a mistaken decision and when you give way to your own feelings of compassion you are being guilty of a kind of weakness which is dangerous to you and which will not make them love you any more. What you do not realize is that your empire is a tyranny exercised over subjects who do not like it and who are always plotting against you; you will not make them obey you by injuring your own interests in order to do them a favour; your leadership depends on superior strength and not on any goodwill of theirs. And this is the very worst thing—to pass measures and then not to abide by them. We should realize that a city is better off with bad laws, so long as they remain fixed, than with good laws that are constantly being altered, that lack of learning combined with sound common sense is more helpful than the kind of cleverness

---

1 This wording is echoed by Thucydides in VI, 35 when he introduces the Syracusan "demagogue" Athenagoras.

that gets out of hand, and that as a general rule states are better governed by the man in the street than by intellectuals. These are the sort of people who want to appear wiser than the laws, who want to get their own way in every general discussion, because they feel that they cannot show off their intelligence in matters of greater importance, and who, as a result, very often bring ruin on their country. But the other kind—the people who are not so confident in their own intelligence—are prepared to admit that the laws are wiser than they are and that they lack the ability to pull to pieces a speech made by a good speaker; they are unbiased judges, and not people taking part in some kind of a competition; so things usually go well when they are in control. We statesmen, too, should try to be like them, instead of being carried away by mere cleverness and a desire to show off our intelligence and so giving you, the people, advice which we do not really believe in ourselves.

"As for me, I have not altered my opinion, and I am amazed at those who have proposed a reconsideration of the question of Mytilene, thus causing a delay which is all to the advantage of the guilty party. After a lapse of time the injured party will lose the edge of his anger when he comes to act against those who have wronged him; whereas the best punishment and the one most fitted to the crime is when reprisals follow immediately. I shall be amazed, too, if anyone contradicts me and attempts to prove that the harm done to us by Mytilene is really a good thing for us, or that when we suffer ourselves we are somehow doing harm to our allies. It is obvious that anyone who is going to say this must either have such confidence in his powers as an orator that he will struggle to persuade you that what has been finally settled was, on the contrary, not decided at all, or else he must have been bribed to put together some elaborate speech with which he will try to lead you out of the right track. But in competitions of this sort the prizes go to others and the state takes all the danger for herself. The blame is yours, for stupidly instituting these competitive displays. You have become regular speech-goers, and as for action, you merely listen to accounts of it; if something is to be done in the future you estimate the possibilities by hearing a good speech on the subject, and as for the past you rely not so much on the facts which you have seen with your own eyes as on what you have heard about them in some clever piece of verbal criticism. Any novelty in an argument deceives you at once, but when the argument is tried and proved you become unwilling to follow it; you look with suspicion on what is normal and are the slaves of every paradox that comes your way. The chief wish of each one of you is to be able to make a speech himself, and, if you cannot do that, the next best thing is to compete with those who can make this sort of speech by not looking as though you were at all out of your depth while you listen to the views put forward, by applauding a good point even before it is made, and by being as quick at seeing how an argument is going to be developed as you are slow at understanding what in the end it will lead to. What you are looking for all the time is something that is, I should say, outside the range of ordinary experience, and yet you cannot even think straight about the facts of life that are before you. You are simply victims of your own pleasure in listening, and are more like an audience sitting at the feet of a professional lecturer than a parliament discussing matters of state.

"I am trying to stop you behaving like this, and I say that no single city has ever done you the harm that Mytilene has done. Personally I can make allowances for those who revolt because they find your rule intolerable or because they have been forced into it by enemy action. Here, however, we have the case of people living on an island, behind their own fortifications, with nothing to fear from our enemies except an attack by sea against which they were adequately protected by their own force of triremes; they had their own independent government and they were treated by us with the greatest consideration. Now, to act as they acted is not what I should call a revolt (for people only revolt when they have been badly treated); it is a case of calculated aggression, of deliberately taking sides with our bitterest enemies in order to destroy us. And this is far worse than if they had made war against us simply to increase their own power. They learned nothing from the fate of those of their neighbours who had already revolted and been subdued; the prosperity which they enjoyed did not make them hesitate before running into danger; confident in the future, they declared war on us, with hopes that indeed extended beyond their means, though still fell short of their desires. They made up their minds to put might first and right second, choosing the moment when they thought they would win, and then making their unprovoked attack upon us.

"The fact is that when great prosperity comes suddenly and unexpectedly to a state, it usually breeds arrogance; in most cases it is safer for people to enjoy an average amount of success rather than something which is out of all proportion; and it is easier, I should say, to ward off hardship than to maintain happiness. What we should have done long ago with the Mytilenians was to treat them in exactly the same way as all the rest; then they would never have grown so arrogant; for it is a general rule of human nature that people despise those who treat them well and look up to those who make no concessions. Let them now therefore have the punishment which their crime deserves. Do not put the blame on the aristocracy and say that the people were innocent. The fact is that the whole lot of them attacked you together, although the people might have come over to us and, if they had, would now be back again in control of their city. Yet, instead of doing this, they thought it safer to share the dangers, and join in the revolt of the aristocracy.

"Now think of your allies. If you are going to give the same punishment to those who are forced to revolt by your enemies and those who do so of their own accord, can you not see that they will all revolt upon the slightest pretext, when success means freedom and failure brings no very dreadful consequences? Meanwhile we shall have to spend our money and risk our lives against state after state; if our efforts are successful, we shall recover a city that is in ruins, and so lose the future revenue from it, on which our strength is based; and if we fail to subdue it, we shall have more enemies to deal with in addition to those we have already, and we shall spend the time which ought to be used in resisting our present foes in making war on our own allies.

"Let there be no hope, therefore, held out to the Mytilenians that we, either as a result of a good speech or a large bribe, are likely to forgive them on the grounds that it is only human to make mistakes. There was nothing involuntary about the harm they did us; they knew what they were about and they planned it all beforehand; and one only forgives actions that were not deliberate. As for me, just as I was at first, so I am now, and I shall continue to impress on you the importance of not altering your previous decisions. To feel pity, to be carried away by the pleasure of hearing a clever argument, to listen to the claims of decency are three things that are entirely against the interests of an imperial power. Do not be guilty of them. As for compassion, it is proper to feel it in the case of people who are like ourselves and who will pity us in their turn, not in the case of those who, so far from having the same feelings towards us, must always and inevitably be our enemies. As for the speech-makers who give such pleasure by their arguments, they should hold their competitions on subjects which are less important, and not on a question where the state may have to pay a heavy penalty for its light pleasure, while the speakers themselves will no doubt be enjoying splendid rewards for their splendid arguments. And a sense of decency is only felt towards those who are going to be our friends in future, not towards those who remain just as they were and as much our enemies as they ever have been.

"Let me sum the whole thing up. I say that, if you follow my advice, you will be doing the right thing as far as Mytilene is concerned and at the same time will be acting in your own interests; if you decide differently, you will not win them over, but you will be passing judgement on yourselves. For if they were justified in revolting, you must be wrong in holding power. If, however, whatever the rights or wrongs of it may be, you propose to hold power all the same, then your interest demands that these too, rightly or wrongly, must be punished. The only alternative is to surrender your empire, so that you can afford to go in for philanthropy. Make up your minds, therefore, to pay them back in their own coin, and do not make it look as though you who escaped their machinations are less quick to react than they who started them. Remember how they would have been likely to have treated you, if they had won, especially as they were the aggressors. Those who do wrong to a neighbour when there is no reason to do so are the ones who persevere to the point of destroying him, since they see the danger involved in allowing their enemy to survive. For he who has suffered for no good reason is a more dangerous enemy, if he escapes, than the one who has both done and suffered injury.

"I urge you, therefore, not to be traitors to your own selves. Place yourselves in imagination at the moment when you first suffered and remember how then you would have given anything to have them in your power. Now pay them back for it, and do not grow soft just at this present moment, forgetting meanwhile the danger that hung over your heads then. Punish them as they deserve, and make an example of them to your other allies, plainly showing that revolt will be punished by death. Once they realize this, you will not have so often to neglect the war with your enemies because you are fighting with your own allies."

So Cleon spoke. After him Diodotus, the son of Eucrates, who in the previous assembly also had vigorously opposed the motion to put the Mytilenians to death, came forward again on this occasion and spoke as follows:

"I do not blame those who have proposed a new debate on the subject of Mytilene, and I do not share the view which we have heard expressed, that it is a bad thing to have frequent discussions on matters of importance. Haste and anger are, to my mind, the two greatest obstacles to wise counsel—haste, that usually goes with folly, anger, that is the mark of primitive and narrow minds. And anyone who maintains that words cannot be a guide to action must be either a fool or one with some personal interest at stake; he is a fool, if he imagines that it is possible to deal with the uncertainties of the future by any other medium, and he is personally interested if his aim is to persuade you into some disgraceful action, and, knowing that he cannot make a good speech in a bad cause, he tries to frighten his opponents and his hearers by some good-sized pieces of misrepresentation. Then still more intolerable are those who go further and accuse a speaker of making a kind of exhibition of himself, because he is paid for it. If it was only ignorance with which he was being charged, a speaker who failed to win his case could retire from the debate and still be thought an honest man, if not a very intelligent one. But when corruption is imputed, he will be suspect if he wins his case, and if he loses it, will be regarded as dishonest and stupid at the same time. This sort of thing does the city no good; her counsellors will be afraid to speak and she will be deprived of their services. Though certainly it would be the best possible thing for the city if these gentlemen whom I have been describing lacked the power to express themselves; we should not then be persuaded into making so many mistakes.

"The good citizen, instead of trying to terrify the opposition, ought to prove his case in fair argument; and a wise state, without giving special honours to its best counsellors, will certainly not deprive them of the honour they already enjoy; and when a man's advice is not taken, he should not even be disgraced, far less penalized. In this way successful speakers will be less likely to pursue further honours by speaking against their own convictions in order to make themselves popular, and unsuccessful speakers, too, will not struggle to win over the people by the same acts of flattery. What we do here, however, is exactly the opposite. Then, too, if a man gives the best possible advice but is under the slightest suspicion of being influenced by his own private profit, we are so embittered by the idea (a wholly unproved one) of this profit of his, that we do not allow the state to receive the certain benefit of his good advice. So a state of affairs has been reached where a good proposal honestly put forward is just as suspect as something thoroughly bad, and the result is that just as the speaker who advocates some monstrous measure has to win over the people by deceiving them, so also a man with good advice to give has to tell lies if he expects to be believed. And because of this refinement in intellectuality, the state is put into a unique position; it is only she to whom no one can ever do a good turn openly and without deception. For if one openly performs a patriotic action, the reward for one's pains is to be thought to have made something oneself on the side. Yet in spite of this we are discussing matters of the greatest importance, and we who give you our advice ought to be resolved to look rather further into things than you whose attention is occupied only with the surface—especially as we can be held to account for the advice we give, while you are not accountable for the way in which you receive it. For indeed you would take rather more care over your decisions, if the proposer of a motion and those who voted for it were all subject to the same penalties. As it is, on the occasions when some emotional impulse on your part has led you into disaster, you turn upon the one man who made the original proposal and you let yourself off; in spite of the fact that you are many and in spite of the fact that you were just as wrong as he was.

"However, I have not come forward to speak about Mytilene in any spirit of contradiction or with any wish to accuse anyone. If we are sensible people, we shall see that the question is not so much whether they are guilty as whether we are making the right decision for ourselves. I might prove that they are the most guilty people in the world, but it does not follow that I shall propose the death penalty, unless that is in your interests; I might argue that they deserve to be forgiven, but should not recommend forgiveness unless that seemed to me the best thing for the state.

"In my view our discussion concerns the future rather than the present. One of Cleon's chief points is that to inflict the death penalty will be useful to us in the future as a means for deterring other cities from revolt; but I, who am just as concerned as he is with the future, am quite convinced that this is not so. And I ask you not to reject what is useful in my speech for the sake of what is specious in his. You may well find his speech attractive, because it fits in better with your present angry feelings about the Mytilenians; but this is not a law-court, where we have to consider what is fit and just; it is a political assembly, and the question is how Mytilene can be most useful to Athens.

"Now, in human societies the death penalty has been laid down for many offences less serious than this one. Yet people still take risks when they feel sufficiently confident. No one has ever yet risked committing a crime which he thought he could not carry out successfully. The same is true of states. None has ever yet rebelled in the belief that it had insufficient resources, either in itself or from its allies, to make the attempt. Cities and individuals alike, all are by nature disposed to do wrong, and there is no law that will prevent it, as is shown by the fact that men have tried every kind of punishment, constantly adding to the list, in the attempt to find greater security from criminals. It is likely that in early times the punishments even for the greatest crimes were not as severe as they are now, but the laws were still broken, and in the course of time the death penalty became generally introduced. Yet even with this, the laws are still broken. Either, therefore, we must discover some fear more potent than the fear of death, or we must admit that here certainly we have not got an adequate deterrent. So long as poverty forces men to be bold, so long as the insolence and pride of wealth nourish their ambitions, and in the other accidents of life they are continually dominated by some incurable master passion or another, so long will their impulses continue to drive them into danger. Hope and desire persist throughout and cause the greatest calamities—one leading and the other following, one conceiving the enterprise, and the other suggesting that it will be successful—invisible factors, but more powerful than the terrors that are obvious to our eyes. Then too, the idea that fortune will be on one's side plays as big a part as anything else in creating a mood of over-confidence; for sometimes she does come unexpectedly to one's aid, and so she tempts men to run risks for which they are inadequately prepared. And this is particularly true in the case of whole peoples, because they are playing for the highest stakes—either for their own freedom or for the power to control others—and each individual, when acting as part of a community, has the irrational opinion that his own powers are greater than in fact they are. In a word it is impossible (and only the most simple-minded will deny this) for human nature, when once seriously set upon a certain course, to be prevented from following that course by the force of law or by any other means of intimidation whatever.

"We must not, therefore, come to the wrong conclusions through having too much confidence in the effectiveness of capital punishment, and we must not make the condition of rebels desperate by depriving them of the possibility of repentance and of a chance of atoning as quickly as they can for what they did. Consider this now: at the moment, if a city has revolted and realizes that the revolt cannot succeed, it will come to terms while it is still capable of paying an indemnity and continuing to pay tribute afterwards. But if Cleon's method is adopted, can you not see that every city will not only make much more careful preparations for revolt, but will also hold out against siege to the very end, since to surrender early or late means just the same thing? This is, unquestionably, against our interests—to spend money on a siege because of the impossibility of coming to terms, and, if we capture the place, to take over a city that is in ruins so that we lose the future revenue from it. And it is just on this revenue that our strength in war depends.

"Our business, therefore, is not to injure ourselves by acting like a judge who strictly examines a criminal; instead we should be looking for a method by which, employing moderation in our punishments, we can in future secure for ourselves the full use of those cities which bring us important contributions. And we should recognize that the proper basis of our security is in good administration rather than in the fear of legal penalties. As it is, we do just the opposite: when we subdue a free city, which was held down by force and has, as we might have expected, tried to assert its independence by revolting, we think that we ought to punish it with the utmost severity. But the right way to deal with free people is this—not to inflict tremendous punishments on them after they have revolted, but to take tremendous care of them before this point is reached, to prevent them even contemplating the idea of revolt, and, if we do have to use force with them, to hold as few as possible of them responsible for this.

"Consider what a mistake you would be making on this very point, if you took Cleon's advice. As things are now, in all the cities the democracy is friendly to you; either it does not join in with the oligarchies in revolting, or, if it is forced to do so, it remains all the time hostile to the rebels, so that when you go to war with them, you have the people on your side. But if you destroy the democratic party at Mytilene, who never took any hand in the revolt and who, as soon as they got arms, voluntarily gave the city up to you, you will first of all be guilty of killing those who have helped you, and, secondly, you will be doing exactly what the reactionary classes want most. For now when they start a revolt, they will have the people on their side from the beginning, because you have already made it clear that the same punishment is laid down both for the guilty and the

54

innocent. In fact, however, even if they were guilty, you should pretend that they were not, in order to keep on your side the one element that is still not opposed to you. It is far more useful to us, I think, in preserving our empire, that we should voluntarily put up with injustice than that we should justly put to death the wrong people. As for Cleon's point—that in this act of vengeance both justice and self-interest are combined—this is not a case where such a combination is at all possible.

"I call upon you, therefore, to accept my proposal as the better one. Do not be swayed too much by pity or by ordinary decent feelings. I, no more than Cleon, wish you to be influenced by such emotions. It is simply on the basis of the argument which you have heard that I ask you to be guided by me, to try at your leisure the men whom Paches has considered guilty and sent to Athens, and to allow the rest to live in their own city. In following this course you will be acting wisely for the future and will be doing something which will make your enemies fear you now. For those who make wise decisions are more formidable to their enemies than those who rush madly into strong action."

This was the speech of Diodotus. And now, when these two motions, each so opposed to each, had been put forward, the Athenians, in spite of the recent change of feeling, still held conflicting opinions, and at the show of hands the votes were nearly equal. However, the motion of Diodotus was passed.

Immediately another trireme was sent out in all haste, since they feared that, unless it overtook the first trireme, they would find on their arrival that the city had been destroyed. The first trireme had a start of about twenty-four hours. The ambassadors from Mytilene provided wine and barley for the crew and promised great rewards if they arrived in time, and so the men made such speed on the voyage that they kept on rowing while they took their food (which was barley mixed with oil and wine) and rowed continually, taking it in turn to sleep. Luckily they had no wind against them, and as the first ship was not hurrying on its distasteful mission, while they were pressing on with such speed, what happened was that the first ship arrived so little ahead of them that Paches had just had time to read the decree and to prepare to put it into force, when the second ship put in to the harbour and prevented the massacre. So narrow had been the escape of Mytilene.

The other Mytilenians whom Paches had sent to Athens as being the ones chiefly responsible for the revolt were, on the motion of Cleon, put to death by the Athenians. There were rather more than 1,000 of them. The Athenians also destroyed the fortifications of Mytilene and took over their navy. Afterwards, instead of imposing a tribute on Lesbos, they divided all the land, except that belonging to the Methymnians, into 3,000 holdings, 300 of which were set apart as sacred for the gods, while the remainder was distributed by lot to Athenian shareholders, who were sent out to Lesbos. The Lesbians agreed with these shareholders to pay a yearly rent of two minae for each holding, and cultivated the land themselves. The Athenians also took over all the towns on the mainland that had been under the control of Mytilene. So for the future the Mytilenians became subjects of Athens. This completes the account of what took place in Lesbos.

The Melian Dialogue

The island of Melos was of no strategic importance in the Peloponnesian War, only a symbolic one. Melos was one of the scant few Greek islands which were not part of the Athenian alliance. Despite its declared neutrality, Melos was openly sympathetic to the Spartans, connected to them by ties of race, culture, and politics. As the war lengthened and some of Athens' allies became restive, the Athenians decided they could not allow such hostile independence: the risk of further rebellions in their empire (like that of Mytilene) was too great. So the Athenians sent a force to Melos with orders to make it a part of their alliance—or destroy it.

The "Melian Dialogue" (415 b.c.e.) is Thucydides' reconstruction of the negotiations between the Athenian generals and the aristocratic leaders of Melos. Bear in mind that "the few" Melians here do not necessarily speak in the interest of "the many." Would the outcome have been different if the Athenians could have presented their demands to the entire town? In any event, there is no mistaking the harsh tone of the Athenians and the brutality of subsequent events. Thucydides wants his readers to see that too much democracy leads to mistakes (like Mytilene), attrocities (like Melos), and eventually disintegration (like the disastrous expedition to Syracuse, which Thucydides introduces on the very next page of his account). We may or may not agree with Thucydides that "democracy" was to blame for what happened at Melos, but the deepening war had certainly driven the Athenians a long way from the vision of their city in Pericles' Funeral Oration.

John Cornell

84 Next summer Alcibiades sailed to Argos with twenty ships and seized 300 Argive citizens who were still suspected of being pro-Spartan. These were put by the Athenians into the nearby islands under Athenian control.

The Athenians also made an expedition against the island of Melos. They had thirty of their own ships, six from Chios, and two from Lesbos; 1,200 hoplites, 300 archers, and twenty mounted archers, all from Athens; and about 1,500 hoplites from the allies and the islanders.

The Melians are a colony from Sparta. They had refused to join the Athenian empire like the other islanders, and at first had remained neutral without helping either side; but afterwards, when the Athenians had brought force to bear on them by laying waste their land, they had become open enemies of Athens.

Now the generals Cleomedes, the son of Lycomedes, and Tisias, the son of Tisimachus, encamped with the above force in Melian territory and, before doing any harm to the land, first of all sent representatives to negotiate. The Melians did not invite these representatives to speak before the people, but asked them to make the statement for which they had come in front of the governing body and the few. The Athenian representatives then spoke as follows:

85 "So we are not to speak before the people, no doubt in case the mass of the people should hear once and for all and without interruption an argument from us which is both persuasive and incontrovertible, and should so be led astray. This, we realize, is your motive in bringing us here to speak before the

few. Now suppose that you who sit here should make assurance doubly sure. Suppose that you, too, should refrain from dealing with every point in detail in a set speech, and should instead interrupt us whenever we say something controversial and deal with that before going on to the next point? Tell us first whether you approve of this suggestion of ours."

86 The Council of the Melians replied as follows:

"No one can object to each of us putting forward our own views in a calm atmosphere. That is perfectly reasonable. What is scarcely consistent with such a proposal is the present threat, indeed the certainty, of your making war on us. We see that you have come prepared to judge the argument yourselves, and that the likely end of it all will be either war, if we prove that we are in the right, and so refuse to surrender, or else slavery."

87 *Athenians:* If you are going to spend the time in enumerating your suspicions about the future, or if you have met here for any other reason except to look the facts in the face and on the basis of these facts to consider how you can save your city from destruction, there is no point in our going on with this discussion. If, however, you will do as we suggest, then we will speak on.

88 *Melians:* It is natural and understandable that people who are placed as we are should have recourse to all kinds of arguments and different points of view. However, you are right in saying that we are met together here to discuss the safety of our country and, if you will have it so, the discussion shall proceed on the lines that you have laid down.

89 *Athenians:* Then we on our side will use no fine phrases saying, for example, that we have a right to our empire because we defeated the Persians, or that we have come against you now because of the injuries you have done us a great mass of words that nobody would believe. And we ask you on your side not to imagine that you will influence us by saying that you, though a colony of Sparta, have not joined Sparta in the war, or that you have never done us any harm. Instead we recommend that you should try to get what it is possible for you to get, taking into consideration what we both really do think; since you know as well as we do that, when these matters are discussed by practical people, the standard of justice depends on the equality of power to compel and that in fact the strong do what they have the power to do and the weak accept what they have to accept.

90 *Melians:* Then in our view (since you force us to leave justice out of account and to confine ourselves to self-interest)—in our view it is at any rate useful that you should not destroy a principle that is to the general good of all men— namely, that in the case of all who fall into danger there should be such a thing as fair play and just dealing, and that such people should be allowed to use and to profit by arguments that fall short of a mathematical accuracy. And this is a principle which affects you as much as anybody, since your own fall would be visited by the most terrible vengeance and would be an example to the world.

91 *Athenians:* As for us, even assuming that our empire does come to an end, we are not despondent about what would happen next. One is not so much frightened of being conquered by a power which rules over others, as Sparta does (not that we are concerned with Sparta now), as of what would happen if a ruling

power is attacked and defeated by its own subjects. So far as this point is concerned, you can leave it to us to face the risks involved. What we shall do now is to show you that it is for the good of our own empire that we are here and that it is for the preservation of your city that we shall say what we are going to say. We do not want any trouble in bringing you into our empire, and we want you to be spared for the good both of yourselves and of ourselves.

92 *Melians:* And how could it be just as good for us to be the slaves as for you to be the masters?

93 *Athenians:* You, by giving in, would save yourselves from disaster; we, by not destroying you, would be able to profit from you.

94 *Melians:* So you would not agree to our being neutral, friends instead of enemies, but allies of neither side?

95 *Athenians:* No, because it is not so much your hostility that injures us; it is rather the case that, if we were on friendly terms with you, our subjects would regard that as a sign of weakness in us, whereas your hatred is evidence of our power.

96 *Melians:* Is that your subjects' idea of fair play—that no distinction should be made between people who are quite unconnected with you and people who are mostly your own colonists or else rebels whom you have conquered?

97 *Athenians:* So far as right and wrong are concerned they think that there is no difference between the two, that those who still preserve their independence do so because they are strong, and that if we fail to attack them it is because we are afraid. So that by conquering you we shall increase not only the size but the security of our empire. We rule the sea and you are islanders, and weaker islanders too than the others; it is therefore particularly important that you should not escape.

98 *Melians:* But do you think there is no security for you in what we suggest? For here again, since you will not let us mention justice, but tell us to give in to your interests, we, too, must tell you what our interests are and, if yours and ours happen to coincide, we must try to persuade you of the fact. Is it not certain that you will make enemies of all states who are at present neutral when they see what is happening here and naturally conclude that in course of time you will attack them too? Does not this mean that you are strengthening the enemies you have already and are forcing others to become your enemies even against their intentions and their inclinations?

99 *Athenians:* As a matter of fact we are not so much frightened of states on the continent. They have their liberty, and this means that it will be a long time before they begin to take precautions against us. We are more concerned about islanders like yourselves, who are still unsubdued, or subjects who have already become embittered by the constraint which our empire imposes on them. These are the people who are most likely to act in a reckless manner and to bring themselves and us, too, into the most obvious danger.

100 *Melians:* Then surely, if such hazards are taken by you to keep your empire and by your subjects to escape from it, we who are still free would show ourselves great cowards and weaklings if we failed to face everything that comes rather than submit to slavery.

101 *Athenians:* No, not if you are sensible. This is no fair fight, with honour on one side and shame on the other. It is rather a question of saving your lives and not resisting those who are far too strong for you.

102 *Melians:* Yet we know that in war fortune sometimes makes the odds more level than could be expected from the difference in numbers of the two sides. And if we surrender, then all our hope is lost at once, whereas, so long as we remain in action, there is still a hope that we may yet stand upright.

103 *Athenians:* Hope, that comforter in danger! If one already has solid advantages to fall back upon, one can indulge in hope. It may do harm, but will not destroy one. But hope is by nature an expensive commodity, and those who are risking their all on one cast find out what it means only when they are already ruined; it never fails them in the period when such a knowledge would enable them to take precautions. Do not let this happen to you, you who are weak and whose fate depends on a single movement of the scale. And do not be like those people who, as so commonly happens, miss the chance of saving themselves in a human and practical way, and, when every clear and distinct hope has left them in their adversity, turn to what is blind and vague, to prophecies and oracles and such things which by encouraging hope lead men to ruin.

104 *Melians:* It is difficult, and you may be sure that we know it, for us to oppose your power and fortune, unless the terms be equal. Nevertheless we trust that the gods will give us fortune as good as yours, because we are standing for what is right against what is wrong; and as for what we lack in power, we trust that it will be made up for by our alliance with the Spartans, who are bound, if for no other reason, then for honour's sake, and because we are their kinsmen, to come to our help. Our confidence, therefore, is not so entirely irrational as you think.

105 *Athenians:* So far as the favour of the gods is concerned, we think we have as much right to that as you have. Our aims and our actions are perfectly consistent with the beliefs men hold about the gods and with the principles which govern their own conduct. Our opinion of the gods and our knowledge of men lead us to conclude that it is a general and necessary law of nature to rule whatever one can. This is not a law that we made ourselves, nor were we the first to act upon it when it was made. We found it already in existence, and we shall leave it to exist forever among those who come after us. We are merely acting in accordance with it, and we know that you or anybody else with the same power as ours would be acting in precisely the same way. And therefore, so far as the gods are concerned, we see no good reason why we should fear to be at a disadvantage. But with regard to your views about Sparta and your confidence that she, out of a sense of honour, will come to your aid, we must say that we congratulate you on your simplicity but do not envy you your folly. In matters that concern themselves or their own constitution the Spartans are quite remarkably good; as for their relations with others, that is a long story, but it can be expressed shortly and clearly by saying that of all people we know the Spartans are most conspicuous for believing that what they like doing is honourable and what suits their interests is just. And this kind of attitude is not going to be of much help to you in your absurd quest for safety at the moment.

106 *Melians:* But this is the very point where we can feel most sure. Their own self-interest will make them refuse to betray their own colonists, the Melians, for that would mean losing the confidence of their friends among the Hellenes and doing good to their enemies.

107 *Athenians:* You seem to forget that if one follows one's self-interest one wants to be safe, whereas the path of justice and honour involves one in danger. And, where danger is concerned, the Spartans are not, as a rule, very venture-some.

108 *Melians:* But we think that they would even endanger themselves for our sake and count the risk more worth taking than in the case of others, because we are so close to the Peloponnese that they could operate more easily, and because they can depend on us more than on others, since we are of the same race and share the same feelings.

109 *Athenians:* Goodwill shown by the party that is asking for help does not mean security for the prospective ally. What is looked for is a positive prepon-derance of power in action. And the Spartans pay attention to this point even more than others do. Certainly they distrust their own native resources so much that when they attack a neighbour they bring a great army of allies with them. It is hardly likely therefore that, while we are in control of the sea, they will cross over to an island.

110 *Melians:* But they still might send others. The Cretan sea is a wide one, and it is harder for those who control it to intercept others than for those who want to slip through to do so safely. And even if they were to fail in this, they would turn against your own land and against those of your allies left unvisited by Brasidas. So, instead of troubling about a country which has nothing to do with you, you will find trouble nearer home, among your allies, and in your own country.

111 *Athenians:* It is a possibility, something that has in fact happened before. It may happen in your case, but you are well aware that the Athenians have never yet relinquished a single siege operation through fear of others. But we are somewhat shocked to find that, though you announced your intention of discuss-ing how you could preserve yourselves, in all this talk you have said absolutely nothing which could justify a man in thinking that he could be preserved. Your chief points are concerned with what you hope may happen in the future, while your actual resources are too scanty to give you a chance of survival against the forces that are opposed to you at this moment. You will therefore be showing an extraordinary lack of common sense if, after you have asked us to retire from this meeting, you still fail to reach a conclusion wiser than anything you have mentioned so far. Do not be led astray by a false sense of honour—a thing which often brings men to ruin when they are faced with an obvious danger that somehow affects their pride. For in many cases men have still been able to see the dangers ahead of them, but this thing called dishonour, this word, by its own force of seduction, has drawn them into a state where they have surrendered to an idea, while in fact they have fallen voluntarily into irrevocable disaster, in dishonour that is all the more dishonourable because it has come to them from their own folly rather than their misfortune. You, if you take the right view, will

be careful to avoid this. You will see that there is nothing disgraceful in giving way to the greatest city in Hellas when she is offering you such reasonable terms—alliance on a tribute-paying basis and liberty to enjoy your own property. And, when you are allowed to choose between war and safety, you will not be so insensitively arrogant as to make the wrong choice. This is the safe rule—to stand up to one's equals, to behave with deference towards one's superiors, and to treat one's inferiors with moderation. Think it over again, then, when we have withdrawn from the meeting, and let this be a point that constantly recurs to your minds—that you are discussing the fate of your country, that you have only one country, and that its future for good or ill depends on this one single decision which you are going to make.

112 The Athenians then withdrew from the discussion. The Melians, left to themselves, reached a conclusion which was much the same as they had indicated in their previous replies. Their answer was as follows:

"Our decision, Athenians, is just the same as it was at first. We are not prepared to give up in a short moment the liberty which our city has enjoyed from its foundation for 700 years. We put our trust in the fortune that the gods will send and which has saved us up to now, and in the help of men—that is, of the Spartans; and so we shall try to save ourselves. But we invite you to allow us to be friends of yours and enemies to neither side, to make a treaty which shall be agreeable to both you and us, and so to leave our country."

113 The Melians made this reply, and the Athenians, just as they were breaking off the discussion, said:

"Well, at any rate, judging from this decision of yours, you seem to us quite unique in your ability to consider the future as something more certain than what is before your eyes, and to see uncertainties as realities, simply because you would like them to be so. As you have staked most on and trusted most in Spartans, luck, and hopes, so in all these you will find yourselves most completely deluded."

114 The Athenian representatives then went back to the army, and the Athenian generals, finding that the Melians would not submit, immediately commenced hostilities and built a wall completely round the city of Melos, dividing the work out among the various states. Later they left behind a garrison of some of their own and some allied troops to blockade the place by land and sea, and with the greater part of their army returned home. The force left behind stayed on and continued with the siege.

115 About the same time the Argives invaded Phliasia and were ambushed by the Phliasians and the exiles from Argos, losing about eighty men.

Then, too, the Athenians at Pylos captured a great quantity of plunder from Spartan territory. Not even after this did the Spartans renounce the treaty and make war, but they issued a proclamation saying that any of their people who wished to do so were free to make raids on the Athenians. The Corinthians also made some attacks on the Athenians because of private quarrels of their own, but the rest of the Peloponnesians stayed quiet.

Meanwhile the Melians made a night attack and captured the part of the Athenian lines opposite the market-place. They killed some of the troops, and then, after bringing in corn and everything else useful that they could lay their hands on, retired again and made no further move, while the Athenians took measures to make their blockade more efficient in future. So the summer came to an end.

116 In the following winter the Spartans planned to invade the territory of Argos, but when the sacrifices for crossing the frontier turned out unfavourably, they gave up the expedition. The fact that they had intended to invade made the Argives suspect certain people in their city, some of whom they arrested, though others succeeded in escaping.

About this same time the Melians again captured another part of the Athenian lines where there were only a few of the garrison on guard. As a result of this, another force came out afterwards from Athens under the command of Philocrates, the son of Demeas. Siege operations were now carried on vigorously and, as there was also some treachery from inside, the Melians surrendered unconditionally to the Athenians, who put to death all the men of military age whom they took, and sold the women and children as slaves. Melos itself they took over for themselves, sending out later a colony of 500 men.[2]

2   That there were Melian survivors, who were restored by Lysander at the end of the war, is stated by Xenophon *(Hellenica,* II, 2, 9).

Ancient China

Meinig Model of China[1]

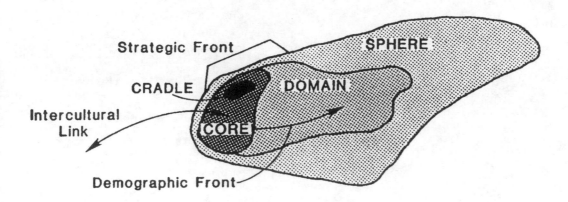

CRADLE—Area of birth of culture

CORE—Focus or heart of the culture defined by:
1. Greatest density of occupance (urbanization)
2. Greatest intensity of movement of people, goods and messages
3. Seat of political, economic and cultural power

DOMAIN—Area in which culture is dominant numerically but with less intensity and homogeneity than the core

SPHERE—Culture is numerical minority but with considerable influence politically, economically and culturally

DEMOGRAPHIC FRONT—Principle zone of expansion of culture; vector of migration

STRATEGIC FRONT—Principle zone of chronic military threat

INTERCULTURAL LINK—Principle zone of contact and interchange with another great cultural tradition

---

1   Developed from Meinig, D. W., "Cultural Geography," *Introduction to Geography: Viewpoints and Themes,* Commission on College Geography Publication #5, Washington, DC: Association of American Geographers, 1967.

Han China, 200 BC–200 AD

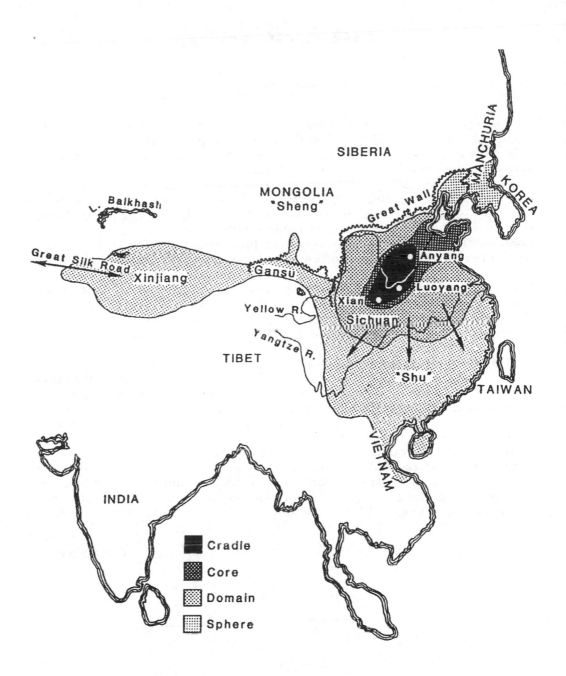

SIBERIA

MONGOLIA
"Sheng"

L. Balkhash

Great Silk Road

Xinjiang

Gansu

Yellow R.

Yangtze R.

TIBET

Great Wall

MANCHURIA

KOREA

Anyang

Luoyang

Xian

Sichuan

"Shu"

TAIWAN

VIETNAM

INDIA

■ Cradle
▨ Core
▨ Domain
▨ Sphere

Yin and Yang

The concepts of *yin and* yang comprise the two basic principles of the universe as understood by the ancient Chinese. *Yin* is the receptive; *yang* the active. Much of Chinese thinking and philosophy is based on the understanding that everything in the universe is a combination of these two principles.

Some Chinese use the image of the mountain—with one side in the sun and the other shaded—to discuss *yin and yang*. In fact, the Chinese character for "mountain" makes up part of both the modern composite characters for the words *yin and yang*. The left-hand column below shows the current Chinese characters for the two words, along with their meanings. The center column shows the two characters which combine to make the composite characters for *yin and yang*. The left-hand characters in this column are the modern ones; the right-hand ones are the older pictographic forms. The composite characters for *yin and yang* both combine the character for mountain with a second character which gives the word its meaning and pronunciation. Finally, the right-hand columns show the two ancient pictograms which combined to make the characters for *yin and yang*.

The *t'ai chi* symbol contains the yang (white) and yin (black) elements enclosed within a circle. They are separated not by a straight line, but by a curved one which shows the idea of a constant flow between the yin and yang. In the midst of each white and black section is a small circle of the opposite color, implying that within every yang there is always a small portion of yin, and within every yin there is likewise a small portion of yang.

The trigrams surrounding the *t'ai chi* are the six main building blocks of the *I Ching* (see Hucker, page 39). It is important to realize that the top of each trigram is always the line farthest from the *t'ai chi* symbol. If you rotate the book, the appropriate line will be on top. This rotation also enhances the *t'ai chi* symbol, because it reinforces the idea of yin and yang in motion, flowing one into the other.

Wayne Wentzel

Yin and Yang

Mai-Mai Sze

陽

yang: clear, light, hot; dryness, fire, red, day; upper, outer, front, open; South; south of a mountain and north of a river; male or positive element, force, and principle, Sun, spring-summer, Heaven, Spirit

阝 厂

fu: mound; hill, mountain

易 昜

yang: sun, light; the sun radiating heat and light

⊙

tan: dawn; sun above the horizon

勿

wu, a phonetic used sometimes as a negative and a prohibition, also in the sense of motion of jerking, flapping, waving, or, as here, radiating

陰

yin: shady, dark, cold; moistness, water, black, night; lower, inner, back, closed; North; south of a river and north of a mountain; female or negative element, force, and principle, Moon, autumn-winter, Earth, Matter

阝 厂

fu: mound; hill, mountain

会 會

yin: cloudy, shaded, dark; a coiled cloud; the moment when clouds cast shadows

今

chin: now, the moment

云 云

yün: cloud

The eight trigrams around the *Yin-Yang* emblem (the *T'ai Chi*)

67

Ode to King Wên

————◆————

This text is one of the 305 songs which comprise the *Shih Ching* (Book of Odes/Songs), one of the five Confucian classics. The collection was compiled around 600 B.C., so the songs themselves come from the Chou period with some perhaps earlier. Ssu-ma Ch'ien, the Grand Historian, says that Confucius selected these from a larger collection of 3000 songs, put them in the present order, and worked over the musical accompaniment. Whether or not Confucius had a hand in the editing as tradition says, he clearly valued the Odes highly as we can tell from his quotes of them (which you will also observe in some other texts in this reader). Another tradition relates the collection of the Odes to the activity of the Chou rulers who sent officials out to record them as a means of discovering the sentiments and complaints of their subjects.

Chinese poetry from the time of the Odes on was an accepted way of expressing political criticism in an oblique (and less dangerous) manner. Like the other Confucian classics (except the *I Ching)*, *the Shih Ching* was victim to the Ch'in dynasty effort to destroy the classics by burning them.

Although there is considerable variation in style, the basic form is a short poem of two to three stanzas, with lines consisting of four characters each, often four to eight lines in a stanza. Especially characteristic is the use of a repeated word or refrain, what is believed to be the earliest use of rhyme in any culture, and the extensive use of metaphor. The songs cover a wide range of subject matters, including a number of songs about the Chou dynasty founders.

King Wen, the "Cultured King," was the founder of the Chou dynasty, although it was his son, King Wu, who in 1122 B.C. actually overthrew the Shang dynasty. Note in this hymn the characteristics of an ideal king, the prosperity and happiness he brings to his people, and the application of the "Mandate of Heaven" concept to explain the reason for the end of the Shang dynasty and to warn future kings that the same fate could befall them.

Malcolm Clark

From *The Book of Songs* translated by Arthur Waley. Copyright © 1937 by Arthur Waley. Used by permission of Grove/Atlantic, Inc.

King Wên is on high;
Oh, he shines in Heaven!
Chou is an old people,
But its charge is new.
The land of Chou became illustrious,
Blessed by God's charge.
King Wên ascends and descends
On God's left hand, on His right.

Very diligent was King Wên,
His high fame does not cease;
He spread his bounties in Chou,
And now in his grandsons and sons,
In his grandsons and sons
The stem has branched
Into manifold generations,
And all the knights of Chou
Are glorious in their generation

Glorious in their generation,
And their counsels well pondered.
Mighty were the many knights
That brought this kingdom to its birth.
This kingdom well they bore;
They were the prop of Chou.
Splendid were those many knights
Who gave comfort to Wên the king.

August is Wên the king;
Oh, to be reverenced in his glittering light!
Mighty the charge that Heaven gave him.
The grandsons and sons of the Shang,[1]
Shang's grandsons and sons,
Their hosts were innumerable.
But God on high gave His command,
And by Chou they were subdued.

By Chou they were subdued;
Heaven's charge is not forever.
The knights of Yin, big and little,
Made libations and offerings at the capital;
What they did was to make libations

---

1   The people overthrown by the Chou.

69

Dressed in skirted robe and close cap.
O chosen servants of the king,
May you never thus shame your ancestors!

May you never thus shame your ancestors,
But rather tend their inward power,
That forever you may be linked to Heaven's charge
And bring to yourselves many blessings.
Before Yin[2] lost its army
It was well linked to God above.
In Yin you should see as in a mirror
That Heaven's high charge is hard to keep.

The charge is not easy to keep.
Do not bring ruin on yourselves.
Send forth everywhere the light of your good fame;
Consider what Heaven did to the Yin.
High Heaven does its business
Without sound, without smell.
Make King Wên your example,
In whom all the peoples put their trust.

---

2   Another name for the Shang.

From
Records of the Historian

━━▷◆◁━━

Ssu-ma Ch'ien

Ssu-ma Ch'ien (or Sima Qian, c. 145–90 B.C.) is the most famous Chinese historian and set the pattern for subsequent Chinese historical writing. He inherited his position as Grand Historian of the Emperor Wu from his father (d. 110 B.C.) who had already become interested in going beyond the traditional duties of the office to compile a history of China. While continuing his father's work on the history, Ssu-ma Ch'ien incurred the disfavor of the emperor by speaking up for a defeated general. Given the choice between committing suicide (the proper choice) or being castrated, Ssu-ma Ch'ien dishonored himself by choosing the latter in order to complete the history. His autobiography concludes the work.

Ssu-ma Ch'ien's history (in Chinese, *Shih Chi*) was unprecedented in its scope and form. It covers the time period from the semi-mythic beginnings of China in the early third millennium to about 100 B.C. The work has five parts: 1) Annals of dynasties; 2) Chronological Tables; 3) Treatises on subjects such as rites, music, astronomy, economics, and religion; 4) Hereditary Houses—chapters on the vassal states of Chou times plus accounts of fiefs of the Han imperial household, and; 5) Biographies of famous statesmen, generals, philosophers (such as Mencius, Hsün-Tzu, and Han Fei Tzu), assassins, fortune tellers, and the like as well as accounts of foreign lands and peoples. The story-telling technique relies on dialogue between characters rather than a neutral observer's description of events and circumstances.

Ssu-ma Ch'ien preferred to let the material speak for itself, although he did inject his own comments at section beginnings with the phrase "the Grand Historian remarks." As a Confucianist, he believed that history taught moral lessons and provided moral exemplars, and that the action of the individual was decisive. Nevertheless, he gave much more attention than had been given previously to the influence of geography, climate, economy, customs, and institutions on the course of history.

From *Records of the Historian,* ed. Burton Watson, © 1969 Columbia University Press. Reprinted with the permission of the publisher.

Two of the selections below are from the Biography section's assassin-retainer tales from the warring states period of the Fifth and Fourth centuries B.C.; the Chou's central feudal control had broken down into constant warfare and jockeying for preeminence among the various emerging states. These two selections exemplify key values of this period. The third selection is from the Hereditary Houses section. The story is set in the period after the fall of the Ch'in dynasty when Han Kao-tzu (Liu Chi) established the new Han dynasty. Hsiao Ho played an important role in the triumph of Kao-tzu and became his chief minister. When reading this selection, note how the historical situation and values replicate or differ from the situation and values of the warring states period.

Malcolm Clark

The Biographies of the Assassin Retainers

Through Master Ts'ao's dagger Lu recovered its lands and Ch'i proved it could be trusted. Yü Jang did not consider it right to harbor treacherous intentions. Thus I made The Biographies of the Assassin-Retainers.

Yü Jang

Some seventy years later there was the affair of Yü Jang in Chin. Yü Jang was a native of the state of Chin. He once served the Fan family, and later the Chung-hang family, but attracted no notice under either of them. He left and became a retainer of Chih Po, who treated him with great respect and honor. Later Chih Po attacked Hsiang-tzu, the lord of Chao. Hsiang-tzu plotted with the lords of Han and Wei, wiped out Chih Po and his heirs, and divided up his land among the three of them. Hsiang-tzu hated Chih Po intensely and had his skull lacquered and made into a drinking cup.[1]

Yü Jang fled and hid in the mountains. He sighed and said, "A man will die for one who understands him, as a woman will make herself beautiful for one who delights in her. Chih Po understood me. Before I die, I will repay him by destroying his enemy! Then my spirit need feel no shame in the world below."

He changed his name, became a convict laborer, and succeeded in entering the palace of the lord of Chao, where he was given the task of replastering the privy. In his breast he concealed a dagger, hoping to stab Hsiang-Tzu with it. Hsiang-tzu entered the privy but suddenly grew uneasy and ordered his men to seize and examine the convict laborer who was plastering the privy. It was Yü

---

1 Fan, Chung-hang, Chih, Chao, Han, and Wei were all ministerial families of Chin. In the middle of the fifth century B.C, when these events took place, Chih Po wiped out the Fan and Chung-hang families and was in turn destroyed by Chao, Han, and Wei, who overthrew the ruling family of Chin and divided the state into three parts.

72

Jang who, clasping the knife to his breast, said, "I intended to avenge Chih Po's death!"

Hsiang-tzu's attendants were about to put him to death on the spot, but Hsiang-tzu said, "He is a righteous man. From now on I will simply take care to keep him at a distance. Chih Po and his heirs were all wiped out. If one of his retainers feels compelled to try to avenge his death, he must be a worthy man such as the world seldom sees." So he pardoned Yü Jang and sent him away.

After some time, Yü Jang painted his body with lacquer to induce sores like those of a leper, destroyed his voice by drinking lye, and completely changed his appearance until no one could recognize him. When he went begging in the market place, even his wife did not know him. But, as he was going along, he met a friend who recognized him and asked, "Aren't you Yü Jang?"

"I am," he said.

His friend began to weep. "With your talent, you could swear allegiance and take service under Hsiang-tzu, and he would be sure to make you one of his close associates. Once you got close to him, you would have a chance to accomplish your aim. Would that not be easier? Destroying your body and inflicting pain on yourself in order to carry out your revenge—is that not doing it the hard way?"

Yü Jang replied, "To seek to kill a man after you have sworn allegiance and taken service with him amounts to harboring traitorous thoughts against your own lord. I have chosen the hard way, it is true. But I have done so in order to bring shame to all men in the future generations who think to serve their lords with treacherous intentions!" Then he took leave of his friend.

Sometime later, word got about that Hsiang-tzu was going out on an excursion, and Yü Jang accordingly went and hid under the bridge he was to pass over. When Hsiang-tzu came to the bridge, his horse suddenly shied. "This must be Yü Jang!" he said, and sent one of his men to investigate. It was indeed Yü Jang.

Hsiang-tzu began to berate him. "You once served both the Fan and Chung-hang families, did you not? And yet when Chih Po wiped them out, you made no move to avenge their deaths, but instead swore allegiance and took service under Chih Po. Now that Chih Po too is dead, why are you suddenly so determined to avenge his death?"

Yü Jang replied, "I served both the Fan and Chung-hang families, and both of them treated me as an ordinary man; therefore I repaid them as an ordinary man would. But when I served Chih Po, he treated me as one of the finest men of the land, and so I have determined to repay him in the same spirit."

Hsiang-tzu sighed a deep sigh and tears came to his eyes. "Ah, Yü Jang," he said, "the world already knows of your loyalty to Chih Po, and I have already pardoned you all I need to. You had best take thought for your end. I can pardon you no more!" He ordered his men to surround Yü Jang.

"They say that a wise ruler does not hide the good deeds of others," said Yü Jang, "and a loyal subject is bound to die for his honor. Formerly you were gracious enough to pardon me, and all the world praised you as a worthy man. For today's business I have no doubt that I deserve to be executed. But I beg you to give me your robe so that I may at least strike at it and fulfill my determination

73

symbolic will to fulfill sense of duty.

everylife becomes a moral lesson.

takes own life. sign of honor assumes punishment for failing

for revenge. Then I may die without regret. It is more than I dare hope for, yet I am bold to speak what is in my heart."

Hsiang-tzu, filled with admiration at Yü Jang's sense of duty, took off his robe and instructed his attendants to hand it to Yü Jang. Yü Jang drew his sword, leaped three times into the air, and slashed at the robe, crying, "Now I can go to the world below and report to Chih Po!" Then he fell on his sword and died. That day, when men of true determination in the state of Chao heard what he had done, they all wept for him.

Death before Dishonor

Nieh Cheng

Some forty years later there was the affair of Nieh Cheng in Chih. Nieh Cheng was from the village of Deep Well in Chih. He killed a man and, in order to escape retaliation, went with his mother and elder sister to the state of Ch'i, where he made a living as a butcher. Some time later Yen Chung-tzu of P'u-yang, an official in the service of Marquis Ai of Han, had a falling out with Han Hsia-lei, the prime minister of Han. Fearful that he might be put to death, Yen Chung-tzu fled from the state and traveled about to other states searching for someone who would be willing to get back to Hsia-lei for him.

sense of obligation to mother & sister

When he arrived in Ch'i, someone told him that Nieh Cheng was a man of valor and daring who, fleeing from his enemies, was hiding out among the butchers. Yen Chung-tzu went to his door and requested an interview, but was several times turned away. He then prepared a gift of wine which he asked to be allowed to offer in the presence of Nieh Cheng's mother. When the drinking was well under way, Yen Chung-tzu brought forth a hundred taels of yellow gold which he laid before Nieh Cheng's mother with wishes for a long life. Nieh Cheng was astounded at such generosity and firmly refused the gift. When Yen Chung-tzu just as firmly pressed it on him, Nieh Cheng repeated his refusal, saying, "I am fortunate enough to have my old mother with me. Though our family is poor and I am living in a strange land and earning my way as a dog butcher,[2] I am still able, come morning and evening, to find some sweet or tasty morsel with which to nourish her. She has everything she needs for her care and comfort—I could not be so bold as to accept your gift."

refusal of gift. to accepting would be a polite can't b/c mother & sister endangerment

Yen Chung-tzu asked the others present all to withdraw and spoke to Nieh Cheng in private. "I have an enemy," he said, "and I have already traveled about to a great many states. When I reached Ch'i, however, I was privileged to learn that you, sir, are a man of extremely high principles. Therefore I have presented these hundred taels of gold, hoping that you may use them to purchase some trifling gift of food for your honored parent and that I may have the pleasure of your friendship. How would I dare hope for anything more?"

Nieh Cheng replied, "I have been content to humble my will and shame my body, living as a butcher here by the market place and well, only because I am

acceptance of loyalty.

---

2   Dogs were raised to be eaten.

fortunate enough to have my old mother to take care of. While she lives, I dare not promise my services to any man!"

Yen Chung-tzu continued every effort to persuade him, but to the end Nieh Cheng was unwilling to accept the gift. Yen Chung-tzu nevertheless did all that etiquette demands of a proper guest before taking his leave.

Some time later Nieh Cheng's mother died and, when she had been buried and the mounring period was over, Nieh Cheng said to himself, "Ah! I am a man of the market place and well, swinging a knife and working as a butcher, while Yen Chung-tzu is chief minister to one of the feudal lords. And yet he did not consider it too far to come a thousand miles, driving far out of his way just to make friends with me. I treated him very shabbily indeed! I have accomplished no great deeds for which I might be praised, yet Yen Chung-tzu presented a hundred taels of gold to my mother with wishes for her continued good health. Though I did not accept it, it is clear that he did so simply because he has a profound appreciation of my worth. Now a worthy gentleman, burning with anger and indignation, has offered friendship and trust to a poor and insignificant man. Can I bear to remain silent and let it end there? Earlier, when he made his request of me, I refused only because my mother was still alive. Now that her years have come to a close, I shall offer my services to one who truly understands me!"

Thereupon he journeyed west to P'u-yang in Wey and went to see Yen Chung-tzu. "The reason I would not agree earlier," he said, "was simply that my mother was still alive. Now, unfortunately, the years Heaven gave her have come to a close. Who is this enemy that you wish to take revenge on? I request permission to undertake the task!"

Yen Chung-tzu then related to him the whole story. "My enemy is Han Hsia-lei, the prime minister of Han. He is also the younger uncle of the ruler of Han. His clan is numerous and powerful and there are many armed guards stationed wherever he happens to be. I had hoped to send someone to stab him to death, but so far no one has been able to accomplish it. Now if you are so kind as not to reject my plea for help, I hope you will allow me to give you additional carriages and men to assist you in the job."

But Nieh Cheng said, "Han and Wey are near neighbors. Now if one is going to murder the prime minister of another state, and the prime minister also happens to be a close relative of the ruler, then the circumstances make it unwise to send a large party of men. If you try to use a lot of men, then there are bound to be differences of opinion on how best to proceed; if there are differences of opinion, then word of the undertaking will leak out; and if word leaks out, then the whole state of Han will be up in arms against you! What could be more dangerous?"

Nieh Cheng therefore declined to accept any carriages or attendants, but instead took leave and set off alone, disguising his sword as a walking stick,[3]

---

3   This phrase is customarily taken simply to mean "using his sword as a walking stick," but this makes little sense here, in addition to being a rather foolish and disrespectful way to handle a sword. Examination of other passages where the

75

until he reached Han. When he arrived, the Han prime minister Hsia-lei happened to be seated in his office, guarded and attended by a large body of men bearing lances and other weapons. Nieh Cheng walked straight in, ascended the steps, and stabbed Hsia-lei to death. Those about the prime minister were thrown into great confusion, and Nieh Cheng, shouting loudly, attacked and killed thirty or forty of them. Then he flayed the skin of his face, gouged out his eyes, and, butchering himself as he had once done animals, spilled out his bowels and in this way died.

The ruler of Han had his corpse taken and exposed in the market place, offering to reward anyone who could identify him, but no one knew who he was. The ruler then hung up the reward, promising to give a thousand pieces of gold to anyone who could say who it was that had killed Prime Minister Hsia-lei. A long time passed but no one came forward with the answer.

Meanwhile Nieh Cheng's elder sister Jung heard that someone had stabbed and killed the prime minister of Han, but that the blame could not be fixed since no one knew the culprit's name. His corpse had been exposed in the market place with a reward of a thousand pieces of gold hanging above it, she was told. Filled with apprehension, she said, "Could it be my younger brother? Ah-Yen Chung-tzu certainly knew what he was capable of!"

Then she set off at once and went to the market place of Han, where she found that the dead man was indeed Nieh Cheng. Throwing herself down beside the corpse, she wept in profound sorrow, crying, "This man is called Nieh Cheng from the village of Deep Well in Chih!"

The people passing back and forth through the market all said to her, "This man has committed an act of violence and treachery against the prime minister of our state and our king has posted a reward of a thousand gold pieces for anyone who can discover his name—have you not heard? How dare you come here and admit that you were acquainted with him? "

Jung replied, "Yes, I have heard. But Cheng was willing to accept shame and disgrace, throwing away his future and making a living in the market place, because our mother was still in good health and I was not yet married. After our mother had ended her years and departed from the world, and I had found a husband, then Yen Chung-tzu, recognizing my brother's worth, lifted him up from hardship and disgrace and became his friend, treating him with kindness and generosity. So there was nothing he could do. A gentleman will always be willing to die for someone who recognizes his true worth. And now, because I am still alive, he has inflicted this terrible mutilation upon himself so as to wipe out all trace of his identity. But how could I, out of fear that I might be put to death, allow so worthy a brother's name to be lost forever?"

Having astounded the people of the market place with these words, she cried three times in a loud voice to Heaven and then died of grief and anguish by the

---

phrase occurs shows that in all cases the person is traveling incognito and I therefore suggest the above translation. Nieh Cheng could hardly have approached the prime minister if his sword had been visible.

dead man's side. When the inhabitants of Chin, Ch'u, Ch'i, and Wey heard of this, they all said, "Cheng was not the only able one—his sister too proved herself a woman of valor!"

If Cheng had in fact known that his sister would be unwilling to stand by in silence but, heedless of the threat of execution and public exposure, would make her way a thousand miles over the steep passes, determined to spread his fame abroad, so that sister and brother would both end as criminals in the market place of Han, then he would surely never have agreed to undertake such a mission for Yen Chung-tzu. And as for Yen Chung-tzu, it can certainly be said that he knew how to recognize a man's ability and win others to his service.

The Hereditary House of Prime Minister Hsiao

When the armies of Ch'u surrounded us at Jung-yang and we were locked in stalemate for three years, Hsiao Ho governed the land west of the mountains, plotting our welfare, sending a constant stream of reinforcements, and supplying rations and provisions without end. He caused the people to rejoice in Han and hate the alliance of Ch'u. Thus I made The Hereditary House of Prime Minister Hsiao.

Prime Minister Hsiao Ho was a native of Feng in the district of P'ei. Because of his thorough understanding of law and letters he was made a director of officials in P'ei. While Kao-tsu was still a commoner, Hsiao Ho on numerous occasions took advantage of his official capacity to help Kao-tsu out. After Kao-tsu became a village head he in turn did all he could to assist Hsiao Ho. When Kao-tsu was sent with a band of corvée laborers to Hsien-yang, each of the other officials presented him with three hundred cash as a parting gift, but Hsiao Ho alone gave five hundred.

As an official of P'ei, Hsiao Ho worked with the secretary of Ch'in who was in charge of overseeing the province. Because he conducted his affairs with consistent discretion and understanding, he was given the position of a provincial secretary of Ssu River, where his record was also of the highest order. The secretary of Ch'in planned on his return to the capital to make a report of Hsiao Ho's good record and have him appointed to a position in the central government, but Hsiao Ho begged not to be transferred.

When Kao-tsu rose to the position of governor of P'ei, Hsiao Ho always served as his aide and looked after official business for him. At the time when Kao-tsu marched into the capital of Hsien-yang, all the generals rushed to the storehouses and fought with each other over Ch'in's goods and treasures. But Hsiao Ho entered ahead of them and gathered up all the maps and official records that had belonged to Ch'in's ministers and secretaries and stored them away. When Kao-tsu became king of Han, Hsiao Ho served as his prime minister. Hsiang Yü arrived later with the other nobles, massacred the inhabitants of Hsien-yang, burned the city, and then marched away. But because of the maps and registries of Ch'in which Hsiao Ho had in his possession, the king of Han was able to inform himself of all the strategic defense points of the empire, the population and relative strength of the various districts, and the ills and grievances of the people.

On the recommendation of Hsiao Ho, the king of Han took Han Hsin into his service and made him a major general. . . .

When the king of Han led his forces east again to conquer the three kingdoms of Ch'in, he left Hsiao Ho behind as his prime minister to govern Pa and Shu, with instructions to ensure their well-being and loyalty, propagandize for his cause, and see that provisions were sent to feed his army.

In the second year of Han [205 B.C.], while the king of Han and the other feudal leaders were attacking Ch'u, Hsiao Ho remained behind to guard the area within the Pass and look after the heir apparent. Establishing the seat of government in Yuehyang, he worked to simplify the laws and statutes and set up dynastic temples and altars, palaces, and district offices. All affairs he reported immediately to the king of Han, and acted only upon his permission and approval. If it was impossible to report to the king at the time, he disposed of the matter as he thought best and asked the king's opinion on his return. He had charge of all affairs within the Pass, drawing up registers of the population and sending supplies by land and water to provision the army. The king of Han several times lost large parts of his army and was forced to retreat in flight, but each time Hsiao Ho raised more troops from the area within the Pass and immediately brought the army back up to strength. For this reason the king entrusted sole charge of the land within the Pass to him.

In the third year of Han [204 B.C.], the king of Han and Hsiang Yü were locked in stalemate in the area So in Ching. The king several times sent envoys to reward and encourage Hsiao Ho for his labors. Master Po spoke to Hsiao Ho, saying, "While His Majesty is forced to camp in the fields and suffer the hardships of exposure, he sends envoys to reward and encourage you. It must be that he doubts your loyalty. I think it would be best for you to summon all your sons and brothers who are fit to take up arms and send them to join the army. Then the king will surely have greater confidence in you." Hsiao Ho followed his suggestion and the king was greatly pleased.

In the fifth year of Han [202 B.C.], after Hsiang Yü had been killed and the empire brought to peace, discussions were begun as to who had won merit and who should be enfeoffed but, because there was a great deal of contention among the officials over their respective achievements, the year passed before the matter could be settled.

The king of Han, now emperor, considered that Hsiao Ho had achieved the highest merit, and hence enfeoffed him as marquis of Tsuan with the revenue from a large number of towns. But the other distinguished officials objected, saying, "We have all buckled on armor and taken up our weapons, some of us fighting as many as a hundred or more engagements, the least of us fighting twenty or thirty. Each, to a greater or lesser degree, has engaged in attacks upon cities or seizures of territory. And yet Hsiao Ho, who has never campaigned on the sweaty steeds of battle, but only sat here with brush and ink deliberating on

78

questions of state instead of fighting, is awarded a position above us. How can this be?"

"Gentlemen," the emperor asked, "do you know anything about hunting?"

"We do," they replied.

"And do you know anything about hunting dogs?"

"We do."

"Now in a hunt," the emperor said, "it is the dog who is sent to pursue and kill the beast. But the one who unleashes the dog and points out the place where the beast is hiding is the huntsman. You, gentlemen, have only succeeded in capturing the beast, and so your achievement is that of hunting dogs. But it is Hsiao Ho who unleashed you and pointed out the place, and his achievement is that of the huntsman. Also in your case only you yourselves, or at most two or three of your family, joined in following me. But Hsiao Ho dispatched his whole family numbering twenty or thirty members to accompany me. This is a service I can hardly forget."

None of the officials dared say anything further. The various marquises having been granted their fiefs, the question of what order of precedence they should take was brought before the emperor. "Ts'ao Ts'an, the marquis of P'ing-yang," the officials stated, "bears on his body the scars of seventy wounds. In attacking cities and seizing territory he has achieved the greatest merit. It is proper that he should be given first place."

The emperor had already contravened the will of his ministers by granting Hsiao Ho such a generous fief, and when it came to the question of precedence he did not feel that he could dispute their judgment a second time, though personally he wanted Hsiao Ho to be given first place. At this point Lord E, a marquis of the area within the Pass came forward. "The opinion of the other ministers," he said, "is in my estimation a mistake. Although Ts'ao Ts'an has won merit by fighting in the field and seizing territory, this was an accomplishment of the moment. While the emperor was locked in battle with Hsiang Yü for five years, he several times lost the major part of his army, and was on occasion forced to flee for his life in retreat. But each time Hsiao Ho sent reinforcements from the area within the Pass to bring the army back to strength. The emperor sent no orders of men and yet, just when his forces were weakest and most in danger of annihilation, a new contingent of some ten thousand recruits would arrive. Again, when Han and Ch'u were stalemated for several years at Jung-yang, our army ran completely out of provisions, but Hsiao Ho sent supplies by land and water from the area within the pass and saved our men from starvation. Though His Majesty several times lost control of land east of the mountains, Hsiao Ho kept firm hold on the area within the Pass and awaited His Majesty's final return. His achievements were not a matter of a moment, but deserve everlasting honor. Han could have done without a hundred men like Ts'ao Ts'an and never felt the loss, nor would their presence have assured inevitable victory by any means. How then can one suggest that the achievements of a moment take precedence over those of all time? Hsiao Ho should clearly be granted first place, and Ts'ao Ts'an ranked second."

79

The emperor approved this suggestion; in addition he granted Hsiao Ho the privilege of wearing his sword and shoes when he ascended to the audience chamber, and absolved him from the duty of hurrying when he entered court.[4]

The emperor announced, "I have heard that he who works for the advancement of worthy men deserves the highest reward. Although Hsiao Ho achieved the most outstanding merit, it was Lord E who made this fact clear." With this he granted Lord E the title of marquis of P'ing-an, awarding him the cities from which he already received the revenue as a marquis within the Pass.[5] On the same day he enfeoffed all of Hsiao Ho's male relatives, some ten or more, with the revenue of various towns, and increased Hsiao Ho's original fief by two thousand households. This last, according to the emperor, was done because when he had once been sent on labor service to Hsien-yang Hsiao Ho had presented him with two hundred cash more than any of the other officials as a parting gift.

In the eleventh year of Han [196 B.C.] Ch'en Hsi revolted. Kao-tsu marched to Han-tan to attack him, but before the campaign was completed Han Hsin, the marquis of Huai-yin, began to plot a rebellion in the area within the Pass. Empress Lu followed Hsiao Ho's advice and executed Han Hsin. . . . When the emperor received word of Han Hsin's execution, he sent a messenger to honor Hsiao Ho with the position of prime minister and increase his fief by five thousand households, granting him at the same time a private retinue of five hundred soldiers headed by a colonel to act as his bodyguard.

All the other ministers went to congratulate Hsiao Ho on his good fortune, but Shao P'ing alone presented condolences as though upon a death. (Shao P'ing had been the marquis of Tung-ling under Ch'in, but when Ch'in was defeated he was made a commoner. Being very poor, he used to raise melons east of the city of Ch'ang-an. His melons were known for their excellent flavor and everyone called them "Tung-ling melons" after the title that Shao P'ing had once held.) Shao P'ing said to him, "Some misfortune will come from this. The emperor is away in battle and has left you to guard the capital area, and yet, though you suffer none of the perils of war, he suddenly increases your fief and grants you a bodyguard. It must be that, because of the recent revolt of Han Hsin in the capital area, he doubts your loyalty. He has granted you a bodyguard not for your own protection but because he does not trust you. I beg you to decline the new enfeoffment and not accept it, but instead to make a contribution to the expenses of the campaign from your own private wealth. Then the emperor's mind will be set at ease." Hsiao Ho followed his advice, to the great pleasure of the emperor.

---

4   Chinese etiquette forbade ministers to wear their swords or shoes when they
    entered the emperor's presence. In addition they were required to scurry into
    court instead of walking at a normal pace. By excepting him from these
    requirements the emperor was conferring upon Hsiao Ho the marks of extreme
    honor.

5   The "marquises within the Pass" ordinarily did not hold possession of any lands,
    but only received the revenues from the cities in their fiefs.

In the autumn of the twelfth year of Han [195 B.C.] Ch'ing Pu revolted. The emperor in person led a force to attack him, from time to time sending envoys back to the capital to ask what Hsiao Ho was doing. While the emperor was away in battle Hsiao Ho continued to look after the wants of the people and encourage them in their labors, sending all the assistance he could to the army as he had done at the time of Ch'en Hsi's revolt. But one of his retainers advised him, saying, "It will not be long before your family is wiped out. You have been made prime minister and given the highest rank in the empire. There is no further honor that can be added to this. Now it has been over ten years since you first entered the Pass and won the hearts of the people. They are all unswervingly loyal to you, for you have ceaselessly and with the greatest diligence worked for their peace and well-being. The reason the emperor keeps sending to ask what you are doing is that he is afraid you will betray him and start an uprising within the Pass. Why don't you buy up a lot of farm land on credit and start speculating in goods at a cheap price so that you will create a reputation for being corrupt? Then the emperor's mind will be set somewhat at ease."[6]

Hsiao Ho followed this suggestion and the emperor was very pleased. When his campaign against Ch'ing Pu was completed and he led his army back to the capital, the people crowded along the roadside presenting petitions to the emperor accusing the prime minister of forcing them to sell their land and houses at an unfair price and accumulating a fortune of twenty or thirty million of cash. After the emperor reached the capital, Hsiao Ho appeared before him. "I see that you have been making a profit from the people," said the emperor laughing. He then handed over to Hsiao Ho the petitions that had been presented, adding, "You must do something to make amends to them!"

Hsiao Ho accordingly made this request on behalf of the people: "The region of Ch'ang-an is very narrow and constricted, and yet there is a great deal of idle land going to waste in the Shang-ling Park.[7] I beg that the people be allowed to use the park for farm land, leaving the straw and other remains of their crops as fodder for beasts."

The emperor flew into a rage. "You have succeeded in getting a lot of money and bribes from the merchants and now for their sake you want to take my park away from me!" He turned Hsiao Ho over to the law officials to be put into chains.

A few days later one of the palace guards named Wang who was in attendance advanced and inquired, "What terrible crime has the prime minister committed that Your Majesty has so suddenly thrown him into prison?"

"I have heard," replied the emperor, "that when Li Ssu was prime minister to the emperor of Ch'in if anything good came about he attributed it to his sovereign, but for anything bad he accepted responsibility himself. But now my

---

6 This would seem an odd way to set the emperor's mind at ease, but all the suggestion means is that Hsiao Ho should do something to decrease his popularity, which had reached dangerous proportions.

7 The emperor's private hunting park.

prime minister has been accepting money from a lot of dirty merchants and in return asks for my park so that he can ingratiate himself with the people. Therefore, I have had him put in chains and punished."

"But if in the course of his duties the prime minister becomes aware of something that will benefit the people," objected Wang, "it is his duty to request it. Why should Your Majesty suppose that he has been accepting money from the merchants? During the years when Your Majesty was battling Ch'u, and later, when Ch'en Hsi and Ch'ing Pu revolted, Your Majesty was away leading the armies, while the prime minister the whole time guarded the area within the Pass. At that time he had no more than to nod his head and Your Majesty would have lost possession of the whole area west of the Pass. But since he did not take that opportunity to scheme for his own profit, why should he now try to profit from the money of the merchants? As for the ruler of Ch'in, the reason he did not become aware of his own faults and eventually lost the empire was that Li Ssu kept accepting the blame for things himself. Ch'in can therefore hardly be taken as a model. Is it not very shortsighted of Your Majesty to suspect the prime minister in this fashion?"

The emperor was deeply perplexed, but before the day was over he dispatched a messenger bearing the imperial seal with orders to pardon Hsiao Ho and release him. Hsiao Ho was by this time well on in years and, being by nature extremely respectful and circumspect in his manner, came before the emperor barefooted and begged for forgiveness. "You may go!" said the emperor. "You asked for the park for the sake of the people. In denying your request I have acted no better than the tyrants Chieh and Chou of old, while you have shown yourself a worthy minister. The reason I had you bound was so that the people might all hear of my fault."

Hsiao Ho had never been on good terms with Ts'ao Ts'an. When Hsiao Ho fell ill Emperor Hui, who had succeeded his father, Kao-tsu, on the throne, came in person to inquire about his illness. "When your hundred years are ended," the emperor asked, "who can fill your place?"

"No one knows his ministers better than their lord," Hsiao Ho replied.

"What about Ts'ao Ts'an?"

Hsiao Ho bowed his head and answered, "As long as my lord has him, I may die without regret."

In selecting his lands and residence, Hsiao Ho always chose to live in an out-of-the-way place with no elaborate walls or roofs to his house.

"This way, if my descendants are worthy men," he used to say, "they will follow my example of frugal living. And if they turn out to be unworthy, they will at least have nothing that the more powerful families can take away from them."

In the second year of Emperor Hui [193 B.C.] Prime Minister Hsiao Ho died. He was granted the posthumous title of Wen-chung or "Civil Fulfillment Marquis." In the fourth generation his heirs, because of some offense, were deprived of the marquisate, but shortly afterwards the emperor sought out Hsiao Ho's descendant and enfeoffed him as marquis of Tsuan to carry on the line. None of the other distinguished ministers received such honor.

The Grand Historian remarks: Prime Minister Hsiao Ho in the time of Ch'in was a petty official, wielding his brush and scraper[8] and going about his business without distinction or honor. But when the Han, like a great sun or moon, rose in the sky, he caught a little of its brilliance. With the gravest care he guarded what was charged to him as though under lock and key and, because the people groaned under the laws of Ch'in, he gratified their wishes by making a new beginning for the empire. When Han Hsin, Ch'ing Pu, and the others had all been wiped out, his glory alone grew ever brighter. First among the ranks of officials, renowned in later ages, his fame rivals that of the ancient ministers Hung Yao and San I.

intellect.

strategize

customs

administrative

humility

frugality

Hsiao tested when he is popular, emperor distrust b/c all the loyalty.

good deeds of a man will affect future generations

. set good example

good emperor will bring good things to the people.

---

8   Writing at this time was done on strips of wood. When the clerk made a mistake, he would scrape the surface of the wood clean and write on it again.

Selections from
The Writings of Confucius

⫷⬦⫸

If we were to characterize in one word the Chinese way of life for the last two thousand years, the word would be "Confucian." No other individual in Chinese history has so deeply influenced the life and thought of his people, as a transmitter, teacher, and creative interpreter of the ancient culture and literature, and as a molder of the Chinese mind and character. The other ancient philosophies, the religious systems of Taoism and Buddhism, all have known their days of glory and neglect; but the doctrines of Confucianism, since their general recognition in the first century before Christ, have never ceased to exert a vital influence on the nation down to our own century. Many Chinese have professed themselves to be Taoists, Buddhists, even Christians, but seldom have they ceased at the same time to be Confucianists. For Confucianism since the time of its general acceptance has been more than a creed to be professed or rejected; it has become an inseparable part of the society and thought of the nation as a whole, of what it means to be a Chinese, as the Confucian Classics are not the canon of a particular sect but the literary heritage of a whole people.

Considering his tremendous influence and importance, the life of Confucius is peculiarly human and undramatic. He was born in 551 B.C. in the small feudal state of Lu in modern Shantung province. His family name was K'ung, his personal name Ch'iu. "Confucius" is the Latinized form of "K'ung Fu-tzu" or "Master K'ung," the title commonly used in referring to him in Chinese. It is probable that his ancestors were members of the lesser aristocracy who had, however, sunk to a position of poverty and insignificance by the time of his birth. His father died when he was very young, leaving him to struggle alone with the problem of securing an education and making his way in the world.

The world he faced was not a bright one. China was divided into a number of small feudal states which were constantly bickering or making war upon each other or upon the barbarian tribes that pressed the Chinese people on all sides. The kings of the central court of the Chou dynasty, who had once given peace and stability to the nation, were weak and ineffective before the might of the more powerful feudal lords. Kings were ordered about by their vassals, rulers deposed or assassinated by their ministers, fathers slain by their sons. All was

---

From *Sources of Chinese Tradition,* ed. Wm. Theodore de Bary, © 1964 Columbia University Press. Reprinted with the permission of the publisher.

violence and disorder among the ruling class and there seemed to be no higher power, temporal or spiritual, to which men might appeal.

With energy and utter selflessness, Confucius set about to bring order and peace to his age. He believed that his place was in the world of politics and with almost pathetic persistence he sought through the states of China for a ruler who would be willing to employ him and his ideas in the government. He managed to find employment for a while in his native state of Lu and, according to tradition, rose to a fairly high position. But his success was short-lived; on the whole his political career was a failure, and more and more he turned his attention to the teaching of young men who, he hoped, might succeed in public life where he had failed. Judging from all accounts he was a teacher of rare enthusiasm and art; he was said to have had some three thousand students, of whom seventy-two were close personal disciples or known for their virtue. In his old age he retired to devote himself, so tradition says, to the editing of the texts of the Confucian Classics. He died in 479 B.C.

What was the solution which Confucius offered for the ills and evil of his day? It was the same solution which the philosophers and prophets of so many ages and cultures have offered: a return to virtue. Unless men individually embraced the ideal of *jen*—humanity, benevolence, or perfect virtue—there was no hope that society could be spared the evil, cruelty, and violence that was destroying it.

If there is nothing unique or arresting about this solution urged by Confucius, the reasons he used to persuade men of its aptness deserve close attention. First of all, he held out no utilitarian persuasions to attract men to the practice of perfect virtue. He knew too well from his own experience that virtue is often despised and persecuted, and he cautioned his disciples that they must be prepared to face frequent poverty and distress. The pursuit of material profit did not coincide, but more often directly conflicted with the dictates of virtue; it was the concern only of the small and unenlightened mind. The gentleman, mindless of comfort and safety, must fix his attention upon higher things.

Again, he was very sparing in the invocation of divine or supernatural sanction for his teachings. Confucius seems to have been a man of deep personal piety and reverence. But he lived in an age that was still dominated by a primitive fear of the supernatural and marred by gross and cruel superstitions. The rulers of his time firmly believed in the prophetic nature of dreams, the efficacy of the arts of divination, the baleful power of the spirits of the dead, and all manner of weird and unnatural portents and prodigies. Men still cowered before the eclipse and the age when human sacrifices were carried out on the death of a ruler was less than a century past. In such an atmosphere, Confucius chose to direct attention away from the supernatural and toward the vital problems of human society and the ordering of the state. Viewing so much of the history of this period through the pages of the literature of the Confucian school itself, it is difficult to realize how very rare this humanism and rationalism of Confucius and his disciples must have been in their own time.

Confucius had a strong belief in a natural order that was also a moral order. Heaven for him was a guiding Providence, and one's fulfillment as a man came from acting in accordance with the will of Heaven. This will, however, could be best understood through the study of history. In the traditions, customs, and literature of the past, in the collective experience of mankind, there was objective confirmation of the moral law written in the heart of man. From the ancient legends Confucius selected the figures of the sage—kings Yao and Shun, King T'ang, the wise founder of the Shang dynasty, and above all the great ancestors of the ruling house of the Chou, Kings Wen and Wu and the Duke of Chou, to be his ideals. These men had embodied the humanity and perfect virtue that he advocated, and their deeds and their reigns represented all that was wise and good in Chinese history and society. In particular Confucius looked back to an age of peace and order at the beginning of the Chou when its founding fathers, in the depth of their wisdom and virtue, had set up the institutions and organized the complex feudal hierarchy of the new dynasty, and created solemn rites and music for its leaders and people. These rites and music-dance compositions of the old feudal society, the *li* and *yüëh* which figure so prominently in Confucian literature, were regarded by Confucius with the utmost gravity. For they were the outward embodiment of the wisdom and virtue of their creators, the expression of reverence and perfect hierarchical order in society. And by the careful observance of these rites, the thoughtful contemplation of this music and its meaning, one could recreate in oneself the wisdom and virtue of the ancients and discipline oneself to the perfect order which they had intended. All the ills of his day Confucius attributed to the fact that the leaders of society had neglected the old rites, were performing them incorrectly, or usurping rites and ceremonies to which they were not entitled. For as a correct observance of the rites was a sign of perfect social order and the source of all spiritual enlightenment, so their neglect and abuse must be no more than the reflection of a deeper moral chaos and the beginning of spiritual darkness. To abuse the forms of the rites was to abuse the reality, the moral order which they represented. It was this abuse of the rites and titles of the social order, and the inner spiritual disorder which it represented, that Confucius deplored. Hence his call for a "rectification of names," that men might be in reality what they claimed to be in title, and his insistence upon a careful and reverent attention to the spirit and letter of the rites.

This emphasis upon ritual—an insistence upon it sometimes even when its original meaning was lost—must strike us as excessively conservative and formalistic, as indeed Confucianism in its later days often became. Yet implicit in this view was an idealization of the past that set a high standard for the present, and provided more of an impetus to reform, than to maintain, the status quo. Confucius' own life is sufficient evidence of his reformist spirit. He sought to conserve or restore what was good, while changing what was bad. Thus more fundamental to him than either conservatism or reformism in itself was a clear sense of moral values, expressed in his warm humanity, optimism, humility, and good sense. Confucius lived in a feudal society and conceived of society in terms of the feudal hierarchy. The common people were to be led, cared for, cherished, even taught, by the rulers; but their position at the base of the social hierarchy should not be modified, indeed, could not be without upsetting the whole vertical order.

Confucius' teachings were for the *chün-tzu,* the gentleman, the potential or actual ruler of society who alone possessed the vision to see beyond personal profit and material interest to the broader interests of the state and mankind. Yet he insisted that it was not mere birth or social position, but precisely this power of vision, this keener and more profound moral sense, which distinguished the gentleman, the true ruler. Like Plato he would have the kings be sages, for only a truly wise and virtuous ruler could fittingly head the hierarchy of society and lead all men, by the example and suasion of his own goodness, to perfect order and a practice of similar virtue. Because of this belief in the importance of character over birth, he gave himself to the teaching of promising young men regardless of their origins. He and his school are responsible for the pedagogic tradition which characterizes all of later Chinese history, for the optimistic belief in the perfectibility of man through learning, and for the reverence for the scholar and the man of letters so pronounced in Chinese society. And it is to a large extent the teachings and example of Confucius and his school which have convinced so many of the great men of later Chinese history that the highest career in life is that of the statesman, that the highest concern of the gentleman-scholar is politics and the proper ordering of the state.

Confucius and his teachings were little respected and less practiced by the men of his day, and for centuries the Confucian school remained only one among many rival schools of philosophy with its greatest strength in the area of Confucius' native state of Lu. But gradually Confucius' humanism began to triumph over the superstition and mysticism of other doctrines, his idealistic emphasis on virtue, kindness, and learning to attract more men than the harsh and cynical philosophies of other states. At last, in the second century B.C., Confucianism was declared the official creed of the nation and the Classics became the principal, if not the sole, study of all scholars and statesmen. Through the centuries the teachings of Confucius continued not only to be revered in China, but also to exert a tremendous influence in Korea, Japan and Annam. Confucius was given the title "Supreme Sage and Foremost Teacher" and his tomb and temple in Ch'u-fu in Shantung became a kind of Mecca for all educated Chinese, while a Confucian temple on less elaborate scale was established in every county seat throughout the land. Under the Nationalist regime his birthday was (and still is on Taiwan) observed as Teachers' Day, a national holiday.

There is a large body of literature in Chinese, of varying degrees of reliability, on the life and teachings of Confucius. Among this the most important work is the record of the Master's activities and conversations compiled probably by his disciples' disciples, the *Analects*. This work is in twenty chapters and 497 verses, some consisting of the briefest aphorisms. From the time when Confucianism became widely accepted, the laconic and provocative sentences of this work, difficult though they often are to interpret, have exercised a profound influence upon the thought and language of the peoples of East Asia, while for the last eight hundred years it has been a basic text in Chinese education known to every schoolboy. We have selected and translated the more important passages and arranged them under a few significant topics.

[from *Sources of Chinese Tradition*, edited by Theodore de Bary, et al.]

From The Analects

———◆———

Confucius the Man

Personality and Character

1. In his leisure hours, Confucius was easy in his manner and cheerful in his expression. [VII:4]

2. Confucius was gentle yet firm, dignified but not harsh, respectful yet well at ease. [VII:37]

3. Confucius fished but not with a net; he shot but not at a roosting bird. [He did not take unfair advantage of inferior creatures.] [VII:26]

4. When the stables were burned down, on returning from court, Confucius asked: "Was anyone hurt?" He did not ask about the horses. [X:12]

5. When Confucius was pleased with the singing of someone he was with, he would always ask to have the song repeated and would join in himself. [VII:31]

6. The Duke of She asked Tzu Lu about Confucius, and Tzu Lu gave him no answer. Confucius said: "Why didn't you tell him that I am a person who forgets to eat when he is enthusiastic about something, forgets all his worries in his enjoyment of it, and is not aware that old age is coming on?" [VII:18]

7. Confucius said: "Having only coarse food to eat, plain water to drink, and a bent arm for a pillow, one can still find happiness therein. Riches and honor acquired by unrighteous means are to me as drifting clouds." [VII:15]

8. Once when Tzu Lu, Tseng Hsi, Jan Yu, and Kung-hsi Hua were seated in attendance upon him, Confucius said: "You no doubt consider me a day or so your senior, but let us not mind that. When out of office you say among yourselves that your merits are not recognized. Now suppose some prince were to recognize your merits, what would be your wishes?" Tzu Lu without hesitation replied: "Take a kingdom of a thousand chariots, hemmed in by great powers, oppressed by invading troops, and suffering from famine in addition—I should like to take charge of it. In three years' time I could make it brave and make it understand the right course to pursue." Confucius smiled at him. "And how about you, Ch'iu [Jan Yu]?" "Take a district of sixty or seventy *li*[1] square," answered

---

1   A *li* is equal to about one-third of an English mile.

Jan Yu, "or say, one of fifty or sixty *li* square. I should like to take charge of it. In three years' time I could make its people live in abundance; but as for the promotion of rites (*li*) and music, I should have to leave that to a real gentleman." "And how about you, Ch'ih [Kung-hsi Hua]?" "Not that I say I could do it," he answered, "but I should like to be trained for it. At the ceremonies in the Ancestral Temple [of the Imperial House] or at the conferences of the princes, I should like to wear the ceremonial cap and gown, and be a minor official assisting in the ceremony." "And how about you, Tien [Tseng Hsi]?" Tseng Hsi paused in his playing of the zither. Putting it aside he rose and replied: "I am afraid my wishes are entirely different from those cherished by these three gentlemen." "What harm is there in that?" said Confucius. "We are just trying to let each express his desire." Then he said: "In the latter days of spring, when the light spring garments are made, I would like to take along five or six grown-ups and six or seven youths to bathe in the River Yi, and after the bath go to enjoy the breeze in the woods among the altars of Wu-yi, and then return home, loitering and singing on our way." Confucius heaved a deep sigh and said: "You are the man after my own heart." [XI:25]

His Sense of Mission

9. Confucius said: "Were any prince to employ me, even in a single year a good deal could be done, and in three years everything could be accomplished." [XIII:10]   *contradicts modesty.*

10. Confucius said: "Ah! There is no one who knows me!" Tzu Kung asked "Why do you say, sir, that no one knows you?" Confucius said: "I make no complaint against Heaven, nor do I lay the blame on men. Though my studies are lowly, they penetrate the sublime on high. Perhaps after all I am known—by Heaven." [XIV:37]

11. When Confucius was in jeopardy in K'uang, he said: "Since the death of King Wen [founder of the Chou dynasty], does not the mission of culture rest here with us? If Heaven were going to destroy this culture, a mortal like me would not have been given such a place in it. And if Heaven is not going to destroy this culture, what can the men of K'uang do to me?" [IX:5]

12. When [Confucius' most worthy disciple] Yen Hui died, Confucius exclaimed: "Alas, Heaven has destroyed me! Heaven has destroyed me!" [XI:8]

13. Ch'ang-chü and Chieh-ni were cultivating their fields together. Confucius was passing that way and told Tzu Lu to go and ask them where the river could be forded. Ch'ang-chü said: "Who is that holding the reins in the carriage?" Tzu Lu said: "It is Kung Ch'iu [Confucius]." He said: "You mean Kung Ch'iu of the state of Lu?" "Yes," Tzu Lu replied. Ch'ang-chü said: "If it is he, then he already knows where the ford is." Tzu Lu then turned to Chieh-ni. Chieh-ni asked: "Who are you, sir?" Tzu Lu said: "Chung-yu is my name." Chieh-ni said: "You are a follower of Kung Ch'iu of Lu, are you not?" He said: "That is so." Chieh-ni said: "The whole world is swept as by a torrential flood, and who can change it? As for you, instead of following one who flees from this man and that, you would do better to follow one who flees the whole world." And with that he went on covering the seed without stopping. Tzu Lu went and told Confucius,

who said ruefully: "One cannot herd together with birds and beasts. If I am not to be a man among other men, then what am I to be? If the Way *(Tao)* prevailed in the world, I should not be trying to alter things." [XVIII:6]

His Love of Learning

14. Confucius said: "When walking in a party of three, I always have teachers. I can select the good qualities of the one for imitation, and the bad ones of the other and correct them in myself." [VII:21]

15. Confucius said: "Sometimes I have gone a whole day without food and a whole night without sleep, giving myself to thought. It was no use. It is better to learn." [XV:30]

16. Confucius said: "At fifteen, I set my heart on learning. At thirty, I was firmly established. At forty, I had no more doubts. At fifty, I knew the will of Heaven. At sixty, I was ready to listen to it. At seventy, I could follow my heart's desire without transgressing what was right." [II:4]

17. Confucius said: "I am a transmitter and not a creator. I believe in and have a passion for the ancients. I venture to compare myself with our old P'eng [China's Methuselah]." [VII:1]

18. When Confucius was in Ch'i, he heard the Shao Music[2] and for three months he forgot the taste of meat, saying: "I never thought music could be so beautiful." [VII:13]

19. There were four things that Confucius was determined to eradicate: a biased mind, arbitrary judgments, obstinacy, and egotism. [IX:4]

20. Confucius said: "Those who know the truth are not up to those who love it; those who love the truth are not up to those who delight in it." [VI:18]

21. Confucius said: "Having heard the Way *(Tao)* in the morning, one may die content in the evening." [IV:8]

Confucius as a Teacher

22. Confucius said: "By nature men are pretty much alike; it is learning and practice that set them apart."[3] [XVII:2]

23. Confucius said: "In education there are no class distinctions."[4] [XV:38]

24. Confucius said: "The young are to be respected. How do we know that the next generation will not measure up to the present one? But if a man has reached forty or fifty and nothing has been heard of him, then I grant that he is not worthy of respect." [IX:22]

25. Confucius said: "When it comes to acquiring perfect virtue *(jen)*, a man should not defer even to his own teacher." [XV:35]

---

2 Classical music of the time of the ancient sage—King Shun (2255–2208 B.C.?).

3 This simple observation by Confucius was agreed upon as the essential truth with regard to human nature and racial difference by a group of international experts in the UNESCO "Statement on Race" published in July, 1950.

4 These four Chinese characters are often found written over the gates or on the auditorium walls of Chinese school buildings.

26. Confucius said: "Those who are born wise are the highest type of people; those who become wise through learning come next; those who learn by overcoming dullness come after that. Those who are dull but still won't learn are the lowest type of people." [XVI:9]

27. Confucius said: "I won't teach a man who is not anxious to learn, and will not explain to one who is not trying to make things clear to himself. If I hold up one corner of a square and a man cannot come back to me with the other three, I won't bother to go over the point again." [VII:8]

28. Confucius said: "Learning without thinking is labor lost; thinking without learning is perilous." [II:15]

29. Confucius said: "Yu, shall I teach you what knowledge is? When you know a thing, say that you know it; when you do not know a thing, admit that you do not know it. That is knowledge." [II:17]

30. Confucius said: "Worthy indeed was Hui! A single bamboo bowl of millet to eat, a gourdful of water to drink, living in a back alley—others would have found it unendurably depressing, but Hui's cheerfulness was not affected at all. Worthy indeed was Hui!" [VI:9]

31. When Yen Hui died Confucius bewailed him with exceeding grief. His followers thereupon said to him: "Sir! You are carrying your grief to excess." Confucius said: "Have I gone to excess? But if I may not grieve exceedingly over this man, for whom shall I grieve?" [XI:9]

32. Confucius said: "A young man's duty is to be filial to his parents at home and respectful to his elders abroad, to be circumspect and truthful, and, while overflowing with love for all men, to associate himself with humanity (jen). If, when all that is done, he has any energy to spare, then let him study the polite arts." [I:6]

33. These were the subjects on which Confucius often discoursed: poetry, history, and the performance of ceremonies—all these were what he often discoursed on. [VII:17]

34. Confucius said: "Personal cultivation begins with poetry, is made firm by rules of decorum (li), and is perfected by music." [VIII:3]

35. Confucius took four subjects for his teaching—literature, conduct, loyalty, and truthfulness. [VII:24]

36. Yen Hui heaved a sigh and said: "You look up to it and it seems so high. You try to drill through it and it seems so hard. You seem to see it in front of you, and all of a sudden it appears behind you. The Master is very good at gently leading a man along and teaching him. He has broadened me with culture, restrained me with ritual (li). I just could not stop myself. But after I have exhausted every resource, there still remains something standing distinct and apart from me. Do what I can to reach his position, I cannot find the way." [IX:10]

37. Shu-sun Wu-shu said to the officials at court: "Tzu Kung is a better man than Confucius." Tzu-fu Ching-po told this to Tzu Kung, and Tzu Kung said: "It is like the matter of house walls. My house wall comes up only to the shoulder, and the people outside are therefore able to see my handsome dwelling, whereas the wall of Confucius rises fathoms high, and unless one is let in by the gate, one

does not see the palatial beauty of the ancestral temple and the grandeur of the hundred ministrants inside. But few are they who have found the gate. What Shu-sun says is therefore perfectly easy to understand." [XIX:23]

The Teachings of Confucius

The Unitary Principle: Reciprocity or Humanity

38. Confucius said: "Tz'u, do you suppose that I merely learned a great deal and tried to remember it all?" The disciple replied: "Yes, is it not so?" Confucius said: "No, I have one principle that runs through it all." [XV:2]

39. Confucius said: "Shen! My teaching contains one principle that runs through it all." "Yes," replied Tseng Tzu. When Confucius had left the room the disciples asked: "What did he mean?" Tseng Tzu replied: "Our Master's teaching is simply this: loyalty and reciprocity." [IV: 15]

40. Tzu Kung asked: "Is there any one word that can serve as a principle for the conduct of life?" Confucius said: "Perhaps the word 'reciprocity': Do not do to others what you would not want others to do to you." [XV:23]

41. Confucius said: "Perfect indeed is the virtue which is according to the Mean. For long people have seldom had the capacity for it." [VI:27]

42. Confucius said: "It is man that can make the Way great, not the Way that can make man great." [XV:28]

43. Chung-kung asked about humanity. Confucius said: "Behave when away from home as though you were in the presence of an important guest. Deal with the common people as though you were officiating at an important sacrifice. Do not do to others what you would not want others to do to you. Then there will be no dissatisfaction either in the state or at home." [XII:2]

44. Confucius said: . . . "The humane man, desiring to be established himself, seeks to establish others; desiring himself to succeed, he helps others to succeed. To judge others by what one knows of oneself is the method of achieving humanity." [VI:28]

Humanity (*jen*)

As the reader will already have judged from its frequent occurrence, *jen* is a key term in Confucius' thought. Sometimes rendered "goodness," "benevolence," or "love," it is the supreme excellence in man or perfect virtue. In later Confucian thought the concept was expanded greatly to suggest a cosmic power. To retain its basically and unmistakably humanistic sense, we have used "humanity" for *jen*, or, when some alternative rendering was clearly called for by the context, have added the romanized original in parentheses (*jen*). By observing the various uses of the same term in different texts, the reader should acquire a sense of both its centrality in Chinese thought and its breadth of meaning.

[*ibid.*]

45. Fan Ch'ih asked about humanity. Confucius said: "Love men." [XII:22]

46. Tzu Chang asked Confucius about humanity. Confucius said: "To be able to practice five virtues everywhere in the world constitutes humanity." Tzu Chang begged to know what these were. Confucius said: "Courtesy, magnanimity, good faith, diligence, and kindness. He who is courteous is not humiliated, he who is magnanimous wins the multitude, he who is of good faith is trusted by the people, he who is diligent attains his objective, and he who is kind can get service from the people." [XVII:6]

47. Confucius said: "Without humanity a man cannot long endure adversity, nor can he long enjoy prosperity. The humane rest in humanity; the wise find it beneficial." [IV:2]

48. Confucius said: "Only the humane man can love men and can hate men." [IV:3]

49. Someone inquired: "What do you think of 'requiting injury with kindness'?" Confucius said: "How will you then requite kindness? Requite injury with justice, and kindness with kindness." [XIV:36]

50. Confucius said: "Is humanity something remote? If I want to be humane, behold, humanity has arrived." [VII:29]

51. Confucius said: . . . "Is there anyone who exerts himself even for a single day to achieve humanity? I have not seen any who had not the strength to achieve it." [IV:6]

52. Confucius said: "As to Hui, for three months his mind did not deviate from humanity. The others can do so, some for a day, some even for a month, but that is all." [VI:5]

53. Confucius said: "Riches and honor are what every man desires, but if they can be obtained only by transgressing the right way, they must not be held. Poverty and lowliness are what every man detests, but if they can be avoided only by transgressing the right way, they must not be evaded. If a gentleman departs from humanity, how can he bear the name? Not even for the lapse of a single meal does a gentleman ignore humanity. In moments of haste he cleaves to it: in seasons of peril he cleaves to it." [IV:5]

54. Confucius said: "The resolute scholar and the humane person will under no circumstance seek life at the expense of humanity. On occasion they will sacrifice their lives to preserve their humanity." [XV:8]

55. Ssu-ma Niu, worrying, said: "All people have brothers, but I alone have none." Tzu Hsia said: "I have heard it said [by Confucius] that death and life rest with Heaven's mandate and that wealth and honor depend on Heaven. Let the gentleman be reverent and make no mistake in conduct, and let him be respectful to others and observant of propriety. Then all within the four seas are brothers." [XII:5]

Filial Piety

56. Tzu Yu asked about filial piety. Confucius said: "Nowadays a filial son is just a man who keeps his parents in food. But even dogs or horses are given food. If there is no feeling of reverence, wherein lies the difference?" [II:7]

57. Tzu Hsia asked about filial piety. Confucius said: "The manner is the really difficult thing. When anything has to be done the young people undertake it; when there is wine and food the elders are served—is this all there is to filial piety?" [II:8]

58. Confucius said: "In serving his parents, a son may gently remonstrate with them. If he sees that they are not inclined to follow his suggestion, he should resume his reverential attitude but not abandon his purpose. If he is belabored, he will not complain." [IV:18]

59. The Duke of She observed to Confucius: "Among us there was an upright man called Kung who was so upright that when his father appropriated a sheep, he bore witness against him." Confucius said: "The upright men among us are not like that. A father will screen his son and a son his father—yet uprightness is to be found in that." [XIII:18]

60. Tsai Wo questioned the three years' mourning and thought one year was long enough: "If the gentlemen for three years abstain from the practice of ritual, ritual will decay; if for three years they make no music, music will go to ruin. In one year the old crops are exhausted and the new crops have come up, the friction-sticks have made the several seasonal fires—one year should be enough." Confucius said: "Would you then feel at ease in eating polished rice and wearing fineries?" "Quite at ease," was the reply. Confucius continued: "If you would really feel at ease, then do so. When a gentleman is in mourning, he does not relish good food if he eats it, does not enjoy music if he hears it, and does not feel at ease in a comfortable dwelling. Hence he abstains from these things. But now since you would feel at ease, then you can have them." When Tsai Wo had gone out, Confucius said: "What lack of humanity in Yü [Tsai Wo]! Only when a child is three years old does it leave its parents' arms. The three years' mourning is the universal observance in the world. And Yü—did he not enjoy the loving care of his parents for three years?" [XVII:21]

Rites and Music

For Confucius the term *li*, which basically means "rites," embraced all those traditional forms which provided an objective standard of conduct. Thus, while li may in given instances refer to "rites," "ceremonial," or "rules of conduct," it has the general meaning of "good form" or "decorum." Confucius insisted, however, that the observance of li should be neither perfunctory nor rigid and inflexible, but should be in keeping with circumstances and also with that spirit of reverence and respect for others which the ceremonies or rules of conduct were meant to embody. By showing their intrinsic significance, he attempted to reassert the value of these traditional forms at a time when they were increasingly neglected or performed as mere pretense. Where the external form is indicated by *li* we shall render it "rites"; where the inward spirit, "decorum."

[*ibid.*]

61. Tzu Kung proposed to do away with the sacrificial lamb offering at the announcement of each new moon. Confucius said: "Tz'u! You love the lamb, but I love the rite." [III:17]

62. Confucius said: "Courtesy without decorum becomes tiresome. Cautiousness without decorum becomes timidity, daring becomes insubordination, frankness becomes effrontery." [VIII:2]

63. Confucius said: "Rites, rites! Does it mean no more than jades and silks? Music, music! Does it mean no more than bells and drums?" [XVII:11]

64. Confucius said: "A man who is not humane, what has he to do with rites? A man who is not humane, what has he to do with music?" [III:3]

65. Lin Fang asked about the fundamental principle of rites. Confucius replied: "You are asking an important question! In rites at large, it is always better to be too simple rather than too lavish. In funeral rites, it is more important to have the real sentiment of sorrow than minute attention to observances." [III:4]

66. Confucius said: "If a ruler can administer his state with decorum (*li*) and courtesy—then what difficulty will he have? If he cannot administer it with decorum and courtesy, what has he to do with rites (*li*)?" [IV:13]

Religious Sentiment

67. Tzu Lu asked about the worship of ghosts and spirits. Confucius said: "We don't know yet how to serve men, how can we know about serving the spirits?" "What about death," was the next question. Confucius said: "We don't know yet about life, how can we know about death?" [XI:11]

68. Fan Ch'ih asked about wisdom. Confucius said: "Devote yourself to the proper demands of the people, respect the ghosts and spirits but keep them at a distance—this may be called wisdom." [VI:20]

69. Po-niu was ill and Confucius went to inquire about him. Having grasped his hand through the window, Confucius said: "It is killing him. It is the will of Heaven, alas! That such a man should have such a malady! That such a man should have such a malady!" [VI:8]

70. Though his food might be coarse rice and vegetable broth, Confucius invariably offered a little in sacrifice, and always with solemnity. [X:8]

71. When Confucius observed sacrificial fasting, his clothing was spotlessly clean, his food was different from the ordinary, and in his dwelling his seat was changed to another place. [X:7]

72. Confucius said: "He who sins against Heaven has none to whom he can pray." [III:13]

73. When Confucius was very ill, Tzu Lu asked that prayers be offered. Confucius asked: "Is there such a thing?" Tzu Lu replied: "Yes, there is. In one of the Eulogies it is said: 'A prayer has been offered for you to the spirits of Heaven and earth.'" Confucius said: "Ah, my praying has been for a long time." [VII:34]

74. Tzu Kung said: "The Master's views on culture and refinement we can comprehend. But his discourses about man's nature and the ways of Heaven none of us can comprehend." [V:12]

75. Confucius said: "I wish I did not have to speak at all." Tzu Kung said: "But if you did not speak, Sir, what should we disciples pass on to others?" Confucius said: "Look at Heaven there. Does it speak? The four seasons run their course and all things are produced. Does Heaven speak?" [XVII:19]

76. Confucius sacrificed [to the dead] as if they were present. He sacrificed to the spirits as if they were present. He said: "I consider my not being present at the sacrifice as if I did not sacrifice." [III :12]

77. The Master did not talk about weird things, physical exploits, disorders, and spirits. [VII:20]

The Gentleman

78. Confucius said: "When nature exceeds art you have the rustic. When art exceeds nature you have the clerk. It is only when art and nature are harmoniously blended that you have the gentleman." [VI:16]

79. Confucius said: . . . "If a gentleman departs from humanity, how can he bear the name? Not even for the lapse of a single meal does a gentleman ignore humanity. In moments of haste he cleaves to it; in seasons of peril he cleaves to it." [IV:5]

80. Confucius said: "The gentleman occupies himself with the Way and not with his livelihood. One may attend to farming, and yet may sometimes go hungry. One may attend to learning and yet may be rewarded with emolument. What the gentleman is anxious about is the Way and not poverty." [XV:31]

81. Ssu-ma Niu asked about the gentleman. Confucius said: "The gentleman has neither anxiety nor fear." Ssu-ma Niu rejoined: "Neither anxiety nor fear—is that what is meant by being a gentleman?" Confucius said: "When he looks into himself and finds no cause for self-reproach, what has he to be anxious about; what has he to fear?" [XII:4]

82. Confucius said: "The way of the gentleman is threefold. I myself have not been able to attain any of them. Being humane, he has no anxieties; being wise, he has no perplexities; being brave, he has no fear." Tzu Kung said: "But, Master, that is your own way." [XIV:30]

83. Confucius said: "You may be able to carry off from a whole army its commander-in-chief, but you cannot deprive the humblest individual of his will." [IX:25]

84. Tzu Kung asked about the gentleman. Confucius said: "The gentleman first practices what he preaches and then preaches what he practices." [II:13]

85. Confucius said: "The gentleman reaches upward; the inferior man reaches downward." [XIV:23]

86. Confucius said: "The gentleman is always calm and at ease; the inferior man is always worried and full of distress." [VII:36]

87. Confucius said: "The gentleman understands what is right; the inferior man understands what is profitable." [IV:16]

88. Confucius said: "The gentleman cherishes virtue; the inferior man cherishes possessions. The gentleman thinks of sanctions; the inferior man thinks of personal favors." [IV:ll]

89. Confucius said: "The gentleman makes demands on himself; the inferior man makes demands on others." [XV:20]

90. Confucius said: "The gentleman seeks to enable people to succeed in what is good but does not help them in what is evil. The inferior man does the contrary." [XII:16]

91. Confucius said: "The gentleman is broad-minded and not partisan; the inferior man is partisan and not broad-minded." [II:14]

92. Confucius said: "There are three things that a gentleman fears: he fears the will of Heaven, he fears great men, he fears the words of the sages. The inferior man does not know the will of Heaven and does not fear it, he treats great men with contempt, and he scoffs at the words of the sages." [XVI:8]

93. Once when Confucius was in Ch'en, the supply of food was exhausted, and some of his followers became so weak that they could not stand up. Tzu Lu came to the Master in disgust, saying: "Then even a gentleman can be reduced to such straits?" Confucius said: "A gentleman may indeed be so reduced. But when an inferior man is in straits he is apt to do anything." [XV:1]

Government by Personal Virtue

94. Chi K'ang Tzu asked Confucius about government. Confucius said: "To govern *(cheng)* is to set things right *(cheng)*.[5] If you begin by setting yourself right, who will dare to deviate from the right?" [XII:17]

95. Confucius said: "If a ruler himself is upright, all will go well without orders. But if he himself is not upright, even though he gives orders they will not be obeyed." [XIII:6]

96. Tzu Lu asked about the character of a gentleman [man of the ruling class]. Confucius said: "He cultivates himself in reverential attention." Tzu Lu asked: "Is that all there is to it?" Confucius said: "He cultivates himself so as to be able to bring comfort to other people." Tzu Lu asked again: "Is that all?" Confucius said: "He cultivates himself so as to be able to bring comfort to the whole populace. He cultivates himself so as to be able to bring comfort to the whole populace—even [sage-kings] Yao and Shun were dissatisfied with themselves about this." [XIV.45]

97. Confucius said: "Lead the people by laws and regulate them by penalties, and the people will try to keep out of jail, but will have no sense of shame. Lead the people by virtue and restrain them by the rules of decorum, and the people will have a sense of shame, and moreover will become good." [II:3]

98. Chi K'ang Tzu asked Confucius about government, saying: "Suppose I were to kill the lawless for the good of the law-abiding, how would that do?" Confucius answered: "Sir, why should it be necessary to employ capital punishment in your government? Just so you genuinely desire the good, the people will be good. The virtue of the gentleman may be compared to the wind and that of

---

5   This is more than just a pun. Confucius was trying to get at the root of the matter by getting at the root of the word.

the commoner to the weeds. The weeds under the force of the wind cannot but bend." [XII:19]

99. The Duke of She asked about good government. Confucius said: "[A government is good when] those near are happy and those far off are attracted." [XIII:16]

100. When Confucius was traveling to Wei, Jan Yu drove him. Confucius observed: "What a dense population!" Jan Yu said: "The people having grown so numerous, what next should be done for them?" "Enrich them," was the reply. "And when one has enriched them, what next should be done?" Confucius said: "Educate them." [XIII:9]

101. Tzu Kung asked about government. Confucius said: "The essentials are sufficient food, sufficient troops, and the confidence of the people." Tzu Kung said: "Suppose you were forced to give up one of these three, which would you let go first?" Confucius said: "The troops." Tzu Kung asked again: "If you are forced to give up one of the two remaining, which would you let go?" Confucius said: "Food. For from of old, death has been the lot of all men, but a people without faith cannot survive." [XII:7]

102. Duke Ching of Ch'i asked Confucius about government. Confucius replied: "Let the prince be prince, the minister be minister, the father father and the son son." "Excellent!" said the duke. "Indeed if the prince is not prince, the minister not minister, the father not father, and the son not son, then with all the grain in my possession shall I ever get to eat any?"[6] [XII:11]

103. Confucius said: "To have done nothing *(wu-wei)* and yet have the state well-governed—[sage-king] Shun was the one! What did he do? He merely made himself reverent and correctly occupied his royal seat." [XV:4]

---

6   For then the country will be ruined.

From The Great Learning

The essays known as "The Great Learning" *(Ta hsüeh)* and "The Mean" *(Chung yung)* constitute two chapters of the Confucian Classic, the *Book of Rites*. Even before the Christian era the particular significance and interest of these texts was noted. The Neo-Confucian scholars of the Sung dynasty, claiming to find in them the psychological and metaphysical foundations for their system of thought, elevated these short texts to a position of prime importance in Confucian litera- ture. The great Sung scholar Chu Hsi (A.D. 1130–1200), to emphasize their worth, combined the texts with the *Analects* and the *Mencius* to form the so-called *Four Books* (in the order: *The Great Learning, The Mean, Analects,* and *Mencius*). These four texts became the primer of Chinese education, the first major course of study before a student began his study of the Five Classics; they were read aloud and committed to memory by the students. And for a period of six centuries (A.D. 1313–1905) these four texts served as the basis of the civil service examinations by which Chinese scholars were selected for posts in the government bureaucracy.

The Great Learning is a brief essay of some 1,750 words. Its Chinese title, *Ta hsüeh,* means education for the adult or higher education. It has been variously attributed to Tzu Ssu (483–402 B.C.?), Confucius' grandson, to Confucius' disci- ple Tseng Tzu, or to one of his pupils. Some scholars, however, especially in the last three decades, have dated it as late as 200 B.C. In all likelihood its basic ideas go back to Confucius, though the essay itself definitely belongs to a later age.

The central theme of the work is self-cultivation. This is, however, no ordinary guide to self-improvement, which can take for granted the intrinsic importance of each man's fulfillment as an individual. Rather *The Great Learning* seeks first of all to establish the value of self-cultivation in terms of accepted social ends, showing its relevance to the problem of good government which underlies much of the thinking of this age. Indeed, the argumentation here often makes sense only if we understand that it is addressed to the ruler and his officials, rather than to any ordinary man in search of moral guidance. Nevertheless, the problem of the ruler proves, upon analysis, to be identical with that of the individual. Not only does good government depend upon the proper conduct of men on the various levels of social organization, and thus upon their individual moral per- fection, but also self-cultivation on the part of the ruler must proceed on essen- tially the same lines as it does for the individual. Before a man can regulate and discipline others he must learn to regulate and discipline himself. To accomplish this *The Great Learning* offers a method or program which became famous for its "eight points," three of them pertaining to social functions and five to personal cultivation. Broad in scope and rather general in meaning, these eight points nevertheless seemed to outline, in neat and concise form, a complete system of education and social organization. No doubt it appealed greatly to the Chinese taste for a balanced, symmetrical, and hierarchical view of things. It served, moreover, as a formulation of those attitudes which are at the very heart of Confucian teaching: the primacy of the moral order, and the delicate balance which must be maintained between individual and social ends. At the same time, however, *The Great Learning* gave impetus to a dangerous form of oversimplification and idealism among Confucianists: the belief that self-cultivation alone could solve all political problems and usher in the perfect society.

It would be difficult to exaggerate the tremendous influence of this short work on Confucian thought, not only in China, but also in Japan, Korea, and elsewhere in the Chinese cultural sphere. Especially in Neo-Confucian thought the interpretation of the "eight points" became one of the central problems of philosophy and ethics. The excerpts which follow include the basic program of *The Great Learning* and selected passages amplifying two of the eight points.

Malcolm Clark

The Way of the Great Learning consists in clearly exemplifying illustrious virtue, in loving the people, and in resting in the highest good.

Only when one knows where one is to rest can one have a fixed purpose. Only with a fixed purpose can one achieve calmness of mind. Only with calmness of mind can one attain serene repose. Only in serene repose can one carry on careful deliberation. Only through careful deliberation can one have achievement. Things have their roots and branches; affairs have their beginning and end. He who knows what comes first and what comes last comes himself near the Way.

The ancients who wished clearly to exemplify illustrious virtue throughout the world would first set up good government in their states. Wishing to govern well their states, they would first regulate their families. Wishing to regulate their families, they would first cultivate their persons. Wishing to cultivate their persons, they would first rectify their minds. Wishing to rectify their minds, they would first seek sincerity in their thoughts. Wishing for sincerity in their thoughts, they would first extend their knowledge. The extension of knowledge lay in the investigation of things. For only when things are investigated is knowledge extended; only when knowledge is extended are thoughts sincere; only when thoughts are sincere are minds rectified; only when minds are rectified are our persons cultivated; only when our persons are cultivated are our families regulated; only when families are regulated are states well governed; and only when states are well governed is there peace in the world.

From the emperor down to the common people, all, without exception, must consider cultivation of the individual character as the root. If the root is in disorder, it is impossible for the branches to be in order. To treat the important as unimportant and to treat the unimportant as important—this should never be. This is called knowing the root; this is called the perfection of knowledge[1] . . .

What is meant by saying that "the cultivation of the person depends on the rectification of the mind" is this: When one is under the influence of anger, one's mind will not be correct; when one is under the influence of fear, it will not be correct; when one is under the influence of fond regard, it will not be correct; when one is under the influence of anxiety, it will not be correct. When the mind is not there, we gaze at things but do not see; we listen but do not hear; we eat but do not know the flavors. This is what is meant by saying that the cultivation of the person depends on the rectification of the mind. . . .

What is meant by saying that "the government of the state depends on the regulation of the family" is this: One can never teach outsiders if one cannot teach one's own family. Therefore the prince perfects the proper teaching for the whole country without going outside his family; the filial piety wherewith one serves his sovereign, the brotherly respect wherewith one treats his elders, the kindness wherewith one deals with the multitude. There is the saying in the "Announcement to K'ang" [in the *Book of History*]: "Act as if you were rearing an infant." If you set yourself to a task with heart and soul you will not go far wrong even if you do not hit the mark. No girl has ever learned to suckle an infant before she got married.

If one family exemplifies humanity, humanity will abound in the whole country. If one family exemplifies courtesy, courtesy will abound in the whole country. On the other hand, if one man exemplifies greed and wickedness, rebellious disorder will arise in the whole country.[2] Therein lies the secret. Hence the proverb: One word ruins an enterprise; one man determines the fate of an empire. Yao and Shun ruled the empire with humanity, and the people followed them. Chieh and Chou ruled the empire with cruelty, and the people only submitted to them. Since these last commanded actions that they themselves would not like to take, the people refused to follow them. Thus it is that what [virtues] a prince finds in himself he may expect in others, and what [vices] he himself is free from he may condemn in others. It is impossible that a man devoid of every virtue which he might wish to have in others could be able effectively to instruct them.

Thus we see why it is that "the government of the state depends on the regulation of the family."

. . .

What is meant by saying that "the establishment of peace in the world depends on the government of the state" is this: When superiors accord to the aged their due, then the common people will be inspired to practice filial piety; when superiors accord to elders their due, then the common people will be inspired to practice brotherly respect; when superiors show compassion to the orphaned, then the common people do not do otherwise. Thus the gentleman has a principle with which, as with a measuring square, he may regulate his conduct.

---

1   Following the order of the original text as found in the *Li chi*, where it constitutes chapter 42.
2   The "one family" and "one man" are the family and person of the ruler.

What a man dislikes in his superiors let him not display in his treatment of his inferiors; what he dislikes in his inferiors let him not display in his service to his superiors; what he dislikes in those before him let him not set before those who are behind him; what he dislikes in those behind him let him not therewith follow those who are before him; what he dislikes from those on his right let him not bestow upon those on his left; what he dislikes from those on his left let him not bestow upon those on his right. This is called the regulating principle of the measuring square.

Mencius

In the study of the character of Confucian thought, it is important to have some ideas of its chief developments in Mencius, because of the clearer exposition of philosophic values in Mencius and because of their actual influence. Mencius represents the "orthodox" development of the Confucian school. The *Book of Mencius,* in seven books, each divided into two parts, is thicker than the *Analects* by almost one-third, and is incomparably better prose than the *Analects.* Mencius was an eloquent writer and speaker, good at debates, and the passages often consist of long and sustained discourses, and there are so many brilliant passages that it is difficult to make a selection. . . .

Nevertheless, the ideas of Mencius represent such an important development of one side of Confucius' teachings, that it is impossible to get a fair conception of the Confucian ideas without reading something from Mencius. Hantse said, "The teachings of Confucius were broad and covered a wide scope, and it was impossible for any of his disciples to master the whole field. Therefore the early students of Confucianism developed each that side of his teachings which lay closest to his mental equipment. These disciples later on dispersed and settled in different countries and began to teach their disciples what they themselves had mastered, and the farther they were separated from the original source, the more divergent became their views or lines of study. Only Mencius studied under Tsesze, whose knowledge of Confucius' teachings came from Tsengtse. Since Confucius' death, only Mencius was able to carry on the orthodox tradition. Therefore, in order to study the teachings of the Sage, one must begin with Mencius." Hantse also said, "Mencius was the purest of the pure in the interpretation of Confucius; Hsuntse and Yangtse were on the whole pure, with certain adulterations."

I have selected for translation, a whole part of one of the Books of Mencius, in my opinion the most important and representative one. The most important ideas in Mencius are, the goodness of human nature, consequently the importance of recovering that original good nature, the recognition that culture or education merely consists in preventing the good nature in us from becoming "beclouded" by circumstances, the theory of nourishing what amounts to an equivalent of Bergson's *elan vital* (the *haojan chih ch'i*), and finally the declaration that all men are equal in their inherent goodness, and that since the Emperors Yao and Shun were also human beings, "any man could become a Yao or Shun."

Mencius also developed the distinction between the ruler by virtue *(wang)* and the ruler by force or cunning *(pa)*—roughly, the distinction between "a kingly ruler" and "a dictator." He further developed Confucius' idea of government by example into a well-defined system, and for the first time used the phrase "benevolent government" which Confucius never used. *(Jen* definitely means "benevolence" in *Mencius.)* He was also probably the best historical scholar of his days and had definite ideas about taxation systems, agricultural systems and the feudal system. We do not get a clear idea of his theory of "benevolent government," developed from Confucius' government by moral example, but in this essay we find practically all his ideas about the goodness of human nature and the importance and method of finding one's "greater self." This essay is translated in full without omissions.

[Lin Yutang in *The Wisdom of Confucius*]

II. How Our Original Nature Is Destroyed

Mencius said, "There was once a time when the forests of the Niu Mountain were beautiful. But can the mountain any longer be regarded as beautiful, since being situated near a big city, the woodsmen have hewed the trees down? The days and nights gave it rest, and the rains and the dew continued to nourish it, and a new life was continually springing up from the soil, but then the cattle and the sheep began to pasture upon it. That is why the Niu Mountain looks so bald, and when people see its baldness, they imagine that there was never any timber on the mountain. Is this the true nature of the mountain? And is there not a heart of love and righteousness in man, too? But how can that nature remain beautiful when it is hacked down every day, as the woodsman chops down the trees with his axe? To be sure, the nights and days do the healing and there is the nourishing air of the early dawn, which tends to keep him sound and normal, but this morning air is thin and is soon destroyed by what he does in the day. With this continuous hacking of the human spirit, the rest and recuperation obtained during the night are not sufficient to maintain its level, and when the night's recuperation does not suffice to maintain its level, then the man degrades himself to a state not far from the beast's. People see that he acts like a beast and imagine that there was never any true character in him. But is this the true nature of man? Therefore with proper nourishment and care, everything grows, and without the proper nourishment and care, everything degenerates or decays." Confucius said, 'Keep it carefully and you will have it, let it go and you will lose it. It appears and disappears from time to time in we do not know what direction.' He was talking about the human soul."[1]

Mencius said, "Do not think that King (Hsuan of Ch'i) is lacking in wisdom or moral consciousness (as a man). Even in the case of the things that grow most easily in this world, they would never grow up properly if for one day of sunshine

---

1   Elsewhere Mencius defines the "great man" as "one who has not lost the heart of a child."

they get ten days of cloudy (or chilly) weather. He seldom sees me, and when I leave, the people who are the 'cloudy days' for him arrive. Even if what I say to him is taking root (literally 'sprouting') in his mind, what can he do about it? Even in a trivial thing like playing chess, one cannot learn it unless he concentrates his mind on learning it. You let Chess-player Ch'iu, who is the best chess player of the country, teach two persons how to play chess. One man will concentrate his mind and energy on it and listen carefully to Chess-player Ch'iu's explanations and advice, and another man will hear the same explanations, but his mind will be thinking of how a wild goose is going to pass by and how he is going to take a bow and shoot at it. Now although the second man studies under the same master, he will never be equal to the other man. But if you say that this man is lacking in original talent of intelligence, you know it isn't true."

III. The Higher Life and the Greater Self

Mencius said, "I like fish, but I also like bear's paw, but if I can't have both at the same time, I will forego the fish and eat the bear's paw. I love life, but I also love righteousness, and if I can't have both at the same time, I will sacrifice life to have righteousness. I love life, but there is something that I love more than life, and therefore I would not have life at any price. I also hate death, but there is something that I hate more than death, and therefore I would not avoid danger at any price. If there is nothing that man loves more than life, then does he not permit himself to do anything in order to save it? And if there is nothing that man hates more than death, then why does he not always avoid dangers that could be avoided? And so there are times when a man would forsake his life, and there are times when a man would not avoid danger. It is not only the good men who have this feeling that there are times when they would forsake life and there are times when they would not avoid danger. All men have this feeling, only the good men have been able to preserve it."[2] A man's life or death may sometimes depend on a bamboo basket of rice and a bowl of soup but if you say to a starving

---

2   In the Chinese text, Mencius used the word "heart," which I have translated here as "feelings" (elsewhere also as the "soul"), because of the limitations of this word "heart" in the English usage. The whole Mencian philosophy centers around "keeping the heart" and not "losing" it. At other places I have found it necessary to render the same word by "mind" or "intelligence." Of course the English word "heart" comes closest to what Mencius calls *hsin,* since it is primarily a matter of feeling and not of thinking. But the same word is used in Chinese to express the "mind" also, and it should be strongly emphasized that the Chinese language does not admit of a clear distinction of, or separation between, the head and the heart. That is not only grammatically, but also historically a true fact. Mencius, however, uses three important words, "the heart" (including the mind or intelligence), "sentiment" (which is interpreted as the heart in action), and "talent" (or innate capacity, which is more or less fully developed in individuals according to the circumstances).

man passing by, "Hey, Mister!" and offer them to him in the most insulting manner, he would refuse to take them, or if you offer them to a beggar with a kick, the beggar would not receive them.

"What is a salary of ten thousand bushels to me, if I come by it against my principles? Shall I take this position because it offers me beautiful mansions and the service of a wife and concubines, or because I shall be able to help my friends who knew me when I was poor? If formerly I refused to accept the post in the face of death (or starvation), and now I accept it in order to have a fine residence, if formerly I refused to accept this post in the face of death, and now I accept it in order to have the service of a wife and concubines, if formerly I refused this post in the face of death, and now I accept it in order to be able to help my friends who knew me when I was poor, would that not be something totally unnecessary? This is called 'losing one's original heart.'"

Mencius said, "Charity is in the heart of man, and righteousness is the path for men. Pity the man who has lost his path and does not follow it and who has lost his heart and does not know how to recover it. When people's dogs and chicks are lost, they go out and look for them, and yet the people who have lost their hearts (or original nature) do not go out and look for them. The principle of self-cultivation consists in nothing but trying to look for the lost heart."

Mencius said, "Suppose there is a man who has a crooked ring finger which cannot stretch out straight. It isn't painful and it doesn't cause him any inconvenience. And yet, if there was someone who could straighten out the finger for him, he would not mind going as far as Ch'in or Ch'u because he is ashamed that his finger is not like that of other men (or not normal). Now a man is wise enough to be ashamed of a finger that is not normal, and yet he is not wise enough to be ashamed of his heart, when his heart is not normal. We say such a man has no sense of the relative importance of things."

Mencius said, "People know that if they want a lindera tree whose circumference is a fathom long to grow and live, they must take proper care of it. But as to their own selves, they do not know how to take proper care of them. Can it be that they love their selves less than they love a lindera tree? It is mere thoughtlessness."

Mencius said, "There is not a part of the body that a man does not love. And because there is not a part that he does not love, there is not a part of it that he does not nourish. Because there is not an inch of his skin that he does not love, there is not an inch of his skin that he does not take care of. The thing that determines whether a thing is good or bad depends only on his regard for it, or the value he places upon it. Now in our constitution there is a higher and a lower nature, and a smaller and a greater self. One should not develop the lower nature at the expense of the higher nature, or develop the smaller self at the expense of the greater self. He who attends to his smaller self becomes a small man, and he who attends to his greater self becomes a great man. A gardener who attends to thorns and bramble to the neglect of his lindera trees will be regarded as a bad gardener. A man who takes good care of his finger and suffers an injury to his shoulder blade is deformed. People look down upon the matter of food and drink because food nourishes our smaller self and does nothing to our greater self. If

106

a man attends to his food, without forgetting about his greater self, then it may be said that the food taken indeed does not only go to nourish any particular small part of the body (an inch of his skin)."

Kungtutse asked Mencius, "We are all human beings. Why is it that some are great men and some are small men?" Mencius replied, "Those who attend to their greater selves become great men, and those who attend to their smaller selves become small men." "But we are all human beings. Why is it that some people attend to their greater selves and some attend to their smaller selves?" Mencius replied, "When our senses of sight and hearing are distracted by the things outside, without the participation of thought, then the material things act upon the material senses and lead them astray. That is the explanation. The function of the mind is thinking; when you think, you keep your mind, and when you don't think, you lose your mind. This is what heaven has given to us (for the purpose of thinking or knowing what is right and wrong). One who cultivates his higher self will find that his lower self follows in accord. That is how a man becomes a great man."

Mencius said, "There is the heaven-made nobility, and there is the man-made nobility. The people who are kind, righteous, faithful and love virtue without fail belong to the heaven-made nobility (or the nobility of God), and the *kung, ch'ing,* and *taifu* (different ranks of officials) belong to the man-made nobility. The ancient people cultivated what belonged to God's noblemen and they obtained without conscious effort the ranks of manmade nobility. People today, on the other hand, cultivate what belongs to this heaven-made nobility in order to secure man-made honors (or man-made nobility), and after they have secured man-made honors, they forsake the things that make for heaven-made nobility. Thus they are led grievously astray and must soon perish after all."

Mencius said, "All people have the common desire to be elevated in honor, but all people have something still more elevated in themselves without knowing it. What people usually consider as an elevated rank or honor is not true honor, for he whom Chao Meng (a powerful ruling family of Chin) has honored, Chao Meng can also bring into dishonor. The *Book of Songs* says, 'I am drunk with wine, and I am filled with virtue.' This figurative expression means that a man is 'filled' with kindness and righteousness, and when he is so filled, he does not care for the flavors of delicate food. And when a man wears a mantle of fame, he does not care for the embroidered gowns." *doesn't care for social honor.*

Mencius said, "The five kinds of grains are considered good plants, but if the grains are not ripe, they are worse than cockles. It is the same with regard to kindness, which must grow into maturity."

Mencius said, "When Yi (a famous archer) taught people to shoot, he told them to pull the string on the bow its full length. The man who wants to cultivate himself must also develop himself to the full extent. A great carpenter teaches his apprentice to use squares and compasses. The man who wants to cultivate himself, must also have squares and compasses for his conduct."

honor upon yourself

Human Nature Is Evil

―――◆◆◆―――

Hsün-Tzu

The most famous teacher of his time, Hsün-Tzu (Xun-zi, or Master Hsün) was a native of the state of Chao. A younger contemporary of Mencius, he was born about 312 B.C. and lived to at least 238 B.C. His two most famous disciples were Han Fei Tzu and Li Ssu (prime minister of the first Ch'in emperor). It was Hsün-Tzu's teaching, modified by other influences, which formed the basis of the political philosophy of the Han dynasty.

In terms of content, Hsün-Tzu's teaching is the most complete and systematic philosophical system up to that time in China. In terms of style, Hsün-Tzu was second only to Chuang Tzu as a writer of expository prose. His writings consisted of well organized and closely argued essays on a broad range of topics. In about 77 B.C, these essays were collected into the thirty-two chapters of the (book of) *Hsün-Tzu*.

Despite his considerable influence on Han Fei Tzu, Hsün-Tzu was no legalist but rather a classical Confucianist. While understandably pessimistic (given the chaos at the end of the warring states period) about basic human nature, he was optimistic about the prospects for improvement of that nature through proper education (including study of the classics), laws, and environment. Like Confucius, his goal was a state which would be governed and ordered on moral principles. The example of the sage rulers of the past (such as King Wen) showed that this was possible and provided a model by which any man in theory could become a sage. Even a king who was not a sage could rule successfully with the support of the people.

We may understand the teachings of Hsün-Tzu better by seeing what views he opposed. Hsün-Tzu was a realist, a rationalist, and a humanist who said that we should not be concerned with the world of the supernatural nor with spirits or demons. Ritual (*li*) is important, but only for its social function. Hsün-Tzu rejected the feudalist-primitivist vision of Mencius and Mo-Tzu's emphasis on social conformity, frugality, and utilitarianism (Mo-Tzu, for example, rejected music). Hsün-Tzu also rejected the nature-mystic focus of Chuang Tzu and the

From *Sources of Chinese Tradition*, ed. Wm. Theodore de Bary, © 1964 Columbia University Press. Reprinted with the permission of the publisher.

Taoists, as well as the Legalists' advocacy of government by force. Law cannot replace the example of the virtuous leader.

Malcolm Clark

The nature of man is evil; his goodness is acquired.

His nature being what it is, man is born, first, with a desire for gain. If this desire is followed, strife will result and courtesy will disappear. Second, man is born with envy and hate. If these tendencies are followed, injury and cruelty will abound and loyalty and faithfulness will disappear. Third, man is born with passions of the ear and eye as well as the love of sound and beauty. If these passions are followed, excesses and disorderliness will spring up and decorum and righteousness will disappear. Hence to give rein to man's original nature and to yield to man's emotions will assuredly lead to strife and disorderliness, and he will revert to a state of barbarism. Therefore it is only under the influence of teachers and laws and the guidance of the rules of decorum and righteousness that courtesy will be observed, etiquette respected, and order restored. From all this it is evident that the nature of man is evil and that his goodness is acquired.

Crooked wood needs to undergo steaming and bending by the carpenter's tools; then only is it straight. Blunt metal needs to undergo grinding and whetting; then only is it sharp. Now the original nature of man is evil, so he must submit himself to teachers and laws before he can be just; he must submit himself to the rules of decorum and righteousness before he can be orderly. On the other hand, without teachers and laws, men are biased and unjust; without decorum and righteousness, men are rebellious and disorderly. In ancient times the sage-kings knew that man's nature was evil and therefore biased and unjust, rebellious and disorderly. Thereupon they created the codes of decorum and righteousness and established laws and ordinances in order to bend the nature of man and set it right, and in order to transform his nature and guide it. All men are thus made to conduct themselves in a manner that is orderly and in accordance with the Way. At present, those men who are influenced by teachers and laws, who have accumulated culture and learning, and who are following the paths of decorum and righteousness, are the gentlemen. On the other hand, those who give rein to their nature, who indulge in their willfulness, and who disregard decorum and righteousness, are the inferior men. From all this it is evident that the nature of man is evil and that his goodness is acquired.

Mencius says: "The reason man is ready to learn is that his nature is originally good."[1] I reply: This is not so. This is due to a lack of knowledge about the original nature of man and of understanding of the distinction between what is natural and what is acquired. Original nature is a heavenly endowment; it cannot be learned, and it cannot be striven after. As to rules of decorum and righteousness, they have been brought forth by the sages, they can be attained

---

1   This saying does not appear in the present *Mencius* but does reflect the doctrine in *Mencius,* VI A:2–6.

by learning, and they can be achieved by striving. That which cannot be learned and cannot be striven after and rests with Heaven is what I call original nature. That which can be attained by learning and achieved by striving and rests with man is what I call acquired character. This is the distinction between original nature and acquired character. Now by the nature of man, the eye has the faculty of seeing and the ear has the faculty of hearing. But the keenness of the faculty of sight is inseparable from the eye, and the keenness of the faculty of hearing is inseparable from the ear. It is evident that keenness of sight and keenness of hearing cannot be learned.

Mencius says: "The original nature of man is good; but because men all ruin it and lose it, it becomes evil."[2] I reply: In this he is gravely mistaken. Regarding the nature of man, as soon as he is born, he tends to depart from its original state and depart from its natural disposition, and he is bent on ruining it and losing it. From all this, it is evident that the nature of man is evil and that his goodness is acquired.

To say that man's original nature is good means that it can become beautiful without leaving its original state and it can become beneficial without leaving its natural disposition. This is to maintain that beauty pertains to the original state and disposition and goodness pertains to the heart and mind in the same way as the keenness of the faculty of sight is inseparable from the eye and the keenness of the faculty of hearing is inseparable from the ear, just as we say that the eye is keen in seeing or the ear is keen in hearing. Now as to the nature of man, when he is hungry he desires to be filled, when he is cold he desires warmth, when he is tired he desires rest. This is man's natural disposition. But now a man may be hungry and yet in the presence of elders he dare not be the first to eat. This is because he has to yield precedence to someone. He may be tired and yet he dare not take a rest. This is because he has to labor in the place of someone. For a son to yield to his father and a younger brother to yield to his older brother, for a son to labor in the place of his father and a younger brother to labor in the place of his older brother—both of these kinds of actions are opposed to man's original nature and contrary to man's feeling. Yet they are the way of the filial son and in accordance with the rules of decorum and righteousness. It appears if a person follows his natural disposition he will show no courtesy, and if he shows courtesy he is acting contrary to his natural disposition. From all this it is evident that the nature of man is evil and that his goodness is acquired.

It may be asked: "If man's original nature is evil, whence do the rules of decorum and righteousness arise?" I reply: All rules of decorum and righteousness are the products of the acquired virtue of the sage and not the products of the nature of man. Thus, the potter presses the clay and makes the vessel—but the vessel is the product of the potter's acquired skill and not the product of his original nature. Or again, the craftsman hews pieces of wood and makes utensils—but utensils are the product of the carpenter's acquired skill and not the

---

2   This saying does not appear in the present *Mencius* but does reflect the doctrine in *Mencius,* VI A:6 and 8.

product of his original nature. The sage gathers many ideas and thoughts and becomes well versed in human affairs, in order to bring forth the rules of decorum and righteousness and establish laws and institutions. So then the rules of decorum and righteousness and laws and institutions are similarly the products of the acquired virtue of the sage and not the products of his original nature. . . .

Man wishes to be good because his nature is evil. If a person is unimportant he wishes to be important, if he is ugly he wishes to be beautiful, if he is confined he wishes to be at large, if he is poor he wishes to be rich, if he is lowly he wishes to be honored—whatever a person does not have within himself, he seeks from without. But the rich do not wish for wealth and the honorable do not wish for position, for whatever a person has within himself he does not seek from without. From this it may be seen that man wishes to be good because his nature is evil. Now the original nature of man is really without decorum and righteousness, hence he strives to learn and seeks to obtain them. . . .

"Straight wood does not require the carpenter's tools to be straight; by nature it is straight. Crooked wood needs to undergo steaming and bending by the carpenter's tools and then only will it be straight; by nature it is not straight." As the nature of man is evil, it must be submitted to the government of the sage-kings and the reforming influence of the rules of decorum and righteousness; then only will everyone issue forth in orderliness and be in accordance with goodness. From all this it is evident that the nature of man is evil and that his goodness is acquired.

It may be objected: "Decorum and righteousness and the accumulation of acquired virtues must be in the nature of man so that the sage could bring them forth." I reply: This is not so. Now the potter pounds and and molds the clay and produces earthenware. Are the earthenware and clay then in the nature of the potter? The workman hews a piece of wood and makes utensils. Are furniture and wood then in the nature of the carpenter? So it is with the sage and decorum and righteousness; he produces them in the same way as earthenware is produced. Are decorum and righteousness and the accumulation of acquired virtues then in the original nature of man? As far as the nature of man is concerned, the sage-kings Yao and Shun have the same nature as the wicked King Chieh and robber Chih; the gentleman has the same nature as the inferior man. Should we now regard decorum and righteousness and the accumulation of acquired virtues as being in the nature of man, then why should we prize the sage-kings Yao and Yü and why should we prize the gentlemen? We prize Yao, Yü, and the gentlemen because they were able to transform nature and produce acquired virtue, and from acquired virtue decorum and righteousness issued forth. . . .

There is a saying: "The man on the street can become a Yü." How would you account for that? I reply: All that made Yü what he was was that he instituted humanity and righteousness, laws, and government. However, there are principles by which humanity and righteousness, laws and government can be known and practiced. At the same time any man on the street has the faculty for knowing them and has the capacity for practicing them. Thus it is evident that he can become a Yü. Should we assume there were really no principles by which humanity and righteousness, laws and government could be known and practiced, then even Yü would not be able to know them or practice them. Or, should we assume the man on the street really had no faculty for knowing humanity and righteousness, laws and government, or the capacity for practicing them, then the man cannot know, on the one hand, the proper relation between father and son and, on the other, the proper discipline between sovereign and minister. Thus it is evident that the man on the street does have the faculty for knowing and the capacity for practicing these virtues. Now let the man on the street take his faculty for knowing and his capacity for practicing humanity and righteousness, laws and government, and bring them to bear upon the principles by which these virtues can be known and can be practiced—then it is self-evident that he can become a Yü. Yes, let the man on the street pursue the path of knowledge and devote himself to learning, with concentration of mind and a singleness of purpose; let him think, search, examine, and re-examine, day in and day out, with persistence and patience—let him thus accumulate good works without cease, then he may be counted among the gods and may form a triad with Heaven and earth. Hence sagehood is a state that any man can achieve by cumulative effort. . . ."

Eminence in Learning

❧❖❧

Han Fei Tzu

Unlike most important early philosophers who came from the ranks of the lower gentry, Han Fei Tzu (Han Fei Zi, or Master Han Fei) was born a prince of the royal family of the small state of Han in about 280 B.C. A student of Hsün-Tzu, his book came into the hands of the future first emperor of Ch'in, who sent for him. Han Fei Tzu's former co-student, Li Ssu (a principal advisor to the future first emperor), intrigued to have him sent to prison where he was forced to commit suicide (taking poison sent by Li Ssu) in 233 B.C.

Han Fei Tzu gave the most developed statement of the Legalist position, which became the official political philosophy of the Ch'in dynasty. His style was clear, polished, sophisticated, and cynical. After the fall of the Ch'in dynasty, his ideas were often condemned although he remained widely read and influential. Some of the ideas of Legalism go back more than two centuries earlier, but the primary influences on Han Fei Tzu were his former teacher Hsün-Tzu, and the legalists Lord Shang (d. 338) and Shen Pu-hai (d. 337). Legalism had a single focus: how to preserve and strengthen the state. Government should not be based on morality, religion, ritual, or tradition. The past does not provide a solution for the problems of the present. Philosophy, understood as the free examination and discussion of ideas, was dangerous to the state.

Han Fei Tzu emphasized four principles for successful rule—1) *fa:* an elaborate system of written and publicized laws; 2) *shu:* the use of policy and method in governing, and; 3) *shih:* the use of power (war, aggression, severe penalties) to achieve the goals of the state. Han Fei Tzu was also influenced by another philosophical school, the Logicians, in 4) the concept of *hsing-ming* ('forms and names'): the name of the office and the list of duties must correspond to the performance of the office-holder. He also believed people should be appointed to office on the basis of merit. In practical terms these ideas meant a strong system of laws coupled with severe penalties for law-breaking, the use of war, the promotion of agriculture, and the provision of government services through an efficient system of taxation.

From *Basic Writings of Han Fei Tzu,* ed. Burton Watson, © 1964 Columbia University Press. Reprinted with the permission of the publisher.

Perhaps from Hsün-Tzu, Han Fei Tzu derived his views on the selfish nature of people. He did not, however, share Hsün-Tzu's optimism regarding moral improvement. Ironically, Legalism drew on the picture of the Taoist Sage as aloof and beyond good and evil to provide a model for the legalist ruler who exercised his control through the impersonal laws and government machinery. The emperor should trust no one.

Malcolm Clark

In the present age, the Confucians and Mo-ists are well known for their learning. The Confucians pay the highest honor to Confucius, the Mo-ists to Mo Ti. Since the death of Confucius, the Tzu-chang School, the Tzu-ssu School, the Yen Family School, the Meng Family School, the Ch'i-tiao Family School, the Chung-liang Family School, the Sun Family School, and the Yueh-cheng Family School have appeared. Since the death of Mo Tzu, the Hsiang-li Family School, the Hsiang-fu Family School, and the Teng-ling Family School have appeared. Thus, since the death of its founder, the Confucian school has split into eight factions, and the Mo-ist school into three. Their doctrines and practices are different or even contradictory, and yet each claims to represent the true teaching of Confucius and Mo Tzu. But since we cannot call Confucius and Mo Tzu back to life, who is to decide which of the present versions of the doctrine is the right one?

Confucius and Mo Tzu both followed the ways of Yao and Shun, and though their practices differed, each claimed to be following the real Yao and Shun.[1] But since we cannot call Yao and Shun back to life, who is to decide whether it is the Confucians or the Mo-ists who are telling the truth?

Now over seven hundred years have passed since Yin and early Chou times, and over two thousand years since Yü and early Hsia times. If we cannot even decide which of the present versions of Confucian and Mo-ist doctrine are the genuine ones, how can we hope to scrutinize the ways of Yao and Shun, who lived three thousands years ago? Obviously we can be sure of nothing! He who claims to be sure of something for which there is no evidence is a fool, and he who acts on the basis of what cannot be proved is an imposter. Hence it is clear that those who claim to follow the ancient kings and to be able to describe with certainty the ways of Yao and Shun must be either fools or imposters. The learning of fools and impostors, doctrines that are motley and contradictory—such things as these the enlightened ruler will never accept.

For funerals, the Mo-ists prescribe that winter mourning garments be worn in winter and summer garments in summer, that the coffin be of paulownia wood three inches thick, and that mourning be observed for three months. The rulers

---

1 Judging from the *Analects,* Confucius himself had little to say about the ancient sage rulers Yao and Shun, and the few references to them may well be later insertions in the text. But Confucian scholars of late Chou times paid great honor to Yao and Shun and compiled the "Canon of Yao," the first section of the *Book of Documents,* as a record of their lives.

of the time regard such ways as frugal and honor them. The Confucians, on the other hand, will bankrupt the family to carry out a funeral, wearing mourning garments for three years, reducing themselves to physical exhaustion and walking about with canes. The rulers of the time regard such ways as filial and honor them. Now if you approve of the frugality of Mo Tzu, you must condemn Confucius for his extravagance, and if you approve of the filial piety of Confucius, you must condemn Mo Tzu for his impiety. Thus the teachings of the Confucians and Mo-ists embrace both piety and impiety, extravagance and frugality, and yet the ruler honors them both!

According to the teaching of Ch'i-tiao,[2] a man should never cringe before others or flinch in the face of danger; if his actions are base, he should not refuse to be treated as a slave, but if his actions are upright, he should not hesitate to defy the feudal lords. The rulers of the time regard such conduct as honorable and praise it. According to the teaching of Sung Jung-tzu,[3] a man should condemn warfare and contention and refuse to take part in acts of vengeance; he should not be embarrassed to go to jail and should consider it no shame to suffer insult. The rulers of the time regard such an attitude as broad-minded and praise it. Now if you approve of the honorable conduct of Ch'i-tiao, you must condemn Sung Jung for being too forgiving, and if you approve of the broad-mindedness of Sung Jung, you must condemn Ch'i-tiao for being too violent. Thus these two codes of behavior embrace both broad-mindedness and a keen sense of honor, forgiveness and violence, and yet the ruler honors them both!

Because the ruler gives equal ear to the learning of fools and impostors and the wranglings of the motley and contradictory schools, the gentlemen of the world follow no fixed policy in their words and no constant code of action in their behavior. As ice and live coals cannot share the same container for long, or winter and summer both arrive at the same time, so, too, motley and contradictory doctrines cannot stand side by side and produce a state of order. If equal ear is given to motley doctrines, false codes of behavior, and contradictory assertions, how can there be anything but chaos? If the ruler listens and acts in such a way, he will surely govern his people in the same absurd fashion.

When the scholars of today discuss good government, many of them say, "Give land to the poor and destitute so that those who have no means of livelihood may be provided for." Now if men start out with equal opportunities and yet there are a few who, without the help of unusually good harvests or outside income, are able to keep themselves well supplied, it must be due either to hard work or to frugal living. If men start out with equal opportunities and yet there are a few who, without having suffered from some calamity like famine or sickness, still sink into poverty and destitution, it must be due either to laziness or to extravagant living. The lazy and extravagant grow poor; the diligent and

---

2   Nothing is known of the identity of this man. He appears to be a different person from the Ch'i-tiao mentioned above as the leader of one school of Confucianism.

3   Referred to in other texts as Sung Chien or Sung K'eng, he seems to have taught a doctrine of passivity, frugality, and few desires.

frugal get rich. Now if the ruler levies money from the rich in order to give alms to the poor, he is robbing the diligent and frugal and indulging the lazy and extravagant. If he expects by such means to induce the people to work industriously and spend with caution, he will be disappointed.

Now suppose there is a man who on principle refuses to enter a city that is in danger, to take part in a military campaign, or in fact to change so much as a hair of his shin, though it might bring the greatest benefit to the world.[4] The rulers of the time are sure to honor him, admiring his wisdom, praising his conduct, and regarding him as a man who despises material things and values his life. Now the ruler hands out good fields and large houses and offers titles and stipends in order to encourage the people to risk their lives in his service. But if he honors and praises a man who despises material things and values life above everything else, and at the same time expects the people to risk their lives and serve him to the death, he will be disappointed.

Then there are other men who collect books, study rhetoric, gather bands of disciples, and devote themselves to literature, learning, and debate. The rulers of the time are sure to treat them with respect, saying, "It is the way of the former kings to honor worthy men." The farmers are the ones who must pay taxes to the officials, and yet the ruler patronizes scholars—thus the farmer's taxes grow heavier and heavier, while the scholars enjoy increasing reward. If the ruler hopes, in spite of this, that the people will work industriously and spend little time talking, he will be disappointed.

There are others who establish a name for chivalrous action and gather bands of followers, who guard their honor from all insult and avenge with ready swords the slightest sullen word that reaches their ears. The rulers of the time are sure to treat such men with courtesy, considering them gentlemen of self-respect. No reward is given to those who strive to cut off the heads of the enemy in battle, and yet the daring that men show in their family feuds brings them honor and renown. If the ruler hopes, in spite of this, that the people will fight fiercely to drive back the enemy and refrain from private quarrels, he will be disappointed. The nation at peace may patronize Confucian scholars and cavaliers, but the nation in danger must call upon its fighting men. Thus those who are patronized are not those who are of real use, and those who are of real use are not those who are patronized. Hence we have disorder.

Moreover, when the ruler listens to a scholar, if he approves of his words, he should give them official dissemination and appoint the man to a post; but if he disapproves of his words, he should dismiss the man and put a stop to his teaching. Now, though the ruler may approve of some doctrine, he does not give it official dissemination, and though he may disapprove of some doctrine, he does not put a stop to it. Not to use what you approve of and not to suppress what you disapprove of—this is the way to confusion and ruin.

---

4   A reference to the followers of Yang Chu. Cf. *Mencius* VIIA, 26: "Mencius said, 'The principle of Yang Tzu was "each one for himself." Though he might have benefited the whole *World* by plucking out a single hair, he would not have done it.'"

T'an-t'ai Tzu-yü had the appearance of a gentleman. Confucius, considering him promising, accepted him as a disciple but, after associating with him for some time, he found that his actions did not come up to his looks. Ts'ai Yü's speech was elegant and refined and Confucius, considering him promising, accepting him as a disciple. But after associating with him, he found that his wisdom did not match his eloquence. Therefore Confucius said, "Should I choose a man on the basis of looks? I made a mistake with Tzu-yü. Should I choose a man on the basis of his speech? I made a mistake with Ts'ai Yü." Thus even Confucius, for all his wisdom, had to admit that he judged the facts wrongly. Now our new orators today are far more voluble than Ts'ai Yü, and the rulers of the age far more susceptible to delusion than Confucius. If they appoint men to office simply because they are pleased with their words, how can they fail to make mistakes?

Wei trusted the eloquence of Meng Mao and met with calamity below Mount Hua.[5] Chao trusted the eloquence of Ma-fu and encountered disaster at Ch'ang-p'ing.[6] These two instances show what mistakes can be made by trusting men because of their eloquence.

If one were only to note the quantity of tin used in the alloy, examine the color of the metal, but apply no other test, then even the famous Smithy Ou could not guarantee the sharpness of a sword. But if one sees it strike off the heads of water birds and cut down horses on land, then even the stupidest slave would not doubt that the sword is sharp. If one were only to look at a horse's teeth and examine[7] its shape, then even the famous judge of horses, Po Lo, could not guarantee the quality of the horse. But if one hitches it to a carriage and observes how it covers a certain distance of ground, then even the stupidest slave can tell whether the horse is good or not. Similarly, if one were only to observe a man's features and dress and listen to his speech, then even Confucius could not be certain what kind of person he is. But if one tries him out in government office and examines his achievements, then even a man of mediocre judgment can tell whether he is stupid or wise.

In the bureaucracy of an enlightened ruler the prime minister has come up from the post of district magistrate and the renowned generals have risen from the ranks. Since achievements are invariably rewarded, the able man rises in title and stipend and works harder than ever; since he keeps moving to a higher office and a better rank, he will in time reach an important position and do his job better than ever. Thus to see to it that titles and stipends are generous[8] and jobs are well done is the way of a true king.

---

5   In 273 B.C. Ch'in attacked Wei and its allies, defeating and routing the army of the Wei general Meng Mao at Hua-yang.

6   The Chao general Chao Ma-fu was defeated at Ch'ang-p'ing by the Ch'in army in 260 B.C.

7   Supplying *hsiang* above *hsing*.

8   Reading *hou* instead of *ta* in accordance with the suggestion of Ch'en Ch'i-yu.

The ruler with a thousand *li* of rocky land cannot be called rich; the ruler with a million funerary dolls cannot be called powerful. It is not that the stony fields are not vast or the dolls not numerous. But such a ruler cannot be called rich or powerful because stony fields will grow no grain and dolls will not fend off an enemy. Now the artists and craftsmen, or the merchants who buy themselves government offices, manage to eat without tilling the land. Thus the land remains as unproductive as though it were in fact a stony field. Likewise the Confucians and cavaliers gain fame and glory without the hardships of service in the army; they are in fact useless citizens, no different from funerary dolls. Now if you recognize the curse[9] of having only stony lands and lifeless dolls, but not the curse of merchants who buy their way into office, or Confucians and cavaliers—men who till no land and serve no purpose—then you have no head for analogies.

Although the ruler of a state whose power is equal to yours may admire your righteousness, you cannot force him to come with tribute and acknowledge your sovereignty; but although one of the marquises within your borders may disapprove of your actions, you can make him bring the customary gifts and attend your court. Thus he who has great power at his disposal may force others to pay him court, but he whose power is weak must pay court to others. For this reason the enlightened ruler works to build up power. In a strict household there are no unruly slaves, but the children of a kindly mother often turn out bad. From this I know that power and authority can prevent violence, but kindness and generosity are insufficient to put an end to disorder.

When a sage rules the state, he does not depend on people's doing good of themselves; he sees to it that they are not allowed to do what is bad. If he depends on people's doing good of themselves, then within his borders he can count less than ten instances of success. But if he sees to it that they are not allowed to do what is bad, then the whole state can be brought to a uniform level of order. Those who rule must employ measures that will be effective with the majority and discard those that will be effective with only a few. Therefore they devote themselves not to virtue but to law.

If you depend on arrow shafts becoming straight of themselves, you will never produce one arrow in a hundred generations. If you depend on pieces of wood becoming round of themselves, you will never get a cartwheel in a thousand years. If in a hundred generations you never find such a thing as an arrow shaft that makes itself straight or a piece of wood that makes itself round, then how it is that people all manage to ride around in carriages and shoot down birds? Because the tools of straightening and bending are used. And even if, without the application of such tools, there were an arrow shaft that made itself straight or a piece of wood that made itself round, a good craftsman would not prize it. Why? Because it is not only one man who wants to ride, and not just one shot that the archer wants to make. And even if, without depending upon rewards and punishments, there were a man who became good of himself, the enlightened

---

9   Reversing the order of *huo and chih*.

ruler would not prize him. Why? Because the laws of the state must not be ignored, and it is more than one man who must be governed. Therefore a ruler who understands policy does not pursue fortuitous goodness, but follows the way of certain success.

If someone were to go around telling people, "I can give you wisdom and long life!", then the world would regard him as an impostor. Wisdom is a matter of man's nature, and long life is a matter of fate, and neither human nature nor fate can be got from others. Because the man tells people he can do what is impossible, the world naturally considers him an impostor. To say you can do something which you cannot do is simply to make an empty assertion, and an empty assertion cannot affect human nature.[10] Likewise, to try to teach people to be benevolent and righteous is the same as saying you can make them wise and long-lived. A ruler who has proper standards will not listen to such an idea.

You may admire the beauty of a lovely woman like Mao-ch'iang or Hsi-shih all you like, but it will not improve your own looks. If you apply rouge, powder, and paint, however, you may make yourself twice as attractive as you were to begin with. You may talk about the benevolence and righteousness of the former kings all you like, but it will not make your own state any better ordered. But if you make your laws and regulations clear and your rewards and punishments certain, it is like applying rouge, powder, and paint to the state.[11] The enlightened ruler pays close attention to such aids to rule and has little time for extolling the ancients. Therefore he does not talk about benevolence and righteousness.

When the shaman priests pray for someone, they say, "May you live a thousand autumns and ten thousands years!" But the "thousand autumns and ten thousand years" are only a noise dinning on the ear—no one has ever proved that such prayers add so much as a day to anyone's life. For this reason people despise the shaman priests. Similarly, when the Confucians of the present time counsel rulers, they do not praise those measures which will bring order today, but talk only of the achievements of the men who brought order in the past. They do not investigate matters of bureaucratic system or law, or examine the realities of villainy and evil, but spend all their time telling tales of the distant past and praising the achievements of the former kings. And then they try to make their words more attractive by saying, "If you listen to our advice, you may become a dictator or a king!" They are the shaman priests of the rhetoricians, and no ruler with proper standards will tolerate them. Therefore the enlightened ruler works with facts and discards useless theories. He does not talk about deeds of benevolence and righteousness, and he does not listen to the words of scholars.

Nowadays, those who do not understand how to govern invariably say, "You must win the hearts of the people!" If you could assure good government merely by winning the hearts of the people, then there would be no need for men like Yi

---

10 Adding a *fei* before *hsing* and translating in accordance with the interpretation of Ch'en Ch'i-yu. But the passage is far from clear.

11 The rhythm of the sentence is awkward and the parallelism faulty; it is probable that something has dropped out of the text.

Yin and Kuan Chung—you could simply listen to what the people say. The reason you cannot rely upon the wisdom of the people is that they have the minds of little children. If the child's head is not shaved, its sores will spread;[12] and if its boil is not lanced, it will become sicker than ever. But when it is having its head shaved or its boil lanced, someone must hold it while the loving mother performs the operation, and it yells and screams incessantly, for it does not understand that the little pain it suffers now will bring great benefit later.

Now the ruler presses the people to till the land and open up new pastures so as to increase their means of livelihood, and yet they consider him harsh; he draws up a penal code and makes the punishments more severe in order to put a stop to evil, and yet the people consider him stern. He levies taxes in cash and grain in order to fill the coffers and granaries so that there will be food for the starving and funds for the army, and yet the people consider him avaricious. He makes certain that everyone within his borders understands warfare and sees to it that there are no private exemptions[13] from military service; he unites the strength of the state and fights fiercely in order to take its enemies captive, and yet the people consider him violent. These four types of undertaking all insure order and safety to the state, and yet the people do not have sense enough to rejoice in them.

The ruler seeks for men of superior understanding and ability precisely because he knows that the wisdom of the people is not sufficient to be of any use. In ancient times Yü opened up channels for the rivers and deepened the waterways, and yet the people gathered tiles and stones to throw at him; Tzu-ch'an opened up the fields and planted mulberry trees, and yet the men of Cheng spoke ill of him.[14] Yü profited the whole world, Tzu-ch'an preserved the state of Cheng, and yet both men suffered slander—it is evident from this, then, that the wisdom of the people is not sufficient to be of use. In appointing men, to seek among the people for those who are worthy and wise; in governing, to try to please the people—methods such as these are the source of confusion. They are of no help in ensuring good government.

---

12 Emending the *fu* in the text to the *fu* which means "increasingly."

13 Adding *she* after *chieh* and translating in accordance with the interpretation of Ch'en Ch'i-yu.

14 Yü, the founder of the Hsia dynasty, was supposed to have fixed the courses of the rivers and rescued China from a great flood. Tzu-ch'an (d. 522 B.C.), chief minister of the state of Cheng, introduced various agricultural reforms which were at first much opposed by the people but which eventually brought benefit to the state.

Selections from Chuang-Tzu

According to our very limited information, Chuan Tzu (Zhuang-zi) may have lived in the state of Sung (present-day Honan, south of the Yellow River) from about 399–295 B.C. A contemporary of Mencius, Chuang Tzu declined an offer to become prime minister and was an "official in the lacquer garden."

In his introduction to our translation, Burton Watson (the translator) notes that Chuang Tzu uses "the Chinese language as it had never been used before. No other text of early times, with the possible exception of the *Tso chuan,* so fully exploits the beauties of ancient Chinese—its vigor, its economy, its richness and symmetry" (p. 19). It is one of those prose texts which is poetic in its use of language. While it is difficult adequately to convey these stylistic features in translation, the brilliance of writing in its use of anecdotes, paradox, humor, and intentionally ambiguous word meanings should impart to the reader some of the flavor of this literary masterpiece.

Although the *Tao Te Ching* is never mentioned in the *Chuang Tzu,* these two works should be regarded as more or less contemporaneous expressions of the Taoist spirit. After the time of the Han dynasty, Chuang Tzu had a major influence on the development of neo-Taoism and of Chan (Zen) Buddhism. He also exerted significant influence on Chinese poetry and landscape painting.

Chuang Tzu attacked the positions of both Confucius and Mo-Tzu. It is true but inadequate to say that the *Chuang Tzu* is a work of nature mysticism—a collection of mystical writings which tries to lead the reader to a vision of reality which ultimately cannot be described or reduced to logical propositions. Its ultimate aim is a spiritual transformation which frees the individual from bondage to all conventional thoughts, social customs and expectations, world views, absolute truth claims and even from one's own attitudes. The sage will also become free from all goal-oriented activity, not withdrawing from the world as would a monk or ascetic, but living a spontaneous existence in the world, a rider of the clouds, a craftsman skilled in the art of living.

Malcolm Clark

From *Basic Writings of Chuang-Tzu,* ed. Burton Watson, © 1996 Columbia University Press. Reprinted with the permission of the publisher.

A

Nieh Ch'ueh asked Wang Ni, "Do you know what all things agree in calling right?"

"How would I know that?" said Wang Ni.

"Do you know that you don't know it?"

"How would I know that?"

"Then do things know nothing?"

"How would I know that? However, suppose I try saying something; What way do I have of knowing that if I say I know something I don't really not know it? Or what way do I have of knowing that if I say I don't know something I don't really in fact know it? Now let me ask you some questions. If a man sleeps in a damp place, his back aches and he ends up half paralyzed, but is this true of a loach? If he lives in a tree, he is terrified and shakes with fright, but is this true of a monkey? Of these three creatures, then, which one knows the proper place to live? Men eat the flesh of grass-fed and grain-fed animals, deer eat grass, centipedes find snakes tasty, and hawks and falcons relish mice. Of these four, which knows how food ought to taste? Monkeys pair with monkeys, deer go out with deer, and fish play around with fish. Men claim that Mao-ch'iang and Lady Li were beautiful, but if fish saw them they would dive to the bottom of the stream, if birds saw them they would fly away, and if deer saw them they would break into a run. Of these four, which knows how to fix the standard of beauty for the world? The way I see it, the rules of benevolence and righteousness and the paths of right and wrong are all hopelessly snarled and jumbled. How could I know anything about such discriminations?"

Nieh Ch'ueh said, "If you don't know what is profitable or harmful, then does the Perfect Man likewise know nothing of such things?"

Wang Ni replied, "The Perfect Man is godlike. Though the great swamps blaze, they cannot burn him; though the great rivers freeze, they cannot chill him, though swift lightning splits the hills and howling gales shake the sea, they cannot frighten him. A man like this rides the clouds and mist, straddles the sun and moon, and wanders beyond the four seas. Even life and death have no effect on him, much less the rules of profit and loss!"

B

Once Chuang Chou dreamt he was a butterfly, a butterfly flitting and fluttering around, happy with himself and doing as he pleased. He didn't know he was Chuang Chou. Suddenly he woke up and there he was, solid and unmistakable Chuang Chou. But he didn't know if he was Chuang Chou who had dreamt he was a butterfly, or a butterfly dreaming he was Chuang Chou. Between Chuang Chou and a butterfly there must be *some* distinction! This is called the Transformation of Things.

C

Your life has a limit but knowledge has none. If you use what is limited to pursue what has no limit, you will be in danger. If you understand this and still strive for knowledge, you will be in danger for certain! If you do good, stay away from fame. If you do evil, stay away from punishments. Follow the middle; go by what is constant, and you can stay in one piece, keep yourself alive, look after your parents, and live out your years.

Cook Ting was cutting up an ox for Lord Wen-hui.[1] At every touch of his hand, every heave of his shoulder, every move of his feet, every thrust of his knee—zip! zoop! He slithered the knife along with a zing, and all was in perfect rhythm, as though he were performing the dance of the Mulberry Grove or keeping time to the Ching-shou music.[2]

"Ah, this is marvelous!" said Lord Wen-hui. "Imagine skill reaching such heights!"

Cook Ting laid down his knife and replied, "What I care about is the Way, which goes beyond skill. When I first began cutting up oxen, all I could see was the ox itself. After three years I no longer saw the whole ox. And now—now I go at it by spirit and don't look with my eyes. Perception and understanding have come to a stop and spirit moves where it wants. I go along with the natural makeup, strike in the big hollows, guide the knife through the big openings, and follow things as they are. So I never touch the smallest ligament or tendon, much less a main joint.

"A good cook changes his knife once a year—because he cuts. A mediocre cook changes his knife once a month—because he hacks. I've had this knife of mine for nineteen years and I've cut up thousands of oxen with it, and yet the blade is as good as though it had just come from the grindstone. There are spaces between the joints, and the blade of the knife has really no thickness. If you insert what has no thickness into such spaces, then there's plenty of room—more than enough for the blade to play about it. That's why after nineteen years the blade of my knife is still as good as when it first came from the grindstone.

"However, whenever I come to a complicated place, I size up the difficulties, tell myself to watch out and be careful, keep my eyes on what I'm doing, work very slowly, and move the knife with the greatest subtlety, until—flop! the whole thing comes apart like a clod of earth crumbling to the ground. I stand there holding the knife and look all around me, completely satisfied and reluctant to move on, and then I wipe off the knife and put it away."[3]

---

1 Identified as King Hui of Wei. . . .

2 The Mulberry Grove is identified as a rain dance from the time of King T'ang of the Shang dynasty, and the Ching-shou music as part of a longer composition from the time of Yao.

3 Waley (*Three Walls of Thought in Ancient China*, p. 73) takes this whole paragraph to refer to the working methods of a mediocre carver and hence translates it very differently. There is a great deal to be said for his interpretation but after much consideration I have decided to follow the traditional interpretation because it seems to me that the extreme care and caution which the cook uses *when he comes to a difficult place* is also a part of Chuang Tzu's "secret of caring for life."

"Excellent!" said Lord Wen-hui. "I have heard the words of Cook Ting and learned how to care for life!"

D

Yen Ho, who had been appointed tutor to the crown prince, son of Duke Ling of Wei, went to consult Ch'ü Po-yü.[4] "Here is this man who by nature is lacking in virtue. If I let him go on with his unruliness I will endanger the state. If I try to impose some rule on him, I will endanger myself. He knows enough to recognize the faults of others, but he doesn't know his own faults. What can I do with a man like this?"

"A very good question," said Ch'ü Po-yü. "Be careful, be on your guard, and make sure that you yourself are in the right! In your actions it is best to follow along with him, and in your mind it is best to harmonize with him. However, these two courses involve certain dangers. Though you follow along, you don't want to be pulled into his doings, and though you harmonize, you don't want to be drawn out too far. If in your actions you follow along to the extent of being pulled in with him, then you will be overthrown, destroyed, wiped out, and brought to your knees. If in your mind you harmonize to the extent of being drawn out, then you will be talked about, named, blamed, and condemned. If he wants to be a child, be a child with him. If he wants to follow erratic ways, follow erratic ways with him. If he wants to be reckless, be reckless with him. Understand him thoroughly, and lead him to the point where he is without fault.[5]

"Don't you know about the praying mantis that waved its arms angrily in front of an approaching carriage, unaware that they were incapable of stopping it? Such was the high opinion it had of its talents. Be careful, be on your guard! If you offend him by parading your store of talents, you will be in danger!

"Don't you know how the tiger trainer goes about it? He doesn't dare give the tiger any living thing to eat for fear it will learn the taste of fury by killing it. He doesn't dare give it any whole thing to eat for fear it will learn the taste of fury by tearing it apart. He gauges the state of the tiger's appetite and thoroughly understands its fierce disposition. Tigers are a different breed from men, and yet you can train them to be gentle with their keepers by following along with them. The men who get killed are the ones who go against them."

E

Carpenter Shih went to Ch'i and, when he got to Crooked Shaft, he saw a serrate oak standing by the village shrine. It was broad enough to shelter several

---

4 Yen Ho was a scholar of Lu, Ch'ü Po-yü a minister of Wei. The crown prince is the notorious K'uai-k'uei, who was forced to flee from Wei because he plotted to kill his mother. He reentered the state and seized the throne from his son in 481 B.C.

5 Waley (*Three Ways of Thought in Ancient China,* p. 109) translates "And if you probe him, do so in a part where his skin is not sore," taking the verb *ta,* which I have translated as "understand thoroughly," to refer to acupuncture.

thousand oxen and measured a hundred spans around, towering above the hills. The lowest branches were eighty feet from the ground, and a dozen or so of them could have been made into boats. There were so many sightseers that the place looked like a fair, but the carpenter didn't even glance around and went on his way without stopping. His apprentice stood staring for a long time and then ran after Carpenter Shih and said, "Since I first took up my ax and followed you, Master, I have never seen timber as beautiful as this. But you don't even bother to look, and go right on without stopping. Why is that?"

"Forget it—say no more!" said the carpenter. "It's a worthless tree! Make boats out of it and they'd sink; make coffins and they'd rot in no time; make vessels and they'd break at once. Use it for doors and it would sweat sap like pine; use it for posts and the worms would eat them up. It's not a timber tree—there's nothing it can be used for. That's how it got to be that old!"

After Carpenter Shih had returned home, the oak tree appeared to him in a dream and said, "What are you comparing me with? Are you comparing me with those useful trees? The cherry apple, the pear, the orange, the citron, the rest of those fructiferous trees and shrubs—as soon as their fruit is ripe, they are torn apart and subjected to abuse. Their big limbs are broken off, their little limbs are yanked around. Their utility makes life miserable for them, and so they don't get to finish out the years Heaven gave them, but are cut off in mid-journey. They bring it on themselves—the pulling and tearing of the common mob. And it's the same way with all other things.

"As for me, I've been trying a long time to be of no use, and though I almost died, I've finally got it. This is of great use to me. If I had been of some use, would I ever have grown this large? Moreover you and I are both of us things. What's the point of this—things condemning things? You, a worthless man about to die—how do you know I'm a worthless tree?"

When Carpenter Shih woke up, he reported his dream. His apprentice said, "If it's so intent on being of no use, what's it doing there at the village shrine?"[6]

"Shhh! Say no more! It's only *resting* there. If we carp and criticize, it will merely conclude that we don't understand it. Even if it weren't at the shrine, do you suppose it would be cut down? It protects itself in a different way from ordinary people. If you try to judge it by conventional standards, you'll be way off!"

F

What do I mean by a True Man?[7] The True Man of ancient times did not rebel against want, did not grow proud in plenty, and did not plan his affairs. A man like this could commit an error and not regret it, could meet with success and not make a show. A man like this could climb the high places and not be

---

6   The shrine, or altar of the soil, was always situated in a grove of beautiful trees. So the oak was serving a purpose by lending an air of sanctity to the spot.

7   Another term for the Taoist sage, synonymous with the Perfect Man or the Holy Man.

frightened, could enter the water and not get wet, could enter the fire and not get burned. His knowledge was able to climb all the way up to the Way like this.

The True Man of ancient times slept without dreaming and woke without care; he ate without savoring and his breath came from deep inside. The True Man breathes with his heels; the mass of men breathe with their throats. Crushed and bound down, they gasp out their words as though they were retching. Deep in their passions and desires, they are shallow in the workings of Heaven.

The True Man of ancient times knew nothing of loving life, knew nothing of hating death. He emerged without delight; he went back in without a fuss. He came briskly, he went briskly, and that was all. He didn't forget where he began; he didn't try to find out where he would end. He received something and took pleasure in it; he forgot about it and handed it back again. This is what I call not using the mind to repel the Way, not using man to help out Heaven. This is what I call the True Man.

Since he is like this, his mind forgets;[8] his face is calm; his forehead is broad. He is chilly like autumn, balmy like spring, and his joy and anger prevail through the four seasons. He goes along with what is right for things and no one knows his limit. Therefore, when the sage calls out the troops, he may overthrow nations but he will not lose the hearts of the people. His bounty enriches ten thousand ages but he has no love for men. Therefore he who delights in bringing success to things is not a sage; he who has affections is not benevolent; he who looks for the right time is not a worthy man; he who cannot encompass both profit and loss is not a gentleman; he who thinks of conduct and fame and misleads himself is not a man of breeding; and he who destroys himself and is without truth is not a user of men. Those like Hu Pu-hsieh, Wu Kuang, Po Yi, Shu Ch'i, Chi Tzu, Hsü Yü, Chi T'o, and Shen-t'u Ti—all of them slaved in the service of other men, took joy in bringing other men joy, but could not find joy in any joy of their own.[9]

This was the True Man of old: his bearing was lofty and did not crumble; he appeared to lack but accepted nothing; he was dignified in his correctness but not insistent; he was vast in his emptiness but not ostentatious. Mild and cheerful, he seemed to be happy; reluctant, he could not help doing certain things; annoyed, he let it show in his face; relaxed, he rested in his virtue. Tolerant,[10] he seemed to be part of the world; towering alone, he could be checked by nothing; withdrawn, he seemed to prefer to cut himself off; bemused, he forgot what he was going to say.[11]

---

8 Reading *wang* instead of *chih* in accordance with the suggestion of Wang Mao-hung.

9 According to legend, these were men who either tried to reform the conduct of others or made a show of guarding their own integrity. All either were killed or committed suicide.

10 Following the Ts'ui text, which reads *kuang*.

11 There are many different interpretations of the words used to describe the True Man in this paragraph. I have followed those adopted by Fukunaga.

G

Yen Hui said, "I'm improving!"

Confucius said, "What do you mean by that?"

"I've forgotten benevolence and righteousness!"

"That's good. But you still haven't got it."

Another day, the two met again and Yen Hui said, "I'm improving!"

"What do you mean by that?"

"I've forgotten rites and music!"

"That's good. But you still haven't got it."

Another day, the two met again and Yen Hui said, "I'm improving!

"What do you mean by that?"

"I can sit down and forget everything!"

Confucius looked very startled and said, "What do you mean, sit down and forget everything?"

Yen Hui said, "I smash up my limbs and body, drive out perception and intellect, cast off form, do away with understanding, and make myself identical with the Great Thoroughfare. This is what I mean by sitting down and forgetting everything."

Confucius said, "If you're identical with it, you must have no more likes! If you've been transformed, you must have no more constancy! So you really are a worthy man after all![12] With your permission, I'd like to become your follower."

H

Once, when Chuang Tzu was fishing in the P'u River, the king of Ch'u sent two officials to go and announce to him: "I would like to trouble you with the administration of my realm."

Chuang Tzu held on to the fishing pole and, without turning his head, said, "I have heard that there is a sacred tortoise in Ch'u that has been dead for three thousand years. The king keeps it wrapped in cloth and boxed, and stores it in the ancestral temple. Now would this tortoise rather be dead and have its bones left behind and honored? Or would it rather be alive and dragging its tail in the mud?"

"It would rather be alive and dragging its tail in the mud," said the two officials.

Chuang Tzu said, "Go away! I'll drag my tail in the mud!"

I

When Hui Tzu was prime minister of Liang, Chuang Tzu set off to visit him. Someone said to Hui Tzu, "Chuang Tzu is coming because he wants to replace you as prime minister!" With this Hui Tzu was filled with alarm and searched all over the state for three days and three nights trying to find Chuang Tzu.

---

12 Chuang Tzu probably intends a humorous reference to the words of Confucius in *Analects* VI, 9: "The Master said, 'What a worthy man was Hui!'"

Chuang Tzu then came to see him and said, "In the south there is a bird called the Yüan-ch'u—I wonder if you've ever heard of it? The Yüan-ch'u rises up from the South Sea and flies to the North Sea, and it will rest on nothing but the Wu-t'ung tree, eat nothing but the fruit of the Lien, and drink only from springs of sweet water. Once there was an owl who had gotten hold of a half-rotten old rat, and as the Yüan-ch'u passed by, it raised its head, looked up at the Yüan-ch'u, and said, 'Shoo!' Now that you have this Liang state of yours, are you trying to shoo me?"

J

Is there such a thing as perfect happiness in the world or isn't there? Is there some way to keep yourself alive or isn't there? What to do, what to rely on, what to avoid, what to stick by, what to follow, what to leave alone, what to find happiness in, what to hate?

This is what the world honors: wealth, eminence, long life, a good name. This is what the world finds happiness in: a life of ease, rich food, fine clothes, beautiful sights, sweet sounds. This is what it looks down on: poverty, meanness, early death, a bad name. This is what it finds bitter: a life that knows no rest, a mouth that gets no rich food, no fine clothes for the body, no beautiful sights for the eye, no sweet sounds for the ear.

People who can't get these things fret a great deal and are afraid—this is a stupid way to treat the body. People who are rich wear themselves out rushing around on business, piling up more wealth than they could ever use—this is a superficial way to treat the body. People who are eminent spend night and day scheming and wondering if they are doing right—this is a shoddy way to treat the body. Man lives his life in company with worry, and if he lives a long while, till he's dull and doddering, then he has spent that much time worrying instead of dying, a bitter lot indeed! This is a callous way to treat the body.

Men of ardor are rewarded by the world as good, but their goodness doesn't succeed in keeping them alive. So I don't know whether their goodness is really good or not. Perhaps I think it's good—but not good enough to save their lives. Perhaps I think it's no good—but still good enough to save the lives of others. So I say, if your loyal advice isn't heeded, give way and do not wrangle. Tzu-hsü wrangled and lost his body.[13] But if he hadn't wrangled, he wouldn't have made a name. Is there really such a thing as goodness or isn't there?

What ordinary people do and what they find happiness in—I don't know whether such happiness is in the end really happiness or not. I look at what ordinary people find happiness in, what they all make a mad dash for, racing around as though they couldn't stop—they all say they're happy with it. I'm not

---

13 Wu Tzu-hsü, minister to the king of Wu, repeatedly warned the king of the danger of attack from the state of Yüeh. He finally aroused the king's ire and suspicion and was forced to commit suicide in 484 B.C.

happy with it and I'm not unhappy with it. In the end is there really happiness or isn't there?

I take inaction to be true happiness, but ordinary people think it is a bitter thing. I say: perfect happiness knows no happiness, perfect praise knows no praise. The world can't decide what is right and what is wrong. And yet inaction can decide this. Perfect happiness, keeping alive—only inaction gets you close to this!

Let me try putting it this way. The inaction of Heaven is its purity, the inaction of earth is its peace. So the two inactions combine and all things are transformed and brought to birth. Wonderfully, mysteriously, there is no place they come out of. Mysteriously, wonderfully, they have no sign. Each thing minds its business and all grow up out of inaction. So I say, Heaven and earth do nothing and there is nothing that is not done. Among men, who can get hold of this inaction?

K

Chuang Tzu's wife died. When Hui Tzu went to convey his condolences, he found Chuang Tzu sitting with his legs sprawled out, pounding on a tub and singing. "You lived with her, she brought up your children and grew old," said Hui Tzu. "It should be enough simply not to weep at her death. But pounding on a tub and singing—this is going too far, isn't it?"

Chuang Tzu said, "You're wrong. When she first died, do you think I didn't grieve like anyone else? But I looked back to her beginning and the time before she was born. Not only the time before she was born, but the time before she had a body. Not only the time before she had a body, but the time before she had a spirit. In the midst of the jumble of wonder and mystery a change took place and she had a spirit. Another change and she had a body. Another change and she was born. Now there's been another change and she's dead. It's just like the progression of the four seasons, spring, summer, fall, winter.

"Now she's going to lie down peacefully in a vast room. If I were to follow after her bawling and sobbing, it would show that I don't understand anything about fate. So I stopped."

Two Women

---◆---

The family has always been considered by the Chinese as the fundamental unit of their society. During the Han, family virtues, especially filial piety and female constancy, were widely celebrated. The *Classic of Filial Piety* gained popularity, and Liu Hsiang (79–8 B.C.), an eminent scholar and bibliographer, wrote *Biographies of Admirable Women,* a collection of accounts of the gallant deeds and unselfish behavior of women of antiquity. Many of these women epitomized a single virtue—for instance, loyalty to the ruler, self-sacrifice to help husband or father, or preservation of chastity under duress. As seen in the account below, however, the mother of the great Confucian philosopher Mencius (372–289 B.C.) had several virtues.

Reading this account does not reveal what women were like in the Han, but it does show us what people admired in women. No fiction has survived from the Han which could give us portrayals of women in ordinary life. We do have, however, one description of a real but far-from-ideal woman written by her husband, Feng Yen. It is found in a letter he addressed to his wife's younger brother to explain his reasons for divorcing her. Hardly a detached observer, Feng Yen nevertheless cannot help but reveal his own attitudes toward female character and the institution of marriage.

[Patricia Buckley Ebrey in *Chinese Civilization and Society*]

The Mother of Mencius

The mother of Mencius lived in Tsou in a house near a cemetery. When Mencius was a little boy he liked to play burial rituals in the cemetery, happily building tombs and grave mounds. His mother said to herself, "This is no place to bring up my son."

She moved near the marketplace in town. Mencius then played merchant games of buying and selling. His mother again said, "This is no place to bring up my son."

So once again she moved, this time next to a school house. Mencius then played games of ancestor sacrifices and practiced the common courtesies between students and teachers. His mother said, "At last, this is the right place for my son!" There they remained.

When Mencius grew up he studied the six arts of propriety, music, archery, charioteering, writing, and mathematics. Later he became a famous Confucian scholar. Superior men commented that Mencius' mother knew the right influences for her sons. The *Book of Poetry* says, "That admirable lady, what will she do for them!"

When Mencius was young, he came home from school one day and found his mother was weaving at the loom. She asked him, "Is school out already?'

He replied, "I left because I felt like it."

His mother took her knife and cut the finished cloth on her loom. Mencius was startled and asked why. She replied, "Your neglecting your studies is very much like my cutting the cloth. The superior person studies to establish a reputation and gain wide knowledge. He is calm and poised and tries to do no wrong. If you do not study now, you will surely end up as a menial servant and will never be free from troubles. It would be just like a woman who supports herself by weaving to give it up. How long could such a person depend on her husband and son to stave off hunger? If a woman neglects her work or a man gives up the cultivation of his character, they may end up as common thieves if not slaves!"

Shaken, from then on Mencius studied hard from morning to night. He studied the philosophy of the Master and eventually became a famous Confucian scholar. Superior men observed that Mencius' mother understood the way of motherhood. The *Book of Poetry* says, "That admirable lady, what will she tell them!"

After Mencius was married, one day as he was going into his private quarters, he encountered his wife not fully dressed. Displeased, Mencius stopped going into his wife's room. She then went to his mother, begged to be sent home, and said, "I have heard that the etiquette between a man and a woman does not apply in their private room. But lately I have been too casual, and when my husband saw me improperly dressed, he was displeased. He is treating me like a stranger. It is not right for a woman to live as a guest; therefore, please send me back to my parents."

Mencius' mother called him to her and said, "It is polite to inquire before you enter a room. You should make some loud noise to warn anyone inside, and as you enter, you should keep your eyes low so that you will not embarrass anyone. Now, you have not behaved properly, yet you are quick to blame others for their impropriety. Isn't that going a little too far?"

Mencius apologized and took back his wife. Superior men said that his mother understood the way to be a mother-in-law.

When Mencius was living in Ch'i, he was feeling very depressed. His mother saw this and asked him, "Why are you looking so low?"

"It's nothing," he replied.

On another occasion when Mencius was not working, he leaned against the door and sighed. His mother saw him and said, "The other day I saw that you were troubled, but you answered that it was nothing. But why are you leaning against the door sighing?"

Mencius answered, "I have heard that the superior man judges his capabilities and then accepts a position. He neither seeks illicit gains nor covets glory or high salary. If the Dukes and Princes do not listen to his advice, then he does not talk to them. If they listen to him but do not use his ideas, then he no longer frequents their courts. Today my ideas are not being used in Ch'i, so I wish to go somewhere else. But I am worried because you are getting too old to travel about the country."

His mother answered, "A woman's duties are to cook the five grains, heat the wine, look after her parents-in-law, make clothes, and that is all! Therefore, she cultivates the skills required in the women's quarters and has no ambition to manage affairs outside of the house. The *Book of Changes* says, 'In her central place, she attends to the preparation of the food.' The *Book Of Poetry* says, 'It will be theirs neither to do wrong nor to do good,/ Only about the spirits and the food will they have to think.' This means that a woman's duty is not to control or to take charge. Instead she must follow the 'three submissions.' When she is young, she must submit to her parents. After her marriage, she must submit to her husband. When she is widowed, she must submit to her son. These are the rules of propriety. Now you are an adult and I am old; therefore, whether you go depends on what you consider right, whether I follow depends on the rules of propriety."

Superior men observed that Mencius' mother knew the proper course for women. The *Book of Poetry* says, "Serenely she looks and smiles,/ Without any impatience she delivers her instructions."

Translated by Nancy Gibb

Letter from Feng Yen to His Brother-in-law

Man is a creature of emotion. Yet it is according to reason that husband and wife are joined together or put asunder. According to the rules of propriety which have been set down by the Sage, a gentleman should have both a primary wife and concubines as well. Even men from poor and humble families long to possess concubines. I am old and approaching the end of my life, but I have never had a concubine. I will carry regret for this into my grave.

My wife is jealous and has destroyed the Way of a good family. Yet this mother of five children is still in my house. For the past five years her conduct has become worse and worse day after day. She sees white as black and wrong as right. I never err in the slightest, yet she lies about me and nags me without end. It is like falling among bandits on the road, for I constantly encounter unpredictable disasters through this woman. Those who slander us good officials seem to have no regard for the deleterious effects this has on the welfare of the country. Likewise, those who indulge their jealousy seem to have no concern for the unjust strain this puts on other people's lives.

Since antiquity it has always been considered a great disaster to have one's household be dominated by a woman. Now this disaster has befallen me. If I eat too much or too little or if I drink too much or too little, she jumps all over me like the tyrant Hsia Chieh. If I play some affectionate joke on her, she will gossip about it to everyone. She glowers with her eyes and clenches her fists tightly in anger over things which are purely the product of her imagination. I feel a severe pang in my heart, as though something is poisoning my five viscera. Anxiety cuts so deeply that I can hardly bear to go on living. My rage is so great that I often forget the calamities I might cause.

When she is at home, she is always lounging in bed. After she gave birth to my principal heir, she refused to have any more children. We have no female servants at our home who can do the work of weaving clothes and rugs. Our family is of modest means and we cannot afford a man-servant, so I have to work myself like a humble commoner. My old friends see my situation and feel very sorry for me, but this woman has not the slightest twinge of sympathy or pity.

Wu Ta, you have seen our one and only female servant. She has no hairpins or hair ornaments. She has no make-up for her face, looks haggard, and is in bad shape. My wife does not extend the slightest pity to her, nor does she try to understand her. The woman flies into a rage, jumps around, and yells at her. Her screaming is so shrill that even a sugar-peddler's concubine would be ashamed to behave in such a manner.

I should have sent this woman back long ago, but I was concerned by the fact that the children were still young and that there was no one else to do the work in our house. I feared that my children, Chiang and Pao, would end up doing servants' work. Therefore I retained her. But worry and anxiety plunge like a dagger into my heart and cause me great pain. The woman is always screaming fiercely. One can hardly bear to listen to it.

Since the servant was so mistreated, within half a year her body was covered with scabs and scars. Ever since the servant became ill, my daughter Chiang has had to hull the grain and do the cooking, and my son Pao has had to do all sorts of dirty work. Watching my children struggle under such labor gives me distress.

Food and clothing are scattered all over the house. Winter clothes which have become frayed are not patched. Even though the rest of us are very careful to be neat, she turns the house into a mess. She does not have the manner of a good wife, nor does she possess the virtue of a good mother. I despise her overbearing aggressiveness, and I hate to see our home turned into a sty.

She relies on the power of Magistrate Cheng to get what she wants. She is always threatening people, and her barbs are numerous. It seems as if she carries a sword and lance to the door. Never will she make a concession, and it feels as if there were a hundred bows around our house. How can we ever return to a happy family life?

When the respectable members of our family try to reason with her, she flings insults at them and makes sharp retorts. She never regrets her scandalous behavior and never allows her heart to be moved. I realize that I have placed myself in a difficult position, and so I have started to plan ahead. I write you this letter lest I be remiss in keeping you informed of what is happening. I believe that I have just cause, and I am not afraid of criticism. Unless I send this wife back, my family will have no peace. Unless I send this wife back, my house will never be clean. Unless I send this wife back, good fortune will not come to my family. Unless I send this wife back, I will never again get anything accomplished. I hate myself for not having made this decision while I was still young. The decision is now made, but I am old, humiliated, and poor. I hate myself for having allowed this ulcer to grow and spread its poison. I brought a great deal of trouble on myself.

Having suffered total ruin as a result of this family catastrophe, I am abandoning the gentry life to live as a recluse. I will sever relationships with my friends and give up my career as an official. I will stay at home all the time and concentrate on working my land to supply myself with food and clothing. How can I think of success and fame?

Translated by Lily Hwa

The Debate on Salt and Iron

The standard histories of the Han are replete with Accounts of the decisions and policies made by the central government. Energetic rulers, such as Emperor Wu (r. 141–82 B.C.), are credited with greatly strengthening the power of the government. Determining how fully these policies were carried out or how they affected the population is often difficult. Sources such as the record of the "Debate on Salt and Iron" nevertheless provide some insight. In 81 B.C., after Emperor Wu's death, Confucian scholars who opposed the fiscal policies he had instituted were invited by his successor to argue their case with the Chief Minister, a man who had been instrumental in establishing them. A record of this debate was made in twenty-four chapters, the first of which is given below.

A major motive for Emperor Wu's fiscal policies had been the need to defend against the non-Chinese nomadic tribes (especially the Hsiung-nu) who lived in the dry regions north of China proper. To protect settlers on the borders from raids by the Hsiung-nu, the government had to mobilize huge armies and build numerous fortifications and encampments. To generate the revenue to pay for these military ventures, Emperor Wu manipulated coinage, confiscated the lands of nobles, sold offices and titles, and increased taxes. He also established government monopolies in the production of iron, salts, and liquor, enterprises that had previously been sources of great profit for private entrepreneurs. Large-scale grain dealing had also been a profitable business, which the government now took over under the name of the system of equable marketing. Grain was to be bought where it was plentiful and its price low and either stored in granaries or transported to areas of scarcity. This procedure was supposed to eliminate speculation in grain, provide more constant prices, and bring profit to the government.

From the start these fiscal ventures were controversial. Those educated in Confucian principles questioned their morality and their effect on the livelihood of the people. They thought that farming was an essential or "root" activity but that trade and crafts produced little of real value and were to be discouraged. Although the government claimed that it was protecting the people from the exploitation of merchants, its critics argued that it was teaching people mercantile tricks by setting itself up in commerce.

Reprinted with the permission of The Free Press, a Division of Simon & Schuster from *Chinese Civilization and Society: A Sourcebook* by Patricia Buckley Ebrey. Copyright © 1981 by The Free Press.

In the selection below both sides argued in general terms. They also both used the same rhetorical style, relying heavily on direct and indirect quotations from earlier books. Yet from their debate we can see some of the ways officials and potential officials thought about their responsibilities. From their descriptions of economic conditions we can also gain insight into the state of the economy in this period and the influence of the state on day-to-day economic affairs.

[Patricia Buckley Ebrey in *Chinese Civilization and Society*]

In 81 B.C. an imperial edict directed the Chancellor and Chief Minister to confer with a group of wise and learned men about the people's hardships.

The learned men responded: We have heard that the way to rule lies in preventing frivolity while encouraging morality, in suppressing the pursuit of profit while opening the way for benevolence and duty. When profit is not emphasized, civilization flourishes and the customs of the people improve.

Recently, a system of salt and iron monopolies, a liquor excise tax, and an equable marketing system have been established throughout the country. These represent financial competition with the people which undermines their native honesty and promotes selfishness. As a result, few among the people take up the fundamental pursuits [agriculture] while many flock to the secondary [trade and industry]. When artificiality thrives, simplicity declines; when the secondary flourishes, the basic decays. Stress on the secondary makes the people decadent; emphasis on the basic keeps them unsophisticated. When the people are unsophisticated, wealth abounds; when they are extravagant, cold and hunger ensue.

We desire that the salt, iron, and liquor monopolies and the system of equable marketing be abolished. In that way the basic pursuits will be encouraged, and the people will be deterred from entering secondary occupations. Agriculture will then greatly prosper. This would be expedient.

The Minister: The Hsiung-nu rebel against our authority and frequently raid the frontier settlements. To guard against this requires the effort of the nation's soldiers. If we take no action, these attacks and raids will never cease. The late Emperor had sympathy for the long-suffering of the frontier settlers who live in fear of capture by the barbarians. As defensive measures, he therefore built forts and beacon relay stations and set up garrisons. When the revenue for the defense of the frontier fell short, he established the salt and iron monopolies, the liquor excise tax, and the system of equable marketing. Wealth increased and was used to furnish the frontier expenses.

Now our critics wish to abolish these measures. They would have the treasury depleted and the border deprived of funds for its defense. They would expose our soldiers who defend the frontier passes and walls to hunger and cold, since there is no other way to supply them. Abolition is not expedient.

The learned men: Confucius observed, "The ruler of a kingdom or head of a family does not worry about his people's being poor, only about their being unevenly distributed. He does not worry about their being few, only about their being dissatisfied." Thus, the Emperor should not talk of much and little, nor the feudal lords of advantage and harm, nor the ministers of gain and loss. Instead they all should set examples of benevolence and duty and virtuously care for people, for then those nearby will flock to them and those far away will joyfully submit to their authority. Indeed, the master conqueror need not fight, the expert warrior needs no soldiers, and the great commander need not array his troops.

If you foster high standards in the temple and courtroom, you need only make a bold show and bring home your troops, for the king who practices benevolent government has no enemies anywhere. What need can he then have for expense funds?

The Minister: The Hsiung-nu are savage and cunning. They brazenly push through the frontier passes and harass the interior, killing provincial officials and military officers at the border. Although they have long deserved punishment for their lawless rebellion, Your Majesty has taken pity on the financial exigencies of the people and has not wished to expose his officers to the wilderness. Still, we cherish the goal of raising a great army and driving the Hsiung-nu back north.

I again assert that to do away with the salt and iron monopolies and equable marketing system would bring havoc to our frontier military policies and would be heartless toward those on the frontier. Therefore this proposal is inexpedient.

The learned men: The ancients honored the use of virtue and discredited the use of arms. Confucius said, "If the people of far-off lands do not submit, then the ruler must attract them by enhancing his refinement and virtue. When they have been attracted, he gives them peace."

At present, morality is discarded and reliance is placed on military force. Troops are raised for campaigns and garrisons are stationed for defense. It is the long-drawn-out campaigns and the ceaseless transportation of provisions that burden our people at home and cause our frontier soldiers to suffer from hunger and cold.

The establishment of the salt and iron monopolies and the appointment of Financial Officers to supply the army were meant to be temporary measures. Therefore, it is expedient that they now be abolished.

The Minister: The ancient founders of our country laid the groundwork for both basic and secondary occupations. They facilitated the circulation of goods and provided markets and courts to harmonize the various demands. People of all classes gathered and goods of all sorts were assembled, so that farmers, merchants, and workers could all obtain what they needed. When the exchange of goods was complete, everyone went home. The *Book of Changes* says, "Facilitate exchange so that the people will not be overworked." This is because without artisans, the farmers are deprived of tools, and without merchants, desired commodities are unavailable. When farmers lack tools, grain is not planted, just as when valued goods are unavailable, wealth is exhausted.

The salt and iron monopolies and the equable marketing system are intended to circulate accumulated wealth and to regulate consumption according to the urgency of need. It is inexpedient to abolish them.

The learned men: If virtue is used to lead the people, they will return to honesty, but if they are enticed with gain, they will become vulgar. Vulgar habits lead them to shun duty and chase profit; soon they throng the roads and markets.

Lao Tzu said, "A poor country will appear to have a surplus." It is not that it possesses abundance, but that when wishes multiply the people become restive. Hence, a true king promotes the basic and discourages the secondary. He restrains the people's desires through the principles of ritual and duty and arranges to have grain exchanged for other goods. In his markets merchants do not circulate worthless goods nor artisans make worthless implements.

The purpose of merchants is circulation and the purpose of artisans is making tools. These matters should not become a major concern of the government.

The Minister: Kuan Tzu[1] said: "If a country possesses fertile land and yet its people are underfed, the reason is that there are not enough tools. If it possesses rich natural resources in its mountains and seas and yet the people are poor, the reason is that there are not enough artisans and merchants."

The scarlet lacquer and pennant feathers from the kingdoms of Lung and Shu; the leather goods, bone, and ivory from Ching and Yang; the cedar, catalpa, bamboo, and reeds from Chiang-nan; the fish, salt, felt, and furs from Yen and Ch'i; the silk yam, linen, and hemp cloth from Yen and Yu—all are needed to maintain our lives or be used in our funerals. We depend upon merchants for their distribution and on artisans for their production. For such reasons the ancient sages built boats and bridges to cross rivers; they domesticated cattle and horses to travel over mountains and plains. By penetrating to remote areas, they were able to exchange all kinds of goods for the benefit of the people.

Thus, the Former Emperor set up iron officials to meet the farmers' needs and started the equable marketing system to assure the people adequate goods. The bulk of the people look to the salt and iron monopolies and the equable marketing system as their source of supply. To abolish them would not be expedient.

The learned men: If a country possesses a wealth of fertile land and yet its people are underfed, the reason is that merchants and workers have prospered while agriculture has been neglected. Likewise, if a country possesses rich natural resources in its mountains and seas and yet its people are poor, the reason is that the people's necessities have not been attended to while luxuries have multiplied. A spring cannot fill a leaking cup; the mountains and seas cannot satisfy unlimited desires. This is why [the ancient emperor] Fan Keng practiced communal living, [the ancient emperor] Shun concealed the gold, and [the Han dynasty founder] Kao-tsu prohibited merchants and shopkeepers from becoming officials. Their purpose was to discourage habits of greed and to strengthen the spirit of sincerity. Now, even with all of the discriminations against commerce, people still do evil. How much worse it would be if the ruler himself were to pursue profit!

The *Tso Chronicle* says: "When the feudal lords take delight in profit, the officers become petty; when the officers are petty, the gentlemen become greedy;

---

1   I.e., Kuan Chung, a famous minister of the seventh century B.C. noted for his economic policies.

when the gentlemen are greedy, the common people steal." Thus to open the way for profit is to provide a ladder for the people to become criminals!

The Minister: Formerly the feudal lords in the commanderies and kingdoms sent in the products of their respective regions as tribute. Transportation was troublesome and disorganized and the goods often of such bad quality as not to be worth the transport cost. Therefore, Transport Officers were appointed in every commandery and kingdom to assist in speeding the delivery of tribute and taxes from distant regions. This was called the equable marketing system. A Receiving Bureau was established at the capital for all the commodities. Because goods were bought when prices were low and sold when prices were high, the government suffered no loss and the merchants could not speculate for profit. This was called the balancing standard.

The balancing standard safeguards the people from unemployment; the equable marketing system distributes their work fairly. Both of these measures are intended to even out goods and be a convenience for the people. They do not provide a ladder for the people to become criminals by opening the way to profit!

The learned men: The ancients in placing levies and taxes on the people would look for what they could provide. Thus farmers contributed their harvest and the weaving women the products of their skill. At present the government ignores what people have and exacts what they lack. The common people then must sell their products cheaply to satisfy the demands of the government. Recently, some commanderies and kingdoms ordered the people to weave cloth. The officials caused the producers various difficulties and then traded with them. They requisitioned not only the silk from Ch'i and Tao and the broadcloth from Shu and Han, but also the ordinary cloth people make. These were then nefariously sold at "equable" prices. Thus the farmers suffered twice over and the weavers were doubly taxed. Where is the equability in this marketing?

The government officers busy themselves with gaining control of the market and cornering commodities. With the commodities cornered, prices soar and merchants make private deals and speculate. The officers connive with the cunning merchants who are hoarding commodities against future need. Quick traders and unscrupulous officials buy when goods are cheap in order to make high profits. Where is the balance in this standard?

The equable marketing system of antiquity aimed at bringing about fair division of labor and facilitating transportation of tribute. It was surely not for profit or commodity trade.

Early Islamic Civilization

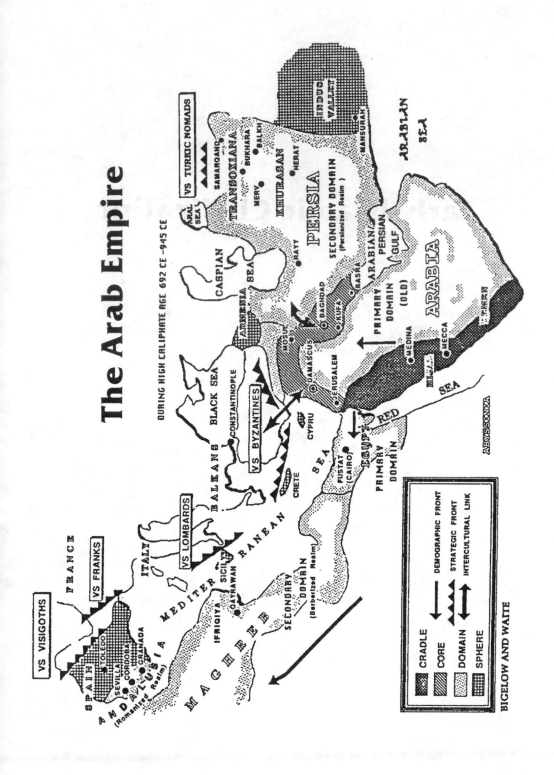

The Arab Empire

DURING HIGH CALIPHATE AGE 692 CE –945 CE

VS TURKIC NOMADS

TRANSOXIANA

SAMARQAND
BUKHARA
BALKH
MERV
HERAT
RAYY
KHURASAN

PERSIA

SECONDARY DOMAIN
(Persianized Realm)

ARAL SEA

CASPIAN

ARMENIA

BLACK SEA

CONSTANTINOPLE

VS BYZANTINES

CYPRUS

CRETE

BALKANS

ITALY

VS LOMBARDS

FRANCE

VS FRANKS

VS VISIGOTHS

SPAIN

TOLEDO
SEVILLA
CORDOBA
GRANADA

ANDALUSIA
(Romanized Realm)

MEDITERRANEAN

SICILY

IFRIQIYA

QAYRAWAN

MAGHREB

SECONDARY DOMAIN
(Berberized Realm)

SEA

RED SEA

EGYPT

FUSTAT
(CAIRO)

PRIMARY DOMAIN

ABYSSINIA

MOSUL

DAMASCUS

JERUSALEM

BAGHDAD

KUFA

BASRA

PERSIAN GULF

PRIMARY DOMAIN (OLD)

ARABIA

MEDINA

MECCA

HIJAZ

YEMEN

INDUS VALLEY

MANSURAH

ARABIAN SEA

ARABIAN

Legend

CRADLE	
CORE	
DOMAIN	
SPHERE	

DEMOGRAPHIC FRONT

STRATEGIC FRONT

INTERCULTURAL LINK

BIGELOW AND WAITE

Early Islamic Civilization

———❦———

I. Pre-Islamic Arabia (1000 B.C.E.–622 C.E.)

II. LIFE OF MUHAMMAD (c. 570–632 C.E.)

c. 570	Birth of Muhammad
c. 595	Muhammad marries Khadija
603–628	Byzantine-Sasanian War
610	Call of Muhammad
619	Deaths of Khadija and Abu Talib
622	Hijra (flight to Medina)
630	Mecca submits to Muhammad
632	"Farewell pilgrimage"; death of Muhammad

III. 632–661 PERIOD OF THE "RIGHTLY GUIDED" CALIPHS

632–634	**Abu Bakr, first caliph:** defeat of rebellious Arab tribes
634–644	**Umar, second caliph:** expansion of empire
636	Capture of Damascus
638	Jerusalem conquered
637–651	Conquest of Persia
641–642	Conquest of Egypt
643	Conquest of Tripoli (N. Africa)
644–56	**Uthman, third caliph:** collector of *Quran*
656	Assassination of Uthman
656–661	First fitnah (civil war)
656	Battle of Camel—Ali victorious
656–61	**Ali, fourth caliph,** cousin/son-in-law of Muhammad
658	Arbitration of 658 (Ali and Muawiya)
661	Ali assassinated by a Kharijite

IV. 661–750 UMAYYAD CALIPHATE (DAMASCUS)

CALIPHS		POLITICAL DATES		OTHER DATES	
661–680	MUAWIYA	680	Husayn martyred at Karbala		
		680–692	Second fitnah (civil war)	692	Completion of Dome of Rock, Jerusalem
685–705	ABD AL-MALIK: Arabization of Islam			696	Arabic coinage
692–715	AL-HAJJAJ, governor of Iraq			701	Death of Jamil, Bedouin ghazal poet
705–715	AL-WALID I			705	Umayyad mosque in Damascus
		711	Completion of N. African conquest; beginning of Muslim conquest of Spain		
717–720	UMAR II: Islamization of government				
724–743	HISHAM				
744–750	MARWAN II	750	Third fitnah (civil war)		

144

V. 750–1258 ABBASID CALIPHATE (BAGHDAD)

A. 750–945 Early Abbasid

CALIPHS	POLITICAL DATES	OTHER DATES
754–775 AL-MANSUR		c. 756 *Kalila wa-Dimna* translated by al-Muqaffa
	756–1031 UMAYYAD dynasty in Spain	762 Foundation of Baghdad
		765 Split between Twelvers and Ismaili (Seveners) Shiites
775–785 AL-MAHDI		785 Great Mosque at Cordoba begun
786–809 HARUN AL-RASHID: Ideal Abbasid Caliph		801 Death of Rabia (female Sufi poet)
813–833 AL-MAMUM: flowering of scholarship; translation of Greek works into Arabic	809–819 Fourth fitnah (civil war)	
833–842 AL-MUTASIM		c. 830 al-Khwarizmi founds science of algebra (al-jabr) *Bayt al-Hikmah* academy founded
842–847 AL-WATHIQ: last ruler of strong, unified Abbasid empire		

A. 750–945 Early Abbasid (continued)

847–851		AL-MUTAWAKKIL: abandons Mutazili thesis; gulf between religious and state communities.
767–869		al-Jahiz (best known prose essayist)
870		Death of al-Bukhari (most important hadith collection)
c. 866		Death of al-Kindi (philosopher)
874		Occultation (hiding) of twelfth Imam
909–972	FATIMID DYNASTY, in North Africa	
922		Execution of al-Hallaj (Sufi mystic)
838–923		al-Tabari (great historian, exegete of *Quran*)
865–925		al-Razi (physician, philosopher, alchemist)
850–929		al-Battani (astronomer)
873–935		al-Ashari (major theologian)

B. 945–1258 Later Abbasid

1. 945–1055 Buyid Dynasty

POLITICAL DATES		OTHER DATES	
945	Buyids occupy Baghdad; end of political power of Abbasids		
		915–965	al-Mutanabbi (great Arab poet)
969–1171	FATIMID independent Islamic state in Egypt	976	Al-Azhar University founded (Cairo)
		980–1037	Avicenna (Ibn Sina; physician, philosopher)

2. 1055–c. 1157 Seljuq Dynasty

POLITICAL DATES		OTHER DATES	
1055–1058	Seljuqs overthrow Buyids, occupy Baghdad	973–1057	al-Maarri; last great Arabic poet of golden age
1071	Battle of Manzikert		
1085	Christian reconquest of Spain begins (Toledo)	1090	First use of compass by Muslims
1095–1291	The Crusades	1100	Omar Khayyam composes the *Rubaiyyat*
1099	Crusaders take Jerusalem	1058–1111	al-Ghazali (important theologian; Sufi)

3. 1157–1258 Seljuq Empire Fragments

CALIPHS	POLITICAL DATES		OTHER DATES	
	1171	Saladin overthrows Fatimids in Egypt		
	1175	First Muslim empire in India		
1180–1225 AL-NASIR, last important Abbasid caliph				
	1187	Saladin recovers Jerusalem from Crusaders	1124–1198	Ibn-Rushd (Averroes); (Islamic Aristotelian)
	1206–27	Reign and Conquests of Genghis Khan	1203	Persian poet Nizami dies
			1238	Alhambra construction begins (Granada)
			1207–1273	Jalal al-Din Rumi (Sufi poet)
	1258	Mongols sack Baghdad; kill last Caliph		
	1280	Osman, First Ottoman sultan		

Early Islamic Civilization Glossary

Abbasid: second great Islamic dynasty (749–1258). Founded by descendants of al-Abbas, an uncle of Muhammad.

Abu Bakr (d.634): companion, prayer leader during Muhammad's life, and his successor as first caliph.

Adab *courtesy, politeness, literature, morals:* more generally culture of the educated upper class.

Aisha (613–678): daughter of Abu Bakr and favorite wife of Muhammad.

Alhambra: the great 14th century palace in Granada, Spain. Peak achievement of Islamic architecture in West.

Allah: Arabic word for God

Amir (Emir) *commander:* military commander, governor, or prince.

Ansar *helpers:* Medinan supporters of Muhammad

Arabesque: originally designates the vegetal style of decoration involving patterns of leaves and stems (the pattern having no beginning or end), sometimes used also to include geometric and calligraphic decorative patterns.

Ashari (Abu-l-Hasan Ali ibn Ismail al-Ashari: 873–935): most important early Muslim theologian. Tried to reconcile pre-destination with free-will; supported eternal *Quran* and literal meaning of anthropomorphic terms used of God. Opponent of Mutazilites.

Baghdad: Abbasid capital founded by al-Mansur in 762 on west bank of Tigris River, near ancient Ctesiphon.

Berbers: native (non-Arab) inhabitants of N. Africa, west of Egypt.

Bismilla (Basmala) *invocation:* "In the name of God, the Beneficent, the Merciful."

Black Stone: in southeast corner of Kaba, set in silver. By tradition originally placed there by Adam.

al-Bukhari, Muhammad Ibn Ismail (d. 875): Compiler of the most important collection of Hadiths.

Byzantine Empire: (eastern) Roman empire with capital at Constantinople.

Caliph: *successor* of Muhammad in his political function as ruler of the Islamic community.

Chador: garment covering female body and head in Iran.

Dar al-Harb *The Abode of War:* those areas not under Islamic government.

Dar al-Islam *The Abode of Islam:* those states under Muslim govenment.

Dome of the Rock (691): octagonal shrine (not a mosque) built on the site of the ancient Jewish temple in Jerusalem over the rock from which Muhammad ascended into heaven during his night journey.

al-Fatiha *The Opening:* the first sura of the *Quran.*

Fatima (d. 632/3): daughter of Khadijah and Muhammad, wife of Ali.

Fatwa: legal opinion given by a mufti; may be used by a judge in making decisions.

Fertile Crescent: area comprising the Tigres-Euphrates river valleys and Levantine coast. More broadly, the middle-eastern lands of Iraq, Syria, Lebanon, Israel, Jordan, and Arabia.

Fiqh: jurisprudence, discipline which deals with laws governing Muslim life.

Fiqh al-Akbar *the greatest Fiqh:* ten point credal statement by Abu Hanifa; defines basic Sunni belief.

Gabriel: key archangel of Islamic traditions; reveals *Quran* to Muhammad and takes him on the "night journey."

Garrison towns: established in conquered areas as military camps and dwellings for Arab troops, apart from native living areas. Kufah and Basra in Iraq are the two most important early ones.

al-Ghazali (1058–1111): reconciled Sufism to Sunni orthodoxy. Most important Islamic theologian.

Hadith *speech, report, account:* A report of what the Prophet did or said, and thus the basis of knowing the tradition (sunna) of the Prophet. A hadith consists of two parts: the account itself (matn), and the chain of transmitters (isnad) which guarantees its genuineness. Hadiths collected in six books; those of al-Bukhari and Muslim are considered the most important.

Hajj: greater pilgrimage to Mecca in the twelfth month. A male pilgrim is a hajji, and a female a hajja.

Hanbalites: most fundamentalist of the four law schools.

Hanif: a monotheist who is not Christian, Jewish, or Muslim, e.g., Abraham of the Bible.

Hanafite: largest (in terms of followers today) of four schools of law. Named after Abu Hanifah (d. 767). Dominant today in Iraq, Syria, Afghanistan, India, and Turkic Central Asia.

Haram *sanctuary:* sacred area (thus also means "forbidden," "taboo," or "holy.") The sacred areas around Mecca and Medina which only Muslims may enter.

Harem: secluded women's quarters in an Arab home.

Hasan al-Basri (642–728): key figure in development of both Sufism and theology (Mutazilites); prominent role in hadith transmission.

Hashimite: the Meccan clan (Banu Hashim) to which Muhammad, Abu Talib, and Ali belonged.

Hijaz: area along central-west coast of Arabia which includes Mecca and Medina.

Hijra *emigration:* especially of Muhammad and his companions from Mecca to Medina in 622.

Husayn (624–680): second son of Ali and Fatima. Killed in battle with forces of Umayyad caliph Yazid at Karbala, Iraq. His martyrdom central to Shiism and celebrated each year in a passion play. (Cf. Muharram).

Iblis: name of the devil in Islam; an angel cast out from heaven.

Ibn Ishaq (d. 767): author of the standard three volume biography of Muhammad.

Ibn Rushd (Averroes, 1126–1198): philosopher; important expositor of Aristotle; wrote on revelation and reason.

Ibn Sina (Avicenna, 980–1037): his *Canon of Medicine* became a standard medical textbook in the West; also a philosopher.

ijma *consensus:* (especially of scholars) one of the four roots of Islamic law.

Ijtihad: reasoning from analogy by which are resolved legal questions not answered by *Quran* or Sunna.

Imam: 1) leader of daily prayer; 2) legitimate successor of Muhammad and Ali and leader of Shiite community.

Iman *faith:* a key virtue (same root as "amen").

Islam *surrender:* the name of the religion taught in the *Quran.* Cf. Muslim.

Ismaili: Shiite branch which traces line of seven imams. Name from Ismail, the sixth imam.

Isnad: chain of hadith transmission, usually beginning with a companion of the Prophet. A science of hadith criticism developed to grade the hadith as to their reliability, based on evaluating the moral character and other factors concerning each person named in the isnad.

Jahiliya: the "age of ignorance" which preceded Islam in Arabia.

Jesus: "Messenger" next in importance to Muhammad; born of the virgin Mary; performed miracles; did not die on cross and is not the son of God; will return at day of judgment to destroy the anti-Christ.

Jihad *striving:* both interior (spiritual) and exterior (holy war).

Jinn: creatures who inhabit the material and immaterial world; both good and evil. (English "genie")

Jizya: tax imposed on non-Muslims living under Muslim rule.

Kaba: cubic structure in middle of the Grand Mosque of Mecca; contains the Black Stone. Ritual center of Islam.

Khadijah (554–619): first (and during her lifetime only) wife of Muhammad.

Kharijites *seceders:* puritanical sect of early Islam; a person who sins is no longer a Muslim; caliph should be sinless and chosen democratically.

al-Khwarizmi (d. 850): astronomer, mathematician, algebraist; popularized use of "Arabic" (actually Hindu) numbers and use of zero.

Levant: the area bordering the eastern shore of the Mediterranean.

Maghreb: lands on north coast of Africa, north of Sahara, from Tunisia to Morocco.

Mahdi: "Messiah" who will come at end of time and restore God's rule prior to the final judgment day. In Imami Shiism, the Mahdi will be the hidden twelfth imam.

Malikite: dominant school of law in Medina, Egypt N. Central and W. Africa, Muslim Spain and some of the E. Arabian coast.

Mecca: commercial and trading city of central Hijaz; home of Muhammad; location of Kaba and thus most sacred site of Islam.

Medina: "City of (the Prophet)" where Muhammad emigrated in 622 and established the Muslim state. Originally Yathrib.

Mevlevi: Sufi order in Turkey founded by Rumi, sometimes referred to in west as "Whirling Dervishes" (after use of dancing and music in their ritual).

Mihrab: the prayer niche in the wall facing Mecca; marks the direction of prayer.

Minaret: tower(s) attached to mosque from which call to prayer is issued.

Minbar: pulpit from which sermon is delivered at Friday service.

Monophysites: a form of eastern Christianity (e.g., the Coptic church in Egypt) which maintained that Christ had a single nature (human body and divine nature).

Mosque *place of prostration:* Muslim house of worship (i.e., prayer).

Muezzin: the person who calls the community to prayer (from the minaret if there is one).

Mufti: a legal official who is consulted to give opinions concerning application of the law. His decision is a fatwa.

Muhammad (570–632): final prophet and messenger of God; founder of Islam.

Mulla: title of religious teachers and scholars in Iran and Central Asia.

Muslim: one who practices Islam (submission to God).

Mutazilite: rationalist, philosophical kalam school in early Islam; tried to reconcile faith with reason; emphasized free will and denied doctrine of eternal *Quran*.

Nestorians: Eastern branch of Christianity which taught that in Jesus there were two natures and two persons, one divine and one human.

Night journey: the occasion in month of Ramadan when Muhammad was taken by Gabriel to Jerusalem, from where he ascended through the seven heavens to the presence of God.

Niyya *intention:* necessary to fulfillment of all religious obligations; may be stated aloud or to oneself.

Pillars (Five): Five basic categories of worship: the shahada; salat; zakat; Ramadan fast; hajj.

Qadi: a judge, appointed by ruler chosen from among scholars of law; decisions are binding.

Qiblah: direction of prayer towards Kabah in Mecca (originally towards Jerusalem). Marked by the mihrab in the mosque.

Quran *recitation:* especially the words of God revealed to Muhammad and existing eternally in heaven.

Quraysh: Leading tribe of Mecca in time of Muhammad; Ummayads were from Quraysh.

Rabia, al-Adawiyyah (713–801): famous female Sufi saint and poet.

Raka: complete cycle of postures in the salat; standing, bowing, prostration, sitting.

Ramadan: ninth month of Muslim calendar. Fasting *(sawn)* dawn to dusk in Ramadan is one of five pillars. *Quran* revealed in a night of Ramadan, which is holiest night of Muslim year.

Rasul *messenger:* a prophet who brings a new revelation; basic role of Muhammad.

Ridda *apostasy* from Islam. The term also designates the period of rebellion following death of Muhammad.

ar-Rumi, Jalal al-Din (1207–1273): great Persian Sufi mystic and poet. His *Mathnawi* is a six volume work of Sufi teaching, stories, etc. in poetic form. Founder of the Mevlevi order.

Salat: formal, ritual prayer performed five times a day.

Sasanian Empire: Persian based empire at time of Muhammad; controlled Iran and Iraq.

Shafiite: One of the four schools of law; founded by ash-Shafii.

Shahada: basic confession of Islam—"There is no God but Allah and Muhammad is the Messenger of God."

Sharia *the way to the water hole:* the revealed law as set forth in *Quran* and Sunna.

Shaykh: elder; tribal chief; Sufi master; religious scholar.

Shia [Shiite/Shiism] *party/faction:* branch of Islam (10–15%) which believed that caliphate should have remained in family of Muhammad (Ali and his descendants).

Shirk *association:* unforgivable sin in Islam is "association" of anything with God; idolatry (see *Quran* 4:48).

Subha: Muslim prayer beads, strung in loops of 11, 33, or 99, used in reciting the 99 names of God.

Sufi/Sufism: Muslim mystic/mysticism; perhaps from Suf (wool).

Sultan: the military ruler in late Abbasid and later times; accepted nominal authority of the caliph.

Sunna *custom, usage:* specifically the custom of Muhammad as a source of sharia. The authentic hadiths provided the content of this custom.

Sunni: the 85% majority branch of Islam who follow the Sunna (custom) of Muhammad and accept the first four caliphs.

Sura: chapters of the *Quran*.

Ulama: the religious scholars (and elite) of Islam.

Umayyads (661–750): first dynasty; capital at Damascus, established by Muawiyah.

Umma: the Muslim community.

Umra: the "lesser" pilgrimage to Mecca made at any time of year; does not fulfill the hajj requirement of five pillars.

Vizier (wazir): chief minister of government of caliph; established by al-Mansur.

Yathrib: oasis town to which Muhammad migrated in 622, known thereafter as Medina.

Zakat: required almsgiving, 1 of 5 pillars; calculated as a portion of one's wealth.

Zamzam: the well near the Kaba in Mecca.

Zoroastrianism: native religion of ancient Persia and official religion of Sasanian state. Believed in creator god, final judgment, fight between principle of good and of evil.

Sacred Biographies

⟶◆⟵

The *Sirat Rasul Allah (Biography of the Messenger of God)* by Ibn Ishaq (d. c. 768 C.E.) was the first biography of Muhammad. The biography is a collection of hadiths (see introductory note to *The Hadith* in this volume) painstakingly investigated for authenticity by Ibn Ishaq around 125 years after Muhammad's death. Ibn Ishaq arranged the hadiths into a chronological order, and wove them together with a continuous narrative.

The biography had three parts: ancient legends (from which the story of Abraham and Ishmael comes), Muhammad's early life and mission (which includes the Birth, Call, Night Journey, and Constitution of Medina) and his military campaigns (from which we get The Lie About Aisha). Much of the first section was lost, and has been reconstructed by scholars from quotations of Ibn Ishaq's work in other Islamic writings.

Malcolm Clark
[Notes interspersed in the text are from the publications
in which the selection originally appeared.]

Abraham and Ishmael

Sa'id b. Salim, who got it from 'Uthman b. Saj, who got it from Muhammad b. Ishaq, told us: It reached me that an angel came to Hagar, the mother of Ishmael, after Abraham settled her in Mecca, before Abraham and Ishmael raised up the edifice of the Temple, and showed her the Temple, which was a round, red hill, and said to her, This is the first temple made for mankind on earth, and it is the Temple of God. Know that Abraham and Ishmael will erect it for mankind.

From Sa'id b. Salim, who got it from 'Uthman b. Saj, Muhammad b. Ishaq said, When God commanded Abraham, the Friend of God, to build the Holy Temple, Abraham came from Armenia on Buraq, along with the Shechinah, which was like a gentle wind and had a face which would talk. With Abraham was an angel which guided him to the place of the Temple, so that he came to Mecca. And there was Ishmael, who was twenty, his mother having died before that, and she was buried in al-Hijr. He said, O Ishmael, God has commanded me to build a temple for Him. Ishmael said to him, Where? And the angel showed him the place of the Temple. The two of them began digging, and there were only two of them, and Abraham reached the first foundation of Adam. He dug around the Temple and found a stone great enough that three men could not surround it. Then he built on the first foundation of Adam. The Shechinah flitted about the first foundations as though it were alive and said, O Abraham, build on me. So he built on it, and for that reason the Arabs do not circumambulate the Temple without seeing the Shechinah on it.

He built the Temple, making its height seven cubits, and its depth in the early thirty-two cubits from the Black Stone to the Syrian corner. From the Syrian corner to the western was twenty-two cubits, and from the western corner to the Yemenite corner, thirty-one cubits. Its southern side from the Black Stone to the Yemenite corner was twenty cubits, and for that reason it was called Cube.

When Abraham, the Friend of God, finished building the Holy Temple, Gabriel came to him and said, Circumambulate it seven times. So he went around it seven times, he and Ishmael, touching the corners on each circuit. When they had competed the seven, they prayed two prostrations. Gabriel stayed with Abraham and showed him all the rites of the Pilgrimage, as-Safa, al-Marwah, Mina, Muzdalifah, and 'Arafah. When he entered Mina and came down from the height, Iblis appeared to him on the height, and Gabriel said to him, Throw at him. Abraham threw seven pebbles, and Iblis disappeared. Then Iblis appeared at the lowest part, and Gabriel said to Abraham, Throw at him. So he threw seven pebbles, and Iblis disappeared. Then Abraham performed his Pilgrimage. Gabriel stopped him at the stations and taught him the rites until he came to 'Arafah. When he arrived, Gabriel said to him, Do you know the rites? And Abraham said, Yes; so it was named 'Arafah because of his statement that he knew the rites.

Then God commanded Abraham to announce the Pilgrimage to mankind. Abraham said, O Lord, my voice will not reach. God said, Announce and it will reach. So he raised his voice up over the place until it went to the tops of the mountains and along their length. The earth, its plains, its mountains, its dry land and sea, its men and Jinn gathered that day so that they all heard it together. He put his fingers in his ears and turned his face to the south and the north, and east and the west. He began with the south, saying, O mankind, the Pilgrimage is ordained for you in the ancient Temple, so respond to your Lord. And they responded from the seven limits and from the east and the west, from the ends of the earth: At your service, O God, Labayka.

The stones were as they are today, except that God wished to make the place a sign, and Abraham's footprints are there today. Everyone who makes the Pilgrimage today is of those who answered Abraham.

Muhammad's Birth

The apostle was born on Monday, 12th Rabî'u'l-awwal, in the year of the elephant. . . .

. . .

After his birth his mother sent to tell his grandfather 'Abdu'l-Muttalib that she had given birth to a boy and asked him to come and look at him. When he came she told him what she had seen when she conceived him and what was said to her and what she was ordered to call him. It is alleged that 'Abdu'l-Muttalib took him . . . in the . . . Ka'ba, where he stood and prayed to Allah thanking him for his gift. Then he brought him out and delivered him to his mother, and he tried to find foster-mothers for him.

. . .

Jahm b. Abû jahm the client of al-Hârith b. Hâtib al-jumahî on the authority of 'Abdullah b. Ja'far b. Abû Tâlib or from one who told him it as from him, informed me[1] that Halîma the apostle's foster-mother used to say that she went forth from her country with her husband and little son whom she was nursing, among the women of her tribe, in search of other babies to nurse. This was a year of famine when they were destitute. She was riding a dusky she-donkey of hers with an old she-camel which did not yield a drop of milk. They could not sleep the whole night because of the weeping of her hungry child. She had no milk to give him, nor could their she-camel provide a morning draught, but we were hoping for rain and relief. "I rode upon my donkey which had kept back the other riders through its weakness and emaciation so that it was a nuisance to them. When we reached Mecca, we looked out for foster children, and the apostle of God was offered to everyone of us, and each woman refused him when she was told he was an orphan,[2] because we hoped to get payment from the child's father. We said, 'An orphan! and what will his mother and grandfather do?', and so we spurned him because of that. Every woman who came with me got a suckling except me, and when we decided to depart I said to my husband: 'By God, I do not like the idea of returning with my friends without a suckling; I will go and take that orphan.' He replied, 'Do as you please; perhaps God will bless us on

---

From *The Islamic World,* edited by William H. McNeill and Marilyn Robinson Waldman. Copyright © 1973. Reprinted by permission of the University of Chicago Press.

1   This series of authorities comprises an *isnâd,* the basic method used by early Islamic historians to validate their information. The editors have simplified the use of *isnâds* in this selection to ensure readability, but it is important to remember that authors like Ibn Ishâq might offer the reader several versions of an event under different *isnâds.*

2   The *Qur'an* repeatedly insists on protecting the orphan: Muhammad, an orphan himself, was very familiar with the kind of treatment orphans received in pre-Islamic Arabia.

his account.' So I went and took him for the sole reason that I could not find anyone else. I took him back to my baggage, and as soon as I put him in my bosom, my breasts overflowed with milk which he drank until he was satisfied, as also did his foster-brother. Then both of them slept, whereas before this we could not sleep with him. My husband got up and went to the old she-camel and lo, her udders were full; he milked it and he and I drank of her milk until we were completely satisfied, and we passed a happy night. In the morning my husband said: 'Do you know, Harîma, you have taken a blessed creature?' I said, 'By God, I hope so.' Then we set out and I was riding my she-ass and carrying him with me, and she went at such a pace that the other donkeys could not keep up so that my companions said to me, 'Confound you! stop and wait for us. Isn't this the donkey on which you started?' 'Certainly it is,' I said. They replied, 'By God, something extraordinary has happened.' Then we came to our dwellings in the Banû Sa'd country and I do not know a country more barren than that.

When we had him with us my flock used to yield milk in abundance. We milked them and drank while other people had not a drop, nor could they find anything in their animals' udders, so that our people were saying to their shepherds, 'Woe to you! send your flock to graze where the daughter of Abû Dhuayb's shepherd goes.' Even so, their flocks came back hungry not yielding a drop of milk, while mine had milk in abundance. We ceased not to recognize this bounty as coming from God for a period of two years, when I weaned him. He was growing up as none of the other children grew and by the time he was two he was a well-made child. We brought him to his mother, though we were most anxious to keep him with us because of the blessing which he brought us. I said to her: 'I should like you to leave my little boy with me until he becomes a big boy, for I am afraid on his account of the pest in Mecca.' We persisted until she sent him back with us.

Some months after our return he and his brother were with our lambs behind the tents when his brother came running and said to us, 'Two men clothed in white have seized that Qurayshî brother of mine and thrown him down and opened up his belly, and are stirring it up.' We ran towards him and found him standing up with a livid face. We took hold of him and asked him what was the matter. He said, 'Two men in white raiment came and threw me down and opened up my belly and searched therein for I know not what.'[3] So we took him back to our tent.

His father said to me, 'I am afraid that this child has had a stroke, so take him back to his family before the result appears.' So we picked him up and took him to his mother who asked why we had brought him when I had been anxious for his welfare and desirous of keeping him with me. I said to her, 'God has let my son live so far and I have done my duty. I am afraid that ill will befall him, so I have brought him back to you as you wished.' She asked me what happened and gave me no peace until I told her. When she asked if I feared a demon possessed him, I replied that I did. She answered that no demon had any power over her son who had a great future before him, and then she told how when she

---

3   Cf. *Qur'an* XCIV: 1. (Tr.)

was pregnant with him a light went out from her which illumined the castles of Busrâ in Syria, and that she had borne him with the least difficulty imaginable. When she bore him he put his hands on the ground lifting his head towards the heavens. 'Leave him then and go in peace,' she said."

Thaur b. Yazîd from a learned person who I think was Khâlid b. Ma'dân al Kalâ'i told me that some of the apostle's companions asked him to tell them about himself. He said: "I am what Abraham my father prayed for and the good news of . . . Jesus. When my mother was carrying me she saw a light proceeding from her which showed her the castles of Syria. I was suckled among the B. Sa'd b. Bakr, and while I was with a brother of mine behind our tents shepherding the lambs, two men in white raiment came to me with a gold basin full of snow. Then they seized me and opened up my belly, extracted my heart and split it; then they extracted a black drop from it and threw it away; then they washed my heart and my belly with that snow until they had thoroughly cleaned them. Then one said to the other, weigh him against ten of his people; they did so and I outweighed them. Then they weighed me against a hundred and then a thousand, and I outweighed them. He said, 'Leave him alone, for by God, if you weighed him against all his people he would outweigh them.'"

The apostle of God used to say, There is no prophet but has shepherded a flock. When they say, "You, too, apostle of God?", he said "Yes."

Muhammad's Call

Ibn Isḥāq: When Muḥammad the Messenger of God, God bless him and give him peace, reached the age of forty, God sent him in mercy to all beings to bring good news to the people.

From Wahb b. Kaysān, from 'Ubayd b. 'Umayr b. Qatāda al-Laythī. The Messenger of God would withdraw to Mt. Ḥirā' every year for a month. This was part of the custom of *taḥannuth* [devotion] practised by Quraysh in pagan times. He would withdraw and feed all poor persons who came to him during this time. When he was finished the first thing he would do was go to the Ka'ba and circumambulate it seven times or as God willed, and then return to his house. In the year in which God sent him as a prophet, in the month of Ramaḍān, he set forth to Mt. Ḥirā' according to his custom, with his family. When it was the night on which God honored him with his mission, Gabriel brought him God's command. The Messenger said later, "He came to me when I was asleep, with a saddle-cloth of brocade on which was writing, and said 'Recite!' I said, 'Recite what?' He wrapped me in it so that I thought this was death, then he let me go, and said, 'Recite!' 'Recite what?' I said. At that, he wrapped me so I thought it was death, then let me go, and said, 'Recite!' Then I said, 'What is it I should recite?' I only said this to deliver myself from him, lest he return to doing to me as he had done before. Then he said,

> Recite: In the Name of your Lord who created,
>   Created Man of a blood-clot.
> Recite: And your Lord is the Most Generous
> Who taught by the Pen. [*Sūra* 96:1-4]

"So I recited it, and he left me. Then I woke from my sleep, and it was as though the words were written on my heart. I left, and when I was halfway down the mountain, I heard a voice from the sky saying, 'Muhammad! You are the Messenger of God, and I am Gabriel!' I raised my head to heaven to look, and lo, there was Gabriel in the form of a man, his feet astride the horizon, saying, 'Muhammad, you are the Messenger of God, and I am Gabriel.' I stood staring at him, neither advancing nor withdrawing, then I began to turn my face away from him, but wherever I looked in the heavens I saw him like that. I did not stop standing like that, moving neither forward not backward, until Khadīja had sent her messengers looking for me. Finally he left me, and I set out to go back to my family, until I came to Khadīja, and sat down by her thigh and drew her close. She said, 'Why, Abū al-Qāsim [Father of al-Qāsim]! Where have you been? By God, I have sent messengers looking for you until they reached the upper part of Mecca and came back to me.' I said, 'I am surely an accursed poet or a man possessed.' She told me, 'I take refuge in God from that, Abū al-Qāsim! God would not do that to you; He knows your truthful speech, your great trustworthiness, your good character, and your abundant kindness. It cannot be, husband. Perhaps you saw something that upset you?' 'Yes, I did,' I told her, and related what I had seen. She said, 'Rejoice, husband, and be steadfast; by Him in whose hand is my soul, I have hope that you will be the prophet of this people!'"

She stood up, gathered her garments about her, and set off for Waraqa b. [ibn] Nawfal b. Asad, her paternal cousin. Waraqa had become a Christian. He recited the scriptures and had learned from the followers of the Torah and the Gospel. When she told him what the Messenger of God had seen and heard, Waraqa cried, "Holy, Holy! By Him in whose hand is my soul, Khadīja, if you are telling the truth, this is the great Nāmūs who has come to him, the Angel Gabriel, peace be upon him, who used to come to Moses, and he will be the prophet of this people! Tell him to take heart." Khadīja went back to the Messenger of God and told him what Waraqa had said, and that soothed his anxiety somewhat.

When he was finished with his seclusion and returned to Mecca, he circumambulated the Ka'ba first of all, according to his custom, and Waraqa met him as he was going around it. He told him, "Cousin, tell me what you saw and heard," so the Messenger of God told him. Then Waraqa said, "By Him in whose hand is my soul, you are the prophet of this community! The great Nāmūs has come to you, who came to Moses. You will surely be called a liar, and treated badly, and they will drive you out and seek to kill you. If I live to see it, I will help

God's cause in ways known to Him." Then he brought his head near and kissed his forehead, and the Messenger of God went home to his house.[1]

The First Converts

Khadīja was the first to have faith in God and His messenger and the truth of what came from Him. By this, God lightened the burden on His prophet. He never met with hateful contradiction and accusations of falsehood which grieved him, that God did not comfort him through her when he went home to her. She strengthened him, lightened his burden, affirmed his words, and belittled people's opposition. May God Most High have mercy on her!

'Alī b. Abī Ṭālib (Muḥammad's young cousin) was the first male to have faith in the Messenger of God, pray with him, and affirm his message. At the time he was a boy of ten. Among the favors God granted 'Alī was that he was being reared in the care of the Messenger of God before Islam.

Ibn Isḥāq, from a learned man of Mecca: When the time of prayer would come, the Messenger of God would go out on one of the mountain paths around Mecca. 'Alī would go with him, unknown to his father, his uncles, or other people, and they would pray the ritual prayers. Abū Ṭālib came upon them once when they were praying thus and said to the Messenger of God, "Nephew, what religion is this I see you practicing?" He replied, "Uncle, this is the religion of God, His angels, and His messengers; the religion of our father Abraham. God has sent me as a messenger to His servants, and you are the most worthy of those I should advise and call to guidance, and most worthy to respond to me and assist me." His uncle replied, "I cannot leave the religion of my forefathers and their practices, but, by God, nothing you hate will reach you so long as I live." They mention that he said to 'Alī, "My son, what is this religion you practice?" He replied, "Father, I have put my faith in God and in the Messenger of God. I affirm that what he has brought is true, and I worship God with him and follow him." They allege that his father said, "Well, he wouldn't call you to anything but good, so stay with him."

Zayd b. Ḥāritha al-Kalbī [who had been bought by Khadīja as a child of eight and presented to Muḥammad, who set him free and adopted him as a son before the revelation came] was the first male to adopt Islam after 'Alī.

Then Abū Bakr, whose name was 'Atīq, son of Abū Quḥāfa, became a Muslim. He professed his faith openly and called others to God and His messenger. He was a man sought-after by his people, well liked and of easy manners, a merchant of excellent character and kindliness. He began to call to God and Islam all those whom he trusted among the people who sought his company.

---

1 Ibn Isḥāq, found in Ibn Hishām: *Sīrat al-Nabī*, 4 bks. (Cairo, 1963, bk. 1:153–156, and al-Tabarī, *Ta'rīkh*, 3 series (Leiden: Brill, 1879–1901) series 1:1150–1152, abridged (my translation and abridgments throughout unless otherwise noted.

Among those who accepted his invitation to Islam were 'Uthmān b. 'Affān the Umawī, al-Zubayr b. 'Awwām, 'Abd al-Raḥmān b. 'Awf, Sa'd b. Abī Waqqāṣ, and Ṭalḥa b. 'Ubaydallāh [all were later among the leading Companions of the Prophet].[2]

Around Muḥammad grew up a party of able men, critical of the tribal leadership, on whom the leaders looked with alarm and disfavor. They were not so much jealous for their gods as distrustful of signs of social and political innovation. There was little they could do to Muḥammad so long as his clan protected him, but his followers in their own and some other clans were more accessible.

The Prophet therefore sent a number of his followers to Abyssinia, where they sought the protection of the Christian king, the Negus. It seems possible that he was contemplating a political alliance with Abyssinia in the event that his followers came to control Mecca. The following story is almost certainly not historical in all particulars, but it is an early apologia for Islam.

The Emigration to Abyssinia

Muḥammad b. Muslim al-Zuhrī, from Abū Bakr b. 'Abd al-Raḥmān al-Makhzūmī, from Umm Salama, wife of Abū Salama [after whose death she married the Prophet]: When we reached Abyssinia, the Negus received us most kindly; we practiced our religion, worshipped God Most High, suffered no harm, and heard nothing to dislike. When that got to the Quraysh, they decided among themselves to send two forceful men, 'Amr b. al-'Āṣ and 'Abdallāh b. Abī Rabī'a, to the Negus about us, and present him gifts of the choicest goods of Mecca. But the Negus summoned the Prophet's Companions, and when they came into his presence they found that he had summoned his bishops and they had spread out their scrolls around him. He asked them, "What is this religion for which you have separated from your people without entering my religion or that of any other community?"

Ja'far b. Abī Ṭālib [the cousin of the Prophet] answered, "O King, we were a barbarous people, worshiping idols, eating carrion, committing enormities, breaking the ties of kinship, mistreating our neighbors, the strong among us devouring the weak. Thus we stayed, until God sent us a messenger of our own, whose descent, truthfulness, trustworthiness, and forbearance we knew. He called us to acknowledge the oneness of God and worship Him, and renounce the stones and idols we and our forefathers had served. He ordered us to speak the truth, keep our word, observe the ties of kinship, be good neighbors, and cease from crime and bloodshed. He forbade us to commit abominations or devour the property of orphans or slander chaste women. He commanded us to serve God alone and associate nothing with him, and gave us commands about ritual prayer, the alms-tax, and fasting [he enumerated the commands of Islam]. We recognized his truth and put our faith in him, and followed him in all he brought us from God. At this, our people turned against us, persecuted us, and tried to seduce us

---

2   Ibn Isḥāq, from Ibn Hishām, *Sīrat*, 1:158–165, abridged.

from our faith, to make us go back to worshiping idols after worshiping God Most High, and consider as lawful the evil practices we had followed. When they oppressed us and came between us and our religion, we left for your country, choosing you above any other. We have sought your protection, and we hope that we shall not be wronged while with you, O King."

The Negus asked if they had anything with them which the Prophet had brought them from God. "Yes," said Ja'far, and he recited a portion of the *Sūra* of Mary. By God, the Negus wept until his beard was wet, and his bishops wept until their scrolls were wet, when they heard what he recited. Then the Negus said, "Truly, this and what Jesus brought both came from the same niche. You two men can go, for I will never hand them over to you, and they will not be betrayed."

The next day 'Amr b. al-'Āṣ told the king that the Muslims said a terrible thing about Jesus: that he was only a created being. The king sent for them and asked them, "What is it that you have said about Jesus, Son of Mary?" Ja'far said, "We say of him what our Prophet has brought us: that he is the servant of God, and His messenger, His spirit, and His word, which He sent into Mary the blessed virgin." The Negus took a twig from the ground, and said, "By God, Jesus does not exceed what you have said about him by this twig."

Some of his patricians around him snorted, but he said, "Though they snort, by God, go freely, for you are safe in my land. Whoever curses you will be fined. Not for a mountain of gold would I let one of you be hurt. Let these two take back their gifts."[3]

---

3   Ibid, 221–225, abridged.

Muhammad's Night Journey

A much loved story connected with the Prophet is that of his night-journey (isrā'), his ascension (mi'rāj), and his vision of the world to come. Art, poetry, and pious imagination have all lavished attention on this theme. It is now generally considered that Dante borrowed not only the general plan but many details of the Divine Comedy from a later fancifully developed treatment of the story, which was translated from Arabic to Latin. Ibn Ishāq presents the earliest form of the story as he pieced it together. Its main elements are the journey from Mecca to Jerusalem, the ascent to the heavens, and the vision of the afterlife.

The Night Journey and the Mi'rāj [Ascent]

Ibn Ishāq: Then the Messenger of God was carried by night from the Mosque of the Ka'ba to the Aqsa Mosque, which is the Holy House of Aelia [Jerusalem].

The following *hadīths* are from 'Abdallāh b. Mas'ūd, Abū Sa'īd al-Khudrī, 'ā'isha, wife of the Prophet, Mu'āwiya b. Abī Sufyān [a brother-in-law of the Prophet], al-Hasan al-Basrī, Ibn Shihāb al-Zuhrī, Qatāda, and other learned men as well as Umm Hāni', daughter of Abū Tālib. The account is pieced together, each contributing something of what he or she was told.

'Abdallāh b. Mas'ūd: the Messenger of God was brought al-Burāq, the steed which the prophets before him used to ride, whose every step carries it as far as the eye can see.

Hasan al-Basrī said, the Messenger of God said: "While I was sleeping in al-Hijr, Gabriel came and stirred me with his foot. He brought me out to the door of the mosque, and there stood a white animal, between a mule and a donkey, with wings on its sides by which it propelled its feet, and each step carried it as far as it could see. He placed me on it, and left with me, not quitting me nor I him." They went their way until they arrived at the temple of Jerusalem, and found there Abraham, Moses, Jesus, and a company of the prophets. The Messenger then acted as their leader in the ritual prayer; He then was brought two vessels, one containing wine and the other milk. He took the vessel of milk and drank from it. Gabriel told him, "You have been guided to the primeval religion, and your community will be so guided, Muhammad. Wine is forbidden to you." Then the Messenger went back to Mecca, and in the morning told the Quraysh what had happened. Most of the people said, "By God, the matter's clear! A caravan takes a month to go from Mecca to Jerusalem and a month to return, so how could Muhammad do the journey there and back in one night?" But Abū Bakr said, "If he says it, it is true." Then he asked the Messenger to describe Jerusalem to him. Hasan says he was lifted up so he could see the Prophet speaking.[4] He began to describe Jerusalem to Abū Bakr, and he would say, "You have spoken truly—I testify that you are the Messenger of God!"

---

4   There is a difficulty here. Al-Hasan of Basra had not been born at this time, so if it is true, it was his source who was lifted up as a child to see this.

Then the Messenger said, "And you, O Abū Bakr, are al-Ṣiddīq, (the Testifier to the Truth]." From that day on, the Muslims called him "al-Ṣiddīq."

'Ā'isha, the Prophet's wife, used to say: The Messenger of God's body remained where it was, but God moved his spirit by night.

I have heard that he used to say, "My eyes sleep while my heart is fully awake." God knows best how what happened happened, and how he saw what he saw. But whether he was asleep or awake, it was a reality, and actually happened.

From one I do not doubt, from Abū Saʿīd al-Khudrī, from the Messenger of God: "When my business in Jerusalem was finished, I was brought a ladder finer than anything I've ever seen. It is what each of you will gaze toward at the hour of death. Gabriel mounted with me until I came to one of the gates of heaven, called the Gate of the Watchers. In charge of it was an angel named Ismāʿīl, in command of twelve thousand angels who each commanded twelve thousand other angels."

A learned man, from one who heard the Messenger say: "All the angels who met me as I entered the lowest heaven smiled in welcome and wished me well, until one angel met me who spoke as they did, but did not smile or show the joyful expression of the others. When I asked Gabriel the reason, he said, 'If he were to smile at anyone, either before you or after you, he would have smiled at you, but he does not smile. That is Mālik, the Keeper of Hell.' I said to Gabriel, who has the position yonder that God describes, 'Obeyed there and charged' [Qur'ān 74:34], 'Will you ask him to show me Hell?' He said, 'Certainly! Mā-lik, show Muḥammad Hell.' At this he removed its cover, and the Fire blazed so high that I thought it would catch all I saw and said to Gabriel, 'Tell him to send it back!' He told him, and Mālik commanded the Fire, 'Subside!' It went back to its place, so it seemed to me most like the falling of a shadow, and he replaced the cover."

Abū Saʿīd al-Khudrī: The Messenger of God said, "When I entered the lowest heaven, I saw a man sitting there, with human souls passing before him. To one he would speak well and rejoice, saying, 'A good soul, from a good body!' To another, he would say 'Uff!' and look grimly, saying, 'A vile spirit, from a vile body!' Gabriel said, 'That is your father Adam, reviewing the souls of his offspring. When a faithful soul passes before him, he is pleased, and when the soul of a rejecter passes, he is disgusted.'

"I saw men with lips like camels, with pieces of fire like stones in their hands. They thrust them in their mouths, and they come out of their posteriors. Gabriel told me these are those who sinfully devour the property of orphans.

"I saw men like those of the family of Pharaoh, 'in the worst of all punishments' [Qur'ān 40:49], with such bellies as I have never seen, with something like thirst-maddened camels passing over them, treading them down as they are cast into Hell, while they cannot move out of the way. These are the usurers.

"I saw men with delicious plump meat before them, side by side with lean and stinking meat. They eat the latter and leave the former. Gabriel told me these are those who leave the women God has made lawful to them and go after those He has forbidden.

"I saw women hanging by their breasts. These are those who have fathered bastards on their husbands.

"Then I was taken up to the second heaven, and there were the two maternal cousins, Jesus, the son of Mary, and John, the son of Zachariah. Then to the third heaven, where there was a man with a face beautiful as the full moon. Gabriel told me, 'It is your brother Joseph, son of Jacob.' In the fourth heaven was Enoch [Idrīs]; 'And We raised him to an exalted place' [Qur'ān 19:58]. In the fifth heaven was a man with white hair and a great beard; never have I seen a handsomer elder. This was the beloved of his people, Aaron. In the sixth heaven was his brother Moses, a tall bronzed man with a hooked nose. In the seventh heaven was an older man sitting on a throne at the gate of the Immortal Mansion. Every day seventy thousand angels enter it, not to return until the Resurrection Day. I have never seen a man who looked more like myself. Gabriel told me, 'This is your father Abraham.' Then he took me into Paradise, and I saw a maiden with dark red lips. I asked her, 'For whom are you destined?' because I admired her when I saw her. She told me, 'For Zayd b. Ḥāritha.'" Thus the Messenger of God gave Zayd the good news that his place in Paradise was sure.

From 'Abdallāh b. Mas'ūd: Finally the Messenger of God came to his Lord, and the duty of five ritual prayers a day was laid on his community.[5]

The Opposition of the Quraysh

Khadīja, the daughter of Khuwaylid, and Abū Ṭālib both died in one year, and troubles followed thick and fast on the Messenger of God with Khadīja's death. She had been a faithful adviser to him in Islam, and he could tell her his problems. With the death of his uncle Abū Ṭālib he lost a support and refuge in his life, a defense and help against his tribe. This was three years before his emigration to Madīna. The Quraysh began to treat him in an offensive way they would never have dared use in his uncle's life. One young ruffian even threw dust on his head.

Hishām b. 'Urwa, from his father, 'Urwa b. Zubayr: When this happened, he went into his house with the dust still on his head, and one of his daughters rose and began to wash the dust away, weeping as she did so. He told her, "Don't weep, little daughter, for God is your father's Defender." At the same time he said, "The Quraysh never did anything hateful to me until Abū Ṭālib died."[6]

---

5   Ibid., 2:268–276, abridged.
6   Ibid., 282–283.

The Constitution of Medina

The constitution of Medina, a treaty between the recent immigrants from Mecca and several groups native to Medina, has been called "the world's first written constitution" and provides an early model for the formation of an Islamic state.

Malcolm Clark

3.2.4 Muhammad as a statesman: the constitution of Medina

Ibn Ishaq said: The messenger of God wrote a document concerning the emigrants and the helpers in which he made a friendly agreement with the Jews and established them in their religion and their property, and stated the conditions, as follows.

In the name of God, the Merciful, the Compassionate. This is a writing from Muhammad the prophet, may the prayers and peace of God be upon him, governing the relations between the believers and Muslims of Quraysh and Yathrib, and those who follow them and join with them and strive with them. They are one community separate from other people. The Quraysh emigrants are responsible for their affairs and shall pay the blood-money among themselves and shall redeem their prisoners according to the custom and sense of justice common among the believers.

The tribe of 'Awf are responsible for their affairs and shall first pay the blood-money among themselves; every group shall redeem its prisoners according to the custom and sense of justice among the believers. The same is true of the tribes of Sa'ida, al-Harith, Jusham, al-Najjar, 'Amr ibn 'Awf, al-Nabit, and al-Aws.

Believers shall not leave anyone destitute among them without paying their redemption money or blood-money as is customary.

A believer shall not make an alliance with a freedman of a believer against that believer. The God-fearing believers shall oppose those who are rebellious and those who seek to spread injustice, sin, enmity, or corruption among the believers; the hand of everyone shall be against such a person even if he should be the son of one of them.

A believer shall not slay a believer for the sake of an unbeliever, nor support an unbeliever against a believer. God's protection is one; the least of them may give protection on behalf of them. Believers are allies to each other to the exclusion of other people. Help and equality shall be given to the Jews who follow us. They shall not suffer injustice nor shall their enemies be aided. The peace of the believers is indivisible; no separate peace shall be made when believers are fighting in the way of God unless the conditions are fair and equitable to all. For each raiding party raiding with us, there shall be one following the other. The believers must avenge on behalf of another for whatever harms their blood in the way of God. The God-fearing believers have the best and most upright guidance.

From *Textual Sources for the Study of Islam,* edited by Andrew Rippin and Jan Knappert. Copyright 1986 by Andrew Rippin and Jan Knappert. Reprinted by permission.

No polytheist shall protect the property or person of the unbelievers of Quraysh nor shall they intervene against a believer. Whoever kills a believer without good reason shall be killed in retaliation unless the next of kin of the deceased is satisfied with blood-money, and the believers shall be against that person altogether, and they are obligated to take action against such a person.

It shall not be lawful for a believer who agrees to what is in this document and who believes in God and the last day, to help or shelter an evil-doer. The curse of God and His wrath on the day of resurrection will be upon whoever does that, and neither repentance nor ransom will be accepted from that person. Whenever you differ about a matter it must be referred to God and to Muhammad.

The Jews shall pay taxes while they are fighting alongside the believers. The Jews of the tribe of 'Awf are one community with the believers, the Jews having their religion and the Muslims having theirs, their clients and themselves, except those who act wrongfully and sinfully, for they harm only themselves and their families. The same applies to the Jews of the tribes of al-Najjar, al-Harith, Sa'ida, Jusham, al-Aws, Tha'laba, Jafna (a clan of the Tha'laba), and al-Shutayba. Loyalty is a protection against treachery. The clients of Tha'laba are to be considered as a group. Those associated with the Jews are likewise to be considered as a group. None of them shall go out to war without the permission of Muhammad, but none shall be prevented from taking revenge for a wound. Whoever kills someone kills themselves and their household, unless the one killed has wronged them, for God will accept this.

The Jews must pay their own taxes and the Muslims their own taxes. There will be help between them against anyone who attacks the people of this document. Between them there will be goodwill and sincerity. Loyalty is a protection against treachery. No one shall violate their ally's pledge. Help is due to the wronged. The Jews must pay the tax with the believers so long as war lasts.

Yathrib shall be a sanctuary for the people of this document. A stranger under protection is like oneself; they shall not be harmed nor shall they commit crime. A woman shall only be given protection with the permission of her family. Whenever a dispute or controversy likely to cause trouble arises among the people of this document it shall be referred to God and to Muhammad, the apostle of God. God is the guarantor of the pious observance of what is in this document.

Unbelievers of Quraysh and whoever helps them shall not be given protection. There shall be help between the people of this document against any attack on Yathrib. If they are called to make peace and keep it, they shall make that peace and keep it; if they are called upon to do something similar to that, the believers are obliged to those who do so to go along with it except in the case of fighting for religion. Everyone shall be responsible for the side of the city in front of them; the Jews of al-Aws, their clients and themselves have the same rights as the people of this document with pure loyalty from the people of this document. Loyalty is a protection against treachery; whoever breaches a treaty only does so against themselves. God is the guarantor of the truth and the observance of what is in this document. This does not protect the unjust nor the sinner. Whoever goes forth to fight is safe and whoever stays at home in Yathrib is safe unless they have been unjust or sinned. God is the protector of the pious and the God-fearing and Muhammad is the messenger of God.

The Lie about Aisha

According to what a man I do not suspect told me from al-Zuhri from 'Urwa from 'A'isha[1] the apostle had gone forward on that journey of his until he was near Medina, 'A'isha having been with him on the journey, when the liars spoke about her.

. . .

She said: "When the apostle intended to go on an expedition he cast lots between his wives which of them should accompany him. He did this on the occasion of the raid on B. al-Mustaliq and the lot fell on me, so the apostle took me out. The wives on these occasions used to eat light rations; meat did not fill them up so that they were heavy. When the camel was being saddled for me I used to sit in my howdah; then the men who saddled it for me would come and pick me up and take hold of the lower part of the howdah and lift it up and put it on the camel's back and fasten it with a rope. Then they would take hold of the camel's head and walk with it.

"When the apostle finished his journey on this occasion he started back and halted when he was near Medina and passed a part of the night there. Then he gave permission to start and the men moved off. I went out for a certain purpose having a string of Zafar beads on my neck. When I had finished, it slipped from my neck without my knowledge, and when I returned to the camel I went feeling my neck for it but could not find it. Meanwhile the main body had already moved off. I went back to the place where I had been and looked for the necklace until I found it. The men who were saddling the camel for me came up to the place I had just left and having finished the saddling they took hold of the howdah thinking that I was in it as I normally was, picked it up and bound it on the camel, not doubting that I was in it. Then they took the camel by the head and went off with it. I returned to the place and there was not a soul there. The men had gone. So I wrapped myself in my smock and then lay down where I was, knowing that if I were missed they would come back for me, and by Allah I had but just lain down when Safwan b. al-Mu'attal al-Sulami passed me; he had fallen behind the main body for some purpose and had not spent the night with the troops. He saw my form and came and stood over me. He used to see me before the veil was prescribed for us,[2] so when he saw me he exclaimed in astonishment 'The apostle's wife' while I was wrapped in my garments. He asked me what had kept me behind but I did not speak to him. Then he brought up his camel and told me

---

1 Al-Zuhri and 'Urwa: Very early (third generation) Muslim authorities. 'A'isha: Muhammad's youngest wife, one of the wives he took after Khadija's death.

2 Muhammad veiled his women as befitting the wives of someone in his position, but the general practice of veiling and secluding women was not an Arab custom and came into vogue much later under different influences.

to ride it while he kept behind. So I rode it and he took the camel's head going forward quickly in search of the army, and by Allah we did not overtake them and I was not missed until the morning. The men had halted and when they were rested up came the man leading me and the liars spread their reports and the army was much disturbed. But by Allah I knew nothing about it.

"Then we came to Medina and immediately I became very ill and so heard nothing of the matter. The story had reached the apostle and my parents, yet they told me nothing of it though I missed the apostle's accustomed kindness to me. When I was ill he used to show compassion and kindness to me, but in this illness he did not and I missed his attentions. When he came in to see me when my mother was nursing me, all he said was, 'How is she?'[3] so that I was pained and asked him to let me be taken to my mother so that she could nurse me. 'Do what you like,' he said, and so I was taken to my mother, knowing nothing of what had happened until I recovered from my illness some twenty days later. Now we were an Arab people: we did not have those privies which foreigners have in their houses; we loathe and detest them. Our practice was to go out into the open spaces of Medina. The women used to go out every night, and one night I went out with Umm Mistah d. Abu Ruhm. b. al-Muttalib b. 'Abdu Manaf. Her mother was d. Sakhr b. 'Amir b. Ka'b b. Sa'd b. Taym aunt of Abu Bakr.[4] As she was walking with me she stumbled over her gown and exclaimed, 'May Mistah stumble,' Mistah being the nickname of 'Auf.[5] I said, 'That is a bad thing to say about one of the emigrants who fought at Badr.' She replied, 'Haven't you heard the news, O daughter of Abu Bakr?' and when I said that I had not heard she went on to tell me of what the liars had said, and when I showed my astonishment she told me that all this really had happened. By Allah, I was unable to do what I had to do and went back. I could not stop crying until I thought that the weeping would burst my liver.[6] I said to my mother, 'God forgive you! Men have spoken ill of me (and you have known of it; Tr.) and have not told me a thing about it.' She replied 'My little daughter, don't let the matter weigh on you. Seldom is there a beautiful woman married to a man who loves her but her rival wives gossip about her and men do the same.'

"The apostle had got up and addressed the men, though I knew nothing about it. After praising God he said: 'What do certain men mean by worrying me about my family and saying false things about them? By Allah, I know only good of them, and they say these things of a man of whom I know naught but good, who never enters a house of mine but in my company.'

. . .

---

3 The form used indicates the plural and, to some extent, the speaker's indifference. (Tr.)

4 I.e., 'A'isha's great aunt.

5 'Auf: relative of Abu Bakr, the first Caliph, and an early convert.

6 Arabic and Persian commonly use "liver" where "heart" would be appropriate in English.

As for 'Ali[7] he said: 'Women are plentiful, and you can easily change one for another. Ask the slave girl, for she will tell you the truth.' So the apostle called Burayra to ask her, and 'Ali got up and gave her a violent beating, saying, 'Tell the apostle the truth,' to which she replied, 'I know only good of her. The only fault I have to find with 'A'isha is that when I am kneading dough and tell her to watch it she neglects it and falls asleep and the sheep . . . comes and eats it!'[8]

"Then the apostle came in to me. My parents and a woman of the Ansar were with me and both of us were weeping. He sat down and after praising God he said, "'A'isha, you know what people say about you. Fear God and if you have done wrong as men say then repent towards God, for He accepts repentance from His slaves.' As he said this my tears ceased and I could not feel them. I waited for my parents to answer the apostle but they said nothing. By Allah I thought myself too insignificant for God to send down concerning me a *Quran* which could be read in the mosques and used in prayer, but I was hoping that the apostle would see something in a dream by which God would clear away the lie from me, because He knew my innocence, or that there would be some communication. As for a *Quran* coming down about me by Allah I thought far too little of myself for that. When I saw that my parents would not speak I asked them why, and they replied that they did not know what to answer, and by Allah I do not know a household which suffered as did the family of Abu Bakr in those days. When they remained silent my weeping broke out afresh and then I said: 'Never will I repent towards God of what you mention. By Allah, I know that if I were to confess what men say of me, God knowing that I am innocent of it, I should admit what did not happen; and if I denied what they said you would not believe me.' Then I racked my brains for the name of Jacob and could not remember it, so I said, 'I will say what the father of Joseph said: "My duty is to show becoming patience and God's aid is to be asked against what you describe." '[9]

"And, by God, the apostle had not moved from where he was sitting when there came over him from God what used to come over him and he was wrapped in his garment and a leather cushion was put under his head. As for me, when I saw this I felt no fear or alarm, for I knew that I was innocent and that God would not treat me unjustly. As for my parents, as soon as the apostle recovered I thought that they would die from fear that confirmation would come from God of what men had said. Then the apostle recovered and sat up and there fell from him as it were drops of water on a winter day, and he began to wipe the sweat from his brow, saying, 'Good news, 'A'isha! God has sent down (word) about your innocence.' I said, 'Praise be to God,' and he went out to the men and

---

7   Ali: son-in-law and early follower of Muhammad, later to become fourth Caliph.
8   The homeliness of Ibn Ishaq's *Sira* is evident here and throughout and seems to correspond to the actual flavor of Muhammad's environment.
9   *Qur'an* XII: 18. (Tr.)

addressed them and recited to them what God had sent down concerning that. . . .[10]

"My father Ishaq b. Yasar told me from some of the men of B. al-Najjar that the wife of Abu Ayyub Khalid b. Zayd said to him, 'Have you heard what people are saying about 'A'isha?' 'Certainly, but it is a lie,' he said. 'Would you do such a thing?'[11] She answered 'No, by Allah, I would not.' He said, 'Well, 'A'isha is a better woman than you.'"

'A'isha continued: When the *Qur'an* came down with the mention of those of the slanderers who repeated what the liars had said, God said: "Those who bring the lie are a band among you. Do not regard it as a bad thing for you; nay it is good for you. Every man of them will get what he has earned from the sin, and he who had the greater share therein will have a painful punishment,"[12] meaning Hassan b. Thabit and his companions who said what they said.

---

10 Descriptions of how Muhammad's revelations actually took place are rare.
11 I.e., what 'A'isha was accused of.
12 *Qur'an* XXIV:12. (Tr.)

Selected Hadiths

————◦◈◦————

Faith and Submission

1

Abu Hurairah reported that The Prophet, peace and blessings of Allah be on him, said:

"Religion is easy, and no one exerts himself too much in religion but it overpowers him; so act aright and keep to the mean and be of good cheer and ask for (Divine) help at morning and at evening and during a part of the night."

(B.2:29.)

2

Nu'man ibn Bashir said, I heard the Messenger of Allah, peace and blessings of Allah be on him, say:

"What is lawful is manifest and what is unlawful is manifest and between these two are doubtful things which many people do not know. So whoever guards himself against the doubtful things, he keeps his religion and his honour unsullied, and whoever falls into doubtful things is like the herdsman who grazes his cattle on the borders of a reserve—he is likely to enter it. Know that every king has a reserve (and) know that the reserve of Allah in His land is what He has forbidden. Know that in the body there is a bit of flesh; when it is sound the whole body is sound, and when it is corrupt the whole body is corrupt. Know, it is the heart."

(B. 2:38)

3

Abu Hurairah said, The Prophet, peace and blessings of Allah be on him, was one day sitting outside among the people when a man came to him and asked, What is faith (Iman)? He said:

"Faith is that thou believe in Allah and His angels and in meeting with Him and (in) His messengers and that thou believe in being raised to life (after death)."

He asked, What is Islam? (The Prophet) said:

"Islam is that thou shalt worship Allah and not associate aught with Him and (that) thou keep up prayer and pay the zakat as ordained and fast in Ramadzan."

He asked, What is *ihsan* (goodness)? (The Prophet) said:

"That thou worship Allah as if thou seest Him; for if thou see Him not, surely He sees thee."

(B. 2:36.)

4

Ibn'Umar said, The Messenger of Allah, peace and blessings of Allah be on him, said:

"Islam is built on five (things), the bearing of witness that there is no god but Allah and that Muhammad is the Messenger of Allah and the keeping up of prayer and the payment of zakat and the pilgrimage and fasting in Ramadan."

(B. 2:1.)

5

Anas reported on the authority of the Prophet, peace and blessings of Allah be on him, He said:

"None of you has faith unless he loves for his brother what he loves for himself."

(B. 2:6.)

6

Anas reported on the authority of the Prophet, peace and blessings of Allah be on him, . . . He said:

"There is none who bears witness with sincerity of heart that there is no god but Allah and that Muhammad is the Messenger of Allah but Allah has forbidden his going to fire."

(M-Msh. 1)

Knowledge

7

Anas said, The Messenger of Allah, peace and blessings of Allah be on him, said:

"The seeking of knowledge is obligatory upon every Muslim."[1]

(Bhl-Msh. 2.)

---

1   The words *every Muslim* include both men and women. . . .

Purification

8

Abu Malik said, The Messenger of Allah, peace and blessings of Allah be on him, said:

"Purification is half the faith."

(M-Msh. 3.)

9

Ibn 'Umar said, The Messenger of Allah, peace and blessings of Allah be on him, said:

"Prayer is not accepted without purification, nor (is) charity (accepted) out of what is acquired by unlawful means."

(M-Msh. 3:1.)

10

Abu Dharr said, The Messenger of Allah, peace and blessings of Allah be on him, said:

"Pure earth serves the purpose of a Muslim's ablution, though he may not find water for three years. When he finds water, he should wash with it his body, for that is better."

(AD-Msh. 3:10.)

11

Yahya al-Mazine reported that

A man said to 'Abd Allah ibn Zaid, Canst thou show me how the Messenger of Allah, peace and blessings of Allah be on him, performed ablution? 'Abd Allah ibn Zaid said, Yes. So he sent for water and poured it over his hands and washed his hands twice, then he rinsed his mouth and sniffed water into his nose thrice, then he washed his face thrice, then he washed his hands up to the elbow twice, then he wiped his head with both his hands so that he carried them from the front and brought them back—he began with his forehead until he carried them to his neck, then he brought them back to the place from which he had started—then he washed his two feet.

(B. 4:38.)

Prayer

12

It is reported about Ibn 'Umar that he used to say,

The Muslims when they came to Madinah used to gather together and they made an appointment for prayers; no call was given for it. So they talked about it one day. Some of them said, Have a bell like the bell of the Christians; others said, Rather a bugle like the horn of the Jews; 'Umar said, Would you not appoint

175

a man who should sound a call for the prayer. The Messenger of Allah, peace and blessings of Allah be on him, said, "O Bilal! get up and give a call for prayer."

(B. 10:1)

13

Abu Mahdhura said,

I said, O Messenger of Allah! Teach me the way of delivering the adhan. He said, So he touched his forehead (and) said:

"Thou shouldst say:

"'Allah is the Greatest, Allah is the Greatest, Allah is the Greatest.' "Thou shouldst raise thy voice with it; then thou shouldst say,

"'I bear witness that there is no God by Allah, I bear witness that there is no God but Allah, I bear witness that Muhammad is the Messenger of Allah, I bear witness that Muhammad is the Messenger of Allah.'

"Thou shouldst lower thy voice with it; then thou shouldst raise thy voice with the bearing of witness,

"'I bear witness that there is no God but Allah, I bear witness that there is no God but Allah, I bear witness that Muhammad is the Messenger of Allah, I bear witness that Muhammad is the Messenger of Allah. Come to prayer, Come to prayer; Come to success, Come to success.'

"Then if it is the morning prayer, thou shouldst say, 'Prayer is better than sleep. Prayer is better than sleep';

"(Then thou shouldst say),

"'Allah is the Greatest, Allah is the Greatest, there is no God but Allah.'"

(AD-Msh. 4:4.)

14

Abu Hurairah reported that

A man entered the mosque, and the Messenger of Allah, peace and blessings of Allah be on him, was sitting in a corner of the mosque; . . . he said, Teach me, O Messenger of Allah! He said:

"When thou risest for the prayer, then perform the ablution in a right manner, then turn thy face towards the Qublah, then say *Allahu Akbar,* then recite what thou canst afford of the *Qur'an*, then bow down until thou art at rest in bowing down (ruku'), then raise thyself up until thou art firm in the standing posture, then fall down in prostration until thou art at rest in prostration, then raise thyself up until thou art at rest in sitting, then fall down in prostration until thou art at rest in prostration, then raise thyself up until thou art at rest in sitting; and, according to one report, then raise thyself up until thou art firm in the standing posture; then do this in the whole of thy prayer."

(B. & M-Msh. 4:10.)

15

'Ubadah reported that The Messenger of Allah, peace and blessings of Allah be on him, said:

"There is not prayer for him who does not recite the Opening (chapter) of the Book."[2]

(B. 10:95.)

The Imam

16

Abu Musa said, The Prophet, peace and blessings of Allah be on him, fell ill and his illness became severe; so he said:

"Tell Abu Bakr that he should lead the prayer for the people." . . . So the messenger came to him, and he (Abu Bakr) led the prayer for the people in the lifetime of the Prophet, peace and blessings of Allah be on him.

(B. 10:46.)

Charity and Zakat

17

Abu Hurairah said on the authority of the Prophet, peace and blessings of Allah be on him, (who said):

"There is a man who gives a charity and he conceals it so much so that his left hand does not know what his right hand spends."

(B. 24:13.)

18

Jabir said, The Messenger of Allah, peace and blessings of Allah be on him, said:

"Every good deed is charity, and it is a good deed that thou meet thy brother with a cheerful countenance and that thou pour water from thy bucket into the vessel of thy brother."

(Ah-Msh. 6:6.)

19

Abu Hurairah said, The Prophet, peace and blessings of Allah be on him, said:

"The man who exerts himself on behalf of the widow and the poor one is like the one who struggles in the way of Allah, or the one who keeps awake in the night (for prayers) and fasts during the day."

(B. 69:1.)

---

2   *The Fatihah* [opening chapter of the *Qur'an*] is thus an essential part of every rak'ah in every prayer.

20

Abu Musa reported, The Prophet, peace and blessings of Allah be on him, said:

"*Sadaqah*[3] is incumbent on every Muslim."

They (his companions) said, O Prophet of Allah! And (what about him) who has not got (anything to give)? He said:

"He should work with his hand and profit himself and give in charity."

They said, If he has nothing (in spite of this). He said:

"He should help the distressed one who is in need."

They said, If he is unable to do this. He said:

"He should do good deeds and refrain from doing evil—this is charity on his part."

(B. 24:31.)

Fasting

21

Abu Hurairah reported, The Messenger of Allah, peace and blessings of Allah be on him, said:

"Fasting is an armour with which one protects oneself; so let not him (who fasts) utter immodest (or foul) speech, nor let him act in an ignorant manner; and if a man quarrels with him or abuses him, he should say twice, I am fasting. And by Him in Whose hand is my soul, the odour of the mouth of one fasting is sweeter in the estimation of Allah than the odour of musk—he gives up his food and his drink and his (sexual) desire for My sake; fasting is for Me and I will grant its reward; and a virtue brings reward ten times like it."

(B. 30:2.)

22

'Ata' said, One should break the fast on account of illness, whatever it may be, as Allah has said. And Hasan and Ibrahim said, concerning the woman who gives suck and the one with child, when they fear about themselves or their child, they should break the fast, then fast on other days. And as to the very old man when he cannot bear fasting—Anas, after he became old, fed one who was needy, for a year or two daily with bread and meat, and broke the fast.

(B. 65: ii, 25.)

---

3   The Arabic word for charity is *sadaqah* (from *sidq,* meaning *truth*). . . .
    Technically *zakat* is a fixed portion of one's Wealth which it is obligatory to give
    away annually for the benefit of the poor. . . . *Zakat* is a tax distinct from
    voluntary charity [*sadaqah*] and the most important obligation next to prayer.

Pilgrimage

23

Ibn 'Abbas reported, Al-Aqra' asked the Prophet, peace and blessings of Allah be on him, O Messenger of Allah! Is the pilgrimage to be performed every year or only once? He said: "Only once; and whoever does it more that once, it is supererogatory."

(AD. 11:1.)

24

Ibn 'Umar reported about the Prophet, peace and blessings of Allah be on him, A man asked him, What should a man wear in the state of ihram[4]? He said:

"He shall not wear shirt, nor turban, nor trousers, nor head-gear, nor any cloth dyed with *wars* or saffron[5]; and if he does not find shoes, let him wear leather stockings, and he should cut them off so that they may be lower than the ankles."

(B. 3:53.)

25

Ibn 'Umar reported, 'Umar said, speaking of the Corner (the Black Stone), I call Allah to witness that I know that thou art a stone—thou canst not harm or profit; and if I had not seen the Messenger of Allah, peace and blessings of Allah be on him, kissing thee, I would not have kissed thee, then he kissed it.

(B. 25:56.)

Marriage and Divorce

26

'Alqamah said, While I was going along with 'Abd Allah, he said, We were with the Prophet, peace and blessings of Allah be on him, and he said:

"He who is able to marry should marry, for it keeps the eye cast down and keeps a man chaste; and he who cannot, should take to fasting, for it will have a castrating effect upon him.

(B. 30:10.)

---

4   *Ihram* (from *haram*, a forbidden thing) signifies entering upon a state that causes what is allowed before to be forbidden or unlawful, and it is technically used to indicate the condition in which the pilgrim is required to put himself.

5   Men wore only two seamless sheets, a sheet reaching from the navel to below the knees . . . and a sheet which covers the upper part of the body . . . while women wore their ordinary simple dress. *Wars* is a plant with which clothes are dyed. Clothes dyed red or yellow are thus forbidden.

27

'Ali reported, The Messenger of Allah, peace and blessings of Allah be on him, forbade temporary marriage with women, and the eating of domestic asses, on the day of Khaibar.

(B. 64:40.)

28

Jabir said, The Messenger of Allah, peace and blessings of Allah be on him, said: "When one of you asks a woman in marriage, then if he is able that he should look into what invites him to have her in marriage, he should do it."

(AD. 12:17.)

29

Mughirah reported, He made a proposal of marriage to a woman, and the Prophet, peace and blessings of Allah be on him, said:

"See her, for this is more likely to bring about agreement between you."

(Tr. 9:5.)

30

Abu Hurairah reported, The Prophet, peace and blessings of Allah be on him, said:

"The widow shall not be married until she is consulted, and the virgin shall not be married until her consent is obtained."

They said, O Messenger of Allah! How shall her consent be obtained? He said, "(It is sufficient) that she remains silent."

(B. 67:42.)

31

Khansa' reported, Her father gave her away in marriage, and she was a *thayyib*[6], and she did not like it. So she came to the Messenger of Allah, peace and blessings of Allah be on him, and he annulled her marriage.

(B. 67:43.)

32

'A'ishah said, The Messenger of Allah, peace and blessings of Allah be on him, said:

"Select (fit) women (in respect of character) for your seed, and marry (your) equals and give (your daughters) in marriage to them."[7]

(IM. 9:46.)

---

6   The word *thayyib* includes both a woman whose husband has died and a woman who has been divorced.

7   Marriage must be contracted so far as possible between equals. . . . Bukhari explains this by heading his chapter as . . . *Equals in religion;* making it clear that all Muslims are equal in one sense. There are examples recorded in Hadith in which a woman of . . . high family . . . was married to a slave or a freed slave.

33

Abu Hurairah reported, The Prophet, peace and blessings of Allah be on him, said:

"A woman is married on account of four things; on account of her wealth, and on account of (the nobility of) her family, and her beauty, and on account of her character, so attain success with the one possessing nobility of character."

(B. 67:16.)

Divorce

34

Ibn 'Umar reported, The Prophet, peace and blessings of Allah be on him, said:
"With Allah, the most detestable of all things permitted is divorce."[8]

(AD. 13:3.)

35

Thauban said, The Messenger of Allah, peace and blessings of Allah be on him, said:

"Whatever woman asks for divorce from her husband without any harm, the sweet odour of paradise shall be forbidden to her."

(Ah. 5, 277.)

36

Ibn 'Umar reported, He divorced his wife while she was menstruating. 'Umar mentioned this to the Messenger of Allah, peace and blessings of Allah be on him, so the Messenger of Allah, peace and blessings of Allah be on him, became displeased on account of this and said:

"He should take her back, then keep her until she is clean, then menstruates and (again) becomes clean; if it then appears to him that he should divorce her, he should divorce her while she is in a clean condition; before he approaches her. This is the *'iddah* as Allah has commanded it."[9]

(B. 65:65.)

---

8   This hadith shows that divorce should be resorted to only in cases of extreme hardship. A Muslim is required to face the difficulties of the married life, and to avoid disruption of family relations, so long as possible, turning to divorce only as a last resort.

9   This hadith . . . shows that divorce is not effective unless it is pronounced when the wife is clean. *'Iddah,* or the period during which a woman must wait before remarrying, is stated in v. 4 (2:228) to be three *quru'*. The word *quru'* is plural of *qar'* which signified *the entering from the state of cleanness into a state of menstruation,* and is in normal cases about four weeks.

37

Ibn 'Abbas said, The (procedure of) divorce in the time of the Messenger of Allah, peace and blessings of Allah be on him, in that of Abu Bakr and for two years in the caliphate of 'Umar ibn al-Khattab, was that divorce uttered thrice (on one occasion) was considered as one divorce. Then 'Umar said, People have made haste in a matter in which there was moderation for them; so we may make it take effect with regard to them. So he made it take effect with regard to them.

(AH. I, 314.)

38

'Ali said, The Messenger of Allah, peace and blessings of Allah be on him, cursed the man who committed *halalah*[10] and the one for whom *halalah* was committed.

(Tr. 9:25.)

39

Ibn Al-Musayyab said, When a person is found missing while fighting, his wife shall wait for one year.

(B. 68:22.)

Buying and Selling

40

Miqdam reported, The Messenger of Allah, peace and blessings of Allah be on him, said:

"No one eats better food than that which he eats out of the work of his hand."

(B. 34:15.)

41

Ma'mar said, The Messenger of Allah, peace and blessings of Allah be on him, said,

"Whoever withholds cereals that they may become scarce and dear, is a sinner."

(M-Msh. 12:8.)

---

10 In pre-Islamic Arabia the divorce was pronounced thrice and was irrevocable, and remarriage between the parties required the wife to go through a temporary marriage with another husband who divorced her after having sexual connection with her. This practice was called *halalah* (literally, *making a thing lawful*). Without going through it, it was not lawful for the divorced pair to return to marital relations. Islam did not recognize temporary marriage, and therefore *halalah* was denounced.

42

Hudhaifah said, The Prophet, peace and blessings of Allah be on him, said:

"The angels met the soul of a man from among those who were before you, (and) they said, Hast thou done any good? He said, I used to give respite to the one in easy circumstances and forgive one who was in straitened circumstances. So they forgave him."

(B. 34:17)

43

Sa'id ibn Huraith said, The Messenger of Allah, peace and blessings of Allah be on him, said:

"Whoever sells a house or a land yielding revenue, then he does not invest the price on a thing akin to it, he is not likely to be blessed therein."

(Ah. IV. 307.)

44

Abu Hurairah reported, The Prophet, peace and blessings of Allah be on him, said:

"Allah says, There are three persons whose adversary in dispute I shall be on the day of resurrection: a person who makes a promise in My name then acts unfaithfully, and a person who sells a free person then devours his price, and a person who employs a servant and receives fully the labour due from him then he does not pay his remuneration."

(B. 34:106)

45

Jabir reported, The Messenger of Allah, peace and blessings of Allah be on him, cursed the usurer and the man who pays usury and the writer of the transaction and the two witnesses thereof and he said:

"They are alike."

(M-Msh. 12:4.)

Cultivation of Land

46

Abu Hurairah reported, The Messenger of Allah, peace and blessings of Allah be on him, said:

"Excess of water should not be withheld, arresting thereby the growth of herbage."

(B. 42:2.)

Gifts

47

Ibn 'Abbas said, The Prophet, peace and blessings of Allah be on him, said:

"The man who takes back what he has gifted is like one who returns to his vomit."

(B. 51:30.)

48

Usamah said, The Messenger of Allah, peace and blessings of Allah be on him, said:

"To whomsoever good is done and he says to the doer of it, May Allah reward thee, he has done his utmost in praising."

(Tr-Msh. 12:17.)

Wills and Inheritance

49

Sa'd ibn Abi Waqqas said, The Messenger of Allah, peace and blessings of Allah be on him, used to visit me at Makkah, in the year of the Farewell pilgrimage, on account of (my) illness which had become very severe. So I said, My illness has become very severe and I have much property and there is none to inherit from me but a daughter, shall I then bequeath two-thirds of my property as a charity? He said, "No." Then he said:

"Bequeath one-third and one-third is much, for if thou leavest thy heirs free from want, it is better than that thou leavest them in want, begging of (other) people; and thou dost not spend anything seeking thereby the pleasure of Allah but thou art rewarded for it, even for that which thou puttest into the mouth of thy wife."

(B. 23:36.)

50

'Amr ibn Shu'aib reported, The Prophet, peace and blessings of Allah be on him, said:

"Whoever holds illicit intercourse with a free woman or a slave-girl, the child (thus born) is illegitimate, and he does not inherit, nor is he inherited."

(Tr-Msh. 12:19.)

Food and Drink

51

Jabir said, The Messenger of Allah, peace and blessings of Allah be on him, said:
"Of whatever thing a large quantity intoxicates, even a small quantity is prohibited."

(AD. 25:5.)

52

Salman reported, The Messenger of Allah, peace and blessings of Allah be on him, said:
"The blessing of food is the washing of hands before it, and the washing of hands after it."

(Tr-Msh. 20.)

53

Abu Sa'id al-Khudri said,
When the Messenger of Allah, peace and blessings of Allah be on him, finished his meal, he used to say: "All praise is due to Allah Who has given us to eat and to drink, and made us Muslims."

(Tr-Msh. 20.)

Ethics

54

Abu Hurairah said, A man came to the Messenger of Allah, peace and blessings of Allah be on him, and said, O Messenger of Allah! Who has the greatest right that I should keep company with him with goodness? He said, "Thy mother." He said, Who then? He said, "Thy mother." He said, Who then? He said, "Thy mother." He said, Who then? He said, "Then thy father."

(B. 78:2)

55

Aswad said, I asked 'A'ishah, What did the Prophet, peace and blessings of Allah be on him, do when in his house? She said, he served his wife, meaning that he did work for his wife.

(B. 10:44.)

56

Ibn 'Umar reported, The Messenger of Allah, peace and blessings of Allah be on him, said:
"A Muslim is the brother of a Muslim; he does him no injustice, nor does he leave him alone (to be the victim of another's injustice); and whoever does the needful for his brother, Allah does the needful for him; and whoever removes

185

the distress of a Muslim, Allah removes from him a distress out of the distresses of the day of resurrection; and whoever covers (the fault of) a Muslim, Allah will cover his sins on the day of resurrection."

(B. 46:3.)

57

Abu Dharr said, . . . The Prophet, peace and blessings of Allah be on him, said to me:

". . . Your slaves are your brethren, Allah has placed them under your control; so whoever has his brother under his control should feed him from what he eats and should give him clothes to wear from what he wears, and do not impose on them a task which should overpower them, and if you impose on them such a task, then help them (in doing it)."

(B. 2:21.)

58

'Abd Allah reported, The Prophet, peace and blessings of Allah be on him, said:

"Surely truth leads to virtue, and virtue leads to paradise, and a man continues to speak the truth until he becomes thoroughly truthful; and surely falsehood leads to vice, and vice leads to the fire, and a man continues to tell lies until he is written down a great liar with Allah."

(B. 78:69.)

The State

59

Ibn 'Umar reported, I heard the Messenger of Allah, peace and blessings of Allah be on him, say:

"Every one of you is a ruler and every one of you shall be questioned about those under his rule; the king is a ruler and he shall be questioned about his subjects; and the man is a ruler in his family and he shall be questioned about those under his care; and the woman is a ruler in the house of her husband, and she shall be questioned about those under her care; and the servant is a ruler so far as the property of his master is concerned, and he shall be questioned about that which is entrusted to him."

(B. 11:11.)

60

Ibn 'Umar reported, The Prophet, peace and blessings of Allah be on him, said:

"To hear and obey (the authorities) is binding, so long as one is not commanded to disobey (God); when one is commanded to disobey (God), he shall not hear or obey."

(B. 56:108.)

61

Abu Hurairah reported, He heard the Messenger of Allah, peace and blessings of Allah be on him, say:

"He who obeys me obeys Allah, and he who disobeys me disobeys Allah; and he who obeys the amir obeys me, and he who disobeys the amir disobeys me; and the imam is an armour for protection—the battle is fought for his defence and through him protection is sought. So if he commands the doing of duty to Allah and does justice, he has a reward for it; and if he does otherwise, he shall suffer the evil consequences of it."

(B. 56:109.)

62

'Ali said, The Prophet, peace and blessings of Allah be on him, said:

"Obedience is due only in that which is good."

(B. 64:61.)

63

Abu Sa'id said, The Messenger of Allah, peace and blessings of Allah be on him, said:

"The most excellent jihad is the uttering of truth in the presence of an unjust ruler."

(Tr-Msh. 17.)

64

Abu Burdah said, The Messenger of Allah, peace and blessings of Allah be on him, sent Abu Musa and Mu'adh ibn Jabal to Yaman, and he appointed each one of them to govern a part of Yaman, and he said, Yaman was divided into two parts; then he said: "Be gentle (to the people) and be not hard (on them), and make (them) rejoice and do not incite (them) to aversion."

(B. 64:62.)

65

It is reported about 'Umar that when he appointed his governors, he laid down upon them certain conditions:

You shall not ride a horse that is not of Arabian breed; you shall not eat bread made of fine flour; you shall not wear fine clothes; and you shall not shut your doors against the needs of the people. If you do any of these things, punishment shall descend on you.

Then he went forth with them to bid them farewell.

(Msh. 17:1.)

Iblis (Satan)

66

Abu Bakr ibn Abi Shayba related that 'Abd al A'la related from Ma'mar from az-Zuhri, from Sa'id, from Abu Hurayra who said that the Messenger of God—may God bless him and grant him peace!—said, "No child is born without Satan (Ash-Shaytan) pricking him. Then he (the child) begins to cry out from the goad of Satan—except the son of Maryam and his mother . . . ."

(Muslim, *al-Jami' as-sahih*, 7:96–97)

67

'Uthman Abu Shayba and Ishaq ibn Ibrahim related that Ishaq told us that 'Uthman said that jarir related from Mansur, from Salim ibn Abi 'l-Ja'd, from his father, from 'Abd Allah ibn Mas'ud who said that the Messenger of God—may God bless him and grant him peace!—said, "There is no one among you who does not have a *jinn* (or *shay* an in other versions) as his companion placed in charge of him." They said, "And you, too, O Messenger of God?" He said, "Even me, except that God came to my assistance against him and he (the *jinn*) has become Muslim. Now he only urges me to good."

(Muslim, *al-Jami' as-sahih*, 8:139)

68

'Abd Allah ibn Maslama related to us from Malik, from 'Abd Allah ibn Dinar, from 'Abd Allah ibn 'Umar—may God be pleased with them both!—who said, "I saw the Messenger of God—may God bless him and grant him peace!—pointing towards the East. And he said, 'Right there, truly discord is right there. Yea, discord is from right there where the horn of Satan rises.'"

(al-Bukhari, *Sahih*, 4:150)

69

Abu Kurayb Muhammad ibn al-A'la' and Ishaq ibn Ibrahim (the formulation belongs to Abu Kurayb) both said, Abu Mu'awiya told us that al-A'mash related to us from Abu Sufyan, from Jabir who said that the Messenger of God—may God bless him and grant him peace!—said, "Iblis places his throne upon the waters. Then he sends forth his flying columns. To those who are best at sowing discord, he has granted a place close to him. One of them comes and says, 'I have done such and such!' Then he replies, 'You have not accomplished anything.'" He said, "Then another of them comes and says, 'I did not leave him until I had caused division between him and his wife.'" He said, "Then he (Iblis) brings him close to himself and says, 'You have done well! . . .'"

(Muslim, *Al-Jami' as-sahih*, 8:138)

Taken from *Satan's Tragedy and Redemption: Iblis in Sufi Psychology* by Peter J. Awn. Copyright © 1983 by E.J. Brill.

Key to Abbreviations used in Hadith

Hadith from Maulana Muhammad Ali's *A Manual of Hadith* are followed by abbreviations in parentheses citing the Hadith collections from which the sayings were taken. The first number represents the number of the book and the second the number of the chapter, except in the case of the *Musnad* of Ahmad ibn Hanbal where the first figure stands for the volume and the second for the page. In all references to *the Mishkat*, the name of the collection from which the *Mishkat* has taken the particular hadith is also indicated. Hadith excerpted from other sources do not use these abbreviations.

AD	Abu Dawud
Ah	*Mushnad* of Ahmad
B	Bukhari
DQ	Dara Qutni
Fr	al-Fara'id al-Durriyyah
H	A Manual of Hadith
h	hadith
IM	Ibn Majah
LL	Lane's Arabic-English Lexicon
M	Muslim
Msh	Mishkat
Mt	Muwatta'
N	Nihayah
Ns	Nasa'i
R	Mufradat of Raghib
Tr	Tirmidhi
v	verse (of the Holy *Qur'an*)

Selected Fiqh

Fiqh is Islamic jurisprudence. *Fiqh Akbar* (or *al-Fiqh al-Akbar)* means "the greatest *fiqh*" and generally means the supreme collection of canonic law. The phrase also refers to several creeds, of which the following Fiqh Akbar I (by Abu Hanifah, d. 767 C. E.) is the most famous.

This doctrine marked the beginning of an important new phase in Islamic theology. Prior to Abu Hanifah's statement, the different sects equated disagreement with heresy. Intolerance and quarrels over belief were the rule. The *Fiqh Akbar* defines Islam broadly enough to make a variety of views possible and acceptable. This broad interpretation identifies the document as representative of the Sunni, the largest Islamic group. The first seven articles deal with who may be considered a Muslim. The last three articles set clear limits to Islamic belief; there are boundaries that one cannot go beyond without falling into error.

Each major Islamic sect has its own collection (or collections) of *fiqh*. Each collection begins with law having to do with human relationships with God (for example, ritual practices). Usually, the next section will cover matters of human relationships, such as personal status (marriage and divorce), then go on to other matters including community relations (including the use of public land and instructions for various occupations), and things and activities that are disapproved or forbidden. The selection from al-Ghazali about birth control provides an example of this type of legal reasoning based on interpretation of the *Quran* and *hadith*. Al-Ghazali is one of Islam's most important philosophers and theologians. Born in 1058 A.D. in the northeast corner of what is now Iran, al-Ghazali came from a family that could enable him to devote his youth to study. He was appointed to one of the most important teaching posts in Baghdad while in his early thirties. He subsequently left the academic life to pursue the Sufi path of personal, mystical experience of God. His autobiography and other later writings reconcile Sufism with orthodox Islamic belief and practice.

Malcolm Clark

The Fiqh Akbar I

Art. 1. We do not consider anyone to be an infidel on account of sin; nor do we deny his faith.

Art. 2. We enjoin what is just and prohibit what is evil.

Art. 3. What reaches you could not possibly have missed you; and what misses you could not possibly have reached you.

Art. 4. We disavow none of the Companions of the Apostle of Allah; nor do we adhere to any of them exclusively.

Art. 5. We leave the question of Uthman and Ali to Allah, who knoweth the secret and hidden things.

Art. 6. Insight in matters of religion is better than insight in matters of knowledge and law.

Art. 7. Difference of opinion in the community is a token of divine mercy.

Art. 8. Whoso believeth all that he is bound to believe, except that he says, I do not know whether Moses and Jesus (peace be upon them) do or do not belong to the Apostles, is an infidel.

Art. 9. Whoso sayeth, I do not know whether Allah is in Heaven or on the earth, is an infidel.

Art. 10. Whoso sayeth, I do not know the punishment in the tomb, belongeth to the sect of the Djahmites, which goeth to perdition.

Al-Ghazali on Birth Control
from His Chapter on the Secrets of Marriage

It is a rule of cohabitation that the emission of semen should not take place outside of the vagina, for what God has decreed must take place. The prophet said likewise. There are differences among the learned class concerning *'azl* or *coitus interruptus*. One group says that *'azl* is lawful in all circumstances while another group says it is unlawful in every circumstance. Another group says it is lawful with the consent of one's wife while another group says it is lawful in the case of female slaves but not in the case of free women. To us, the custom of *'azl* is lawful but is not commendable for the reason that the merits of ejaculation in the vagina are lost. A similar example is found in the person who sits idly in the mosque without remembering God. The point is that the person is not doing something which is intended to be done in the situation; that is not commendable. There is virtue in producing a child but that is lost in *'azl*.

From *Textual Sources for the Study of Islam,* edited by Andrew Rippin and Jan Knappert. Copyright 1986 by Andrew Rippin and Jan Knappert. Reprinted by permission.

Muhammad said: 'If a man cohabits with his wife, the reward of producing a child is decreed for him—such a child will become a martyr fighting in the way of God'. He said this in consideration of reward, because if a child is born like this, he will get the reward for producing a martyr in the way of God. This is only possible with full intercourse.

That birth control by *'azl* is lawful is supported by legal analogy from the *Qur'an*. Though there is no clear verse regarding the matter, it can be gathered by analogy such as the following. It is not unlawful to give up marriage or to give up intercourse after marriage or to give up ejaculation of semen after intercourse. It is true that rewards are given up on these actions but absence of actions is not unlawful. There is no difference between these three things. A child is born after ejaculation into the vagina. Before it there are four stages: (1) to marry; (2) to cohabit; (3) to have patience to ejaculate after intercourse; (4) to ejaculate into the vagina and then to stay in that condition until the semen is settled therein. The life of a child coming into existence has a number of stages: (1) semen in the vagina must be mixed with the female egg. If both are mixed, it is a sin to destroy it. There is no sin if they are not allowed to mix; (2) if it is created into a clot of blood and a lump of flesh, it is more hateable to destroy it; (3) if life is infused into that lump of flesh, it is most hateable to destroy it; (4) the last limit of sin is to destroy the child when it is born. If the male semen is mixed with the menstrual blood of a woman, it is condensed, as happens when something is mixed with milk. It is just like proposal and acceptance which constitute an agreement or contract. Both things are necessary for a contract. If there is a proposal but no acceptance, there is no sin in breaking it. The ejaculation of semen is like a proposal and doing that in the vagina is like its acceptance. If it is ejaculated outside the vagina, the proposal is lost. There is no sin with it. Therefore, to ejaculate outside the vagina before the semen is mixed with female egg is not a sin.

Question: if there is no sin in ejaculating outside of the vagina, it must still be considered bad because the object of semen is to produce a child and if that is not done, it is secret polytheism.

Answer: There are four aims of *'azl*. (1) to preserve the beauty and health of one's wife and thus to enjoy her always. If semen is destroyed with this object, then it is not unlawful. (2) To prevent the birth of too many children. It is not unlawful; to maintain too many children is very difficult. The verse in the *Qur'an* which guarantees maintenance of all creatures means perfection of God—reliance and perfection of merits and rewards but it is no sin to give up the highest stage of merits just as it is no sin to protect one's wealth and properties and to hoard things for a limited period of time. This is the meaning of the verse: *There is no animal in the earth of which the maintenance is not upon God* (*Qur'an* 11:6). (3) To practise birth control for fear of the birth of daughters. This is unlawful. The Arabs before Islam used to bury their daughters alive and they feared the birth of daughters. This was prohibited in the *Qur'an*. If with the above object, marriage or intercourse is given up, it will be committing a sin but these actions without that object are not sinful. (4) To protect the honour of a woman, to keep her neat and clean, and to save her from maintaining children. This too is unlawful use of *'azl*.

192

Islamic Prayer

Muslims around the world perform the ritual of prayer (*salat*) five times daily. In cities, Muslims are reminded to pray by the *muezzin,* who sings the call to prayer from the minaret of the mosque. The prayers themselves are performed the same way by all believers and incorporate intention, movement of the body, and repetition of the centuries-old Arabic words of prayer.

Ellen Hodge

Call to Prayer

1. *Allahu akbar:* "God is most great."
2. *Ashhadu an la ilaha ilia 'llah:* "I testify that there is no god besides God."
3. *Ashhadu anna Muhammad rasul Allah:* "I testify that Muhammad is the apostle of God."
4. *Haiya 'ala 'l-salat:* "Come to prayer!"
5. *Haiya 'ala 'l-falah:* "Come to salvation!"
6. *Allahu akbar:* "God is most great"
7. *La ilaha ilia 'llah:* "There is no god besides God."

The first statement is repeated four times. The other statements are each repeated twice, except the last, which is called only once. For the morning call to prayer, the words, "Prayer is better than sleep" are often inserted between the fifth and sixth statements or added at the end.

From *The Concise Encyclopedia of Islam* by Cyril Glasse. Copyright © 1989 by Stacey International and Cyril Glasse. Reprinted by permission of HarperCollins Publishers, Inc.

Salat

Opening

1. *Niyyah* **(Intention)**
    Standing, eyes downcast, hands to sides, feet somewhat apart.
    Nawaito an assali _____ (give the name of the particular salat, depending on the time of day)

2. *Takbir*
    Raise hands to ear level, eyes still focused on the ground.
    Allahu Akbar.
    God is great.

Cycle (*Rakat*, a bowing)

3. Clasp hands, woman above breast, man below, and keep eyes on hands. Say the *fatihah* (opening prayer of the *Quran*):
    Bismi 'llahi 'r-Rahmani 'r-Rahim
    Al-hamdu li'llahi Rabbi'l-alamin
    Ar-Rahmani 'r-Rahim
    Maliki yawmi'd-din
    Iyyaka na budu wa-iyyaka nasta in
    Ihdi-na 's-sirata 'l-mustaqim
    Sirata 'lladhina an amta alay-him
    Ghairi'l-maghdubi 'alay-him wa-la'd-dhallin. Amin.
    In the name of God the All-Merciful, The Bestower of Mercy
    Praise be to God, the Lord of the Worlds
    The All-Merciful, the Bestower of Mercy
    The Lord of the Day of Judgment
    You alone we worship and in You alone we seek support
    Guide us upon the straight path
    The path of those upon whom you are gracious
    Not of those who are astray nor of those upon whom Your anger has fallen.
    Amen.

    Optional: Extra verses of *Quran*, especially verse 112, "The Sincerity":

    Qul Huwa-llahu ahad; allahu-s-samad
    Lam yalid wa lam yulad
    Wa lam yakum lahu kufuwan ahad
    Say, He, God, is One; God is everlasting.
    He never begot nor was begotten
    Nor is there any equal to him.

Finish with a *takbir:*
Alahu Akbar.
God is great.

4. Bow. Hands on knees, head lowered.
Say silently three times:
Subhana—llahir'l'azim
Glory to God the Mighty

(or a similar statement)

5. Stand.
Say aloud:
Sami'a—llahu liman hamidah
God listens to him who praises him

Say aloud:
Rabbana wa laka-l-hamd
Our Lord, and to thee belongs praise

Say the *takbir:*
Allahu akbar
God is great

6. Prostration.
Go into seated position, knees on ground, and from there go into a bow, forehead and nose touching mat, both palms on mat.

Say silently three times:
Subhana rabbiya-l'a'la
Glory to my Lord the most high

7. Seated Position.

Pause. Then say *takbir* aloud:
Allahu Akbar
God is great

8. Prostration again.

Say silently three times:
Subhana rabbiya-l'a'la
Glory to my Lord the most high

This completes the first *Rakat* or cycle. To begin next cycle, if there is one, stand, say the *takbir* and start again, going through steps 3–8.

Closing

9. In seated position, say the following aloud. (Malikis and others move forefingers of right hand in a counter-clockwise circle while hand rests on knee. Stop circling and point fingers upward when saying the *shahadah.*)

    At tahiya li-llahi wa-s-salawatu wa-t-tayyabutu.
    As-salamu 'alayka ayyuha-n-nabiyyu
    Wa rarmatu-llahi wa barakatuh
    Wa-s-salamu 'alayha wa 'ala 'ibadi-llahi-s-salahin
    Ashadu an la ilaha illa-Illa
    Wa ashadu anna Muhammadan 'abduhu wa rasuluh
    Salutations, prayers, and good works are all for God.
    Peace on thee, oh Prophet,
    and God's mercy and His blessings.
    Peace be on us and on all God's righteous servants.
    I testify that there is no god but God
    And I testify that Muhammad is his servant and his messenger.

10. **The "sealing"**
    Still seated, turn the head to the right and then to the left. Say toward each side (as if speaking to the angel on each side):
    As-salamu-alaykum
    Peace be with you.

11. **Dhikr (Remembrance)**
    Still seated. You may use prayer beads or count your knuckles. (Use the right hand, starting with thumb on tip of little finger. Keep going, 12 counts on the hand. Do 12 + 12 + 9.) You may name any attribute—for example *Ar-rahim,* the Merciful—or choose to say the 99 names of God.

12. *Dua* **(Call or Plea)**
    Hands upraised slightly, palms open upwards. Still seated, make a *dua,* which is a personal prayer, made silently. This is often a spontaneous prayer, although a formula can be used. It always includes a *fatihah*.

    At the end, the hands are drawn across the face as if a blessing had fallen into them, as closing words are said:
    Al-hamdu-li-llah
    Praise to God.

    Then rise, greet other worshippers with
    As-salamu 'alaykum
    Peace be with you.

Hajj Map and Diagram

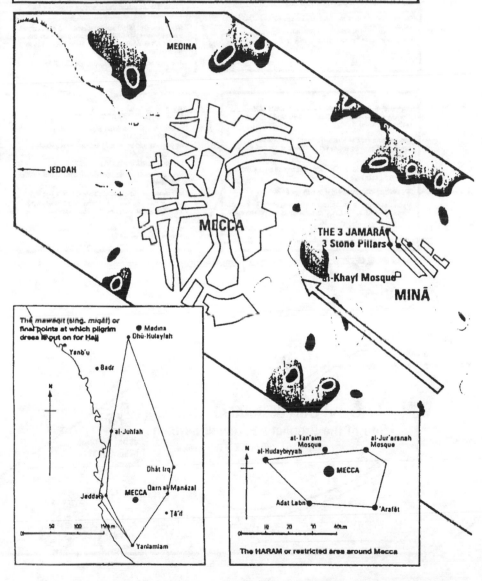

THE HAJJ the pilgrimage to Mecca

Before arrival in Mecca the pilgrim puts on *ihrām* (consecration and pilgrim clothing) at one of the *mawāqit* (see box below), or before, even at the point of departure, and the appropriate intentions (*an-niyyāt*) are formulated.

Note: a day runs from sunset to sunset

MEDINA

JEDDAH

MECCA

THE 3 JAMARĀT
3 Stone Pillars

al-Khayf Mosque

MINĀ

The *mawāqit* (sing. *miqāt*) or final points at which pilgrim dress is put on for Hajj

● Medina
Dhū-Hulaylah

Yanb'u

● Badr

N

● al-Juhfah

Dhāt Irq
Qarn al-Manāzal

Jeddah   ● MECCA

● Ta'd

50   100   150 km

Yanlamlam

N

al-Tan'aim
Mosque   al-Jur'aranah
al-Hudaybiyyah   Mosque

● MECCA

Adat Labn   'Arafāt

0   10   20   30   40 km

The HARAM or restricted area around Mecca

197

DAY 1: 8th DHÜ-1-ḤIJJAH
YAWM at-TARWIYAH (DAY OF DELIBERATION)

TAWĀF al-QUDŪM: The initial circumambulation of the Ka'bah is performed

Personal prayer is made (du'ā)

Prayer is made at the station of Abraham (MAQĀM IBRĀHĪM)

The pilgrim drinks the water of ZAMZAM

The pilgrim performs the SA'Y or courses between ṢAFĀ' and MARWAH

The pilgrim spends the night at MINĀ

DAY 2: 9th DHÜ-1-ḤIJJAH
YAWM 'ARAFĀT (DAY OF 'ARAFĀT)

WUQŪF (a presence, like the multitudes on the Day of Judgement, between noon and sunset on the plain of 'Arafāt or on the "Mount of Mercy" (JABAL RAHMAH)

Frequent recitation of the Abrahamic TALBIYAH ("Here I am, O Lord . . .")

After sunset the IFĀḌAH ("overflowing") or NAFRAH ("rush") takes place; this is a rapid departure for MUZDALIFAH

Night prayers ('ISHĀ) are combined with the delayed sunset prayer (MAGHRIB) and performed near the MASH'AR al-ḤARAM, a station of the pilgrimage in Muzdalifah

The pilgrims spend the night at MUZDALIFAH

DAYS 4, 5, 6: 11th, 12th, 13th DHÜ-1-ḤIJJAH
AYYĀM at-TASHRĪQ (DAYS OF DRYING MEAT, that is, taking provision)

The pilgrims stay at MINĀ, and each day between sunset and sunrise throw seven stones at each of the 3 JAMARĀT

It is permissible to terminate the Pilgrimage on the 12th if departure takes place by sunset

A new covering (kiswah) is put on the Ka'bah

Upon departure, a final circumambulation of the Ka'bah is made: ṬAWĀF al-WADĀ' ("circumambulation of farewell")

DAY 3: 10th DHÜ-1-ḤIJJAH
YAWM an-NAHR (DAY OF SACRIFICE)

The pilgrim prays the dawn prayer (ṢUBH) and visits the MASH'AR al-ḤARAM

The pilgrims gather 49 or 70 pebbles at Muzdalifah to stone the JAMARĀT

They go to MINĀ via WĀDĪ MUHASSAR

They cast seven stones (RAMĪ-I-JIMĀR) at the JAMRAT al-'AQABAH

The animal sacrifice is made between now and day 6

A lock of hair can be clipped terminating most of the conditions of consecration (IHRĀM) between now and the final day

The pilgrims return to Mecca and circumambulate the Ka'bah (TAWĀF al-IFĀḌAH)

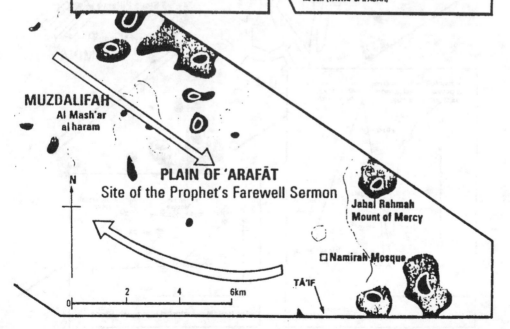

MUZDALIFAH
Al Mash'ar al haram

PLAIN OF 'ARAFĀT
Site of the Prophet's Farewell Sermon

Jabal Rahmah
Mount of Mercy

N

□ Namirah Mosque

TĀ'IF

0   2   4   6km

The Alternative of Socratic Faith and Abrahamic Faith

Al-Ghazali

"The alternatives of Socratic faith and Abrahamic faith" is the record of a debate between two Islamic thinkers, Faylasuf (Philosopher) Razi and Ismalli Razi.[1] In the debate over how truth can be known, Faylasuf Razi represents the radical philosophical school which championed personal, intellectual quest for truth over the collective historical experience of truth in the community as.

The other side of the debate is represented by Ismaili Razi. The Ismaili were marginal to the Sunni mainstream of Islamic thought at the time. They believed that the Imam possessed an esoteric understanding of the Quran, and they promoted a reliance on the collective, historical experience of the truth. The source of truth is the Revelation; the inspired leader (the Imam) is the one authoritative interpreter. Al-Ghazali responds to the tension presented in the debate by trying to hold together the two poles of reason and revelation.

Malcolm Clark

The dilemma is illustrated in conversations recorded by Abu-Hatim al-Razi, an Isma'ili da't preacher, as taking place publicly between himself and the Faylasuf Razi, Ibn-Zakariyya of all those who shared the Qur'anic tradition, the Isma'ilis were the most actively interested in the doctrines associated with Falsafah; their symbolism presupposed the old Hellenistic image of the world, and in the following centuries they were to adapt the old Philosophic cosmology to their own purposes. But the Isma'ili was as shocked as any other adherent of a monotheistic revelation at what he regarded as the dangerous and arrogant rejection of historical revelation recognized by the community, in favour of the momentary speculation of an individual.

From The Venture of Islam, Vol. 1 by Marshall G.S. Hodgson. Copyright © 1974. Reprinted by permission of the University of Chicago Press.

1   Both were from the city of Rayy, hence were called Razi.

The Faylasuf Razi began by objecting to reliance on revelation on the ground that, since more than one doctrine is supported by revelation and there is no way to decide between the conflicting claims, such an appeal can only lead to destructive conflict among mankind—which cannot be God's purpose. All humans alike being endowed with reason, this alone has any hope of settling disputes, and it must be God's intention that we use it for reaching truth. The Isma'ili Razi retorted that while we all have reason, we do not have it all alike; some persons are so much more intelligent than others that it is inevitable that some lead and that others follow. Hence here must be an ultimately authoritative leader if truth is to be found at all as surely God desires it to be; this leader (to be identifiable by the less intelligent) must be a prophet bringing revelation.

But then he turned the Faylasuf's point against him, noting that in fact the proponents of individual reason differed among themselves just as did the proponents of revelation. He noted that the Faylasuf Razi had himself condemned important conclusions of great earlier rationalistic Philosophers and asked if he, their disciple, thought himself wiser than they who had taught him—implying that even the wisest Philosophers make mistakes and have no way of coming to a final settlement. The Faylasuf declared that the later thinker, having the benefit of all that the earlier ones had done, could add his own inquiries and so improve on their work; on which the Isma'ili pointed out that there would always be still later thinkers to improve further on al-Razi's own improvements, so that al-Razi had no assurance that he was right; and (since in fact the various opinions were all retained in the books side by side) the result was simply a multiplication of the number of diverse opinions about which people could dispute.

But at this point the Faylasuf turned to the heart of the matter. He was not immediately concerned with an indefinite progress in knowledge for the benefit of hypothetical future generations (when supposedly the range of diverse opinions might have been narrowed by exhaustive selection). Rather he was concerned with the pursuit of truth in any one generation. He maintained, then, that what counts is that each thinker be putting forth his own best effort; he will then be on the way to truth, even if he does not attain it, and it is being on the way that is desirable. For what is wanted is to purify the soul of its 'turbidness', of the confusion of mind induced by the sensory impressions and passions of living, so that it can judge and act objectively. And 'souls are not purified of the turbidness of this world or freed for that other world [the life of spirituality]' except through independent study and examination; 'when someone studies it [rationalistic Philosophy] and attains something of it, however little it be, he purifies his soul from this turbidness and renders it free. And if the common crowd who ruin their souls and are neglectful of study would devote but the slightest concern to it, this would liberate them from this turbidness. . . ."

The Isma'ili, however, convinced of human intellectual inequality, was less optimistic about the common crowd. He asked if a person who continued to believe in the doctrine of revelation could be purified by studying (rationalistic) Philosophy a little on the side; to which the Faylasuf responded that no one who persevered in submission to established opinion could become even a student of

'Philosophy' (thus indicating what he really was demanding when he asked for even a little bit of independent study). But the Isma'ili pointed out that, in practice, those who went into rationalistic Philosophy less than very deeply (which would be most of the would-be rationalists) might indeed reject revelation, but only to submit to a different tradition—a different set of established opinions—those to be found in the books of the Philosophers, which the Faylasuf had admitted were not necessarily in themselves true. Such a person would lose the benefit of the historical revelation without achieving the purification the Faylasuf called for; none could be in a worse state than that.

Both the Faylasuf and the Isma'ili were concerned with the moral dimensions of living, to which sheer knowledge was only an instrument. The Faylasuf Razi looked to the process of inquiry to make a good man, and was (exceptionally among the Faylasufs) ready to see a relatively large public join in this process—he wrote a book on treating the ailments of the soul, aimed partly at persuading the adib to look beyond his polite and superficial culture. The Isma'ili Razi demanded, as a good Shariah-conscious Muslim, that responsible living be based on something more objective than on an inner 'purity'; he looked for the most tangible possible assurance of a socially valid position—which meant turning to a historically accepted revelation, that of Muhammad and the *Qur'*an. Most Faylasufs acknowledged that, as regards the common masses at least, the Isma'ili had a point.

Layla and Majnun

———◆———

Nizami

The folktale of the love-mad poet and the beautiful but inaccessible object of his affection existed for centuries in the poetry and songs of the Arabian bedouines. The story may have been based on the life of a poet who lived around 850 CE. In about 1188 CE the Persian poet, Nizami, turned the tale of Layla and Majnun into a poem of some 8,000 lines. The prose translation you will read is based on Nizami's poem.

Nizami chose a lively meter to contrast with the melancholy tale, and set the theme of unfulfilled love against lavish descriptions of nature. Nizami established an important poetic form (the *masnavi,* used by centuries of poets after Nizami) to sustain long and continuous narrative. Nizami's name is still revered in many parts of the world, and the story of Layla and Majnun remains one of the most popular romances in the Islamic world.

Ellen Hodge

Long ago, in the desert of Arabia, lived many great chieftains, and the greatest was the chieftain of the tribe of the Banu Amir. Now this *sayyid,* as he was reverently called, had wealth beyond imagining; his gold and jewels were as countless as the grains of desert sand, and in his tent hung the most precious silks and carpets, and the finest herds grazed upon his land. But rich as he was in worldly goods, he was richer still in the goodness of his heart. He ruled with perfect justice and was generous to all; to those in need he readily opened his purse, and every traveler was welcome in his camp. His tribesmen prospered, and they loved and honored him. The *sayyid* was well content, but for one thing: he had no son and heir.

As the years passed and no son was born, he prayed to God with all his heart and brooded on the fortune that denied to him what he most desired. "What care I for my jewels and gold if I should die without an heir?" he asked. "Indeed, he truly lives who lives in the memory of his son!" And thus he prayed even more fervently, until, at last, his prayers were answered, and God gave to him a son.

There was great celebration in the camp of the Banu Amir, and the *sayyid* opened his treasury so that all might share in his happiness. The desert was filled with shouts of joy, for the child was a boy of unsurpassing handsomeness, even from the very moment of his birth. When he was but two weeks old, his face was as round and as beaming as the moon, and every year his comeliness increased. And the good *sayyid* was known to exclaim, "Of all men on this earth, surely none is more fortunate than I!"

Now when Qays, for so the boy was named, was of school age, he was sent to study under a learned teacher. So quick of mind was he that scarcely did he take a pen in hand than he had mastered script; no sooner did he hold a book than he could read. He was eager for new knowledge, and in all the learned disciplines he excelled, but his greatest skill by far was in the art of discourse. When he spoke, his words were sweeter than the music of a lute; his wit sharper than an arrow; his wisdom more lustrous than a pearl. All his schoolmates gathered round and listened with delight.

Now the pupils in this school were from the noblest families, and so it was that one morning the daughter of a mighty chieftain, second only to the *sayyid* himself, was brought into the classroom. This little girl was very beautiful. She was as slender as a cypress tree and as graceful as a bird; her skin was white as milk, her cheeks and lips were red as roses, and she had the darting black eyes of a gazelle. But even darker than her eyes was her raven hair; her hair was more lustrous than the sky at midnight, and indeed she was called Layla, or Night.

The moment Layla came into the schoolroom love awakened in Qays' heart. All that day he could neither read nor write, but only stare at her and wonder at her beauty and at her long black hair. Enraptured, he whispered "Layla, Layla," softly as if in prayer, and all the next day, and the next, and for many days after, he could say no word but "Layla!" Even at this tender age, Qays claimed her for his own and vowed that he would love her all his life.

And Layla loved Qays in return. Yet they spoke not, for their souls were so perfectly attuned that they had no need of words. Thus Qays would gaze at Layla while the other pupils studied or played in the courtyard. And Layla would blush deeply, lower her lashes, then open her eyes and gaze at him and sweetly smile. And every evening, when the sun set and the heavens darkened and the two were apart, they sighed and wept and eagerly went to their beds, all the sooner to dream of one another. When the sun rose they would hasten joyfully to school. Thus did they love, and every day their love increased.

Now love shines more brightly even than the sun, and Qays loved Layla so intensely that after a while the other children noticed what was plain to see. They were too young to know of love, and so they laughed at Qays and pointed at him, and cried, "Our friend has lost his heart and head! He cares not for his books but thinks only of Layla. See how he stares at her like a love-stricken sheep!"

Then Qays tried to hide his love, but his eyes refused to stray from Layla's face. His schoolmates would follow him taunting, "Have you not heard that Qays loves Layla? Like a madman he stares at her, and chants her name!"

At last Qays could contain himself no longer and surrendered to his passion. In the classroom, as the others recited their lessons, he shouted "Layla! Layla!" And he ran through the streets and the bazaars, calling out her name, praising her black eyes and her raven hair. People looked after him and shook their heads. "Indeed, he is a madman, a *majnun,*" they said. And so it was that Qays came to be called Majnun.

Now it was not long before word of Majnun's infatuation reached the ears of Layla's father, and the chieftain was greatly incensed. "Who is this Majnun, that he should speak Layla's name in the bazaars and thus insult my daughter and my tribe?" And so the chieftain ordered that Layla be taken from the school at once and brought to the desert camp and confined in a tent alone.

Majnun was sick at heart. For several days he sat listlessly before his open books, staring sadly at her empty place. When he could no longer bear Layla's absence, he closed his books and fled to the bazaars. From dawn to dusk he wandered among the stalls, murmuring her name and sobbing with grief. So deeply did he suffer, and so strongly did he love, that his ravings became poems. Walking in the markets, Majnun, the possessed, composed love songs of the most exquisite beauty. And as he sang, the wind lifted his words, like leaves, and carried them into the desert. "Layla, Layla! May my songs fall at your feet!" he cried.

And every night, when darkness fell, Majnun followed his songs into the desert. With two or three faithful companions who were still his friends, he crept into the camp of Layla's tribe. Approaching her tent, he hid behind a tree, hoping for a glimpse of his beloved. One night Layla, restless and sleepless, sat at the door of her tent. Majnun suddenly appeared. In the moonlight they gazed at one another, unbelievingly and trembling with love; neither could say a word. It was not until the sky reddened with dawn that Majnun turned and hastened back to his own camp lest he be discovered.

From that day on, his passion burned even more fiercely; like a thorn-bush set afire Majnun was consumed by love. And as he lost his heart, so he lost his reason. Leaving the camp of the Banu Amir, he wandered in the desert and the mountains of Najd. And as he went he tore his robes, shouted Layla's name, and wildly sang his songs. He went alone, for his friends despaired of him and left. From afar people would point to him and say, "There goes Majnun, that madman who was once called Qays. For love of Layla does he wander in the wilderness and bring dishonor on his father and his tribe."

Now when Majnun fled into the wilderness, the good *sayyid* grieved greatly. He called his counselors to him. "Indeed, my son has lost his heart," he said. "His senses are confused, for without Layla does he live in darkness. If he should win her, surely he will find his light." And thus did the *sayyid* resolve to go to Layla's father and ask the chieftain for her hand. The next morning, as the sun rose in the sky, a search party went into the desert to find Majnun. At the same time the *sayyid* set out for Layla's camp. His camels were laden with many precious gifts, and his hopes were brighter even than the rising sun.

But when he went before the chieftain and told why he had come, the chieftain spoke harshly, for he was a proud man. "Who has not heard of Majnun's madness?" he declared. "My daughter will not marry him! See first that your son is cured, then come to me again. For even if I were to grant your wish, as surely as the sun beats down upon the desert sand, Layla's name will soon again be heard in the bazaars, and every man in all Arabia will laugh at me!"

The *sayyid* sadly shook his head and returned to his own camp. There he found Majnun, and told his son what Layla's father had said. "Why must you worship only Layla?" he asked. "Indeed, among our tribe there are a thousand lovely maidens. Choose one as your wife, and forget Layla. Then you will be happy!"

But Majnun only cried out in despair and fled once more into the wilderness. He stumbled across the burning sand, thorns caught at his robes, and still he called "Layla! Layla!" And he tore at his hair and sang his songs until the desert resounded with his words. As he passed through one village and then another, all who heard him marveled at his eloquence; they pitied him and wept. Yet Majnun saw them not, nor did he hear their weeping, or even the sound of his own voice, for he could think only of Layla. At last, like a burnt-out candle, he fell exhausted to his knees and, whispering Layla's name once more, prayed to God for death. "I am an outcast. I bring only shame upon my tribe. Let me die now, for there is no hope for me in life!" Thus he sighed and sank onto the sand.

No sooner had he fainted than a group of shepherds gathered. They prepared a litter for him and carried him gently across the desert to the camp of the Banu Amir. There he lay in his own tent singing his songs and calling Layla's name. And his father's sorrow was no less than Majnun's. "Would that Majnun had never set eyes on Layla, for no longer do I have a son!" he lamented.

With a heavy heart, he called his counselors to him once more. To the eldest he said, "Does not the whole world go to Mecca, to ask God's blessing? Let us, too, make a pilgrimage, and pray to God that Majnun should be cured."

And so it was that in the month of pilgrimage, the last month of the year, the *sayyid* and his closest kinsmen departed from their camp and traveled to Mecca. For this journey the *sayyid* chose his best camels. A litter was devised for Majnun, and as the caravan crossed the desert, Majnun was carried as gently as if he were an infant in his cradle. At last they entered Mecca, and the *sayyid* showered gold coins, as alms, upon the crowds of people in the streets. Then, trembling with hope, he brought Majnun before the shrine, and, taking his hand, said softly, "My son, ask God to save you from your passion; pray to Him to end your madness. Surely you will be cured."

When Majnun heard these words, he wept bitterly. Then he laughed wildly and stretched out his hands toward the shrine, the Kaaba. In supplication, he touched the shrine. "I pray to You, let me not be cured of love, but let my passion grow!" he cried. "Take what is left of my life and give it to Layla's, yet let me never demand from her so much as a single hair! Let me love for love's sake, and make my love a hundred times as great as it is this very day!"

As Majnun so prayed the *sayyid* listened silently and bowed his head with grief. Then they returned to their camp. When they arrived, the *sayyid* told his kinsmen, "I have tried, but never will Majnun be cured, for before the holy Kaaba he has blessed Layla and cursed himself."

Now everyone in the city of Mecca heard of Majnun's prayer, and there was none in the land of Arabia who did not speak of it. When word reached the camp of Layla's tribe, the chieftain thundered with rage and vowed to kill Majnun. But first he sent two messengers to the court of the sultan to register his complaint. "Magnificence," they said, "this Majnun is a man possessed and does dishonor to our tribe. Order him to be punished at once, so that the name of Layla will be unstained."

Then the sultan's prefect drew his sword. "So be it; let him be punished as you wish."

Now it happened that a kinsman of the Banu Amir was in the sultan's court and heard what had been said. He hastened to the *sayyid* to warn him of the threat to Majnun's life, but Majnun had again fled into the desert. Greatly alarmed, the *sayyid* with his tribesmen searched the wilderness until Majnun was found, in a desolate gorge, writhing like a snake, moaning and sighing, and rising and falling upon the rocks. Tenderly the good *sayyid* gathered his son into his arms, weeping bitterly. So too did Majnun weep. "My father, there is no creature on earth who is not ruled by destiny," he said. "To love Layla is my fate, and never can I throw off my burden. But listen to me, for I have a tale to tell.

"Once upon a time, a partridge went hunting in a field and spied an ant, which she seized in her beak by one of its legs. The ant laughed and said, 'You are a skillful hunter, partridge, yet it is a pity that you cannot laugh as I do!' Whereupon the partridge opened her beak to laugh, and the ant escaped. Then the partridge saw how foolish she had been. So it is with man, for he will regret his laughter with bitter tears. Yet I will have nothing to regret, for I have no cause to laugh." And Majnun wept and called out Layla's name.

Then Majnun was carried from the rocky gorge to his own tent, and his kinswomen brought food and water, and his mother whispered many soothing words. But Majnun, staring blankly into the cool darkness of the tent, did not even know her. Several days passed, and when he could rest no longer, he tore open the curtain of his tent and fled again into the desert of the Najd; he roamed under the blistering sun until his face was black and his feet bled from the thorns and rocks. "Let Layla's father threaten, for I fear him not! What lover fears a sword?" he asked. "He who goes in search of his beloved cares not for his life!"

So Majnun sang his songs, and from villages and towns both near and far the people came to hear him. They copied down the words, even as they were moved to tears, and carried the poems away with them. And when they knew love themselves, it was with Majnun's words that they sang of the stirrings and the passion of their hearts, for Majnun spoke for lovers everywhere.

Meanwhile, Layla grew more and more beautiful. Indeed, she was the most beautiful maiden in all Arabia. But every day she grew more sorrowful, for from that evening when she had seen Majnun in the moonlight, she had never ceased to love him. From sunrise until sunset, she secretly whispered his name, and in the darkness of night, weeping and sighing, she would go to the door of her tent and listen for his step and watch for his shadow. But she heard only the desert wind, stirring the sand and leaves of the distant trees. She did not have to wait long before she heard his love poems, for they were on the lips of every child in the bazaars and every traveler in the desert. By day, she would repeat them to herself; then, in the secrecy of night, she would fashion songs in response. And indeed, her songs were no less eloquent than Majnun's, for as true as Majnun's was her love. She wrote her songs on scraps of paper, and strew them on the sand; the wind carried them into the villages. Thus did people come upon them, as one stumbles on a precious jewel, and sing them. Soon the songs reached Majnun's ears, and he would sing a reply. As their words were carried back and forth across the desert, so did Layla and Majnun promise one another their undying love.

Now there was a palm grove a short distance from Layla's tent, and every day Layla would go there with her companions. One afternoon, while her friends played among the trees and danced on the green grass which spread around them like an emerald carpet, Layla sat apart, thinking of Majnun and weeping with longing. Suddenly she heard a voice singing loudly outside the garden walls. "How can it be," the voice rang out, "that Layla can dance joyfully in her garden, while her beloved wanders in the wilderness alone?"

When Layla heard this reproach, she wept so bitterly and so mournfully spoke Majnun's name, that none who saw her, not even the most obdurate stone, could remain unmoved. Indeed, one of her companions happened to hear the song, and came upon the weeping Layla; tears of pity filled her eyes. She went to Layla's mother and told what she had heard and seen. Thus did the good woman learn of her daughter's suffering, for never had Layla spoken a word to her about it.

That very day, as it happened, a young man of the tribe of Assad was journeying across the desert and passed by the grove. This Ibn Salam, for such was the young man's name, happened to catch a glimpse of Layla through a chink in the garden wall and immediately fell in love with her. Now Ibn Salam was of a rich and noble family, and he went at once before the chieftain to ask for Layla's hand. The chieftain was well pleased and readily agreed, but asked only that the youth curb his eagerness. "Be patient for a while, my friend," he said. "In but a few months more the bud will blossom into a full-blown rose; then shall the wedding feast be set."

"Meanwhile, Majnun still wandered in the desert, dressed in his rags, singing his songs, and crying 'Layla! Layla!' He took shelter among some rocks in a gorge where wild animals lived. And one day, a Bedouin prince named Nowfal came upon the gorge and the unhappy Majnun. When he asked his attendants who the mournful creature was, they told of Majnun's suffering. The prince was deeply moved, for while he was brave in battle, he was gentle and kind of heart. Thus he caused a banquet to be set before Majnun. But Majnun would eat no food and drink no wine, and he uttered no word but "Layla!" Then the good prince took his hand and gently said, "My friend, listen to me, for I have heard your story and I wish only to help you. Trust me, and you shall find Layla and shall have her for your own, to love all of your life. Indeed, you shall have Layla, even if I must do battle!"

At these kind words, Majnun arose and embraced Nowfal and went with him to his camp. Under the prince's gracious influence, Majnun became the cheerful youth he had once been. He wore fine robes and a silk turban. Every morning, as the sky brightened with the first rays of the sun, he rode into the wilderness with Nowfal and they would ride all day. Every evening, when darkness fell, he feasted with the prince and called for wine and listened to the songs of minstrels. Happy were these days, when Majnun's sorrow was allayed. When he looked upon his friend, none was more joyful than Nowfal.

Thus did several months pass, until, one afternoon, the two friends sat together in the shade of a tree, resting from their ride. Majnun sighed bitterly and said, "Good prince, my patience has come to its end. I beg of you, help me find Layla as you promised, for if I must wait even a moment longer, surely I shall die." So mournful did he look that Nowfal leaped to his feet at once, took up his sword, and summoned his men to arms. The next day, at dawn, he rode across the desert with Majnun at his side. When they reached the pasturelands of Layla's tribe and saw the tents on the horizon, they pitched camp. Then Nowfal sent a messenger to Layla's father. "Tell the chieftain that you come to him in Majnun's name and that Majnun must have Layla. Tell him, too, that if he should refuse, in Majnun's name will I attack!"

When the chieftain heard this threat, he was enraged. "Rather than give my daughter to this madman, I will fight like a lion and even die!"

Then Nowfal sent an even stronger threat to the chieftain, and with many curses the chieftain refused. So Nowfal set upon Layla's people, and the desert resounded with the clash of war. In the midst of the fighting, Majnun huddled and wept and prayed for peace. He could not fight, for every injury to Layla's tribesmen was as a wound to him. Indeed, he would have drawn his bow and arrow against his own army had not shame stayed his hand. At last, as the sun descended in all its crimson glory, a truce was called and both armies retreated to their camps. Nowfal again sent a messenger to the chieftain, offering many jewels and precious gifts in return for Layla, the most precious jewel of all. The chieftain scornfully refused. His army greatly outnumbered Nowfal's, for he had summoned many tribesmen from surrounding pastures and hunting grounds. But the next morning Nowfal left his camp and went to amass an even greater force, enlisting tribesmen from Medina all the way to Baghdad, and the fighting began anew. At dawn one day Nowfal attacked; by dusk the chieftain was defeated and knelt at Nowfal's feet. "I am a weak old man," he said. "I have no strength; my men are all dispersed. Do what you will with me, but there is only one thing I ask. Give Layla not to Majnun, for he is a fool and has disgraced his name and hers!"

Now Nowfal, as we have said, was gentle of heart, and when the chieftain spoke, tears of compassion rose to the prince's eyes. Had not Nowfal gone to battle for the sake of Majnun? And had not Majnun kissed the bodies of Layla's kinsmen as they fell dead? Was Majnun not a traitor as well as a madman? Thus, with a heavy sigh, Nowfal agreed to the chieftain's request and bid him farewell.

Then he gave the order to break camp. Whereupon Majnun turned to the prince and spoke many bitter words; he then took his few possessions and rode off into the desert. Trembling with rage and weeping with despair, he cried out "Layla! Layla!" And his cries echoed across the dunes. Greatly alarmed, Nowfal went in search of Majnun the next morning, but he was nowhere to be found, and Nowfal saw him not that day, or the day after, or ever again.

For many days Majnun rode deep into the desert; he saw not a living soul, only stones and thorn-bushes and miles of sand. Suddenly he came upon two gazelles caught in a trap. A hunter was standing over them with his dagger raised. When Majnun looked into the gentle eyes of the gazelles he remembered Layla's soft black eyes, and he cried, "I beg of you, good hunter, do not kill!"

"Indeed, I am a poor man with a wife and family to feed," the hunter said. "For two months have I waited for this catch. What will you give me in exchange for the gazelles?"

Whereupon Majnun dismounted from his horse and placed the reins in the hunter's hands. The hunter rode off. Majnun freed the gazelles, and they ran gracefully away. Now Majnun walked in the desert. Thorn tore at his robes and scratched his feet, but he noticed not as he stumbled through the hot sand calling out Layla's name.

The next day Majnun came upon a stag caught in a net and wounded in the neck. Standing over the stag was a hunter with his knife drawn. "I beg of you, good hunter, release this stag at once!" cried Majnun. "Do you not think of the pain of those whose suffering you cause?"

"I do not wish to kill the stag," the hunter said, "but how will I survive? What will you give me if I let the stag go free?" Whereupon Majnun gave to the hunter all that remained of his possessions, and the hunter went off. Then Majnun freed the stag and watched it make its way across the sand. Majnun continued walking in the desert calling out Layla's name.

On the third day, the sun glared down so fiercely that the sand seemed to shimmer, and Majnun sat in the shade of a date palm tree. Now on a branch of the tree there sat a crow, and Majnun spoke to the bird. "Why are you dressed in black? Do you share my sorrow, that your feathers are as black as Layla's hair? If you do mourn, like me, why don't you leave me." The crow did not answer, but hopped onto another branch, then flew away into the stifling air. And so Majnun sat alone all day, until the sun set and the sky turned red, then blue, till it became blacker even than the feathers of the crow.

Then Majnun slept, and at the dawn, when he awoke, he saw an old woman dragging by a rope an old man whose legs and arms were bound with chains. When the old woman came near, Majnun asked her who she was and why the old man was in chains. She replied that she was a widow and he was a dervish and that they traveled through the desert in this way and begged for food and shared what scraps were thrown to them. Then Majnun fell to his knees. "It is I who should be in chains, not he!" he cried. "Free this man, and put this rope round my neck instead, and you shall have all of our food!"

The woman agreed, and she led Majnun through the wilderness. Whenever they came to a village, or even a shepherd's hut, Majnun would sing his songs and dance and hit his head upon the ground and cry out "Layla! Layla!" and they would be given scraps of food. Thus they wandered through the desert until, one day, they happened upon a camp. Majnun saw Layla's tent. He hit his head against a rock; tears streamed from his eyes, and he cried, "Layla! Layla! I have caused your people to suffer at the hands of Nowfal. As punishment I am in chains. Behold me and my grief!" And, with a howl, he tore his chains apart and flung them from him. Then he cast away the rope and fled into the mountains.

Now it happened that after Nowfal's victory, the chieftain had told Layla of Nowfal's agreement. Layla had listened in silence and then had gone to her tent and wept, for never, not even for a moment, had her love for Majnun faltered. Soon after that, Ibn Salam came back to claim Layla as his bride. He came with many caravans laden with gifts and showered silks and gold upon the chieftain. Carpets were spread, and a wedding feast was set. For seven days and seven nights, and for seven days more, there was great celebration: fires were lit; incense of aloe was burned; silver coins were thrown into the air. Then, the next morning, when barely had the stars yielded to the rising sun, Ibn Salam departed with his bride. When the caravan reached the lands of the tribe of Assad, the joyful bridegroom said to Layla, "Everything you see is yours, my love!"

But that night, when he went to embrace her, Layla withdrew. When he still would take her in his arms, she struck him. "Come not within arm's length of me," she said, "for I have vowed never to give myself to you. Take your sword and kill me if you will, but I will not submit, not even in a hundred years!" So great was Ibn Salam's love for Layla, that he fell to his knees and asked her forgiveness, gently saying, "Rather would I be allowed to look upon your face than lose you forever." And thus did they live and so a year passed.

During that year Majnun wandered in the wilderness. One day, while he was lying in the sand exhausted, a stranger, a black-skinned man, passed by. Now he knew well who Majnun was and said to him, "Have you not heard? Layla is married! Her husband is rich and noble, and even this very moment does he hold her in his arms! Better to turn your back on Layla than to scorn the world, my friend!"

At these words, Majnun moaned with despair and fainted. When he at last opened his eyes, the stranger was overcome with pity. "My friend, forgive me, for I have been wicked and have spoken falsely. Layla is married, yet she loves you still and shares not her husband's bed. She is chaste and longs for you with all her heart and soul!"

Then the stranger departed, and Majnun stumbled through the desert, weeping and shaking to the depths of his being. In one breath, he called out Layla's name and sang his songs; in the next, he reproached her for betraying him; then he wept and cried out his forgiveness.

Now in all this time, the good *sayyid* grew weak with age. He grieved greatly for his son and resolved to go once more into the desert to find him. Taking a walking stick, he set out with two companions. After journeying for many days, he came upon a desolate cave where he found Majnun, wasted and drawn. When Majnun heard his father's voice, he wept. Then the *sayyid* said, "I beg of you, my son, come home, for I am close to death. When I die, I wish to have you at my side."

But Majnun shook his head; he heard his father's words but understood them not, for he knew only that he loved, not who he was or what was his name. And, weeping, he replied, "My father, I am lost to you and can never return. I live like the wild animals that roam around me; I am a stranger to my tribe." With sorrow in his heart, the *sayyid* saw that this was so. He left Majnun in his forsaken cave and returned to the camp of the Banu Amir, and shortly thereafter he died.

One day, while hunting in the desert, a kinsman came upon Majnun and told him of his father's death and spoke many bitter words. "Wicked son of a good father, may you pray for forgiveness for your sins!" At this doleful news Majnun wept; he went at once to his father's grave, and prayed for a day and a night for forgiveness. Then he went back into the wilderness.

When he returned to the cave, the animals of the desert came to his side. First the lion, then the very stag that he had saved, and then the antelope, and the wolf, and the fox; the wild ass joined their company, and the hare, and the timid gazelle. Majnun ruled over them all; a king was he, and his cave was his court. All around were rocks and thorns and burning sand. No place on earth was more desolate than this, yet Majnun called it paradise, for here he lived in peace with all his friends. Among the animals there was perfect harmony; the lion lay with the lamb; the wolf chased not the hare; the gazelle went undisturbed before the fox.

Every day, Majnun and his animals wandered in the wilderness and dug among the stones for roots and herbs. As the sun descended, they would feast together. Majnun would speak of Layla and sing his songs, and the beasts would listen quietly and sadly bow their heads. Then darkness fell. Majnun lay down to sleep; with his great bushy tail the fox swept clean Majnun's resting place. The wild ass was Majnun's pillow; his knees rested on the haunches of the antelope, and the gazelle caressed his feet. Throughout the night, until the break of dawn, the wolf kept watch.

For many hours at a time, Majnun would gaze fondly on his animals, and he was wont to say, "Now that I am among my friends, surely I am the happiest man of all!" And he would think upon a story he had heard, years before, of a young courtier at the palace of the king of Merv. This king kept a pack of ferocious dogs, and it was his wont, whenever anyone displeased him, to throw that person to the dogs to be devoured. When the youth heard the dogs' barking and the victims' cries and moans, he resolved to cultivate the friendship of the keeper of the dogs, and then he won the friendship of the dogs themselves. One day, the courtier aroused the king's anger, and the king ordered him thrown to the dogs. But the dogs would not harm the youth, for he was their friend. When the king saw this, he tamed the beast of his own soul.

So did the wild animals guard Majnun against harm. After some time, two visitors came into the wilderness and approached the cave. The first was an old man; he had flowing white hair and a face so kind and gentle that the lion's growling ceased and the wolf showed not his teeth. They let the old man pass. Majnun greeted him and asked, "My friend, what good news do you bring?"

211

Whereupon the old man brought forth a letter. Majnun seized it eagerly. "Know that I have seen Layla," the old man said. "One day I came upon her grieving in a garden; so great was her sorrow that I bade her speak. She wept and said, 'A thousand times madder am I than Majnun, for he is free to wander where he pleases, while I am but a prisoner in my camp. A thousand times greater than Majnun's are my torments. Though I cannot be with him, I hunger for news of him. Where does he go? What does he say? Has he companions? I beg of you, search for him until you find him, and tell me how he is!' Indeed, these are her very words. When I promised to search for you, she wrote this letter and gave it to me to give to you."

Then Majnun read Layla's letter; his heart quickened with joy, for all that the old man said was true. At once, he asked the old man for a paper and pen, and he wrote a reply. "I beg of you, take this to Layla, with my love!" he cried. And the old man rode into the desert, to Layla's camp, and brought the letter to her.

Now the second visitor to the cave was Majnun's uncle Salim Amiri. He came into the desert bringing food and clothing. Majnun was glad to see him, for his uncle was a good man and as a boy Majnun had loved him dearly. He put on the robes but gave the food to the wild beasts. When he did this his uncle sighed and said, "Listen to me, for I have a story to tell.

"Once upon a time, in this very land of Arabia, a king was riding in this very desert, and he happened to pass a hut. He learned that in this miserable dwelling there lived a dervish who hardly ate and never slept, and he sent an attendant to speak to the dervish. The dervish said that he ate only herbs gathered from the fields. 'Indeed, you should have far better food if you were in the service of the king,' said the attendant, but the dervish shook his head. When the king heard of this, he said, 'The dervish is a wise man, and he is superior even to me. He knows well the worth of what he has and is satisfied.' Then the king went into the hut and kissed the dervish's feet."

When Salim Amiri had finished his tale, he said that he would bring Majnun's mother to the desert, for she had grown old and greatly longed to see her son. When the good woman was brought to the cave, she wept and washed the dust from Majnun's body and plucked the thorns from his feet. All the while she pleaded with him to return to his people, but to no avail. "The Banu Amir are your people; they are mine no longer," Majnun said. "I know only the desert and my animals." Bent with sorrow, the old woman returned to her tribe. Shortly thereafter, she breathed her last. Then Salim Amiri again visited Majnun, and told him of his mother's death. Majnun went to her tomb and mourned and wept. There he met some of his kinsmen, and they spoke bitterly to him and reproached him angrily. After a day and a night, he again fled to the desert.

All this time Layla waited eagerly for an answer to her letter. Every night she slipped from her tent and stood at the crossroads of her village, watching and listening for the old man. At last, one night, he came and gave her Majnun's letter. When she read it, she rewarded the good man with jewels and a sack of coins and asked him to bring Majnun to a grove nearby. "The trees grow as thickly as a wall, so we shall not be seen. Tell my beloved that Layla longs to hear him sing his songs!"

And so it was that one night the old man led Majnun into the grove. The faithful animals followed and stood patiently outside. The old man brought Layla into the grove. She stayed at a distance from Majnun, for like a moth fatally drawn to a flame, she feared that she would perish. Instead she sat beneath a tree and listened, but heard not a sound, for Majnun had fainted. The old man revived him, and then he sang the most beautiful love poem he had ever composed. Then the lovers gazed upon each other with joy and wonder, as they had when they were children. But all too soon the moment passed; Majnun fled, and Layla went back to her tent.

When Majnun returned to his desolate cave, a young man came to him. Now this youth, whose name was Salam Baghdadi, begged Majnun to teach him his songs and poems. He stayed with Majnun in the desert and learned them all. Then he went to Baghdad and many other villages and cities and sang Majnun's words wherever he went, that all who loved might hear.

Soon after, Ibn Salam was taken ill with a fever as violent as the desert wind, and in a few days he was dead. At last Layla could weep without restraint, for all who looked upon her thought that she wept for her young husband, and they pitied her with all their hearts. Yet for Majnun only did she mourn. Now in Arabia it was the custom for a widow to seclude herself in her tent for two years, speaking to no one. Layla went dutifully to her tent; she welcomed the solitude and vowed that every moment she would think of Majnun.

This ritual she performed until autumn, when the trees blazed with color and the wind rose. During her many months of solitude Layla became so weak that she could no longer rise from her bed. Her weakness turned to fever, and she called her mother to her and told her what the good woman had known for many years. "Grant me one wish, my mother," Layla said. "When I die, for I am like an autumn leaf on the branches of the tree of life, I will be dressed in bridal robes. Thus shall I wait for my beloved, for surely Majnun will come to my grave. And I would have you comfort him as you would comfort me."

The next day, as the scarlet leaves fluttered to the ground, Layla died, and her mother did as she had promised. When Majnun heard of Layla's death, he went at once to her grave and wept from the depths of his soul. Indeed, he wept his heart's blood, and some say that as he wept, the flowers that grew at Layla's grave turned red. He sang his songs and again likened Layla to the graceful gazelle. For a month did Majnun stay at Layla's grave, guarded by his animals. As time passed he grew weaker and weaker. It was in a voice barely a whisper that he prayed to God to release him from his earthly form and bring him to Layla's side. Soon after his prayers were answered; his animals guarded his body with fierce growls, so that none could touch him. Only when he crumbled into dust did the animals go back to the wilderness. Then Majnun's tribesmen came forth and gathered his bones and buried them by Layla's side. All that day, and for many days after, there was mourning in the camp of the Banu Amir and in the camp of Layla's people. For many years the story of Layla and Majnun has been told and told again, for never did there live two lovers as true as they.

Poetry of Rumi

Mevlana Jalal ad-Din Rumi

Jalal ad-Din ar-Rumi, 1207–1273 C. E., is one of the greatest mystics of Islamic history. The son of a Persian scholar, Rumi lived most of his childhood in Konya in western Turkey, a city founded by the Romans; hence his name, Rumi, literally "The Roman."

In his adulthood Rumi became a religious teacher and a Sufi. The Sufis are the mystics of Islam; their practices aim at direct knowledge of God. At the age of 39 Rumi met a Sufi teacher who led him to a transformation—a taste of immediate, intimate experience of the Divine as the source of sure and certain knowledge. After this awakening, Rumi produced a six volume work of stories and poetry, the *Mathnawi,* that embodied Sufi spiritual teachings and lore.

Sufis seek extinction of the self, that is, to die to the world and to subsist only in God. Rumi was a *mevlevi* (*mawlawi*) Sufi, often called "whirling dervishes" for their use of song and dance to induce spiritual states.

Rumi's spiritual influence spread throughout the Persian-speaking world, Turkey, and India. To this day, his *Mathnawi* is revered by Persian speakers, most of whom memorize portions. The singing of the work has been raised to an art form.

Aron Aji

1

O lovers, lovers, this day you and we are fallen into a whirlpool: who knows how to swim?

Though the world's torrent should overflow and every wave become like a dromedary, why shall the waterfowl worry? It is the bird of the air that should be anxious.

Originally published in *Open Secret,* by Threshold Books, 129 Main Street, Brattleboro, VT 05301.

Our faces are lighted up with gratitude, schooled as we are in wave and sea, inasmuch as ocean and flood are life-increasing to the fish.

Elder, hand us a towel; water, let us plunge into you; Moses son of 'Imran, come, smite the water of the sea with your staff!

This wind concocts in every head a different passion; let my passion be for yonder cupbearer, and you may have all the rest!

Yesterday yon saki on the way snatched the caps of the drunkards; today he is giving yet more wine, preparing to strip us of our robes.

O envy of the Moon and of Jupiter, with us, yet hidden from sight like a peri, gently, gently you are drawing me on—will you not say whither?

Wherever you go, you are with me still, you who are my eyes and my brightness; if you will, draw me to drunkenness, if you will, transport me to annihilation.

Know that the world is like Mount Sinai, and we like Moses are seekers; every moment an epiphany arrives and cleaves the mountain asunder.

One portion becomes green, one portion becomes narcissus-white; one portion becomes a pearl, one portion ruby and amber.

You who seek to behold Him, gaze upon this mountainchain of His. O mountain, what wind has blown upon you? We have become intoxicated with the echo.

O gardener, gardener, why have you come to grapple with us? If we have carried off your grapes, you have carried off our purse!

2

Die now, die now, in this Love die; when you have died in this Love, you will all receive new life.

Die now, die now, and do not fear this death, for you will come forth from this earth and seize the heavens.

Die now, die now, and break away from this carnal soul, for this carnal soul is as a chain and you are as prisoners.

Take an axe to dig through the prison; when you have broken the prison you will all be kings and princes.

Die now, die now before the beauteous King; when you have died before the King, you will all be kings and renowned.

Die now, die now, and come forth from this cloud; when you come forth from this cloud, you will all be radiant full moons.

Be silent, be silent; silence is the sign of death; it is because of life that you are fleeing from the silent one.

Little by little the drunkards congregate, little by little the wine-worshippers arrive.

The heart-cherishers coquettishly come along the way, the rosy-cheeked ones are arriving from the garden.

Little by little from the world of being and not-being the not-beings have departed and the beings are arriving.

All with skirts full of gold as a mine are arriving for the sake of the destitute.

The lean and sick from the pasturage of love are arriving fat and hale.

The souls of the pure ones like the rays of the sun are arriving from such a height to the lowly ones.

Blessed is that garden, where, for the sake of the Mary's, new fruits are arriving even in winter.

Their origin is grace, and their return is grace; even from the garden to the garden they are coming.

I beheld the lovely rosebower face, that eye and lamp of all brightness,

That altar before which the soul prostrates, that gladness and place of security.

The heart said, "I will yield up my soul there, I will let go of being and selfhood."

The soul also joined in the concert and began to clap hands.

Reason came and said, "What shall I say regarding this good fortune and sublime felicity,

This scent of a rose that made upright as a cypress every back that was curved and bent double?"

In love all things are transformed; Armenian is changed to Turk.

Soul, you have attained to the Soul of the soul; body, you have abandoned bodyhood.

The ruby is the alms of our Beloved; the dervish eats the gold of the Rich;

That Mary in anguish discovers anew dates fresh and ripe.

Lest the eye of a stranger should fall upon it, do not show off your good deed to men;

If your desire from faith is security, seek your security in seclusion.

What is the place of seclusion? The house of the heart; become habituated to dwell in the heart;

In the heart's house is delivered that bowl of wholesome and everlasting wine.

Be silent, and practise the art of silence; let go all artful bragging;

For the heart is the place of faith, there in the heart hold fast to faithfulness.

5

Hark, for I am at the door! Open the door; to bar the door is not the sign of good pleasure.

In the heart of every action is a courtyard for You; until You unbar it, it will remain in concealment.

You are the Splitter of Dawn, the Lord of the Daybreak; You open a hundred doors and say, "Come in!"

It is not I at the door, but You; grant access, open the door to Yourself.

Sulphur came to a fire; it said, "Come out to me, beloved!

My form is not your form, but I am all you, my form is as a veil.

I become you in form and reality when you arrive, my form is blotted out in the encounter."

The fire replied, "I have come forth; why should I veil my face from my very self?"

Hark, receive from me and deliver my message to all the companions and all the kinsmen.

If it is a mountain, draw it like a straw; I have given you the quality of amber.

My amber draws the mountain; did I not bring forth Mount Hira out of nonexistence?

I am wholly and completely within your heart, for the pearl of the heart was born of my ocean.

I move my shadow, otherwise how is it that my shadow is apart from me? But I transport it from its place so that, at the time of unveiling, its union may become manifest,

So that it may realize that it is a branch of me, so that it may become separated from all other.

Go to the saki and hear the rest of it, that he may tell you it with the tongue of immortality.

6

Today I beheld the beloved, that ornament of every affair; he went off departing to heaven like the spirit of Mustafa.

The sun is put to shame by his countenance, heaven's sphere is as confused as the heart; through his glow, water and clay are more resplendent than fire.

I said, "Show me the ladder, that I may mount up to heaven." He said, "Your head is the ladder; bring your head down under your feet."

When you place your feet on your head, you will place your feet on the head of the stars; when you cleave through the air, set your foot on the air, so, and come!

A hundred ways to heaven's air become manifest to you; you go flying up to heaven every dawning like a prayer.

7

Walk to the well.
Turn as the earth and the moon turn,
circling what they love.
Whatever circles comes from the center.

8

Grapes under feet that crush them
turn whichever way they are turned.

You ask why I turn around you?
Not around you, I turn around myself.

9

Gone, inner and outer,
no moon, no ground or sky.
Don't hand me another glass of wine.
Pour it in my mouth.
I've lost the way to my mouth.

10

A secret turning in us
makes the universe turn.
Head unaware of feet,
and feet head. Neither cares.
They keep turning.

11

One day you will take me completely out of my self,
I'll do what the angels cannot do.

Your eyelash will write on my cheek
the poem that hasn't been thought of.

12

My turban, my robe, my head, those three
for less than a penny.
My self, my name, not to be mentioned,
less than nothing.

Originally published in *Unseen Rain*, by Threshold Books, 129 Main Street, Brattleboro, VT 05301.

13

This moment this love comes to rest in me,
many beings in one being.
In one wheat-grain a thousand sheaf stacks.
Inside the needle's eye, a turning night of stars.

14

Two hands, two feet, two eyes, good,
as it should be, but no separation
of the Friend and your loving.

Any dividing there
makes other untrue distinctions like "Jew,"
and "Christian," and "Muslim."

15

When your love reaches the core,
earth-heavals and bright irruptions spew in the air.

The universe becomes one spiritual thing, that simple,
love mixing with spirit.

16[5]

Don't forget the nut, being so proud of the shell.
The body has its inward ways,

the five senses. They crack open,
and the Friend is revealed.
Crack open the Friend, you become
the All-One.

17

We don't need wine to get drunk,
or instruments and singing to feel ecstatic.
No poets, no leaders, no songs,
yet we jump around totally wild.

18

From the wet source someone
cuts a reed to make a flute.
The reed sips breath like wine
sips more, practicing. Now dry
it starts the high clear notes.

19

Who ever saw such drunkards?
Barrels broken open, the ground and starry
ceiling soaked. And look,
this full glass in my hand.

20

During the day I was singing with you.
At night we slept in the same bed.
I wasn't conscious day or night.
I thought I knew who I was,
but I was you.

21

The sufi opens his hands to the universe
and gives away each instant, free.
Unlike someone who begs on the street for money to
survive,
a dervish begs to give you his life.

22

Drinking wine with you, getting warmer and warmer,
I think why not trade in this overcoat
made of leaves and dirt.
Then I look out the window.
For what? Both worlds are here.

23

Today, like every other day, we wake up empty
and frightened. Don't open the door to the study
and begin reading. Take down the dulcimer.

Let the beauty we love be what we do.
There are hundreds of ways to kneel and kiss the
ground.

24

They say that Paradise will be perfect
with lots of clear white wine and all the beautiful women.
We hold on to times like this then,
since this is how it's going to be.

Fasting

There's hidden sweetness in the stomach's emptiness.
We are lutes, no more, no less. If the soundbox
is stuffed full of anything, no music.
If the brain and the belly are burning clean
with fasting, every moment a new song comes out of the fire.
The fog clears, and new energy makes you
run up the steps in front of you.
Be emptier and cry like reed instruments cry.
Emptier, write secrets with the reed pen.
When you're full of food and drink, Satan sits
where your spirit would, an ugly metal statue
in place of the Kaaba. When you fast,
good habits gather like friends who want to help.
Fasting is Solomon's ring. Don't give it
to some illusion and lose your power,
but even if you have, if you've lost all will and control,
they come back when you fast, like soldiers appearing
out of the ground, pennants flying above them.
A table descends to your tents,
Jesus's table.
Expect to see it, when you fast, this table
spread with other food, better than the broth of cabbages.

Revolutionary France

Cahiers of Dourdan

When Louis XVI convoked the Estates-General in the fall of 1788, he also called upon his subjects to draft *cahiers de doléances,* or grievance lists, expressing their views about needed reforms in the kingdom. When the clergy, nobility, and commoners convened their separate electoral assemblies in the spring of 1789, they drafted their *cahiers,* most of which still exist in the French National Archives. These grievance lists tell us a great deal about what was on the minds of French men as the Old Regime teetered on the brink of revolution.

This extraordinary gesture of the king had two important impacts. First, it served to politicize the populace, heightening awareness about the problems confronting the country and giving people the sense that something could, and ought to, be done about them. Second, it raised expectations among the people, and when the deputies at Versailles failed to move swiftly on a program of reform the people grew impatient and restive.

Paul Hanson

Cahier of the Clergy of Dourdan
27 March, 1789

Although not as reactionary in tone as many of the cahiers of the clergy, this document indicates adequately the conservative point of view which characterized the first estate of France. . . .

When the King summons his subjects about him to consult them concerning the needs of the State, the ministers of religion are among the most eager to give him proof of their respectful gratitude. Their dual role as citizens and ecclesiastics entitles them to bring to the foot of the throne the most comprehensive wishes for the welfare of the monarchy and the maintenance of a religion that assures its tranquility. Accordingly, His Majesty shall be humbly supplicated:

Chapter I Religion

1. To preserve in its integrity the precious depository of the Catholic, Apostolic, and Roman religion, the most stable support of the fundamental laws of the State, to effect the enforcement of ordinances concerning the respect which is due churches, sanctification of feast days and Sundays, and, in general, whatever affects public worship.

2. To give consideration to the representations made by the last assembly of the clergy concerning the edict on non-Catholics[1] and not to permit any religion other than the Catholic to hold worship or give public instruction. . . .

5. Imbued with profound grief at the sight of the appalling deterioration of religion and the depravation of morals in the kingdom, we direct to His Majesty the most ardent and humble representations concerning the disastrous and widely acknowledged cause of this deplorable subversion of all principles. It obviously derives from the disgraceful excess of writings in which the spirit of libertinage, incredulity, and independence prevails, in which faith, modesty, reason, the throne, and the altar are attacked with equal audacity—impious and corrupting books circulated on all sides with the most revolting profusion and licence, to which the strongest resistance could not be too promptly opposed.

6. Since diversity of religious opinion in the schools for French youth is the greatest danger in the world, His Majesty shall be humbly supplicated also to order all necessary precautions lest there be admitted into any of the universities and academic societies of the kingdom any teacher or member who has not previously given proofs of the greatest ability and of his respectful devotion to the Catholic religion.

7. Since national education is degenerating daily, the King will be willing to take into consideration a matter so pertinent to morals and to the glory of the kingdom, and in his wisdom to provide resources for the talents of indigence by the endowment of the provincial colleges, almost all of which are insufficiently endowed, because a good education is the only means of assuring the State of good citizens, and religion of virtuous ministers. . .

Chapter II Constitution

1. Since monarchical government is the steadfast constitution of the nation the most conducive to its internal tranquility and external security the most suitable for the extent of its provinces, and the most consistent with the character of its people, who always have distinguished themselves by their love for and devotion to their sovereigns, we will never countenance anything that would tend to alter this form of government. We are inviolably attached to it by the most sacred duties of obedience, by ties of oath and fidelity, by love and respect for our masters, and by the happiness of being subject thereto.

---

1   Representation refers to the vigorous protests of the Catholic clergy on the occasion of the granting, by the second Assembly of Notables, of the famous Edict of Toleration of 1787. For the edict itself see Jourdan, *Recueil général des anciennes lois françaises,* v. 28, pp. 472–482.

2. We desire that in matters brought under deliberation in the Estates General relative to all orders, voting be by head; but in those concerning more especially one of the three orders, we request that voting be by order. . . .

Cahier of the Nobles of Dourdan
29 March, 1789

This cahier *represents a more enlightened attitude than is usually found in the requests made by the nobility. It is interesting to note that just as the clergy of Dourdan had criticisms to make of the nobles, so, in turn, the nobles saw faults in their privileged ecclesiastical contemporaries. The inclusion of a section dealing with commerce is suggestive of new interests on the part of the Second Estate. The last section of the document indicates that the "nobles of the sword" were not yet willing to give full recognition to "the nobles of the robe."*

Constitution

The citizens comprising the order of the nobility of the *bailliage* of Dourdan consider that, as soon as the Estates General is convened and the assembly constituted, an address should be voted to the King to thank him for the magnanimous act of justice he has just accorded the nation in restoring its rights, and to pledge to him, in the name of all Frenchmen, unlimited gratitude and love, inviolable submission and fidelity to his sacred person, his legitimate authority, and his august royal house. They would doubtless wish to use this liberty first in paying him new homage of their blood and fortune; but they wish more, they wish to contribute with all their power to the personal happiness of His Majesty, as well as to the general welfare of his people, by working in concert with him to bolster the tottering edifice of the French Constitution, by rendering his faithful commons happier through a just distribution of the taxes necessary to the State, by freeing him of the troubles and anxieties which extensive and absolute legislation necessarily entails; finally, by leaving to him only favors to grant and benefits to dispense throughout the free nation that he governs; thus the subjects of all orders, encompassing the Monarch with their liberty, their happiness, and their unlimited devotion, will render him, if possible, still more beloved throughout his realm, and assuredly more respected abroad.

Accordingly the noble citizens of the *bailliage* of Dourdan request:

That the legislative power reside collectively in the hands of the King and the united nation. . . .

Since the constitutional laws assure each and every one of his liberty, fortune, position, and property, the nobility requests:

That every arbitrary order prejudicial to the liberty of citizens be abolished entirely;

That individual liberty be assured and guaranteed, so that every citizen arrested may be placed in the prisons of the courts which are to take cognizance of his offence within twenty-four hours of the time of his arrest; that, immediately upon his detention, he be permitted to choose a counsel or advocate. . . .

That liberty of the press be granted, upon condition that author and printer are responsible; and the Estates General shall determine the most severe restrictions in order to prevent such liberty from degenerating into licence.

The nobility of the *bailliage* of Dourdan requests, likewise, that, according to the formal wish of His Majesty, no tax be established and no loan be made without the concurrence of the legislative power.

That the administrator of finances be not permitted to make any anticipation or assignment other than on the annual income, under penalty for *lése-patrie,* the lenders to forfeit all claim. . . .

That all property, whoever be the owner, be inviolable and sacred, property being whatever one owns on public faith and on the affirmation of the law; that no one be deprived thereof except for public interest, and that he then be compensated therefor without delay, and at the highest possible price.

Finally, that ministers henceforth be responsible and accountable to the Estates General. . . .

The order of nobility desires further that the distinction of three orders in the Estates General be strengthened and regarded as inherent in the Constitution of the French monarchy, and that opinions be given therein only by order.

That in the event, however, that vote by order be absolutely rejected by the Estates General, and the deputy of the *bailliage* of Dourdan see that further resistance to vote by head is useless, he then request that vote by head be taken in the separate chamber of every order and not in the assembly of the three orders united.

That vote by head never take place on matters of particular interest to one of the three orders alone. . . .

Justice

That venality of offices be generally abolished, and that the Estates General consider the wisest means of reimbursing officeholders, at the same time undertaking to fill the vacant offices by election. . . .

Finally, the nobility declares that, in order to evince its sentiments of esteem, natural equity, and affection for its fellow citizens of the third estate, it wishes to share with them, in proportion to the property and possessions of all orders, whatever imposts and taxes are approved by the nation; claiming to reserve only the sacred rights of property, the prerogatives of rank, honor, and dignity which must appertain to it according to the constitutional principles of the French monarchy.

Cahier of the Third Estate of Dourdan
29 March, 1789

The demands made in this cahier should be compared with Sieyes' attitude concerning the Third Estate. . . .

The order of the third estate of the City, *Bailliage,* and County of Dourdan, imbued with gratitude prompted by the paternal kindness of the King, who deigns to restore its former rights and its former constitution, forgets at this moment its misfortunes and impotence, to harken only to its foremost sentiment and its foremost duty, that of sacrificing everything to the glory of the *Patrie* and the service of His Majesty. It supplicates him to accept the grievances, complaints, and remonstrances which it is permitted to bring to the foot of the throne, and to see therein only the expression of its zeal and the homage of its obedience.
It wishes:

1. That his subjects of the third estate, equal by such status to all other citizens, present themselves before the common father without other distinction which might degrade them.

2. That all the orders, already united by duty and a common desire to contribute equally to the needs of the State, also deliberate in common concerning its needs.

3. That no citizen lose his liberty except according to law; that, consequently, no one be arrested by virtue of special orders, or, if imperative circumstances necessitate such orders, that the prisoner be handed over to the regular courts of justice within forty-eight hours at the latest.

4. That no letters or writings intercepted in the post be the cause of the detention of any citizen, or be produced in court against him, except in case of conspiracy or undertaking against the State.

5. That the property of all citizens be inviolable, and that no one be required to make sacrifice thereof for the public welfare, except upon assurance of indemnification based upon the statement of freely selected appraisers. . . .

9. That the national debt be verified; that the payment of arrears of said debt be assured by such indirect taxes as may not be injurious to the husbandry, industry, commerce, liberty, or tranquility of the citizens.

10. That an annual reimbursement fund be established to liquidate the capital of the debt.

11. That as one part of the debt is liquidated, a corresponding part of the indirect tax also be liquidated.

12. That every tax, direct or indirect, be granted only for a limited time, and that every collection beyond such term be regarded as peculation, and punished as such. . . .

15. That every personal tax be abolished; that thus the *capitation* and the *taille* and its accessories be merged with the *vingtièmes* in a tax on land and real or nominal property.

16. That such tax be borne equally, without distinction, by all classes of citizens and by all kinds of property, even feudal and contingent rights.

Justice

3. That seigneurial courts of justice created by purely gratuitous right be suppressed. . . .

7. That venality of offices be suppressed by successive reimbursement in proportion to their disestablishment; that, accordingly, a fund be constituted forthwith to effect such reimbursement. . . .

9. That all exceptional jurisdictions, *élections, maîtrises,* salt stores, and financial bureaux be suppressed as useless and productive of lawsuits and jurisdictional conflicts; . . .

13. That military ordinances which restrict entrance to the service to those possessing nobility be reformed.

What Is the Third Estate?

Emmanuel-Joseph Sieyès

By February, 1789, the elections had begun. They took place, for the most part, in an atmosphere of turmoil intensified by the complex electoral technique and the continued economic distress. Of all the external forces affecting the elections one of the most vital was the growing intellectual ferment which had derived a powerful stimulus from the Order in Council of 5 July, 1788. One of the most significant aspects of this ferment was the appearance of numerous critical pamphlets. One of the most outstanding of these pamphlets was Abbé Sieyès' *What is the Third Estate?* . . .

This pamphlet appeared in January, 1789, and attracted a wide public. Sieyès' treatment of the already familiar gospel of the importance of the Third Estate imparted a new vitality to his theme. The sixth chapter of the pamphlet provided the basis of the plan eventually followed in transforming the Estates General into a National Constituent Assembly.

[From *A Documentary Survey of the French Revolution*, John Hall Steward, editor]

The plan of this pamphlet is very simple. We have three questions to ask:

1st. What is the third estate? Everything.

2nd. What has it been heretofore in the political order? Nothing.

3rd. What does it demand? To become something therein.

We shall see if the answers are correct. Then we shall examine the measures that have been tried and those which must be taken in order that the third estate may in fact become *something*. Thus we shall state:

4th. What the ministers have *attempted,* and what the privileged classes themselves propose in its favor.

5th. What *ought* to have been done.

6th. Finally, what remains to be done in order that the third estate may take its rightful place.

Chapter I   The Third Estate Is a Complete Nation

What are the essentials of national existence and prosperity? *Private* enterprise and *public* functions.

Private enterprise may be divided into four classes: 1st. Since earth and water furnish the raw material for man's needs, the first class will comprise all families engaged in agricultural pursuits. 2nd. Between the original sale of materials and their consumption or use, further workmanship more or less manifold, adds to these materials a second value, more or less compounded. Human industry thus succeeds in perfecting the benefits of nature and in increasing the gross produce twofold, tenfold, one hundredfold in value. Such is the work of the second class. 3rd. Between production and consumption, as well as among the different degrees of production, a group of intermediate agents useful to producers as well as to consumers, comes into being; these are the dealers and merchants. . . . 4th. In addition to these three classes of industrious and useful citizens concerned with goods for consumption and use, a society needs many private undertakings and endeavors which are *directly* useful or agreeable to the *individual*. This fourth class includes from the most distinguished scientific and liberal professions to the least esteemed domestic services. Such are the labors which sustain society. Who performs them? The third estate.

Public functions likewise under present circumstances may be classified under four well known headings: the Sword, the Robe, the Church, and the Administration. It is unnecessary to discuss them in detail in order to demonstrate that the third estate everywhere constitutes nineteen-twentieths of them, except that it is burdened with all that is really arduous, with all the tasks that the privileged order refuses to perform. Only the lucrative and honorary positions are held by members of the privileged order . . . nevertheless they have dared lay the order of the third estate under an interdict. They have said to it: "Whatever be your services, whatever your talents, you shall go thus far and no farther. It is not fitting that you be honored."

. . .

It suffices here to have revealed that the alleged utility of a privileged order to public service is only a chimera; that without it, all that is arduous in such service is performed by the third estate; that without it, the higher positions would be infinitely better filled; that they naturally ought to be the lot of and reward for talents and recognized services; and that if the privileged classes have succeeded in usurping all the lucrative and honorary positions, it is both an odious injustice to the majority of citizens and a treason to the commonwealth.

Who, then, would dare to say that the third estate has not within itself all that is necessary to constitute a complete nation? It is the strong and robust man whose one arm remains enchained. If the privileged order were abolished, the nation would be not something less but something more. Thus, what is the third estate? Everything; but an everything shackled and oppressed. What would it be without the privileged order? Everything; but an everything free and flourishing.

Nothing can progress without it; everything would proceed infinitely better without the others. It is not sufficient to have demonstrated that the privileged classes, far from being useful to the nation, can only enfeeble and injure it; it is necessary, moreover, to prove that the nobility does not belong to the social organization at all; that, indeed, it may be a burden upon the nation, but that it would not know how to constitute a part thereof. [1]

What is a nation? a body of associates living under a common law and represented by the same legislature.

Is it not exceedingly clear that the noble order has privileges, exemptions, even rights separate from the rights of the majority of citizens? Thus it deviates from the common order, from the common law. Thus its civil rights already render it a people apart in a great nation. It is indeed *imperium in imperio.*

Also, it enjoys its political rights separately. It has its own representatives, who are by no means charged with representing the people. Its deputation sits apart; and when it is assembled in the same room with the deputies of ordinary citizens, it is equally true that its representation is essentially distinct and separate; it is foreign to the nation in principle, since its mandate does not emanate from the people, and in aim, since its purpose is to defend not the general but a special interest.

The third estate, then, comprises everything appertaining to the nation; and whatever is not the third estate may not be regarded as being of the nation. What is the third estate? Everything!

• • •

Chapter III   What Does the Third Estate Demand? To Become Something

. . . The true petitions of this order may be appreciated only through the authentic claims directed to the government by the large municipalities of the kingdom. What is indicated therein? That the people wishes to be *something,* and, in truth, the very least that is possible. It wishes to have real representatives in the Estates General, that is to say, deputies *drawn from its order,* who are competent to be interpreters of its will and defenders of its interests. But what will it avail it to be present at the Estates General if the predominating interest there is contrary to its own! Its presence would only consecrate the oppression of which it would be the eternal victim. Thus, it is indeed certain that it cannot come to vote at the Estates General unless it is to have in that body *an influence at least equal to that of the privileged classes;* and it demands a number of representatives equal

---

1   In a footnote, Sieyès says that he does not include the clergy because he considers it not an order, but a potentially useful profession in the public service.

to that of the first two orders together.[2] Finally, this equality of representation would become completely illusory if every chamber voted separately. The third estate demands, then, that votes be taken *by head and not by order*. This is the essence of those claims so alarming to the privileged classes, because they believed that thereby the reform of abuses would become inevitable. The real intention of the third estate is to have an influence in the Estates General equal to that of the privileged classes. I repeat, can it ask less? And is it not clear that if its influence therein is less than equality, it cannot be expected to emerge from its political nullity and become *something?*

• • •

Chapter VI   What Remains To Be Done. Development of Some Principles

The time is past when the three orders, thinking only of defending themselves from ministerial despotism, were ready to unite against the common enemy....

• • •

The third estate awaits, to no purpose, the meeting of all classes, the restitution of its political rights, and the plenitude of its civil rights; the fear of seeing abuses reformed alarms the first two orders far more than the desire for liberty inspires them. Between liberty and some odious privileges, they have chosen the latter. Their soul is identified with the favors of servitude. Today they dread this Estates General which but lately they invoked so ardently. All is well with them; they no longer complain except of the spirit of innovation. They no longer lack anything; fear has given them a constitution.

The third estate must perceive in the trend of opinions and circumstances that it can hope for nothing except from its own enlightenment and courage. Reason and justice are in its favor; . . . there is no longer time to work for the conciliation of parties. What accord can be anticipated between the energy of the oppressed and the rage of the oppressors?

They have dared pronounce the word secession. They have menaced the King and the people. Well! Good God! How fortunate for the nation if this so desirable secession might be made permanently! How easy it would be to dispense with the privileged classes! How difficult to induce them to be citizens!

• • •

---

2   Sieyès has a footnote on the fact that this has been granted, but, in his opinion, it is meaningless.

In vain would they close their eyes to the revolution which time and force of circumstances have effected; it is none the less real. Formerly the third estate was serf, the noble order everything. Today the third estate is everything, the nobility but a word. . . .

In such a state of affairs, what must the third estate do if it wishes to gain possession of its political rights in a manner beneficial to the nation? There are two ways of attaining this objective. In following the first, the third estate must assemble apart: it will not meet with the nobility and the clergy at all; it will not remain with them, either by *order* or by *head*. I pray that they will keep in mind the enormous difference between the assembly of the third estate and that of the other two orders. The first represents 25,000,000 men, and deliberates concerning the interests of the nation. The two others, were they to unite, have the powers of only about 200,000 individuals, and think only of their privileges. The third estate alone, they say, cannot constitute the *Estates General*. Well! So much the better! It will form a *National Assembly*.

Declaration of the Rights of Man and Citizen Adopted August 26, 1789

⤙⬥⤚

This declaration was one of the first tasks undertaken by the Estates-General, now calling itself the National Assembly. Lafayette, Mirabeau, and Sieyès all had a hand in its drafting. Intended as a universal statement of human rights, it can also be read as an indictment of the failings of the Old Regime. One sees clearly the influence of Rousseau and Montesquieu, and also of John Locke. It is interesting to compare this document to the Declaration of Independence of the United States. It is also interesting to consider not only what this document says, but also what it very pointedly does not say.

Paul Hanson

The representatives of the French people, constituted as a National Assembly, considering that ignorance, disregard or contempt of the rights of man are the sole causes of public misfortunes and governmental corruption, have resolved to set forth a solemn declaration of the natural, inalienable and sacred rights of man, in order that this declaration, by being constantly present to all members of the social body, may keep them at all times aware of their rights and duties; that the acts of both the legislative and executive powers, by being liable at every moment to comparison with the aim of all political institutions, may be the more fully respected; and that demands of the citizens, by being founded henceforward on simple and incontestable principles, may always redound to the maintenance of the constitution and the general welfare.

The Assembly consequently recognizes and declares, in the presence and under the auspices of the Supreme Being, the following rights of man and the citizen:

I.   Men are born and remain free and equal in rights. Social distinctions may be based only on common utility.

II. The aim of all political association is to preserve the natural and imprescriptible rights of man. These rights are liberty, property, security and resistance to oppression.

235

III. The principle of all sovereignty rests essentially in the nation. No body and no individual may exercise authority which does not emanate from the nation expressly.

IV. Liberty consists in the ability to do whatever does not harm another; hence the exercise of the natural rights of each man has no limits except those which assure to other members of society the enjoyment of the same rights. These limits can only be determined by law.

V. Law may rightfully prohibit only those actions which are injurious to society. No hindrance should be put in the way of anything not prohibited by law, nor may any man be forced to do what the law does not require.

VI. Law is the expression of the general will. All citizens have the right to take part, in person or by their representatives, in its formation. It must be the same for all whether it protects or penalizes. All citizens being equal in its eyes are equally admissible to all public dignities, offices and employments, according to their capacity, and with no other distinction than that of their virtues and talents.

VII. No man may be indicted, arrested or detained except in cases determined by law and according to the forms which it has prescribed. Those who instigate, expedite, execute or cause to be executed arbitrary orders should be punished; but any citizen summoned or seized by virtue of the law should obey instantly, and renders himself guilty by resistance.

VIII. Only strictly necessary punishments may be established by law, and no one may be punished except by virtue of a law established and promulgated before the time of the offence, and legally put into force.

IX. Every man being presumed innocent until judged guilty, if it is deemed indispensable to keep him under arrest, all rigor not necessary to secure his person should be severely repressed by law.

X. No one may be disturbed for his opinions, even in religion, provided that their manifestation does not trouble public order as established by law.

XI. Free communication of thought and opinion is one of the most precious of the rights of man. Every citizen may therefore speak, write and print freely, on his own responsibility for abuse of this liberty in cases determined by law.

XII. Preservation of the rights of man and the citizen requires the existence of public forces. These forces are therefore instituted for the advantage of all, not for the private benefit of those to whom they are entrusted.

XIII. For maintenance of public forces and for expenses of administration common taxation is necessary. It should be apportioned equally among all citizens according to their capacity to pay.

XIV. All citizens have the right, by themselves or through their representatives, to have demonstrated to them the necessity of public taxes, to consent to them freely, to follow the use made of the proceeds and to determine the shares to be paid, the means of assessment and collection and the duration.

XV. Society has the right to hold accountable every public agent of administration.

XVI. Any society in which the guarantee of rights is not assured or the separation of powers not determined has no constitution.

XVII. Property being an inviolable and sacred right, no one may be deprived of it except for an obvious requirement of public necessity, certified by law, and then on condition of a just compensation in advance.

The Declaration of the Rights of Woman

Olympe de Gouges

De Gouges was a butcher's daughter from Montauban who wrote several plays and a number of pamphlets on the coming Estates General. In this work de Gouges states that the Declaration of the Rights of Man and Citizen is not being applied to women. She implies the vote for women, demands a national assembly of women, stresses that men must yield rights to women, and emphasizes women's education. She addresses *Les Droits de la Femme* to the Queen, trusting perhaps that the Queen could be converted to the cause of political rights for women and become principal spokeswoman for a feminist program. De Gouges' allegiances are complexly divided between royalty and the national legislature.

[From *Women in Revolutionary Paris,*
1789–1795, edited by Darlene Gay, et al]

To the Queen: Madame,

Little suited to the language one holds to with kings, I will not use the adulation of courtiers to pay you homage with this singular production. My purpose, Madame, is to speak frankly to you; I have not awaited the epoch of liberty to thus explain myself; I bestirred myself as energetically in a time when the blindness of despots punished such noble audacity.

When the whole empire accused you and held you responsible for its calamities, I alone in a time of trouble and storm, I alone had the strength to take up your defense. I could never convince myself that a princess, raised in the midst of grandeur, had all the vices of baseness.

Yes, Madame, when I saw the sword raised against you, I threw my observations between that sword and you, but today when I see who is observed near the crowd of useless hirelings, and [when I see] that she is restrained by fear of the laws, I will tell you, Madame, what I did not say then.

If the foreigner bears arms into France, you are no longer in my eyes this falsely accused Queen, this attractive Queen, but an implacable enemy of the French. Oh, Madame, bear in mind that you are mother and wife; employ all your credit for the return of the Princes. This credit, if wisely applied, strengthens the father's crown, saves it for the son, and reconciles you to the love of the French. This worthy negotiation is the true duty of a queen. Intrigue, cabals, bloody projects will precipitate your fall, if it is possible to suspect that you are capable of such plots.

Madame, may a nobler function characterize you, excite your ambition, and fix your attentions. Only one whom chance has elevated to an eminent position can assume the task of lending weight to the progress of the Rights of Woman and of hastening its success. If you were less well informed, Madame, I might fear that your individual interests would outweigh those of your sex. You love glory; think, Madame, the greatest crimes immortalize one as much as the greatest virtues, but what a different fame in the annals of history! The one is ceaselessly taken as an example, and the other is eternally the execration of the human race.

It will never be a crime for you to work for the restoration of customs, to give your sex all the firmness of which it is capable. This is not the work of one day, unfortunately for the new regime. This revolution will happen only when all women are aware of their deplorable fate, and of the rights they have lost in society. Madame, support such a beautiful cause; defend this unfortunate sex, and soon you will have half the realm on your side, and at least one-third of the other half.

Those, Madame, are the feats by which you should show and use your credit. Believe me, Madame, our life is a pretty small thing, especially for a Queen, when it is not embellished by people's affection and by the eternal delights of good deeds.

If it is true that the French arm all the powers against their own Fatherland, why? For frivolous prerogatives, for chimeras. Believe, Madame, if I judge by what I feel—the monarchical party will be destroyed by itself, it will abandon all tyrants, and all hearts will rally around the fatherland to defend it.

There are my principles, Madame. In speaking to you of my fatherland, I lose sight of the purpose of this dedication. Thus, any good citizen sacrifices his glory and his interests when he has none other than those of his country.

I am with the most profound respect, Madame,

Your most humble and most obedient servant,
de Gouges

The Rights of Woman

Man, are you capable of being just? It is a woman who poses the question; you will not deprive her of that right at least. Tell me, what gives you sovereign empire to oppress my sex? Your strength? Your talents? Observe the Creator in his wisdom; survey in all her grandeur that nature with whom you seem to want to be in harmony, and give me, if you dare, an example of this tyrannical empire. Go back to animals, consult the elements, study plants, finally glance at all the modifications of organic matter, and surrender to the evidence when I offer you the means; search, probe, and distinguish, if you can, the sexes in the administration of nature. Everywhere you will find them mingled; everywhere they cooperate in harmonious togetherness in this immortal masterpiece.

Man alone has raised his exceptional circumstances to a principle. Bizarre, blind, bloated with science and degenerated—in a century of enlightenment and wisdom—into the crassest ignorance, he wants to command as a despot a sex which is in full possession of its intellectual faculties; he pretends to enjoy the Revolution and to claim his rights to equality in order to say nothing more about it.

Declaration of the Rights of Woman and the Female Citizen

For the National Assembly to decree in its last sessions, or in those of the next legislature:

Preamble

Mothers, daughters, sisters [and] representatives of the nation demand to be constituted into a national assembly. Believing that ignorance, omission, or scorn for the rights of woman are the only causes of public misfortunes and of the corruption of governments, [the women] have resolved to set forth in a solemn declaration the natural, inalienable, and sacred rights of woman in order that this declaration, constantly exposed before all the members of the society, will ceaselessly remind them of their rights and duties; in order that the authoritative acts of women and the authoritative acts of men may be at any moment compared with and respectful of the purpose of all political institutions; and in order that citizens' demands, henceforth based on simple and incontestable principles, will always support the constitution, good morals, and the happiness of all.

Consequently, the sex that is as superior in beauty as it is in courage during the sufferings of maternity recognizes and declares in the presence and under the auspices of the Supreme Being, the following Rights of Woman and of Female Citizens.

Article I

Woman is born free and lives equal to man in her rights. Social distinctions can be based only on the common utility.

Article II

The purpose of any political association is the conservation of the natural and imprescriptible rights of woman and man; these rights are liberty, property, security, and especially resistance to oppression.

Article III

The principle of all sovereignty rests essentially with the nation, which is nothing but the union of woman and man; no body and no individual can exercise any authority which does not come expressly from it [the nation].

Article IV

Liberty and justice consist of restoring all that belongs to others; thus, the only limits on the exercise of the natural rights of woman are perpetual male tyranny; these limits are to be reformed by the laws of nature and reason.

Article V

Laws of nature and reason proscribe all acts harmful to society; everything which is not prohibited by these wise and divine laws cannot be prevented, and no one can be constrained to do what they do not command.

Article VI

The law must be the expression of the general will; all female and male citizens must contribute either personally or through their representatives to its formation; it must be the same for all: male and female citizens, being equal in the eyes of the law, must be equally admitted to all honors, positions, and public employment according to their capacity and without other distinctions besides those of their virtues and talents.

Article VII

No woman is an exception; she is accused, arrested, and detained in cases determined by law. Women, like men, obey this rigorous law.

Article VIII

The law must establish only those penalties that are strictly and obviously necessary, and no one can be punished except by virtue of a law established and promulgated prior to the crime and legally applicable to women.

Article IX

Once any woman is declared guilty, complete rigor is [to be] exercised by the law.

Article X

No one is to be disquieted for his very basic opinions; woman has the right to mount the scaffold; she must equally have the right to mount the rostrum, provided that her demonstrations do not disturb the legally established public order.

Article XI

The free communication of thoughts and opinions is one of the most precious rights of woman, since that liberty assures the recognition of children by their fathers. Any female citizen thus may say freely, I am the mother of a child which belongs to you, without being forced by a barbarous prejudice to hide the truth; [an exception may be made] to respond to the abuse of this liberty in cases determined by the law.

Article XII

The guarantee of the rights of woman and the female citizen implies a major benefit; this guarantee must be instituted for the advantage of all, and not for the particular benefit of those to whom it is entrusted.

Article XIII

For the support of the public force and the expenses of administration, the contributions of woman and man are equal; she shares all the duties [*corvées*] and all the painful tasks; therefore, she must have the same share in the distribution of positions, employment, of offices, honors, and jobs [*industrie*].

Article XIV

Female and male citizens have the right to verify, either by themselves or through their representatives, the necessity of the public contribution. This can only apply to women if they are granted an equal share, not only of wealth, but also of public administration, and in the determination of the proportion, the base, the collection, and the duration of the tax.

Article XV

The collectivity of women, joined for tax purposes to the aggregate of men, has the right to demand an accounting of his administration from any public agent.

Article XVI

No society has a constitution without the guarantee of rights and the separation of powers; the constitution is null if the majority of individuals comprising the nation have not cooperated in drafting it.

Article XVII

Property belongs to both sexes whether united or separate; for each it is an inviolable and sacred right; no one can be deprived of it, since it is the true patrimony of nature, unless the legally determined public need obviously dictates it, and then only with a just and prior indemnity.

Postscript

Woman, wake up; the tocsin of reason is being heated throughout the whole universe; discover your rights. The powerful empire of nature is no longer surrounded by prejudice, fanaticism, superstition, and lies. The flame of truth has dispersed all the clouds of folly and usurpation. Enslaved man has multiplied his strength and needs recourse to yours to break his chains. Having become free, he has become unjust to his companion. Oh, women, women! When will you cease to be blind? What advantage have you received from the Revolution? A more pronounced scorn, a more marked disdain. In the centuries of corruption you ruled only over the weakness of men. The reclamation of your patrimony, based on the wise decrees of nature—what have you to dread from such a fine undertaking? The *bon mot* of the legislator of the marriage of Cana? Do you fear that our French legislators, correctors of that morality, long ensnared by political practices now out of date, will only say again to you: women, what is there in common between you and us? Everything, you will have to answer. If they persist in their weakness in putting this non sequitur in contradiction to their principles, courageously oppose the force of reason to the empty pretentions of superiority; unite yourselves beneath the standards of philosophy; deploy all the energy of your character, and you will soon see these haughty men, not groveling at your feet as servile adorers, but proud to share with you the treasures of the Supreme Being. Regardless of what barriers confront you, it is in your power to free yourselves; you have only to want to. Let us pass now to the shocking tableau of what you have been in society; and since national education is in question at this moment, let us see whether our wise legislators will think judiciously about the education of women.

Women have done more harm than good. Constraint and dissimulation have been their lot. What force had robbed them of, ruse returned to them; they had recourse to all the resources of their charms, and the most irreproachable person did not resist them. Poison and the sword were both subject to them; they commanded in crime as in fortune. The French government, especially, depended throughout the centuries on the nocturnal administration of women; the cabinet kept no secret from their indiscretion; ambassadorial post, command, ministry, presidency, pontificate, college of cardinals; finally, anything which characterizes the folly of men, profane and sacred, all have been subject to the cupidity and ambition of this sex, formerly contemptible and respected, and since the revolution, respectable and scorned.

In this sort of contradictory situation, what remarks could I not make! I have but a moment to make them, but this moment will fix the attention of the remotest posterity. Under the Old Regime, all was vicious, all was guilty; but could not the amelioration of conditions be perceived even in the substance of vices? A woman only had to be beautiful or amiable; when she possessed these two advantages, she saw a hundred fortunes at her feet. If she did not profit from them, she had a bizarre character or a rare philosophy which made her scorn

243

wealth; then she was deemed to be like a crazy woman; the most indecent made herself respected with gold; commerce in women was a kind of industry in the first class [of society], which, henceforth, will have no more credit. If it still had it, the revolution would be lost, and under the new relationships we would always be corrupted; however, reason can always be deceived [into believing] that any other road to fortune is closed to the woman whom a man buys, like the slave on the African coasts. The difference is great; that is known. The slave is commanded by the master; but if the master gives her liberty without recompense, and at an age when the slave has lost all her charms, what will become of this unfortunate woman? The victim of scorn, even the doors of charity are closed to her; she is poor and old, they say; why did she not know how to make her fortune? Reason finds other examples that are even more touching. A young, inexperienced woman, seduced by a man whom she loves, will abandon her parents to follow him; the ingrate will leave her after a few years, and the older she has become with him, the more inhuman is his inconstancy; if she has children, he will likewise abandon them. If he is rich, he will consider himself excused from sharing his fortune with his noble victims. If some involvement binds him to his duties, he will deny them, trusting that the laws will support him. If he is married, any other obligation loses its rights. Then what laws remain to extirpate vice all the way to its root? The law of dividing wealth and public administration between men and women. It can easily be seen that one who is born into a rich family gains very much from such equal sharing. But the one born into a poor family with merit and virtue—what is her lot? Poverty and opprobrium. If she does not precisely excel in music or painting, she cannot be admitted to any public function when she has all the capacity for it. I do not want to give only a sketch of things; I will go more deeply into this in the new edition of all my political writings, with notes, which I propose to give to the public in a few days.

I take up my text again on the subject of morals. Marriage is the tomb of trust and love. The married woman can with impunity give bastards to her husband, and also give them the wealth which does not belong to them. The woman who is unmarried has only one feeble right; ancient and inhuman laws refuse to her for her children the right to the name and the wealth of their father; no new laws have been made in this matter. If it is considered a paradox and an impossibility on my part to try to give my sex an honorable and just consistency, I leave it to men to attain glory for dealing with this matter; but while we wait, the way can be prepared through national education, the restoration of morals, and conjugal conventions.

Form for a Social Contract Between Man and Woman

We, _____ and _____, moved by our own will, unite ourselves for the duration of our lives, and for the duration of our mutual inclinations, under the following conditions: We intend and wish to make our wealth communal, meanwhile reserving to ourselves the right to divide it in favor of our children and of those toward whom we might have a particular inclination, mutually recognizing that our property belongs directly to our children, from whatever bed they come, and that all of them without distinction have the right to bear the name of the fathers and mothers who have acknowledged them, and we are charged to subscribe to the law which punishes the renunciation of one's own blood. We likewise obligate ourselves, in case of separation, to divide our wealth and to set aside in advance the portion the law indicates for our children, and in the event of a perfect union, the one who dies will divest himself of half his property in his children's favor, and if one dies childless, the survivor will inherit by right, unless the dying person has disposed of half the common property in favor of one whom he judged deserving.

That is approximately the formula for the marriage act I propose for execution. Upon reading this strange document, I see rising up against me the hypocrites, the prudes, the clergy, and the whole infernal sequence. But how it [my proposal] offers to the wise the moral means of achieving the perfection of a happy government! I am going to give in a few words the physical proof of it. The rich, childless Epicurean finds it very good to go to his poor neighbor to augment his family. When there is a law authorizing a poor man's wife to have a rich one adopt their children, the bonds of society will be strengthened and morals will be purer. This law will perhaps save the community's wealth and hold back the disorder which drives so many victims to the almshouses of shame, to a low station, and into degenerate human principles where nature has groaned for so long. May the detractors of wise philosophy then cease to cry out against primitive morals, or may they lose their point in the source of their citations.[1]

Moreover, I would like a law which would assist widows and young girls deceived by the false promises of a man to whom they were attached; I would like, I say, this law to force an inconstant man to hold to his obligations or at least [to pay] an indemnity equal to his wealth. Again, I would like this law to be rigorous against women, at least those who have the effrontery to have recourse to a law which they themselves had violated by their misconduct, if proof of that were given. At the same time, as I showed in *Le Bonheur primitif de l'homme,* in 1788, that prostitutes should be placed in designated quarters. It is not prostitutes who contribute the most to the depravity of morals, it is the women of society. In regenerating the latter, the former are changed. This link of fraternal union will first bring disorder, but in consequence it will produce at the end a perfect harmony.

I offer a foolproof way to elevate the soul of women; it is to join them to all the activities of man; if man persists in finding this way impractical, let him share his fortune with woman, not at his caprice, but by the wisdom of laws. Prejudice falls, morals are purified, and nature regains all her rights. Add to this the marriage of priests and the strengthening of the king on his throne, and the French government cannot fail.

It would be very necessary to say a few words on the troubles which are said to be caused by the decree in favor of colored men in our islands. There is where nature shudders with horror; there is where reason and humanity have still not

---

1 Abraham had some very legitimate children by Agar, the servant of his wife.

touched callous souls; there, especially, is where division and discord stir up their inhabitants. It is not difficult to divine the instigators of these incendiary fermentations; they are even in the midst of the National Assembly; they ignite the fire in Europe which must inflame America. Colonists make a claim to reign as despots over the men whose fathers and brothers they are; and, disowning the rights of nature, they trace the source of [their rule] to the scantiest tint of their blood. These inhuman colonists say: our blood flows in their veins, but we will shed it all if necessary to glut our greed or our blind ambition. It is in these places nearest to nature where the father scorns the son; deaf to the cries of blood, they stifle all its attraction; what can be hoped from the resistance opposed to them? To constrain [blood] violently is to render it terrible; to leave [blood] still enchained is to direct all calamities towards America. A divine hand seems to spread liberty abroad throughout the realms of man; only the law has the right to curb this liberty if it degenerates into license, but it must be equal for all; liberty must hold the National Assembly to its decree dictated by prudence and justice. May it act the same way for the state of France and render her as attentive to new abuses as she was to the ancient ones which each day become more dreadful. My opinion would be to reconcile the executive and legislative power, for it seems to me that the one is everything and the other is nothing—whence comes, unfortunately perhaps, the loss of the French Empire. I think that these two powers, like man and woman, should be united but equal in force and virtue to make a good household. . . .

Speeches at the Trial of Louis XVI

The trial and execution of Louis XVI were among the most momentous events of the French Revolution. The deputies of the National Convention took this grave responsibility very seriously. Virtually all of them gave speeches, some more than once, during the preliminary deliberations, the trial itself, and the final votes on verdict and sentence. These three speeches from the preliminary phase of the trial focus on the essential questions of whether or not the King could even be tried, on what terms and by whom, and the implications of this decision for the Revolution itself. The deputies had to consider not only the fate of an individual, but also the fate of their government and of the nation itself.

Paul Hanson

Saint-Just
13 November 1792

I shall undertake, citizens, to prove that the king can be judged, that the opinion of Morisson which would respect inviolability and that of the committee which would have him judged as a citizen are equally false, and that the king ought to be judged according to principles foreign to both. . . .

Some day men will be astonished that in the eighteenth century humanity was less advanced than in the time of Caesar. Then, a tyrant was slain in the midst of the Senate, with no formality but thirty dagger blows, with no law but the liberty of Rome. And today, respectfully, we conduct a trial for a man who was the assassin of a people, taken *in flagrante,* his hand soaked with blood, his hand plunged in crime.

Those same men who are to judge Louis are charged with founding the Republic. Those who attach any importance to the just punishment of a king will never found a Republic. Among us, subtlety of spirit and of character is a great

---

From *Regicide and Revolution: Speeches at the Trial of Louis XVI* by Michael Walzer, ed. Copyright © 1974. Reprinted by permission of Cambridge University Press.

obstacle to liberty; we embellish all error and, more often than not, truth for us is only the seduction of taste. . . .

The social contract is between citizen and citizen, not between citizen and government. A contract affects only those whom it binds. As a consequence, Louis, who was not bound, cannot be judged in civil law. The contract was so oppressive as to bind the people and not the king; such a contract was of necessity void, since nothing is legitimate which is not sanctioned by ethics and nature. . . .

For myself, I can see no mean: this man must reign or die. He will prove to you that all his acts were acts of state, to sustain an entrusted power; for in treating with him so, you cannot make him answer for his hidden malice: he will lose you in the vicious circle created of your very accusations. . . .

A man of great spirit might say, in another age, that a king should be accused, not for the crimes of his administration, but for the crime of having been king, as that is an usurpation which nothing on earth can justify. With whatever illusions, whatever conventions, monarchy cloaks itself, it remains an eternal crime against which every man has the right to rise and to arm himself. Monarchy is an outrage which even the blindness of an entire people cannot justify; that people, by the example it gave, is guilty before nature, and all men hold from nature the secret mission to destroy such domination wherever it may be found.

No man can reign innocently. The folly is all too evident. Every king is a rebel and an usurper. . . .

Condorcet
3 December 1792

. . . It is important to the happiness of mankind that the conduct of France towards the man it too long called its king should be the final step in curing other nations of whatever superstition in favor of monarchy may remain among them. Above all, we should beware lest we increase that superstition among those still ruled by it. All nations do not recognize the eternal truths, the unshakable foundation of the French Republic; and whereas our philosophers and our soldiers spread them to foreign nations; whereas tyranny trembles as much before our maxims as before our armies, we would be imprudent to surprise, to frighten perhaps, by the boldness of our actions, those whom we may cause to respect severe but impartial equity. Thus, it is to the laws of universal justice, common to all constitutions, unalterable in the midst of clashing opinions and the revolutions of empires, that we must submit our decisions.

Can the former king be judged?

An action can be grounds for legitimate punishment only if a previous law defined that action expressly as a crime; and it can be punished only with a penalty which likewise was prescribed by a previous law. This is an axiom of humanity and justice.

If, however, the law failed to distinguish in the list of crimes those which circumstances made more heinous, one ought not to conclude that the law wished to exempt them from punishment, but only that the aggravating circumstances did not seem to require the prescription of a specific penalty. The laws of Solon include none against parricide. Shall we conclude that the monster who was guilty of this crime was intended to remain unpunished? No, surely he was to be punished as for a murder.

If then, the laws of France say nothing specifically about a king who conspired against the people, although he be much more guilty than a citizen, it does not follow that he should be spared, but only that those who wrote the laws did not wish to distinguish him from other conspirators. He should be judged then by the usual law, if another law did not specifically exclude him.

Was such an exclusion expressed by the Constitution? Citizens, if such an impunity had been made law, if the Constituent Assembly had committed such a crime against humanity, if the nation had been weak enough to accept that dishonorable law by its silence, by the election of representatives, by the oaths which were demanded of them, then, as a friend of justice, as a friend of liberty, I would say: "the king cannot be judged and punished."

But that scandalous impunity was never enacted.

Two articles make this clear. In one, the person of the king is declared inviolable and sacred. The other declared that for all crimes committed after his legal abdication, he would be judged like other citizens. . . .

Robespierre
3 December 1792

Citizens, the Assembly has unwittingly been brought far from the true question. There is no trial to be conducted here. Louis is not an accused man. You are not judges. You are, and you can only be, statesmen and representatives of the nation. You do not have a verdict to give for or against a man, but a measure to take for the public safety, a precautionary act to execute for the nation. A deposed king in a Republic is good only for two things: either to trouble the tranquility of the state and to undermine liberty, or to strengthen both. And I maintain that the character of the deliberations hitherto goes directly against this latter aim. In fact, what course of action is wanted to unite the new-born Republic? Is it not to engrave on the hearts of all eternal contempt for royalty, and to strike dumb all the partisans of the king? Thus, presenting his crime to the world as a problem, his case as the subject of the most serious discussion, the most religious and the most difficult which might occupy the representatives of the French people, placing an immeasurable distance between even the memory of what he was and the dignity of a citizen—therein lies the secret of making him once more dangerous to liberty.

Louis was king, and the Republic is founded. The great question with which you are occupied is settled by this argument: Louis has been deposed by his crimes. Louis denounced the French people as rebels; to punish them he called upon the arms of his fellow tyrants. Victory and the people have decided that he alone was a rebel. Therefore, Louis cannot be judged; he has already been condemned, else the Republic is not cleared of guilt. To propose a trial for Louis XVI of any sort whatever is to step backward toward royal and constitutional despotism. Such a proposal is counter-revolutionary since it would bring the revolution itself before the court. In fact, if Louis could yet be tried, he might be found innocent. Do I say "found"? He is presumed innocent until the verdict. If Louis is acquitted, where then is the revolution? If Louis is innocent, all defenders of liberty are slanderers. . . .

Speeches of Robespierre

———◦◆◦———

Maximilien Robespierre, a leader of the Paris Jacobin club, served as spokesperson for the Committee of Public Safety before the National Convention during most of the Year II, the year of the Terror. In that capacity, Robespierre introduced legislation and made a number of important policy statements. In these two excerpts, he addresses the principles of revolutionary government, the nature of public virtue, and the relationship between virtue and terror. In the second speech in particular, we hear echoes of Rousseau's *Second Discourse* (*On the Origin of Inequality*). Also resonating in this speech are the ominous words penned by Sieyès over five years before: "How easy it would be to dispense with the privileged classes! How difficult to induce them to be citizens!"

Paul Hanson

On Revolutionary Government
December 25, 1793

. . . The theory of revolutionary government is as new as the Revolution that created it. It is as pointless to seek its origins in the books of the political theorists, who failed to foresee this revolution, as in the laws of the tyrant, who are happy enough to abuse their exercise of authority without seeking out its legal justification.

It is the function of government to guide the moral and physical energies of the nation toward the purposes for which it was established.

The object of constitutional government is to preserve the Republic; the object of revolutionary government is to establish it.

Revolution is the war waged by liberty against its enemies; a constitution is that which crowns the edifice of freedom once victory has been won and the nation is at peace.

The revolutionary government has to summon extraordinary activity to its aid precisely because it is at war. It is subjected to less binding and less uniform regulations, because the circumstances in which it finds itself are tempestuous

---

and shifting, above all because it is compelled to deploy, swiftly and incessantly, new resources to meet new and pressing danger.

The principal concern of constitutional government is civil liberty: that of revolutionary government, public liberty. Under a constitutional government little more is required than to protect the individual against abuses by the state, whereas revolutionary government is obliged to defend the state itself against the factions that assail it from every quarter.

To good citizens revolutionary government owes the full protection of the state; to the enemies of the people it owes only death.

These ideas are in themselves sufficient to explain the origin and the nature of the laws that we term revolutionary. Those who call them arbitrary or tyrannical are foolish or perverse sophists who seek to reconcile white with black and black with white: they prescribe the same system for peace and war, for health and sickness; or rather their only object is to resurrect tyranny and to destroy the fatherland. When they invoke the literal application of constitutional principles, it is only to violate them with impunity. They are cowardly assassins who, in order to strangle the Republic in its infancy without danger to themselves, try to throttle it with vague maxims which they have no intention of observing. . . .

Is a revolutionary government the less just and the less legitimate because it must be more vigorous in its actions and freer in its movements than an ordinary government? No! for it rests on the most sacred of all laws, the safety of the people, and on necessity, which is the most indisputable of all rights.

It also has its rules, all based on justice and on public order. It has nothing in common with anarchy or disorder; on the contrary, its purpose is to repress them and to establish and consolidate the rule of law. It has nothing in common with arbitrary rule; it is public interest that governs it and not the whims of private individuals.

It must adopt the general principles of ordinary government whenever these can be rigorously applied without endangering public liberty. But its force to repress must be commensurate with the audacity or treachery of those who conspire against it. The greater its terrors for the wicked, the greater must be its favors for the good. The more it is compelled by circumstance to act with necessary rigor, the more it must refrain from measures that needlessly interfere with freedom and offend private interests without any advantage to the public.

It must sail between the twin reefs of weakness and temerity, of moderatism and exaggeration: moderatism which is to moderation as impotence is to chastity, and exaggeration whose resemblance to energy it like that of dropsy to good health. . . .

On the Moral and Political Principles of Domestic Policy

. . . What is the end toward which we are aiming? The peaceable enjoyment of liberty and equality; the reign of that eternal justice whose laws have been graven not on marble and stone but in the hearts of all men, even the slave who forgets them and the tyrant who denies them. [Applause.] . . .

We want to substitute, in our land, morality for egotism; probity for honor; principles for customs; ethics for propriety; the rule of reason for the tyranny of fashion; disdain for vice for disdain for misfortune; self-respect for insolence; spiritual grandeur for vanity; love of glory for love of money; good men for good society; merit for intrigue; genius for wit; truth for brilliance; the charm of happiness for the boredom of sensual pleasure; human greatness for the pettiness of the great; a magnanimous, powerful, happy people for an easy, frivolous, and miserable people: that is, all the virtues and all the miracles of the republic for all the vices and all the absurdities of the monarchy. [Applause] . . .

What is the nature of the government that can elect these prodigies? Only that government which is democratic or republican: these two words are synonyms, despite the abuses of common diction; for aristocracy is no more republican than is monarchy. Democracy is not a state in which the whole people, continually assembled, itself rules on all public business, still less is it one in which a hundred thousand fractions of the people decide, by unrelated, hasty, and contradictory measures, on the fate of the entire society; such a government has never existed, and it could exist only to lead the people back to despotism.

Democracy is a state in which the sovereign people, guided by laws which are its own work, itself does all it can do well, and through delegates all it cannot do itself. . . .

Now, what is the fundamental principle of the democratic or popular government—that is, the essential spring which makes it move? It is virtue; I am speaking of the public virtue which effected so many prodigies in Greece and Rome and which ought to produce much more surprising ones in republican France; of that virtue which is nothing other than the love of country and of its laws.

But as the essence of the republic or of democracy is equality, it follows that the love of country necessarily includes the love of equality.

It is also true that this sublime sentiment assumes a preference for the public interest over every particular interest; hence the love of country presupposes or produces all the virtues: for what are they other than that spiritual strength which renders one capable of those sacrifices? And how could the slave of avarice or ambition, for example, sacrifice his idol to his country?

Not only is virtue the soul of democracy; it can exist only in that government. . . .

Republican virtue can be considered in relation to the people and in relation to the government; it is necessary in both. When only the government lacks virtue, there remains a resource in the people's virtue; but when the people itself is corrupted, liberty is already lost. . . .

If the spring of popular government in time of peace is virtue, the springs of popular government in revolution are at once virtue and terror: virtue, without which terror is fatal; terror, without which virtue is powerless. Terror is nothing other than justice, prompt, severe, inflexible; it is therefore an emanation of virtue; it is not so much a special principle as it is a consequence of the general principle of democracy applied to our country's most urgent needs.

VICTORIAN ENGLAND

From Natural Theology

<hr>

William Paley

William Paley (1743–1805) was an influential theologian, Anglican priest, and philosopher (influenced by utilitarianism). In 1794 he published *View of the Evidences of Christianity* which was required reading for entrance into Cambridge University into the twentieth century. His most popular work, *Natural Theology; or, Evidences of the Existence and Attributes of the Deity* (1802) became the standard rationalist defense for the existence of God in nineteenth century England. In this work Paley updated the teleological argument for God's existence, including his famous analogy of the watch and the watchmaker included in this excerpt.

Malcolm Clark

State of the Argument

In crossing a heath, suppose I pitched my foot against a *stone,* and were asked how the stone came to be there, I might possibly answer, that for any thing I knew to the contrary it had lain there for ever; nor would it, perhaps, be very easy to show the absurdity of this answer. But suppose I had found a *watch* upon the ground, and it should be inquired how the watch happened to be in that place, I should hardly think of the answer which I had before given, that for any thing I knew the watch might have always been there. Yet why should not this answer serve for the watch as well as for the stone; why is it not as admissible in the second case as in the first? For this reason, and for no other, namely, that when we come to inspect the watch, we perceive—what we could not discover in the stone—that its several parts are framed and put together for a purpose, e.g. that they are so formed and adjusted as to produce motion, and that motion so regulated as to point out the hour of the day, that if the different parts had been differently shaped from what they are, or placed after any other manner or in any other order than that in which they are placed, either no motion at all would have been carried on in the machine, or none which would have answered the use that is now served by it. To reckon up a few of the plainest of these parts and of their offices, all tending to one result: We see a cylindrical box containing a coiled elastic spring, which, by its endeavor to relax itself, turns round the box. We next observe a flexible chain—artificially wrought for the sake of flexure—communicating the action of the spring from the box to the fusee. We then find a series of wheels, the teeth of which catch in and apply to each other, conducting the motion from the fusee to the balance and from the balance to the pointer, and at the same time, by the size and shape of those wheels, so regulating that motion as to terminate in causing an index, by an equable and measured progression, to pass over a given space in a given time. We take notice that the wheels are made of brass, in order to keep them from rust; the springs of steel, no other metal being so elastic; that over the face of the watch there is placed a glass, a material employed in no other part of the work, but in the room of which, if there had been any other than a transparent substance the hour could not be seen without opening the case. This mechanism being observed—it requires indeed an examination of the instrument and perhaps some previous knowledge of the subject to perceive and understand it; but being once, as we have said, observed and understood, the inference we think is inevitable that the watch must have had a maker—that there must have existed at some time and at some place or other an artificer or artificers who formed it for the purpose which we find it actually to answer, who comprehended its construction and designed its use. . . .

Suppose in the next place that the person who found the watch should after some time discover, that in addition to all the properties which he had hitherto observed in it, it possessed the unexpected property of producing in the course of its movement another watch like itself—the thing is conceivable; that it contained within it a mechanism, a system of parts—a mould, for instance, or a complex adjustment of lathes, files, and other tools—evidently and separately calculated for this purpose; let us inquire what effect ought such a discovery to have upon his former conclusion.

I. The first effect would be to increase his admiration of the contrivance, and his conviction of the consummate skill of the contriver. Whether he regarded the object of the contrivance, the distinct apparatus, the intricate, yet in many parts intelligible mechanism by which it was carried on, he would perceive in this new observation nothing but an additional reason for doing what he had already done—for referring the construction of the watch to design and to supreme art. If that construction *without* this property, or which is the same thing, before this property had been noticed, proved intention and art to have been employed about it, still more strong would the proof appear when he came to the knowledge of this further property, the crown and perfection of all the rest.

II. He would reflect, that though the watch before him were *in some sense* the maker of the watch which was fabricated in the course of its movements, yet it was in a very different sense from that in which a carpenter, for instance, is the maker of a chair—the author of its contrivance, the cause of the relation of its parts to their use. With contrivance, the cause of the relation of its parts to their use. With respect to these, the first watch was no cause at all to the second; in no such sense as this was it the author of the constitution and order, either of the parts which the new watch contained, or of the parts by the aid and instrumentality of which it was produced. We might possibly say, but with great latitude of expression, that a stream of water ground corn; but no latitude of

257

expression would allow us to say, no stretch of conjecture could lead us to think, that the stream of water built the mill, though it were too ancient for us to know who the builder was. What the stream of water does in the affair is neither more nor less than this: by the application of an unintelligent impulse to a mechanism previously arranged, arranged independently of it and arranged by intelligence, an effect is produced, namely, the corn is ground. But the effect results from the arrangement. The force of the stream cannot be said to be the cause or the author of the effect, still less of the arrangement. Understanding and plan in the formation of the mill were not the less necessary for any share which the water has in grinding the corn; yet is this share the same as that which the watch would have contributed to the production of the new watch, upon the supposition assumed in the last section. Therefore,

III. Though it be now no longer probable that the individual watch which our observer had found was made immediately by the hand of an artificer, yet doth not this alteration in anywise affect the inference, that an artificer had been originally employed and concerned in the production. The argument from design remains as it was. Marks of design and contrivance are no more accounted for now than they were before. In the same thing, we may ask for the cause of different properties. We may ask for the cause of the color of a body, of its hardness, of its heat; and these causes may be all different. We are now asking for the cause of that subserviency to a use, that relation to an end, which we have remarked in the watch before us. No answer is given to this question, by telling us that a preceding watch produced it. There cannot be design without a designer; contrivance, without a contriver; order, without choice; arrangement, without any thing capable of arranging, subserviency and relation to a purpose, without that which could intend a purpose; means suitable to an end, and executing their office in accomplishing that end, without the end ever having been contemplated, or the means accommodated to it. Arrangement, disposition of parts, subserviency of means to an end, relation of instruments to a use, imply the presence of intelligence and mind. No one, therefore, can rationally believe that the insensible, inanimate watch, from which the watch before us issued, was the proper cause of the mechanism we so much admire in it—could be truly said to have constructed the instrument, disposed its parts, assigned their office, determined their order, action, and mutual dependency, combined their several motions into one result, and that also a result connected with the utilities of other beings. All these properties therefore are as much unaccounted for as they were before. . . .

The conclusion which the *first* examination of the watch, of its works, construction, and movement, suggested, was, that it must have had, for cause and author of that construction, an artificer who understood its mechanism and designed its use. This conclusion is invincible. A *second* examination presents us with a new discovery. The watch is found, in the course of its movement, to produce another watch similar to itself; and not only so, but we perceive in it a system or organization separately calculated for that purpose. What effect would this discovery have, or ought it to have, upon our former inference? What, as hath already been said, but to increase beyond measure our admiration of the skill which had been employed in the formation of such a machine? Or shall it, instead of this, all at once turn us round to an opposite conclusion, namely, that no art or skill whatever has been concerned in the business, although all other evidences of art and skill remain as they were, and this last and supreme piece of art be now added to the rest? Can it be maintained without absurdity? Yet this is atheism.

Application of the Argument

This is atheism; for every indication of contrivance, every manifestation of design which existed in the watch, exists in the works of natures, with the difference on the side of nature of being greater and more, and that in a degree which exceeds all computation. I mean, that the contrivances of nature surpass the contrivances of art, in the complexity, subtlety, and curiosity of the mechanism; and still more, if possible, do they go beyond them in number and variety; yet, in a multitude of cases are not less evidently mechanical, not less evidently contrivances, not less evidently accommodated to their end or suited to their office, than are the most perfect productions of human ingenuity.

I know no better method of introducing so large a subject, than that of comparing a single thing with a single thing; an eye, for example, with a telescope. As far as the examination of the instrument goes, there is precisely the same proof that the eye was made for vision, as there is that the telescope was made for assisting it. They are made upon the same principles; both being adjusted to the laws by which the transmission and refraction of rays of light are regulated. I speak not of the origin of the laws themselves; but such laws being fixed, the construction in both cases is adapted to them. For instance, these laws require, in order to produce the same effect, that the rays of light, in passing from water into the eye, should be refracted by a more convex surface than when it passes out of air into the eye. Accordingly we find that the eye of a fish, in that part of it called the crystalline lens, is much rounder than the eye of terrestrial animals. What plainer manifestation of design can there be than this difference? What could a mathematical instrument maker have done more to show his knowledge of his principle, his application of that knowledge, his suiting of his means to his end—I will not say to display the compass or excellence of his skill and art, for in these all comparison is indecorous, but to testify counsel, choice, consideration, purpose?

Selections from the Writings of Charles Darwin

———————◆———————

Charles Robert Darwin (1809–1882) was born into an elite and wealthy family. First intending to become a physician, and then a clergyman, after his graduation from Cambridge in 1831 he was hired as the naturalist on the English survey vessel, HMS Beagle. His observations on this trip of geological formations at various coastal sites led him to accept the views of Charles Lyell regarding the gradual formation of the planet over a long period of time (*Principles of Geology,* 1830–1833). Especially influenced by observations of variations among finches he had observed in the Galapagos Islands and examination of the practices of commercial animal breeders in England, he applied Lyell's concept of gradual change to the evolution of species. As to the mechanism of change, he was influenced by the arguments of Thomas Malthus *(Essay on the Principle of Population,* 1798) about how competition for available food led to war, famine and disease which acted as a control on human population. By 1838, Darwin had arrived at his basic thesis that species evolve over time through a process of natural selection in which those individuals fitted by natural variation with the best characteristics for survival under the particular conditions in which they find themselves will be selected by nature and pass on their characteristics to subsequent generations. The first publication of this theory (*On the Origin of the Species,* 1859) was spurred by the impending publication by a young biologist, Russel Wallace, of a theory of natural selection which he had developed independently of Darwin. Darwin's ideas produced an uproar, with attacks by many scientists and theologians who saw Darwin's ideas as contradicting the Bible. Darwin had himself moved away from his earlier orthodox Christian beliefs. Much of the public advocacy of Darwin's position was done by others (e.g., Thomas Huxley). Darwin, who never had to earn a living, had married in 1839 and lived with his wife and children for most of the rest of his life on a small estate outside of London. He devoted his time to refining and expanding his ideas in a series of published works such as *The Descent of Man* (1871). In this work he turned his attention to the evolution of the human species arguing that the development of certain moral sentiments and intellectual abilities favored group survival, consequently lessening the role of physical (bodily) change as a means of adaptive change. Darwin ventured further in speculating how natural selection at a cultural level had favored the emergence and dominance of some nations (such as the Protestant, northern English) while recognizing that progress was not an inevitable historical process.

Malcolm Clark

From Notebook B

When one sees nipple on man's breast. one does not say some use, but sex not having been determined.—so with useless wings under elytra of beetles.—born from beetles with wings .& modified.—if simple creation, surely would have been born without them.=

In some of the lower orders a perfect gradation can be found from forms marking good genera—by steps so insensible, that each is not more change than we know *varieties* can produce.—Therefore all genera MAY have had intermediate steps.

From
The Origin of Species

❖

Struggle for Existence

Before entering on the subject of this chapter, I must make a few preliminary remarks, to show how the struggle for existence bears on Natural Selection. . . . Amongst organic beings in a state of nature there is some individual variability; indeed I am not aware that this has ever been disputed. It is immaterial for us whether a multitude of doubtful forms be called species or sub-species or varieties; what rank, for instance, the two or three hundred doubtful forms of British plants are entitled to hold, if the existence of any well-marked varieties be admitted. But the mere existence of individual variability and of some few well-marked varieties, though necessary as the foundation for the work, helps us but little in understanding how species arise in nature. How have all those exquisite adaptations of one part of the organisation to another part, and to the conditions of life, and of one distinct organic being to another being, been perfected? We scc these beautiful co-adaptations most plainly in the woodpecker and mistletoe; and only a little less plainly in the humblest parasite which clings to the hairs of a quadruped or feathers of a bird; in the structure of the beetle which dives through the water; in the plumed seed which is wafted by the gentlest breeze; in short, we see beautiful adaptations everywhere and in every part of the organic world.

Again, it may be asked, how is it that varieties, which I have called incipient species, become ultimately converted into good and distinct species, which in most cases obviously differ from each other far more than do the varieties of the same species? How do those groups of species, which constitute what are called distinct genera, and which differ from each other more than do the species of the same genus, arise? All these results, as we shall more fully see in the next chapter, follow inevitably from the struggle for life. Owing to this struggle for life, any variation, however slight and from whatever cause proceeding, if it be in any degree profitable to an individual of any species, in its infinitely complex relations to other organic beings and to external nature, will tend to the preservation of that individual, and will generally be inherited by its offspring. The offspring, also, will thus have a better chance of surviving, for, of the many individuals of any species which are periodically born, but a small number can survive. I have called this principle, by which each slight variation, if useful, is preserved, by the term of Natural Selection, in order to mark its relation to man's power of selection. . . . Man by selection can certainly produce great results, and can adapt organic beings to his own uses, through the accumulation of slight but useful variations, given to him by the hand of Nature. But Natural Selection, as we shall hereafter see, is a power incessantly ready for action, and is as immeasurably superior to man's feeble efforts, as the works of Nature are to those of Art.

We will now discuss in a little more detail the struggle for existence. In my future work this subject shall be treated, as it well deserves, at much greater length. The elder De Candolle and Lyell have largely and philosophically shown that all organic beings are exposed to severe competition. In regard to plants, no one has treated this subject with more spirit and ability than W. Herbert, Dean of Manchester, evidently the result of his great horticultural knowledge. Nothing is easier than to admit in words the truth of the universal struggle for life, or more difficult—at least I have found it so—than constantly to hear this conclusion in mind. Yet unless it be thoroughly engrained in the mind, I am convinced that the whole economy of nature, with every fact on distribution, rarity, abundance, extinction, and variation, will be dimly seen or quite misunderstood. We behold the face of nature bright with gladness, we often see superabundance of food; we do not see, or we forget, that the birds which are idly singing round us mostly live on insects or seeds, and are thus constantly destroying life, or we forget how largely these songsters, or their eggs, or their nestlings, are destroyed by birds and beasts of prey; we do not always bear in mind, that though food may be now superabundant, it is not so at all seasons of each recurring year.

I should premise that I use the term Struggle for Existence in a large and metaphorical sense, including dependence of one being on another, and including (which is more important) not only the life of the individual, but success in leaving progeny. Two canine animals in a time of dearth, may be truly said to struggle with each other which shall get food and live. But a plant on the edge of a desert is said to struggle for life against the drought, though more properly it should be said to be dependent on the moisture. A plant which annually produces a thousand seeds, of which on an average only one comes to maturity, may be more truly said to struggle with the plants of the same and other kinds which already clothe the ground. The mistletoe is dependent on the apple and a few other trees, but can only in a far-fetched sense be said to struggle with these trees, for if too many of these parasites grow on the same tree, it will languish and die. But several seedling mistletoes, growing close together on the same branch, may more truly be said to struggle with each other. As the mistletoe is disseminated by birds, its existence depends on birds; and it may metaphorically be said to struggle with other fruit-bearing plants, in order to tempt birds to devour and thus disseminate its seeds rather than those of other plants. In these several senses, which pass into each other, I use for convenience sake the general term of struggle for existence.

A struggle for existence inevitably follows from the high rate at which all organic beings tend to increase. Every being, which during its natural lifetime produces several eggs or seeds, must suffer destruction during some period of its life, and during some season or occasional year, otherwise, on the principle of geometrical increase, its numbers would quickly become so inordinately great that no country could support the product. Hence, as more individuals are produced than can possibly survive, there must in every case be a struggle for existence, either one individual with another of the same species, or with the individuals of distinct species, or with the physical conditions of life. It is the doctrine of Malthus applied with manifold force to the whole animal and vegetable kingdoms; for in this case there can be no artificial increase of food, and no prudential restraint from marriage. Although some species may be now increasing, more or less rapidly, in numbers, all cannot do so, for the world would not hold them.

There is no exception to the rule that every organic being naturally increases at so high a rate, that if not destroyed, the earth would soon be covered by the progeny of a single pair. Even slow-breeding man has doubled in twenty-five years, and at this rate, in a few thousand years, there would literally not be standing room for his progeny. Linnaeus has calculated that if an annual plant produced only two seeds—and there is no plant so unproductive as this—and their seedlings next year produced two, and so on, then in twenty years there would be a million plants. The elephant is reckoned to be the slowest breeder of all known animals, and I have taken some pains to estimate its probable minimum rate of natural increase: it will be under the mark to assume that it breeds when thirty years old, and goes on breeding till ninety years old, bringing forth three pairs of young in this interval; if this be so, at the end of the fifth century there would be alive fifteen million elephants, descended from the first pair.

But we have better evidence on this subject than mere theoretical calculations, namely, the numerous recorded cases of the astonishingly rapid increase of various animals in a state of nature, when circumstances have been favourable to them during two or three following seasons. Still more striking is the evidence from our domestic animals of many kinds which have run wild in several parts of the world: if the statements of the rate of increase of slow-breeding cattle and horses in South-America, and latterly in Australia, had not been well authenticated, they would have been quite incredible. So it is with plants: cases could be given of introduced plants which have become common throughout whole islands in a period of less than ten years. Several of the plants now most numerous over the wide plains of La Plata, clothing square leagues of surface almost to the exclusion of all other plants, have been introduced from Europe; and there are plants which now range in India, as I hear from Dr Falconer, from Cape Comorin to the Himalaya, which have been imported from America since its discovery. In such cases, and endless instances could be given, no one supposes that the fertility of these animals or plants has been suddenly and temporarily increased in any sensible degree. The obvious explanation is that the conditions of life have been very favourable, and that there has consequently been less destruction of the old and young, and that nearly all the young have been enabled to breed. In such cases the geometrical ratio of increase, the result of which never fails to be surprising, simply explains the extraordinarily rapid increase and wide diffusion of naturalised productions in their new homes.

• • •

What checks the natural tendency of each species to increase in number is most obscure. Look at the most vigorous species; by as much as it swarms in numbers, by so much will its tendency to increase be still further increased. We know not exactly what the checks are in even one single instance. Nor will this surprise any one who reflects how ignorant we are on this head, even in regard to mankind, so incomparably better known than any other animal. . . . Here I will make only a few remarks, just to recall to the reader's mind some of the chief points. Eggs or very young animals seem generally to suffer most, but this is not invariably the case. With plants there is a vast destruction of seeds, but, from some observations which I have made, I believe that it is the seedlings which suffer most from germinating in ground already thickly stocked with other plants. Seedlings, also, are destroyed in vast numbers by various enemies; for instance, on a piece of ground three feet long and two wide, dug and cleared, and where there could be no choking from other plants, I marked all the seedlings of our native weeds as they came up, and out of the 357 no less than 295 were destroyed, chiefly by slugs and insects. If turf which has long been mown, and the case would be the same with turf closely browsed by quadrupeds, be let to grow, the more vigorous plants gradually kill the less vigorous, though fully grown, plants: thus out of twenty species growing on a little plot of turf (three feet by four) nine species perished from the other species being allowed to grow up freely.

The amount of food for each species of course gives the extreme limit to which each can increase; but very frequently it is not the obtaining food, but the serving as prey to other animals, which determines the average numbers of a species. Thus, there seems to be little doubt that the stock of partridges, grouse, and hares on any large estate depends chiefly on the destruction of vermin. If not one head of game were shot during the next twenty years in England, and, at the same time, if no vermin were destroyed, there would, in all probability, be less game than at present, although hundreds of thousands of game animals are now annually killed. On the other hand, in some cases, as with the elephant and rhinoceros, none are destroyed by beasts of prey: even the tiger in India most rarely dares to attack a young elephant protected by its dam.

Climate plays an important part in determining the average numbers of a species, and periodical seasons of extreme cold or drought, I believe to be the most effective of all checks. I estimated that the winter of 1854–55 destroyed four-fifths of the birds in my own grounds; and this is a tremendous destruction, when we remember that ten per cent is an extraordinarily severe mortality from epidemics with man. The action of climate seems at first sight to be quite independent of the struggle for existence; but in so far as climate chiefly acts in reducing food, it brings on the most severe struggle between the individuals, whether of the same or of distinct species, which subsist on the same kind of food. Even when climate, for instance extreme cold, acts directly, it will be the least vigorous, or those which have got least food through the advancing winter, which will suffer most. When we travel from south to north or from a damp region to a dry, we invariably see some species gradually getting rarer and rarer, and finally disappearing; and the change of climate being conspicuous, we are tempted to attribute the whole effect to its direct action. But this is a very false view: we forget that each species, even where it most abounds, is constantly suffering enormous destruction at some period of its life, from enemies or from competitors for the same place and food; and if these enemies or competitors be in the least degree favoured by any slight change of climate, they will increase in numbers, and, as each area is already fully stocked with inhabitants, the other species will decrease. When we travel southward and see a species decreasing in numbers, we may feel sure that the cause lies quite as much in other species being favoured, as in this one being hurt. So it is when we travel northward, but in a somewhat lesser degree, for the number of species of all kinds, and therefore of competitors, decreases northwards; hence in going northward, or in ascending a mountain, we far oftener meet with stunted forms, due to the *directly* injurious action of climate, than we do in proceeding southwards or in descending a mountain. When we reach the Arctic regions, or snow-capped summits, or absolute deserts, the struggle for life is almost exclusively with the elements.

That climate acts in main part indirectly by favouring other species, we may clearly see in the prodigious number of plants in our gardens which can perfectly well endure our climate, but which never become naturalised, for they cannot compete with our native plants, nor resist destruction by our native animals.

Natural Selection

How will the struggle for existence, discussed too briefly in the last chapter, act in regard to variation? Can the principle of selection, which we have seen is so potent in the hands of man, apply in nature? I think we shall see that it can act most effectually. Let it be borne in mind in what an endless number of strange peculiarities our domestic productions, and, in a lesser degree, those under nature, vary; and how strong the hereditary tendency is. Under domestication, it may be truly said that the whole organisation becomes in some degree plastic. Let it be borne in mind how infinitely complex and close-fitting are the mutual relations of all organic beings to each other and to their physical conditions of life. Can it, then, be thought improbable, seeing that variations useful to man have undoubtedly occurred, that other variations useful in some way to each being in the great and complex battle of life, should sometimes occur in the course of thousands of generations? If such do occur, can we doubt (remembering that many more individuals are born than can possibly survive) that individuals having any advantage, however slight, over others, would have the best chance of surviving and of procreating their kind? On the other hand, we may feel sure that any variation in the least degree injurious would be rigidly destroyed. This preservation of favourable variations and the rejection of injurious variations, I call Natural Selection. Variations neither useful nor injurious would not be attracted by natural selection, and would be left a fluctuating element, as perhaps we see in the species called polymorphic.

We shall best understand the probable course of natural selection by taking the case of a country undergoing some physical change, for instance, of climate. The proportional numbers of its inhabitants would almost immediately undergo a change, and some species might become extinct. We may conclude, from what we have seen of the intimate and complex manner in which the inhabitants of each country are bound together, that any change in the numerical proportions of some of the inhabitants, independently of the change of climate itself, would most seriously affect many of the others. If the country were open on its borders, new forms would certainly immigrate, and this also would seriously disturb the relations of some of the former inhabitants. Let it be remembered how powerful the influence of a single introduced tree or mammal has been shown to be. But in the case of an island, or of a country partly surrounded by barriers, into which new and better adapted forms could not freely enter, we should then have places in the economy of nature which would assuredly be better filled up, if some of the original inhabitants were in some manner modified; for, had the area been open to immigration, these same places would have been seized on by intruders. In such case, every slight modification, which in the course of ages chanced to arise, and which in any way favoured the individuals of any of the species, by better adapting them to their altered conditions, would tend to be preserved; and natural selection would thus have free scope for the work of improvement.

· · ·

As man can produce and certainly has produced a great result by his methodical and unconscious means of selection, what may not nature effect? Man can act only on external and visible characters: nature cares nothing for appearances, except in so far as they may be useful to any being. She can act on every internal organ, on every shade of constitutional difference, on the whole machinery of life. Man selects only for his own good; Nature only for that of the being which she tends. Every selected character is fully exercised by her; and the being is placed under well-suited conditions of life. Man keeps the natives of many climates in the same country; he seldom exercises each selected character in some peculiar and fitting manner; he feeds a long and a short beaked pigeon on the same food; he does not exercise a long-backed or long-legged quadruped in any peculiar manner; he exposes sheep with long and short wool to the same climate. He does not allow the most vigorous males to struggle for the females. He does not rigidly destroy all inferior animals, but protects during each varying season, as far as lies in his power, all his productions. He often begins his selection by some half-monstrous form; or at least by some modification prominent enough to catch his eye, or to be plainly useful to him. Under nature, the slightest difference of structure or constitution may well turn the nicely balanced scale in the struggle for life, and so be preserved. How fleeting are the wishes and efforts of man! how short his time! and consequently how poor will his products be, compared with those accumulated by nature during whole geological periods. Can we wonder, then, that nature's productions should be far "truer" in character than man's productions; that they should be infinitely better adapted to the most complex conditions of life, and should plainly bear the stamp of far higher workmanship?

It may be said that natural selection is daily and hourly scrutinising, throughout the world, every variation, even the slightest; rejecting that which is bad, preserving and adding up all that is good; silently and insensibly working, whenever and wherever opportunity offers, at the improvement of each organic being in relation to its organic and inorganic conditions of life. We see nothing of these slow changes in progress, until the hand of time has marked the long lapses of ages, and then so imperfect is our view into long past geological ages, that we only see that the forms of life are now different from what they formerly were.

Although natural selection can act only through and for the good of each being, yet characters and structures, which we are apt to consider as of very trifling importance, may thus be acted on. When we see leaf-eating insects green, and bark-feeders mottled-grey: the alpine ptarmigan white in winter, the red-grouse the colour of heather, and the black-grouse that of peaty earth, we must believe that these tints are of service to these birds and insects in preserving them from danger. Grouse, if not destroyed at some period of their lives, would increase in countless numbers; they are known to suffer largely from birds of prey; and hawks are guided by eyesight to their prey,—so much so, that on parts of the Continent persons are warned not to keep white pigeons, as being the most liable to destruction. Hence I can see no reason to doubt that natural selection might be most effective in giving the proper colour to each kind of grouse, and in keeping that colour, when once acquired, true and constant. Nor ought we to think that the occasional destruction of an animal of any particular colour would produce little effect: we should remember how essential it is in a flock of white sheep to destroy every lamb with the faintest trace of black. In plants the down on the fruit and the colour of the flesh are considered by botanists as characters of the most trifling importance: yet we hear from an excellent horticulturist, Downing, that in the United States smooth-skinned fruits suffer far more from a beetle, a *Curculio*, than those with down; that purple plums suffer far more from a certain disease than yellow plums; whereas another disease attacks yellow-fleshed peaches far more than those with other coloured flesh. If, with all the aids of art, these slight differences make a great difference in cultivating the several varieties, assuredly, in a state of nature, where the trees would have to struggle with other trees and with a host of enemies, such differences would effectually settle which variety, whether a smooth or downy, a yellow or purple fleshed fruit, should succeed.

Divergence of character. The principle, which I have designated by this term, is of high importance on my theory, and explains, as I believe, several important facts. In the first place, varieties, even strongly-marked ones, though having somewhat of the character of species—as is shown by the hopeless doubts in many cases how to rank them—yet certainly differ from each other far less than do good and distinct species. Nevertheless, according to my view, varieties are species in the process of formation, or are, as I have called them, incipient species. How, then, does the lesser difference between varieties become augmented into the greater difference between species? That this does habitually happen, we must infer from most of the innumerable species throughout nature presenting well-marked differences; whereas varieties, the supposed prototypes and parents of future well-marked species, present slight and ill-defined differences. Mere chance, as we may call it, might cause one variety to differ in some character from its parents, and the offspring of this variety again to differ from its parent in the very same character and in a greater degree; but this alone would never account for so habitual and large an amount of difference as that between varieties of the same species and species of the same genus.

As has always been my practice, let us seek light on this head from our domestic productions. We shall here find something analogous. A fancier is struck by a pigeon having a slightly shorter beak; another fancier is struck by a pigeon having a rather longer beak; and on the acknowledged principle that "fanciers do not and will not admire a medium standard, but like extremes," they both go on (as has actually occurred with tumbler-pigeons) choosing and breeding from birds with longer and longer beaks, or with shorter and shorter beaks. Again, we may suppose that at an early period one man preferred swifter horses; another stronger and more bulky horses. The early differences would be very slight; in the course of time, from the continued selection of swifter horses by some breeders, and of stronger ones by others, the differences would become greater, and would be noted as forming two sub-breeds; finally, after the lapse of centuries, the sub-breeds would become converted into two well-established and distinct breeds. As the differences slowly become greater, the inferior animals with intermediate characters, being neither very swift nor very strong, will have been neglected, and will have tended to disappear. Here, then, we see in man's productions the action of what may be called the principle of divergence, causing differences, at first barely appreciable, steadily to increase, and the breeds to diverge in character both from each other and from their common parent.

But how, it may be asked, can any analogous principle apply in nature? I believe it can and does apply most efficiently, from the simple circumstance that the more diversified the descendants from any one species become in structure, constitution, and habits, by so much will they be better enabled to seize on many and widely diversified places in the polity of nature and so be enabled to increase in numbers.

. . .

The advantage of diversification in the inhabitants of the same region is, in fact, the same as that of the physiological division of labour in the organs of the same individual body—a subject so well elucidated by Milne Edwards. No physiologist doubts that a stomach by being adapted to digest vegetable matter alone, or flesh alone, draws most nutriment from these substances. So in the general economy of any land, the more widely and perfectly the animals and plants are diversified for different habits of life, so will a greater number of individuals be capable of there supporting themselves. A set of animals, with their organisation but little diversified, could hardly compete with a set more perfectly diversified in structure. It may be doubted, for instance, whether the Australian marsupials, which are divided into groups differing but little from each other, and feebly representing, as Mr. Waterhouse and others have re-marked, our carnivorous, ruminant, and rodent mammals, could successfully compete with these well-pronounced orders. In the Australian mammals, we see the process of diversification in an early and incomplete stage of development.

After the foregoing discussion, which ought to have been much amplified, we may, I think, assume that the modified descendants of any one species will succeed by so much the better as they become more diversified in structure, and are thus enabled to encroach on places occupied by other beings. Now let us see how this principle of great benefit being derived from divergence of character, combined with the principles of natural selection and of extinction, will tend to act. The accompanying diagram will aid us in understanding this rather perplexing subject. Let A to L represent the species of a genus large in its own country; these species are supposed to resemble each other in unequal degrees, as is so generally the case in nature, and as is represented in the diagram by the letters standing at unequal distances. I have said a large genus, because we have seen in the second chapter, that on an average more of the species of large genera vary than of small genera; and the varying species of the large genera present a greater number of varieties. We have, also, seen that the species, which are the common-est and the most widely-diffused, vary more than rare species with restricted ranges. Let (A) be a common, widely-diffused, and varying species, belonging to a genus large in its own country. The little fan of diverging dotted lines of unequal lengths proceeding from (A), may represent its varying offspring. The variations are supposed to be extremely slight, but of the most diversified nature; they are not supposed all to appear simultaneously, but often after long intervals of time; nor are they all supposed to endure for equal periods. Only those variations which are in some way profitable will be preserved or naturally selected. And here the importance of the principle of benefit being derived from divergence of character comes in; for this will generally lead to the most different or divergent variations (represented by the outer dotted lines) being preserved and accumulated by natural selection. When a dotted line reaches one of the horizontal lines, and is there marked by a small numbered letter, a sufficient amount of variation is supposed to have been accumulated to have formed a fairly well-marked variety, such as would be thought worthy of record in a systematic work.

The intervals between the horizontal lines in the diagram, may represent each a thousand generations; but it would have been better if each had represented ten thousand generations. After a thousand generations, species (A) is supposed to have produced two fairly well-marked varieties, namely a^1 and m^1. These two varieties will generally continue to be exposed to the same conditions which made their parents variable, and the tendency to variability is in itself hereditary, consequently they will tend to vary, and generally to vary in nearly the same manner as their parents varied. Moreover, these two varieties, being only slightly modified forms, will tend to inherit those advantages which made their common parent (A) more numerous than most of the other inhabitants of the same country; they will likewise partake of those more general advantages which made the genus to which the parent-species belonged, a large genus in its own country. And these circumstances we know to be favourable to the production of new varieties.

If, then, these two varieties be variable, the most divergent of their variations will generally be preserved during the next thousand generations. And after this interval, variety a^1 is supposed in the diagram to have produced variety a^2, which will, owing to the principle of divergence, differ more from (A) than did variety a^1. Variety m^1 is supposed to have produced two varieties, namely m^2 and s^1, differing from each other, and more considerably from their common parent (A). We may continue the process by similar steps for any length of time; some of the varieties, after each thousand generations, producing only a single variety, but in a more and more modified condition, some producing two or three varieties, and some failing to produce any. Thus the varieties or modified descendants proceeding from the common parent (A), will generally go on increasing in number and diverging in character. In the diagram the process is represented up to the ten-thousandth generation, and under a condensed and simplified form up to the fourteen-thousandth generation.

But I must here remark that I do not suppose that the process ever goes on so regularly as is represented in the diagram, though in itself made somewhat irregular. I am far from thinking that the most divergent varieties will invariably prevail and multiply: a medium form may often long endure, and may or may not produce more than one modified descendant; for natural selection will always act according to the nature of the places which are either unoccupied or not perfectly occupied by other beings; and this will depend on infinitely complex relations. But as a general rule, the more diversified in structure the descendants from any one species can be rendered, the more places they will be enabled to seize on, and the more their modified progeny will be increased. In our diagram the line of succession is broken at regular intervals by small numbered letters marking the successive forms which have become sufficiently distinct to be recorded as varieties. But these breaks are imaginary, and might have been inserted anywhere, after intervals long enough to have allowed the accumulation of a considerable amount of divergent variation.

As all the modified descendants from a common and widely diffused species, belonging to a large genus, will tend to partake of the same advantages which made their parent successful in life, they will generally go on multiplying in number as well as diverging in character: this is represented in the diagram by the several divergent branches proceeding from (A). The modified offspring from the later and more highly improved branches in the lines of

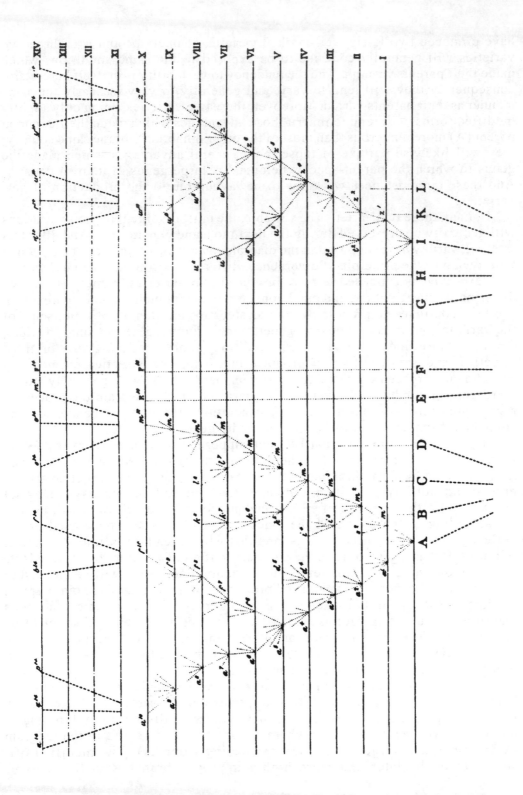

descent, will, it is probable, often take the place of, and so destroy, the earlier and less improved branches: this is represented in the diagram by some of the lower branches not reaching to the upper horizontal lines. In some cases I do not doubt that the process of modification will be confined to a single line of descent, and the number of the descendants will not be increased; although the amount of divergent modification may have been increased in the successive generations. This case would be represented in the diagram, if all the lines proceeding from (A) were removed, excepting that from a^1 to a^{10}. In the same way, for instance, the English race-horse and English pointer have apparently both gone on slowly diverging in character from their original stocks, without either having given off any fresh branches or races. After ten thousand generations, species (A) is supposed to have produced three forms, a^{10}, f^{10}, and m^{10}, which, from having diverged in character during the successive generations, will have come to differ largely, but perhaps unequally, from each other and from their common parent. If we suppose the amount of change between each horizontal line in our diagram to be excessively small, these three forms may still be only well-marked varieties; or they may have arrived at the doubtful category of sub-species; but we have only to suppose the steps in the process of modification to be more numerous or greater in amount, to convert these three forms into well-defined species: thus the diagram illustrates the steps by which the small differences distinguishing varieties are increased into the larger differences distinguishing species. By continuing the same process for a greater number of generations (as shown in the diagram in a condensed and simplified manner), we get eight species, marked by the letters between a^{14} and m^{14}, all descended from (A). Thus, as I believe, species are multiplied and genera are formed.

· · ·

But during the process of modification, represented in the diagram, another of our principles, namely that of extinction, will have played an important part. As in each fully stocked country natural selection necessarily acts by the selected form having some advantage in the struggle for life over other forms, there will be a constant tendency in the improved descendants of any one species to supplant and exterminate in each stage of descent their predecessors and their original parent. For it should be remembered that the competition will generally be most severe between those forms which are most nearly related to each other in habits, constitution, and structure.

Summary of Chapter

If under changing conditions of life organic beings present individual differences in almost every part of their structure, and this cannot be disputed; if there be, owing to their geometrical rate of increase, a severe struggle for life at some age, season, or year, and this certainly cannot be disputed; then, considering the infinite complexity of the relations of all organic beings to each other and to their conditions of life, causing an infinite diversity in structure, constitution, and habits, to be advantageous to them, it would be a most extraordinary fact if no variations had ever occurred useful to each being's own welfare, in the same manner as so many variations have occurred useful to man. But if variations useful to any organic being ever do occur, assuredly individuals thus characterised will have the best chance of being preserved in the struggle for life; and from the strong principle of inheritance, these will tend to produce offspring similarly characterised. This principle of preservation, or the survival of the fittest, I have called Natural Selection. It leads to the improvement of each creature in relation to its organic and inorganic conditions of life; and consequently, in most cases, to what must be regarded as an advance in organization. Nevertheless, low and simple forms will long endure if well fitted for their simple conditions of life.

Natural selection, on the principle of qualities being inherited at corresponding ages, can modify the egg, seed, or young, as easily as the adult. Amongst many animals, sexual selection will have given its aid to ordinary selection, by assuring to the most vigorous and best adapted males the greatest number of offspring. Sexual selection will also give characters useful to the males alone, in their struggles or rivalry with other males; and these characters will be transmitted to one sex or to both sexes, according to the form of inheritance which prevails.

Whether natural selection has really thus acted in adapting the various forms of life to their several conditions and stations, must be judged by the general tenor and balance of evidence given in the following chapters. But we have already seen how it entails extinction; and how largely extinction has acted in the world's history, geology plainly declares. Natural selection, also leads to divergence of character; for the more organic beings diverge in structure, habits, and constitution, by so much the more can a large number be supported on the area,—of which we see proof by looking to the inhabitants of any small spot, and to the productions naturalised in foreign lands. Therefore, during the modification of the descendants of any one species, and during the incessant struggle of all species to increase in numbers, the more diversified the descendants become, the better will be their chance of success in the battle for life. Thus the small differences distinguishing varieties of the same species, steadily tend to increase, till they equal the greater differences between species of the same genus, or even of distinct genera.

We have seen that it is the common, the widely-diffused and widely-ranging species, belonging to the larger genera within each class, which vary most; and these tend to transmit to their modified offspring that superiority which now makes them dominant in their own countries. Natural selection, as has just been remarked, leads to divergence of character and to much extinction of the less improved and intermediate forms of life. On these principles, the nature of the affinities and the generally well-defined distinctions between the innumerable organic beings in each class throughout the world, may be explained. It is a truly wonderful fact—the wonder of which we are apt to overlook from familiarity— that all animals and all plants throughout all time and space should be related to each other in groups, subordinate to groups, in the manner which we everywhere behold—namely, varieties of the same species most closely related, species of the same genus less closely and unequally related, forming sections and sub-genera, species of distinct genera much less closely related, and genera related in different degrees, forming sub-families, families, orders, sub-classes and classes. The several subordinate groups in any class cannot be ranked in a single file, but seem clustered round points, and these round other points, and so on in almost endless cycles. If species had been independently created, no explanation would have been possible of this kind of classification; but it is explained through inheritance and the complex action of natural selection, entailing extinction and divergence of character, as we have seen illustrated in the diagram.

The affinities of all the beings of the same class have sometimes been represented by a great tree. I believe this simile largely speaks the truth. The green and budding twigs may represent existing species; and those produced during former years may represent the long succession of extinct species. At each period of growth all the growing twigs have tried to branch out on all sides, and to overtop and kill the surrounding twigs and branches, in the same manner as species and groups of species have at all times overmastered other species in the great battle for life. The limbs divided into great branches, and these into lesser and lesser branches, were themselves once, when the tree was young, budding twigs, and this connection of the former and present buds by ramifying branches may well represent the classification of all extinct and living species in groups subordinate to groups. Of the many twigs which flourished when the tree was a mere bush, only two or three, now grown into great branches, yet survive and bear the other branches, so with the species which lived during long-past geological periods, very few have left living and modified descendants. From the first growth of the tree, many a limb and branch has decayed and dropped off; and these fallen branches of various sizes may represent those whole orders, families, and genera which have now no living representatives, and which are known to us only in a fossil state. As we here and there see a thin straggling branch springing from a fork low down in a tree, and which by some chance has been favoured and is still alive on its summit, so we occasionally see an animal like the Ornithorhynchus or Lepidosiren, which in some small degree connects by its affinities two large branches of life, and which has apparently been saved from fatal competition by having inhabited a protected station. As buds give rise by growth to fresh buds, and these, if vigorous, branch out and overtop on all sides many a feebler branch, so by generation I believe it has been with the great Tree of Life, which fills with its dead and broken branches the crust of the earth, and covers the surface with its ever-branching and beautiful ramifications.

Recapitulation

I have already recapitulated, as fairly as I could, the opposed difficulties and objections: now let us turn to the special facts and arguments in favour of the theory.

On the view that species are only strongly marked and permanent varieties, and that each species first existed as a variety, we can see why it is that no line of demarcation can be drawn between species, commonly supposed to have been produced by special acts of creation, and varieties which are acknowledged to have been produced by secondary laws. On this same view we can understand how it is that in each region where many species of a genus have been produced, and where they now flourish, these same species should present many varieties; for where the manufactory of species has been active, we might expect, as a general rule, to find it still in action, and this is the case if varieties be incipient species. Moreover, the species of the large genera, which afford the greater number of varieties or incipient species, retain to a certain degree the character of varieties; for they differ from each other by a less amount of difference than do the species of smaller genera. The closely allied species also of the larger genera apparently have restricted ranges, and they are clustered in little groups round other species—in which respects they resemble varieties. These are strange relations on the view of each species having been independently created, but are intelligible if all species first existed as varieties.

As each species tends by its geometrical ratio of reproduction to increase inordinately in number; and as the modified descendants of each species will be enabled to increase by so much the more as they become more diversified in habits and structure, so as to be enabled to seize on many and widely different places in the economy of nature, there will be a constant tendency in natural selection to preserve the most divergent offspring of any one species. Hence during a long-continued course of modification, the slight differences, characteristic of varieties of the same species, tend to be augmented into the greater differences characteristic of species of the same genus. New and improved varieties will inevitably supplant and exterminate the older, less improved and intermediate varieties; and thus species are rendered to a large extent defined and distinct objects. Dominant species belonging to the larger groups tend to give birth to new and dominant forms; so that each large group tends to become still larger, and at the same time more divergent in character. But as all groups cannot thus succeed in increasing in size for the world would not hold them, the more dominant groups beat the less dominant. This tendency in the large groups to go on increasing in size and diverging in character, together with the almost inevitable contingency of much extinction, explains the arrangement of all the forms of life, in groups subordinate to groups, all within a few great classes, which we now see everywhere around us, and which has prevailed throughout all time. This grand fact of the grouping of all organic beings seems to me utterly inexplicable on the theory of creation.

As natural selection acts solely by accumulating slight, successive, favourable variations, it can produce no great or sudden modification; it can act only by very short and slow steps. Hence the canon of *Natura non facit saltum*, which every fresh addition to our knowledge tends to make more strictly correct, is on this theory simply intelligible. We can plainly see why nature is prodigal in variety, though niggard in innovation. But why this should be a law of nature if each species has been independently created, no man can explain.

Many other facts are, as it seems to me, explicable on this theory. How strange it is that a bird, under the form of woodpecker, should have been created to prey on insects on the ground; that upland geese, which never or rarely swim, should have been created with webbed feet; that a thrush should have been created to dive and feed on sub-aquatic insects; and that a petrel should have been created with habits and structure fitting it for the life of an auk or grebe! and so on in endless other cases. But on the view of each species constantly trying to increase in number, with natural selection always ready to adapt the slowly varying descendants of each to any unoccupied or ill-occupied place in nature, these facts cease to be strange, or perhaps might even have been anticipated.

As natural selection acts by competition, it adapts the inhabitants of each country only in relation to the degree of perfection of their associates; so that we need feel no surprise at the inhabitants of any one country, although on the ordinary view supposed to have been specially created and adapted for that country, being beaten and supplanted by the naturalised productions from another land. Nor ought we to marvel if all the contrivances in nature be not, as far as we can judge, absolutely perfect; and if some of them be abhorrent to our ideas of fitness. We need not marvel at the sting of the bee causing the bee's own death; at drones being produced in such vast numbers for one single act, and being then slaughtered by their sterile sisters; at the astonishing waste of pollen by our fir-trees; at the instinctive hatred of the queen bee for her own fertile daughters; at ichneumonidae feeding within the live bodies of caterpillars; and at other such cases. The wonder indeed is, on the theory of natural selection, that more cases of the want of absolute perfection have not been observed.

From
The Descent of Man

◆━◆◆◆━◆

On the Development of the Intellectual and Moral Faculties During Primeval and Civilised Times

The subjects to be discussed in this chapter are of the highest interest, but are treated by me in a most imperfect and fragmentary manner. Mr. Wallace, in an admirable paper before referred to, argues that man after he had partially acquired those intellectual and moral faculties which distinguish him from the lower animals, would have been but little liable to have had his bodily structure modified through natural selection or any other means. For man is enabled through his mental faculties "to keep with an unchanged body in harmony with the changing universe." He has great power of adapting his habits to new conditions of life. He invents weapons, tools and various stratagems, by which he procures food and defends himself. When he migrates into a colder climate he uses clothes, builds sheds, and makes fires; and, by the aid of fire, cooks food otherwise indigestible. He aids his fellow-men in many ways, and anticipates future events. Even at a remote period he practised some subdivision of labour.

The lower animals, on the other hand, must have their bodily structure modified in order to survive under greatly changed conditions. They must be rendered stronger, or acquire more effective teeth or claws, in order to defend themselves from new enemies; or they must be reduced in size so as to escape detection and danger. When they migrate into a colder climate they must become clothed with thicker fur, or have their constitutions altered. If they fail to be thus modified, they will cease to exist.

The case, however, is widely different, as Mr. Wallace has with justice insisted, in relation to the intellectual and moral faculties of man. These faculties are variable; and we have every reason to believe that the variations tend to be inherited. Therefore, if they were formerly of high importance to primeval man and to his ape-like progenitors, they would have been perfected or advanced through natural selection. Of the high importance of the intellectual faculties there can be no doubt, for man mainly owes to them his predominant position in the world. We can see that, in the rudest state of society, the individuals who were the most sagacious, who invented and used the best weapons or traps, and who were best able to defend themselves, would rear the greatest number of offspring. The tribes which included the largest number of men thus endowed would increase in number and supplant other tribes. Numbers depend primarily on the means of subsistence, and this, depends partly on the physical nature of the country, but in a much higher degree on the arts which are there practised. As a tribe increases and is victorious, it is often still further increased by the absorption of other tribes. The stature and strength of the men of a tribe are likewise of some importance for its success, and these depend in part on the nature and amount of the food which can be obtained. In Europe the men of the Bronze period were supplanted by a more powerful and, judging from their sword-handles, larger-handed race; but their success was probably due in a much higher degree to their superiority in the arts.

All that we know about savages, or may infer from their traditions and from old monuments, the history of which is quite forgotten by the present inhabitants shew that from the remotest times successful tribes have supplanted other tribes. Relics of extinct or forgotten tribes have been discovered throughout the civilized regions of the earth, on the wild plains of America, and on the isolated islands in the Pacific Ocean. At the present day civilised nations are everywhere supplanting barbarous nations, excepting where the climate opposes a deadly barrier; and they succeed mainly, though not exclusively, through their arts, which are the products of the intellect. It is, therefore, highly probable that with mankind the intellectual faculties have been gradually perfected through natural selection; and this conclusion is sufficient for our purpose. Undoubtedly it would be interesting to have traced the development of each separate faculty from the state in which it exists in the lower animals to that in which it exists in man; but neither my ability nor knowledge permit the attempt.

It deserves notice that as soon as the progenitors of man became social (and this probably occurred at a very early period), the advancement of the intellectual faculties will have been aided and modified in an important manner, of which we see only traces in the lower animals, namely, through the principle of imitation, together with reason and experience. Apes are much given to imitation, as are the lowest savages; and the simple fact previously referred to, that after a time no animal can be caught in the same place by the same sort of trap, shews that animals learn by experience, and imitate each others' caution. Now, if some one man in a tribe, more sagacious than the others, invented a new snare or weapon, or other means of attack or defence, the plainest self-interest, without the assistance of much reasoning power, would prompt the other members to imitate him; and all would thus profit. The habitual practice of each new art must likewise in some slight degree strengthen the intellect. If the new invention were an important one, the tribe would increase in number, spread, and supplant other tribes. In a tribe thus rendered more numerous there would always be a rather better chance of the birth of other superior and inventive members. If such men left children to inherit their mental superiority, the chance of the birth of still more ingenious members would be somewhat better, and in a very small tribe decidedly better. Even if they left no children, the tribe would still include their blood-relations; and it has been ascertained by agriculturists that by preserving and breeding from the family of an animal, which when slaughtered was found to be valuable, the desired character has been obtained.

• • •

Natural Selection as affecting Civilised Nations.—In the last and present chapters I have considered the advancement of man from a former semi-human condition to his present state as a barbarian. But some remarks on the agency of natural selection on civilized nations may be here worth adding. This subject has been ably discussed by Mr. W. R. Greg, and previously by Mr. Wallace and Mr. Galton. Most of my remarks are taken from these three authors. With savages, the weak in body or mind are soon eliminated; and those that survive commonly exhibit a vigorous state of health. We civilised men, on the other hand, do our utmost to check the process of elimination; we build asylums for the imbecile, the maimed, and the sick; we institute poor-laws; and our medical men exert their utmost skill to save the life of every one to the last moment. There is reason to believe that vaccination has preserved thousands, who from a weak constitution would formerly have succumbed to small-pox. Thus the weak members of civilised societies propagate their kind. No one who has attended to the breeding of domestic animals will doubt that this must be highly injurious to the race of man; it is surprising how soon a want of care, or care wrongly directed, leads to the degeneration of a domestic race; but excepting in the case of man himself, hardly any one is so ignorant as to allow his worst animals to breed.

The aid which we feel impelled to give to the helpless is mainly an incidental result of the instinct of sympathy, which was originally acquired as part of the social instincts, but subsequently rendered, in the manner previously indicated, more tender and more widely diffused. Nor could we check our sympathy, if so urged by hard reason, without deterioration in the noblest part of our nature. The surgeon may harden himself whilst performing an operation, for he knows that he is acting for the good of his patient; but if we were intentionally to neglect the weak and helpless, it could only be for a contingent benefit, with a certain and great present evil. Hence we must bear without complaining the undoubtedly bad effects of the weak surviving and propagating their kind; but there appears to be at least one check in steady action, namely the weaker and inferior members of society not marrying so freely as the sound; and this check might be indefinitely increased, though this is more to be hoped for than expected, by the weak in body or mind refraining from marriage.

In all civilised countries man accumulates property and bequeaths it to his children. So that the children in the same country do not by any means start fair in the race for success. But this is far from an unmixed evil; for without the accumulation of capital the arts could not progress; and it is chiefly through their power that the civilised races have extended, and are now everywhere extending, their range, so as to take the place of the lower races. Nor does the moderate accumulation of wealth interfere with the process of selection. When a poor man becomes moderately rich, his children enter trades or professions in which there is struggle enough, so that the able in body and mind succeed best. The presence of a body of well-instructed men, who have not to labour for their daily bread, is important to a degree which cannot be over-estimated; as all high intellectual work is carried on by them, and on such work material progress of all kinds mainly depends, not to mention other and higher advantage. No doubt wealth when very great tends to convert men into useless drones, but their number is never large; and some degree of elimination here occurs, for we daily see rich men, who happen to be fools or profligate, squandering away their wealth.

Primogeniture with entailed estates is a more direct evil, though it may formerly have been a great advantage by the creation of a dominant class, and any government is better than anarchy. The eldest sons, though they may be weak in body or mind, generally marry, whilst the younger sons, however superior in these respects, do not so generally marry. Nor can worthless eldest sons with entailed estates squander their wealth. But here, as elsewhere, the relations of civilised life are so complex that some compensatory checks intervene. The men who are rich through primogeniture are able to select generation after generation the more beautiful and charming women; and these must generally be healthy in body and active in mind. The evil consequences, such as they may be, of the continued preservation of the same line of descent, without any selection, are checked by men of rank always wishing to increase their wealth and power; and this they effect by marrying heiresses. But the daughters of parents who have produced single children, are themselves, as Mr. Galton has shewn, apt to be sterile; and thus noble families are continually cut off in the direct line, and their wealth flows into some side channel; but unfortunately this channel is not determined by superiority of any kind.

Although civilisation thus checks in many ways the action of natural selection, it apparently favours, by means of improved food and the freedom from occasional hardships, the better development of the body. This may be inferred from civilised men having been found, wherever compared, to be physically stronger than savages. They appear also to have equal powers of endurance, as has been proved in many adventurous expeditions. Even the great luxury of the rich can be but little detrimental; for the expectation of life of our aristocracy, at all ages and of both sexes, is very little inferior to that of healthy English lives in the lower classes.

We will now look to the intellectual faculties alone. If in each grade of society the members were divided into two equal bodies, the one including the intellectually superior and the other the inferior, there can be little doubt that the former would succeed best in all occupations, owing to the great division of labour, a very small one. Hence in civilised nations there will be some tendency to an increase both in the number and in the standard of the intellectually able. But I do not wish to assert that this tendency may not be more than counterbalanced in other ways, as by the multiplication of the reckless and improvident; but even to such as these, ability must be some advantage.

It has often been objected to views like the foregoing, that the most eminent men who have ever lived have left no offspring to inherit their great intellect. Mr. Galton says, "I regret I am unable to solve the simple question whether, and how far, men and women who are prodigies of genius are infertile. I have, however, shewn that men of eminence are by no means so." Great lawgivers, the founders of beneficent religions, great philosophers and discoverers in science, aid the progress of mankind in a far higher degree by their works than by leaving a numerous progeny. In the case of corporeal structures, it is the selection of the slightly better-endowed and the elimination of the slightly less well-endowed individuals, and not the preservation of strongly-marked and rare anomalies, that leads to the advancement of a species.[1] So it will be with the intellectual faculties, namely from the somewhat more able men in each grade of society succeeding rather better than the less able, and consequently increasing in number, if not otherwise prevented. When in any nation the standard of intellect and the number of intellectual men have increased, we may expect from the law of the deviation from an average, as shown by Mr. Galton, that prodigies of genius will appear somewhat more frequently than before.

In regard to the moral qualities, some elimination of the worst dispositions is always in progress even in the most civilised nation. Malefactors are executed, or imprisoned for long periods, so that they cannot freely transmit their bad qualities. Melancholic and insane persons are confined, or commit suicide. Violent and quarrelsome men often come to a bloody end. Restless men who will not follow any steady occupation—and this relic of barbarism is a great check to civilisation—emigrate to newly-settled countries, where they prove useful pioneers. Intemperance is so highly destructive, that the expectation of life of the intemperate, at the age for instance, of thirty is only 13.8 years; whilst for the rural labourers of England at the same age it is 40.59 years. Profligate women bear few children, and profligate men rarely marry; both suffer from disease. In the breeding of domestic animals, the elimination of those individuals, though few in number, which are in any marked manner inferior, is by no means an unimportant element towards success. This especially holds good with injurious characters which tend to reappear through reversion, such as blackness in sheep; and with mankind some of the worst dispositions, which occasionally without any assignable cause make their appearance in families, may perhaps be reversions to a savage state, from which we are not removed by very many generations. This view seems indeed recognised in the common expression that such men are the black sheep of the family.

With civilised nations, as far as an advanced standard of morality, and an increased number of fairly well-endowed men are concerned, natural selection apparently effects but little; though the fundamental social instincts were originally thus gained. But I have already said enough, whilst treating of the lower races, on the causes which lead to the advance of morality, namely, the approbation of our fellow-men—the strengthening of our sympathies by habit—example and imitation—reason—experience, and even self-interest—instruction during youth, and religious feelings.

A most important obstacle in civilised countries to an increase in the number of men of a superior class has been strongly urged by Mr. Greg and Mr. Galton,

---

1   "Origin of Species" (fifth edition, 1869), p. 104.

namely, the fact that the very poor and reckless, who are often degraded by vice, almost invariably marry early, whilst the careful and frugal, who are generally otherwise virtuous, marry late in life, so that they may be able to support themselves and their children in comfort. Those who marry early produce within a given period not only a greater number of generations, but, as shewn by Dr. Duncan, they produce many more children. The children, moreover, that are born by mothers during the prime of life are heavier and larger, and therefore probably more vigorous, than those born at other periods. Thus the reckless, degraded, and often vicious members of society, tend to increase at a quicker rate than the provident and generally virtuous members. Or as Mr. Greg puts the case: "The careless, squalid, unaspiring Irishman multiplies like rabbits: the frugal, fore-seeing, self-respecting, ambitious Scot, stern in his morality, spiritual in his faith, sagacious and disciplined in his intelligence, passes his best years in struggle and in celibacy, marries late, and leaves few behind him. Given a land originally peopled by a thousand Saxons and a thousand Celts—and in a dozen generations five-sixths of the population would be Celts, but five-sixths of the property, of the power, of the intellect, would belong to the one-sixth of Saxons that remained. In the eternal 'struggle for existence,' it would be the inferior and *less* favoured race that had prevailed—and prevailed by virtue not of its good qualities but of its faults."

There are, however, some checks to this downward tendency. We have seen that the intemperate suffer from a high rate of mortality, and the extremely profligate leave few offspring. The poorest classes crowd into towns, and it has been proved by Dr. Stark from the statistics of ten years in Scotland, that at all ages the death-rate is higher in towns than in rural districts, "and during the first five years of life the town death-rate is almost exactly double that of rural districts." As these returns include both the rich and the poor, no doubt more than twice the number of births would be requisite to keep up the number of the very poor inhabitants in the towns, relatively to those in the country. With women, marriage at too early an age is highly injurious; for it has been found in France that, "twice as many wives under twenty die in the year, as died out of the same number unmarried." The mortality, also, of husbands under twenty is "excessively high," but what the cause of this may be seems doubtful. Lastly, if the men who prudently delay marrying until they can bring up their families in comfort, were to select, as they often do, women in the prime of life, the rate of increase in the better class would be only slightly lessened.

It was established from an enormous body of statistics, taken during 1853, that the unmarried men throughout France, between the ages of twenty and eighty, die in a much larger proportion than the married: for instance, out of every 1000 unmarried men, between the ages of twenty and thirty, 11.3 annually died, whilst of the married, only 6.5 died. A similar law was proved to hold good during the years 1863 and 1864, with the entire population above the age of twenty in Scotland: for instance, out of every 1000 unmarried men, between the ages of twenty and thirty, 14.97 annually died, whilst of the married only 7.24 died, that is less than half. Dr. Stark remarks on this, "Bachelorhood is more destructive to life than the most unwholesome trades, or than residence in an unwholesome house or district where there has never been the most distant attempt at sanitary improvement." He considers that the lessened mortality is the direct result of "marriage, and the more regular domestic habits which attend that state." He admits, however, that the intemperate, profligate, and criminal classes, whose duration of life is low, do not commonly marry; and it must likewise be admitted that men with a weak constitution, ill health, or any great infirmity in body or mind, will often not wish to marry, or will be rejected. Dr. Stark seems to have come to the conclusion that marriage in itself is a main cause of prolonged life, from finding that aged married men still have a considerable advantage in this respect over the unmarried of the same advanced age; but every one must have known instances of men, who with weak health during youth did not marry, and yet have survived to old age, though remaining weak, and therefore always with a lessened chance of life. There is another remarkable circumstance which seems to support Dr. Stark's conclusion, namely, that widows and widowers in France suffer in comparison with the married a very heavy rate of mortality; but Dr. Farr attributes this to the poverty and evil habits consequent on the disruption of the family, and to grief. On the whole we may conclude with Dr. Farr that the lesser mortality of married than of unmarried men, which seems to be a general law, "is mainly due to the constant elimination of imperfect types, and to the skilful selection relating only to the marriage state, and acting on all corporeal, intellectual, and moral qualities. We may, therefore, infer that sound and good men who out of prudence remain for a time unmarried do not suffer a high rate of mortality.

If the various checks specified in the two last paragraphs, and perhaps others as yet unknown, do not prevent the reckless, the vicious and otherwise inferior members of society from increasing at a quicker rate than the better class of men, the nation will retrograde, as has occurred too often in the history of the world. We must remember that progress is no invariable rule. It is most difficult to say why one civilised nation rises, becomes more powerful, and spreads more widely, than another; or why the same nation progresses more at one time than at another. We can only say that it depends on an increase in the actual number of the population, on the number of men endowed with high intellectual and moral faculties, as well as on their standard of excellence. Corporeal structure, except so far as vigour of body leads to vigour of mind, appears to have little influence.

It has been urged by several writers that as high intellectual powers are advantageous to a nation, the old Greeks, who stood some grades higher in intellect than any race that has ever existed, ought to have risen, if the power of natural selection were real, still higher in the scale, increased in number, and stocked the whole of Europe. Here we have the tacit assumption, so often made with respect to corporeal structures, that there is some innate tendency towards continued development in mind and body. But development of all kinds depends on many concurrent favourable circumstances. Natural selection acts only in a tentative manner. Individuals and races may have acquired certain indisputable advantages, and yet have perished from failing in other characters. The Greeks may have retrograded from a want of coherence between the many small states, from the small size of their whole country, from the practice of slavery, or from extreme sensuality; for they did not succumb until "they were enervated and corrupt to the very core." The western nations of Europe, who now so immeasurably surpass their former savage progenitors and stand at the summit of civilisation, owe little or none of their superiority to direct inheritance from the old Greeks; though they owe much to the written works of this wonderful people.

Who can positively say why the Spanish nation, so dominant at one time, has been distanced in the race? The awakening of the nations of Europe from the dark ages is a still more perplexing problem. At this early period, as Mr. Galton has remarked, almost all the men of a gentle nature, those given to meditation or culture of the mind, had no refuge except in the bosom of a Church which demanded celibacy; and this could hardly fail to have had a deteriorating influence on each successive generation. During this same period the Holy Inquisition selected with extreme care the freest and boldest men in order to burn or imprison them. In Spain alone some of the best men—those who doubted and questioned, and without doubting there can be no progress—were eliminated during three centuries at the rate of a thousand a year. The evil which the Catholic Church has thus effected, though no doubt counterbalanced to a certain, perhaps large extent in other ways, is incalculable; nevertheless, Europe has progressed at an unparalleled rate.

The remarkable success of the English as colonists over other European nations, which is well illustrated by comparing the progress of the Canadians of English and French extraction, has been ascribed to their "daring and persistent energy"; but who can say how the English gained their energy? There is apparently much truth in the belief that the wonderful progress of the United States, as well as the character of the people, are the results of natural selection; the more energetic, restless, and courageous men from all parts of Europe have emigrated during the last ten or twelve generations to that great country, and having there succeeded best. Looking to the distant future, I do not think that the Rev. Mr. Zincke takes an exaggerated view when he say: "All other series of events as that which resulted in the culture of mind in Greece, and that which resulted in the empire of Rome—only appear to have purpose and value when viewed in connection with, or rather as subsidiary to . . . the great stream of Anglo-Saxon emigration to the west." Obscure as is the problem of the advance of civilization, we can at least see that a nation which produced during a lengthened period the greatest number of highly intellectual, energetic, brave, patriotic, and benevolent men, would generally prevail over less favoured nations.

Natural selection follows from the struggle for existence; and this from a rapid rate of increase. It is impossible not bitterly to regret, but whether wisely is another question, the rate at which man tends to increase; for this leads in barbarous tribes to infanticide and many other evils, and in civilised nations to abject poverty, celibacy, and to the late marriages of the prudent. But as man suffers from the same physical evils with the lower animals, he has no right to expect an immunity from the evils consequent on the struggle for existence. Had he not been subjected to natural selection, assuredly he would never have attained to the rank of manhood. When we see in many parts of the world enormous areas of the most fertile land peopled by a few wandering savages, but which are capable of supporting numerous happy homes, it might be argued that the struggle for existence had not been sufficiently severe to force man upwards to his highest standard. Judging from all that we know of man and the lower animals, there has always been sufficient variability in their intellectual and moral faculties, for their steady advancement through natural selection. No doubt such advance demands many favourable concurrent circumstances; but it may well be doubted whether the most favourable would have sufficed, had not the rate of increase been rapid, and the consequent struggle for existence severe to an extreme degree.

Religious Belief

During these two years[1] I was led to think much about religion. Whilst on board the *Beagle* I was quite orthodox, and I remember being heartily laughed at by several of the officers (though themselves orthodox) for quoting the Bible as an unanswerable authority on some point of morality. I suppose it was the novelty of the argument that amused them. But I had gradually come, by this time, to see that the Old Testament from its manifestly false history of the world, with the Tower of Babel, the rainbow as a sign, etc., etc., and from its attributing to God the feelings of a revengeful tyrant, was no more to be trusted than the sacred books of the Hindoos, or the beliefs of any barbarian. The question then continually rose before my mind and would not be banished,—is it credible that if God were now to make a revelation to the Hindoos, would he permit it to be connected with the belief in Vishnu, Siva, &c., as Christianity is connected with the Old Testament. This appeared to me utterly incredible.

By further reflecting that the clearest evidence would be requisite to make any sane man believe in the miracles by which Christianity is supported,—that the more we know of the fixed laws of nature the more incredible do miracles become,—that the men at that time were ignorant and credulous to a degree almost incomprehensible by us,—that the Gospels cannot be proved to have been written simultaneously with the events,—that they differ in many important details, far too important as it seemed to me to be admitted as the usual inaccuracies of eyewitnesses;—by such reflections as these, which I give not as having the least novelty or value, but as they influenced me, I gradually came to disbelieve in Christianity as a divine revelation. The fact that many false religions have spread over large portions of the earth like wild-fire had some weight with me. Beautiful as is the morality of the New Testament, it can hardly be denied that its perfection depends in part on the interpretation which we now put on metaphors and allegories.

But I was very unwilling to give up my belief;—I feel sure of this for I can well remember often and often inventing day-dreams of old letters between distinguished Romans and manuscripts being discovered at Pompeii or elsewhere which confirmed in the most striking manner all that was written in the Gospels. But I found it more and more difficult, with free scope given to my imagination,

---

1   October 1836 to January 1839.—F.D.

to invent evidence which would suffice to convince me. Thus disbelief crept over me at a very slow rate, but was at last complete. The rate was so slow that I felt no distress, and have never since doubted even for a single second that my conclusion was correct. I can indeed hardly see how anyone ought to wish Christianity to be true; for if so the plain language of the text seems to show that the men who do not believe, and this would include my Father, Brother and almost all my best friends, will be everlastingly punished.

And this is a damnable doctrine.[2]

Although I did not think much about the existence of a personal God until a considerably later period of my life, I will here give the vague conclusions to which I have been driven. The old argument of design in nature, as given by Paley, which formerly seemed to me so conclusive, fails, now that the law of natural selection has been discovered. We can no longer argue that, for instance, the beautiful hinge of a bivalve shell must have been made by an intelligent being, like the hinge of a door by man. There seems to be no more design in the variability of organic beings and in the action of natural selection, than in the course which the wind blows. Everything in nature is the result of fixed laws. But I have discussed this subject at the end of my book on the *Variation of Domestic Animals and Plants,*[3] and the argument there given has never, as far as I can see, been answered.

But passing over the endless beautiful adaptations which we everywhere meet with, it may be asked how can the generally beneficent arrangement of the world be accounted for? Some writers indeed are so much impressed with the amount of suffering in the world, that they doubt if we look to all sentient beings, whether there is more of misery or of happiness;—whether the world as a whole is a good or a bad one. According to my judgment happiness decidedly prevails, though this would be very difficult to prove. If the truth of this conclusion be

---

2   Mrs. Darwin annotated this passage (from "and have never since doubted" . . . to "damnable doctrine") in her own handwriting. She writes:—"I should dislike the passage in brackets to be published. It seems to me raw. Nothing can be said too severe upon the doctrine—of everlasting punishment for disbelief—but very few now wd. call that 'Christianity,' (tho' the words are there.) There is the question of verbal inspiration comes in too. E.D." Oct. 1882. This was written six months after her husband's death, in a second copy of the Autobiography in Francis's handwriting. The passage was not published. . . .—N.B.

3   My father asks whether we are to believe that the forms are preordained of the broken fragments of rock which are fitted together by man to build his houses. If not, why should we believe that the variations of domestic animals or plants are preordained for the sake of the breeder? "But if we give up the principle in one case, . . . no shadow of reason can be assigned for the belief that the variations alike in nature and the result of the same general laws, which have been the groundwork through natural selection of the formation of the most perfectly adapted animals in the world, man included, were intentionally and specially guided."—*Variations of Animals and Plants,* 1st Edit. vol. ii p. 431.—F.D.

granted, it harmonises well with the effects which we might expect from natural selection. If all the individuals of any species were habitually to suffer to an extreme degree they would neglect to propagate their kind; but we have no reason to believe that this has ever or at least often occurred. Some other considerations, moreover, lead to the belief that all sentient beings have been formed so as to enjoy, as a general rule, happiness.

Every one who believes, as I do, that all the corporeal and mental organs (excepting those which are neither advantageous or disadvantageous to the possessor) of all beings have been developed through natural selection, or the survival of the fittest, together with use or habit,[4] will admit that these organs have been formed so that their possessors may compete successfully with other beings, and thus increase in number. Now an animal may be led to pursue that course of action which is the most beneficial to the species by suffering, such as pain, hunger, thirst, and fear,—or by pleasure, as in eating and drinking and in the propagation of the species, &c. or by both means combined, as in the search for food. But pain or suffering of any kind, if long continued, causes depression and lessens the power of action; yet is well adapted to make a creature guard itself against any great or sudden evil. Pleasurable sensations, on the other hand, may be long continued without any depressing effect; on the contrary they stimulate the whole system to increased action. Hence it has come to pass that most or all sentient beings have been developed in such a manner through natural selection, that pleasurable sensations serve as their habitual guides. We see this in the pleasure from exertion, even occasionally from great exertion of the body or mind,—in the pleasure of our daily meals, and especially in the pleasure derived from sociability and from loving our families. The sum of such pleasures as these, which are habitual or frequently recurrent, give, as I can hardly doubt, to most sentient beings an excess of happiness over misery, although many occasionally suffer much. Such suffering, is quite compatible with the belief in Natural Selection, which is not perfect in its action, but tends only to render each species as successful as possible in the battle for life with other species, in wonderfully complex and changing circumstances.

That there is much suffering in the world no one disputes. Some have attempted to explain this in reference to man by imagining that it serves for his moral improvement. But the number of men in the world is as nothing compared with that of all other sentient beings, and these often suffer greatly without any moral improvement. A being so powerful and so full of knowledge as a God who could create the universe, is to our finite minds omnipotent and omniscient, and it revolts our understanding to suppose that his benevolence is not unbounded, for what advantage can there be in the sufferings of millions of the lower animals throughout almost endless time? This very old argument from the existence of suffering against the existence of an intelligent first cause seems to me a strong one;

---

4   "together with use or habit" added later. The many corrections and alterations in this sentence show his increasing preoccupation with the possibility of other forces at work besides Natural Selection.—N.B.

whereas, as just remarked, the presence of much suffering agrees well with the view that all organic beings have been developed through variation and natural selection.

At the present day the most usual argument for the existence of an intelligent God is drawn from the deep inward conviction and feelings which are experienced by most persons. But it cannot be doubted that Hindoos, Mahomadans and others might argue in the same manner and with equal force in favour of the existence of one God, or of many Gods, or as with the Buddists of no God. There are also many barbarian tribes who cannot be said with any truth to believe in what we call God: they believe indeed in spirits or ghosts, and it can be explained, as Tyler and Herbert Spencer have shown, how such a belief would be likely to arise.

Formerly I was led by feelings such as those just referred to, (although I do not think that the religious sentiment was ever strongly developed in me), to the firm conviction of the existence of God, and of the immortality of the soul. In my Journal I wrote that whilst standing in the midst of the grandeur of a Brazilian forest, "it is not possible to give an adequate idea of the higher feelings of wonder, admiration, and devotion which fill and elevate the mind." I well remember my conviction that there is more in man than the mere breath of his body. But now the grandest scenes would not cause any such convictions and feelings to rise in my mind. It may be truly said that I am like a man who has become colour-blind, and the universal belief by men of the existence of redness makes my present loss of perception of not the least value as evidence. This argument would be a valid one if all men of all races had the same inward conviction of the existence of one God; but we know that this is very far from being the case. Therefore I cannot see that such inward convictions and feelings are of any weight as evidence of what really exists. The state of mind which grand scenes formerly excited in me, and which was intimately connected with a belief in God, did not essentially differ from that which is often called the sense of sublimity; and however difficult it may be to explain the genesis of this sense, it can hardly be advanced as an argument for the existence of God, any more than the powerful though vague and similar feelings excited by music.

With respect to immortality,[5] nothing shows me how strong and almost instinctive a belief it is, as the consideration of the view now held by most physicists, namely that the sun with all the planets will in time grow too cold for life, unless indeed some great body dashes into the sun and thus gives it fresh life.—Believing as I do that man in the distant future will be a far more perfect creature than he now is, it is an intolerable thought that he and all other sentient beings are doomed to complete annihilation after such long-continued slow progress. To those who fully admit the immortality of the human soul, the destruction of our world will not appear so dreadful.

Another source of conviction in the existence of God, connected with the reason and not with the feelings, impresses me as having much more weight. This follows from the extreme difficulty or rather impossibility of conceiving this immense and wonderful universe, including man with his capacity of looking far

---

5   Addendum added later to end of paragraph—N.B.

backwards and far into futurity, as the result of blind chance or necessity. When thus reflecting I feel compelled to look to a First Cause having an intelligent mind in some degree analogous to that of man; and I deserve to be called a Theist.

This conclusion[6] was strong in my mind about the time, as far as I can remember, when I wrote the *Origin of Species;* and it is since that time that it has very gradually with many fluctuations become weaker. But then arises the doubt—can the mind of man, which has, as I fully believe, been developed from a mind as low as that possessed by the lowest animal, be trusted when it draws such grand conclusions? May not these be the result of the connection between cause and effect which strikes us as a necessary one, but probably depends merely on inherited experience? Nor must we overlook the probability of the constant inculcation in a belief in God on the minds of children producing so strong and perhaps an inherited effect on their brains not yet fully developed, that it would be as difficult for them to throw off their belief in God, as for a monkey to throw off its instinctive fear and hatred of a snake.[7]

I cannot pretend to throw the least light on such abstruse problems. The mystery of the beginning of all things is insoluble by us; and I for one must be content to remain an Agnostic.

---

6   Addendum of four lines added later. In Charles's MS. copy the interleaved addition is in his eldest son's hand. In Francis's copy it is in Charles's own hand.—N.B.

7   Added later. Emma Darwin wrote and asked Frank to omit this sentence when he was editing the Autobiography in 1885. The letter is as follows:—
    "Emma Darwin to her son Francis. 1885
My dear Frank,

There is one sentence in the Autobiography which I very much wish to omit, no doubt partly because your father's opinion that *all* morality has grown up by evolution is painful to me; but also because where this sentence comes in, it gives one a sort of shock—and would give an opening to say, however unjustly, that he considered all spiritual beliefs no higher than hereditary aversions or liking, such as the fear of monkeys toward snakes.

I think the disrespectful aspect would disappear if the first part of the conjecture was left without the illustration of the instance of monkeys and snakes. I don't think you need consult William about this omission, as it would not change the whole gist of the Autobiography. I should wish if possible to avoid giving pain to your father's religious friends who are deeply attached to him, and I picture to myself the way that sentence would strike them, even those so liberal as Ellen Tollett and Laura, much more Admiral Sullivan, Aunt Caroline, &c., and even the old servants.

Yours, dear Frank,
        E.D."
This letter appeared in *Emma Darwin* by Henrietta Litchfield in the privately printed edition from the Cambridge University Press in 1904. In John Murray's public edition of 1915 it was omitted.—N.B.

291

A man who has no assured and ever present belief in the existence of a personal God or of a future existence with retribution and reward, can have for his rule of life, as far as I can see, only to follow those impulses and instincts which are the strongest or which seem to him the best ones. A dog acts in this manner, but he does so blindly. A man, on the other hand, looks forwards and backwards, and compares his various feelings, desires and recollections. He then finds, in accordance with the verdict of all the wisest men that the highest satisfaction is derived from following certain impulses, namely the social instincts. If he acts for the good of others, he will receive the approbation of his fellow men and gain the love of those with whom he lives; and this latter gain undoubtedly is the highest pleasure on this earth. By degrees it will become intolerable to him to obey his sensuous passions rather than his higher impulses, which when rendered habitual may be almost called instincts. His reason may occasionally tell him to act in opposition to the opinion of others, whose approbation he will then not receive; but he will still have the solid satisfaction of knowing that he has followed his innermost guide or conscience.—As for myself I believe that I have acted rightly in steadily following and devoting my life to science. I feel no remorse from having committed any great sin, but have often and often regretted that I have not done more direct good to my fellow creatures. My sole and poor excuse is much ill-health and my mental constitution, which makes it extremely difficult for me to turn from one subject or occupation to another. I can imagine with high satisfaction giving up my whole time to philanthropy, but not a portion of it; though this would have been a far better line of conduct.

Nothing[8] is more remarkable than the spread of scepticism or rationalism during the latter half of my life. Before I was engaged to be married, my father advised me to conceal carefully my doubts, for he said that he had known extreme misery thus caused with married persons. Things went on pretty well until the wife or husband became out of health, and then some women suffered miserably by doubting about the salvation of their husbands, thus making them likewise to suffer. My father added that he had known during his whole long life only three women who were sceptics; and it should be remembered that he knew well a multitude of persons and possessed extraordinary power of winning confidence. When I asked him who the three women were, he had to own with respect to one of them, his sister-in-law Kitty Wedgwood, that he had no good evidence, only the vaguest hints, aided by the conviction that so clear-sighted a woman could not be a believer. At the present time, with my small acquaintance, I know (or have known) several married ladies, who believe very little more than their husbands. My father used to quote an unanswerable argument, by which an old lady, a Mrs. Barlow, who suspected him of unorthodoxy, hoped to convert him:—"Doctor, I know that sugar is sweet in my mouth, and I know that my Redeemer liveth."

---

8   This paragraph has a note by Charles:—"Written in 1879—copied out Apl. 22, 1881." Probably refers also to previous paragraph.—N.B.

From Poor Laws

━━━◆━━━

Herbert Spencer

Herbert Spencer (1820–1903) is the best known advocate of "Social Darwinism." Born in a family of religious dissenters, he was largely self-educated and eventually gave up his Christian faith. He had a varied career as a civil railway engineer, teacher, journalist, and editor until an inheritance received in 1853 enabled him to work full time on his philosophical works. Spencer was a supporter of the theory of evolution as advocated by Lamarck and the theory of evolution lay at the basis of his philosophical writings. Shortly after the appearance of the writings of Darwin and Wallace, he accepted and became an advocate of their view of natural selection as the mechanism of evolution. Spencer's major project, which occupied him from 1860 until his death, was writing The *Synthetic Philosophy,* a massive work intended to integrate all scientific, sociological, psychological, economic, and political knowledge. Spencer was more interested in grand theory than in moving from empirical data to theory. His work emphasized in all areas the growth of variety and individualization. In the area of government, his basic distinction was between military (despotic) government and a truly minimal, liberal (in the classic sense) government which would interfere in society only to the extent necessary to protect individual natural rights. Just as animals evolve in such a way as to ensure the "survival of the fittest" (a phrase coined by Spencer), Spencer argued that the same is true of human society ("social Darwinism"). To interfere in this evolution is to cause less fit forms to survive to the detriment of both society and the individual. Thus, as in our reading, Spencer opposed various government efforts to lessen the misery of the poor ("Poor Laws" is from Spencer's *Social Statics,* 1851—thus before Darwin's publication of his theory of evolution through natural selection). Spencer was active in the intellectual life of England and included among his friends, Thomas Huxley, John Stuart Mill, George Eliot, and Beatrice Webb.

Malcolm Clark

§6. Pervading all nature we may see at work a stern discipline, which is a little cruel that it may be very kind. That state of universal warfare maintained throughout the lower creation, to the great perplexity of many worthy people, is at bottom the most merciful provision which the circumstances admit of. It is much better that the ruminant animal, when deprived by age of the vigour which made its existence a pleasure, should be killed by some beast of prey, than that it should linger out a life made painful by infirmities, and eventually die of starvation. By the destruction of all such, not only is existence ended before it becomes burdensome, but room is made for a younger generation capable of the fullest enjoyment; and, moreover, out of the very act of substitution happiness is derived for a tribe of predatory creatures. Note further, that their carnivorous enemies not only remove from herbivorous herds individuals past their prime, but also weed out the sickly, the malformed, and the least fleet or powerful. By the aid of which purifying process, as well as by the fighting, so universal in the pairing season, all vitiation of the race through the multiplication of its inferior samples is prevented; and the maintenance of a constitution completely adapted to surrounding conditions, and therefore most productive of happiness, is ensured.

The development of the higher creation is a progress toward a form of being capable of a happiness undiminished by these drawbacks. It is in the human race that the consummation is to be accomplished. Civilization is the last stage of its accomplishment. And the ideal man is the man in whom all the conditions of that accomplishment are fulfilled. Meanwhile the well-being of existing humanity, and the unfolding of it into this ultimate perfection, are both secured by that same beneficent, though severe discipline, to which the animate creation at large is subject: a discipline which is pitiless in the working out of good: a felicity-pursuing law which never swerves for the avoidance of partial and temporary suffering. The poverty of the incapable, the distresses that come upon the imprudent, the starvation of the idle, and those shoulderings aside of the weak by the strong, which leave so many "in shallows and in miseries," are the decrees of a large, far-seeing benevolence. It seems hard that an unskilfulness which with all his efforts he cannot overcome, should entail hunger upon the artisan. It seems hard that a labourer incapacitated by sickness from competing with his stronger fellows, should have to bear the resulting privations. It seems hard that widows and orphans should be left to struggle for life or death. Nevertheless, when regarded not separately, but in connection with the interests of universal humanity, these harsh fatalities are seen to be full of the highest beneficence—the same beneficence which brings to early graves the children of diseased parents, and singles out the low-spirited, the intemperate, and the debilitated as the victims of an epidemic.

There are many very amiable people—people over whom in so far as their feelings are concerned we may fitly rejoice—who have not the nerve to look this matter fairly in the face. Disabled as they are by their sympathies with present suffering, from duly regarding ultimate consequences, they pursue a course which is very injudicious, and in the end even cruel. We do not consider it true kindness in a mother to gratify her child with sweetmeats that are certain to make it ill. We should think it a very foolish sort of benevolence which led a surgeon to let his patient's disease progress to a fatal issue, rather than inflict pain by an operation. Similarly, we must call those spurious philanthropists, who, to prevent present misery, would entail greater misery upon future generations. All defenders of a poor-law must, however, be classed amongst such. That rigorous necessity which, when allowed to act on them, becomes so sharp a spur to the lazy, and so strong a bridle to the random, these paupers friends would repeal, because of the wailings it here and there produces. Blind to the fact, that under the natural order of things society is constantly excreting its unhealthy, imbecile, slow, vacillating, faithless members, these unthinking, though well-meaning, men advocate an interference which not only stops the purifying process, but even increases the vitiation—absolutely encourages the multiplication of the reckless and incompetent by offering them an unfailing provision, and discourages the multiplication of the competent and provident by heightening the prospective difficulty of maintaining a family. And thus, in their eagerness to prevent the really salutary sufferings that surround us, these sigh-wise and groan-foolish people bequeath to posterity a continually increasing curse.

Returning again to the highest point of view, we find that there is a second and still more injurious mode in which law-enforced charity checks the process of adaptation. To become fit for the social state, man has not only to lose his savageness, but he has to acquire the capacities needful for civilized life. Power of application must be developed; such modification of the intellect as shall qualify it for its new tasks must take place; and, above all, there must be gained the ability to sacrifice a small immediate gratification for a future great one. The state of transition will of course be an unhappy state. Misery inevitably results from incongruity between constitution and conditions. All these evils, which afflict us, and seem to the uninitiated the obvious consequences of this or that removable cause, are unavoidable attendants on the adaptation now in progress. Humanity is being pressed against the inexorable necessities of its new position—is being moulded into harmony with them, and has to bear the resulting, unhappiness as best it can. The process *must* be undergone, and the sufferings *must* be endured. No power on earth, no cunningly-devised laws of statesmen, no world-rectifying schemes of the humane, no communist panaceas, no reforms that man ever did broach or ever will broach, can diminish them one jot. Intensified they may be, and are; and in preventing their intensification, the philanthropic will find ample scope for exertion. But there is bound up with the change a *normal* amount of suffering, which cannot be lessened without altering the very laws of life. Every attempt at mitigation of this eventuates in exacerbation of it. All that a poor-law, or any kindred institution can do, is to partially suspend the transition—to take off for awhile, from certain members of society, the painful pressure which is effecting their transformation. At best this is merely to postpone what must ultimately be borne. But it is more than this: it is to undo what has already been done. For the circumstances to which adaptation is taking place cannot be superseded without causing a retrogression—a partial loss of the adaptation previously effected; and as the whole process must some time or other be passed through, the lost ground must be gone over again, and the attendant pain borne afresh. Thus, besides retarding adaptation, a poor-law adds to the distresses inevitably attending it.

At first sight these considerations seem conclusive against all relief to the poor—voluntary as well as compulsory; and it is no doubt true that they imply a condemnation of whatever private charity enables the recipients to elude the necessities of our social existence. With this condemnation, however, no rational man will quarrel. That careless squandering of pence which has fostered into perfection a system of organized begging—which has made skillful mendicancy more profitable than ordinary manual labour—which induces the simulation of palsy, epilepsy, cholera, and no end of diseases and deformities—which has called into existence warehouses for the sale and hire of impostor's dresses—which has given to pity—inspiring babes a market value of 9d. per day—the unthinking benevolence which has generated all this, cannot but be disapproved by every one. Now it is only against this injudicious charity that the foregoing argument tells. To that charity which may be described as helping men to help themselves, it makes no objection——countenances it rather. And in helping men to help themselves, there remains abundant scope for the exercise of a people's sympathies. Accidents will still supply victims on whom generosity may be legitimately expended. Men thrown upon their backs by unforeseen events, men who have failed for want of knowledge inaccessible to them, men ruined by the dishonesty of others, and men in whom hope long delayed has made the heart sick, may, with advantage to all parties, be assisted. Even the prodigal, after severe hardship has branded his memory with the unbending conditions of social life to which he must submit, may properly have another trial afforded him. And, although by these ameliorations the process of adaptation must be remotely interfered with, yet in the majority of cases, it will not be so much retarded in one direction as it will be advanced in another.

From
Evolution and Ethics

⟹◆⟸

Thomas Henry Huxley

Thomas Henry Huxley (1825–1895) was the most forceful and successful public advocate of Darwin's views and played the major role in gaining public acceptance of those views. Self-educated, he had only two years of formal schooling, ending when he was 10. When he was 21, he went on a four year ocean voyage, collecting and analyzing marine specimens. The scientific papers he sent back to England during the voyage had established his reputation by the time he returned home and he was elected a fellow of the Royal Society within the year. Huxley remained active in biological research and taught at the Royal School of Mines in London playing a leading role in its transformation into a major institution of higher education. While there, he pioneered the use of laboratories in science education and the practical training of science teachers. Huxley (along with Joseph Dalton Hooker and Charles Lyell) was one of three scientists whom Darwin submitted his work to for review before its publication. Huxley became the major publicist, both to popular and scientific circles, of Darwin's views. His debate with Samuel Wilberforce in 1860 is cited as a major turning point in the public acceptance of evolutionary theory. Wilberforce was the son of anti-slavery activist William Wilberforce, a major figure in the Oxford Movement for religious revival within the Church of England, bishop of Oxford, and defender of Christianity against the dangerous views of evolution. From 1870 on, Huxley became the dominant figure in the movement which led to far reaching reforms in the English system of primary school education. Huxley was also interested in theology and he invented the word "agnosticism" to designate the position he arrived at concerning the existence of God. (The Huxley selection on "Evolution and Ethics" is from a public lecture given in 1893).

Malcolm Clark

Modern thought is making a fresh start from the base whence Indian and Greek philosophy set out; and, the human mind being very much what it was six-and-twenty centuries ago, there is no ground for wonder if it presents indications of a tendency to move along the old lines to the same results.

We are more than sufficiently familiar with modern pessimism, at least as a speculation, for I cannot call to mind that any of its present votaries have sealed their faith by assuming the rags and the bowl of the mendicant Bhikku, or the cloak and the wallet of the Cynic. The obstacles placed in the way of sturdy vagrancy by an unphilosophical police have, perhaps, proved too formidable for philosophical consistency. We also know modern speculative optimism, with its perfectibility of the species, reign of peace, and lion and lamb transformation scenes; but one does not hear so much of it as one did forty years ago; indeed, I imagine it is to be met with more commonly at the tables of the healthy and wealthy, than in the congregations of the wise. The majority of us, I apprehend, profess neither pessimism nor optimism. We hold that the world is neither so good, nor so bad, as it conceivably might be; and, as most of us have reason, now and again, to discover that it can be. Those who have failed to experience the joys that make life worth living are, probably, in as small a minority as those who have never known the griefs that rob existence of its savour and turn its richest fruits into mere dust and ashes.

Further, I think I do not err in assuming that, however diverse their views on philosophical and religious matters, most men are agreed that the proportion of good and evil in life may be very sensibly affected by human action. I never heard anybody doubt that the evil may be thus increased or diminished; and it would seem to follow that good must be similarly susceptible of addition or subtraction. Finally, to my knowledge, nobody professes to doubt that, so far forth as we possess a power of bettering things, it is our paramount duty to use it and to train all our intellect and energy to this supreme service of our kind.

Hence the pressing interest of the question, to what extent modern progress in natural knowledge, and, more especially, the general outcome of that progress in the doctrine of evolution, is competent to help us in the great work of helping one another?

The propounders of what are called the "ethics of evolution," when the "evolution of ethics" would usually better express the object of their speculations, adduce a number of more or less interesting facts and more or less sound arguments, in favour of the origin of the moral sentiments, in the same way as other natural phenomena, by a process of evolution. I have little doubt, for my own part, that they are on the right track; but as the immoral sentiments have no less been evolved, there is, so far, as much natural sanction for one as the other. The thief and murderer follow nature just as much as the philanthropist. Cosmic evolution may teach us how the good and the evil tendencies of man may have come about; but, in itself, it is incompetent to furnish any better reason why what we call good is preferable to what we call evil than we had before. Some day, I doubt not, we shall arrive at an understanding of the evolution of the aesthetic faculty; but all the understanding in the world will neither increase nor diminish the force of the intuition that this is beautiful and that is ugly.

There is another fallacy which appears to me to pervade the so-called "ethics of evolution." It is the notion that because, on the whole, animals and plants have advanced in perfection or organization by means of the struggle for existence and the consequent "survival of the fittest"; therefore men in society, men as ethical beings, must look to the same process to help them towards perfection. I suspect that this fallacy has arisen out of the unfortunate ambiguity of the phrase "survival of the fittest." "Fittest" has a connotation of "best"; and about "best" there hangs a moral flavour. In cosmic nature, however, what is "fittest" depends upon the conditions. Long since,[1] I ventured to point out that if our hemisphere were to cool again, the survival of the fittest might bring about, in the vegetable kingdom, a population of more and more stunted and humbler and humbler organisms, until the "fittest" that survived might be nothing but lichens, diatoms, and such microscopic organisms as those which give red snow its colour; while, if it became hotter, the pleasant valleys of the Thames and Isis might be uninhabitable by any animated beings save those that flourish in a tropical jungle. They, as the fittest, the best adapted to the changed conditions, would survive.

Men in society are undoubtedly subject to the cosmic process. As among other animals, multiplication goes on without cessation, and involves severe competition for the means of support. The struggle for existence tends to eliminate those less fitted to adapt themselves to the circumstances of their existence. The strongest, the most self-assertive, tend to tread down the weaker. But the influence of the cosmic process on the evolution of society is the greater the more rudimentary its civilization. Social progress means a checking of the cosmic process at every step and the substitution for it of another, which may be called the ethical process; the end of which is not the survival of those who may happen to be the fittest, in respect of the whole of the conditions which obtain, but of those who are ethically the best.[2]

As I have already urged, the practice of that which is ethically best—what we call goodness or virtue—involves a course of conduct which, in all respects, is opposed to that which leads to success in the cosmic struggle for existence. In place of ruthless self-assertion it demands self-restraint; in place of thrusting

---

1   "Criticisms on the Origin of Species," 1864. *Collected Essays,* vol. ii, p. 91.

2   Of course, strictly speaking, social life, and the ethical process in virtue of which it advances towards perfection, are part and parcel of the general process of evolution just as the gregarious habit of innumerable plants and animals, which has been of immense advantage to them, is so. A hive of bees is an organic polity, a society in which the part played by each member is determined by organic necessities. Queens, workers, and drones are, so to speak, castes, divided from one another by marked physical barriers. Among birds and mammals, societies are formed, of which the bond in many cases seems to be to be purely psychological; that is to say, it appears to depend upon the linking of the individuals for one another's company. The tendency of individuals of over self-assertion is kept down by fighting. Even in these rudimentary forms of society, love and fear come into play, and enforce a greater or less renunciation of self-will. To this extent the general cosmic process begins to be checked by a rudimentary ethical process, which is, strictly speaking, part of the former, just as the "governor" in a steam-engine is part of the mechanism of the engine.

aside, or treading down, all competitors, it requires that the individual shall not merely respect, but shall help his fellows; its influence is directed, not so much to the survival of the fittest, as to the fitting of as many as possible to survive. It repudiates the gladiatorial theory of existence. It demands that each man who enters into the enjoyment of the advantages of a polity shall be mindful of his debt to those who have laboriously constructed it; and shall take heed that no act of his weakens the fabric in which he has been permitted to live. Laws and moral precepts are directed to the end of curbing the cosmic process and reminding the individual of his duty to the community, to the protection and influence of which he owes, if not existence itself, at least the life of something better than a brutal savage.

It is from neglect of these plain considerations that the fanatical individualism[3] of our time attempts to apply the analogy of cosmic nature to society. Once more we have a misapplication of the stoical injunction to follow nature; the duties of the individual to the State are forgotten, and his tendencies to self-assertion are dignified by the name of rights. It is seriously debated whether the members of a community are justified in using their combined strength to constrain one of their number to contribute his share to the maintenance of it; or even to prevent him from doing his best to destroy it. The struggle for existence, which has done such admirable work in cosmic nature, must, it appears, be equally beneficent in the ethical sphere. Yet if that which I have insisted upon is true, if the cosmic process has no sort of relation to moral ends, if the imitation of it by man is inconsistent with the first principles of ethics; what becomes of this surprising theory?

Let us understand, once for all, that the ethical progress of society depends, not on imitating the cosmic process, still less in running away from it, but in combating it. It may seem an audacious proposal thus to pit the microcosm against the macrocosm and to set man to subdue nature to his higher ends; but I venture to think that the great intellectual difference between the ancient times with which we have been occupied and our day, lies in the solid foundation we have acquired for the hope that such an enterprise may meet with a certain measure of success.

The history of civilization details the steps by which men have succeeded in building up an artificial world within the cosmos. Fragile reed as he may be, man, as Pascal says, is a thinking reed; there lies within him a fund of energy, operating intelligently and so far akin to that which pervades the universe, that it is competent to influence and modify the cosmic process. In virtue of his intelligence, the dwarf bends the Titan to his will. In every family, in every polity that has been established, the cosmic process in man has been restrained and otherwise modified by law and custom; in surrounding nature, it has been similarly influenced by the art of the shepherd, the agriculturalist, the artisan.

---

3   See "Government: Anarchy or Regimentation," *Collected Essays*, vol. i, pp. 413–418. It is this form of political philosophy to which I conceive the epithet of "reasoned savagery" to be strictly applicable.

As civilization has advanced, so has the extent of this interference increased; until the organized and highly developed sciences and arts of the present day have endowed man with a command over the course of nonhuman nature greater than that once attributed to the magicians. The most impressive, I might say startling, of these changes have been brought about in the course of the last two centuries; while a right comprehension of the process of life and of the means of influencing its manifestations is only just dawning upon us. We do not yet see our way beyond generalities; and we are befogged by the obtrusion of false analogies and crude anticipations. But Astronomy, Physics, Chemistry, have all had to pass through similar phases, before they reached the stage at which their influence became an important factor in human affairs. Physiology, Psychology, Ethics, Political Science, must submit to the same ordeal. Yet it seems to me irrational to doubt that, at no distant period, they will work as great revolution in the sphere of practice.

The theory of evolution encourages no millennial anticipation. If, for millions of years, our globe has taken the upward road, yet, some time, the summit will be reached and the downward route will be commenced. The most daring imagination will hardly venture upon the suggestion that the power and the intelligence of man can ever arrest the procession of the great year.

Moreover, the cosmic nature born with us and, to a large extent, necessary for our maintenance, is the outcome of millions of years of severe training, and it would be folly to imagine that a few centuries will suffice to subdue its masterfulness to purely ethical ends. Ethical nature may count upon having to reckon with a tenacious and powerful enemy as long as the world lasts. But, on the other hand, I see no limit to the extent to which intelligence and will, guided by sound principles of investigation, and organized in common effort, may modify the conditions of existence, for a period longer than that now covered by history. And much may be done to change the nature of man himself.[4] The intelligence which has converted the brother of the wolf into the faithful guardian of the flock ought to be able to do something towards curbing the instincts of savagery in civilized men.

But if we may permit ourselves a larger hope of abatement of the essential evil of the world than was possible to those who, in the infancy of exact knowledge, faced the problem of existence more than a score of centuries ago, I deem it as essential condition of the realization of hope that we should cast aside the notion that the escape from pain and sorrow is the proper object of life.

We have long since emerged from the heroic childhood of our race, when good and evil could be met with the same "frolic welcome"; the attempts to escape from evil, whether Indian or Greek, have ended in flight from the battle-field; it remains to us to throw aside the youthful over-confidence and the

---

4   The use of the word "Nature" here may be criticized. Yet the manifestation of the natural tendencies of men is so profoundly modified by training that it is hardly too strong. Consider the suppression of the sexual instinct between near relations.

no less youthful discouragement of nonage. We are grown men, and must play the man.

strong in will

To strive, to seek to find, and not to yield,

cherishing the good that falls in our way, and bearing the evil, in and around us, with stout hearts set on diminishing it. So far, we all may strive in one faith towards one hope:

> It may be that the gulfs will wash us down,
> It may be we shall touch the Happy Isles,
>   . . . but something ere the end,
> Some work of noble note may yet be done.[5]

---

5   A great proportion of poetry is addressed by the young to the young; only the great masters of the art are capable of divining, or think it worth while to enter into, the feelings of retrospective age. The two great poets whom we have so lately lost, Tennyson and Browning, have done this, each in his own inimitable way; the one in the *Ulysses,* from which I have borrowed; the other in that wonderful fragment "Childe Roland to the dark Tower came."

Minute on Indian Education

Thomas Babington Macaulay

Shortly after he reached India in 1834, Macaulay found himself embroiled in the struggle over the future of Indian education which had been raging within the General Committee on Public Instruction for some time. The committee was divided into two factions—the "Orientalists" who felt that the British government should continue to foster instruction in Sanskrit and Arabic as well as in English for students in institutions of higher learning sponsored by the committee; and the "Anglicists" who were convinced that the available funds should be employed more or less exclusively for the teaching of English. Both sides believed in varying degrees in the necessity for "Westernization" and in the importance of the Indian vernaculars for carrying out this purpose. But the Anglicist party, unlike the Orientalist, believed strongly that the principal effort on the part of the government had to be put into the teaching of English. Macaulay's minute, written in his capacity of Legal Member of Council, strongly favored the Anglicist side. In the event, the governor-general, Lord William Bentinck, adopted in principle (though not in every detail) the policies recommended by Macaulay. The correctness of these policies is still being argued about today, but there is no doubt that their consequences for India were immense.

John Clive and Thomas Pinney

I hold this lac of rupees to be quite at the disposal of the Governor-General in Council, for the purpose of promoting learning in India, in any way which may be thought most advisable. I hold his Lordship to be quite as free to direct that it shall no longer be employed in encouraging Arabic and Sanscrit, as he is to direct that the reward for killing tigers in Mysore shall be diminished, or that no more public money shall be expended on the chanting at the cathedral.

We now come to the gist of the matter. We have a fund to be employed as Government shall direct for the intellectual improvement of the people of this country. The simple question is, what is the most useful way of employing it?

All parties seem to be agreed on one point, that the dialects commonly spoken among the natives of this part of India contain neither literary nor scientific information, and are, moreover so poor and rude that, until they are enriched from some other quarter, it will not be easy to translate any valuable work into them. It seems to be admitted on all sides that the intellectual improvement of those classes of the people who have the means of pursuing higher studies can at present be effected only by means of some language not vernacular amongst them.

What, then, shall that language be? One half of the Committee maintain that it should be the English. The other half strongly recommend the Arabic and Sanscrit. The whole question seems to me to be, which language is the best worth knowing?

I have no knowledge of either Sanscrit or Arabic.—But I have done what I could to form a correct estimate of their value. I have read translations of the most celebrated Arabic and Sanscrit works. I have conversed both here and at home with men distinguished by their proficiency in the Eastern tongues. I am quite ready to take Oriental learning at the valuation of the Orientalists themselves. I have never found one among them who could deny that a single shelf of a good European library was worth the whole native literature of India and Arabia. The intrinsic superiority of the Western literature is, indeed, fully admitted by those members of the Committee who support the Oriental plan of education.

It will hardly be disputed, I suppose, that the department of literature in which the Eastern writers stand highest is poetry. And I certainly never met with any Orientalist who ventured to maintain that the Arabic and Sanscrit poetry could be compared to that of the great European nations. But, when we pass from works of imagination to works in which facts are recorded and general principles investigated, the superiority of the Europeans becomes absolutely immeasurable. It is, I believe, no exaggeration to say, that all the historical information which has been collected from all the books written in the Sanscrit language is less valuable than what may be found in the most paltry abridgments used at preparatory schools in England. In every branch of physical or moral philosophy the relative position of the two nations is nearly the same.

How, then, stands the case? We have to educate a people who cannot at present be educated by means of their mother tongue. We must teach them some foreign language. The claims of our own language it is hardly necessary to recapitulate. It stands preeminent even among the languages of the West. It abounds with works of imagination not inferior to the noblest which Greece has bequeathed to us; with models of every species of eloquence; with historical compositions, which, considered merely as narratives, have seldom been surpassed, and which, considered as vehicles of ethical and political instruction, have never been equalled; with just and lively representations of human life and human nature; with the most profound speculations on metaphysics, morals, government, jurisprudence, and trade; with full and correct information respecting every experimental science which tends to preserve the health, to increase the comfort, or to expand the intellect of man. Whoever knows that language, has ready access to all the vast intellectual wealth, which all the wisest nations of the earth have created and hoarded in the course of ninety generations. It may safely be said that the literature now extant in that language is of far greater value than all the literature which three hundred years ago was extant in all the languages of the world together. Nor is this all. In India, English is the language spoken by the ruling class. It is spoken by the higher class of natives at the seats of Government. It is likely to become the language of commerce throughout the seas of the East. It is the language of two great European communities which are rising, the one in the south of Africa, the other in Australasia; communities which are every year becoming more important, and more closely connected with our Indian empire. Whether we look at the intrinsic value of our literature, or at the particular situation of this country, we shall see the strongest reason to think that, of all foreign tongues, the English tongue is that which would be the most useful to our native subjects.

The question now before us is simply whether, when it is in our power to teach this language, we shall teach languages in which, by universal confession, there are no books on any subject which deserve to be compared to our own; whether, when we can teach European science, we shall teach systems which, by universal confession, whenever they differ from those of Europe, differ for the worse; and whether, when we can patronise sound Philosophy and true History, we shall countenance, at the public expense, medical doctrines which would disgrace an English Farrier—Astronomy; which would move laughter in girls at an English boarding school—History, abounding with kings thirty feet high, and reigns thirty thousand years long—and Geography, made up of seas of treacle and seas of butter.

We are not without experience to guide us. History furnishes several analogous cases, and they all teach the same lesson. There are in modern times, to go no further, two memorable instances of a great impulse given to the mind of a whole society—of prejudices overthrown—of knowledge diffused—of taste purified—of arts and sciences planted in countries which had recently been ignorant and barbarous.

The first instance to which I refer is the great revival of letters among the Western nations at the close of the fifteenth and the beginning of the sixteenth century. At that time almost everything that was worth reading was contained in the writings of the ancient Greeks and Romans. Had our ancestors acted as the Committee of Public Instruction has hitherto acted; had they neglected the language of Cicero and Tacitus; had they confined their attention to the old dialects of our own island; had they printed nothing and taught nothing at the universities but Chronicles in Anglo-Saxon and Romances in Norman-French, would England have been what she now is? What the Greek and Latin were to the contemporaries of More and Ascham, our tongue is to the people of India. The literature of England is now more valuable than that of classical antiquity. I doubt whether the Sanscrit literature be as valuable as that of our Saxon and Norman progenitors. In some departments—in History, for example—I am certain that it is much less so.

Another instance may be said to be still before our eyes. Within the last hundred and twenty years, a nation which had previously been in a state as barbarous as that in which our ancestors were before the Crusades, has gradually emerged from the ignorance in which it was sunk, and has taken its place among civilised communities—I speak of Russia. There is now in that country a large educated class, abounding with persons fit to serve the state in the highest functions, and in nowise inferior to the most accomplished men who adorn the best circles of Paris and London. There is reason to hope that this vast empire, which in the time of our grandfathers was probably behind the Punjab, may, in the time of our grandchildren, be pressing close on France and Britain in the career of improvement. And how was this change effected? Not by flattering national prejudices; not by feeding the mind of the young Muscovite with the old woman's stories which his rude fathers had believed: not by filling his head with lying legends about St. Nicholas: not by encouraging him to study the great question, whether the world was or was not created on the 13th of September: not by calling him "a learned native," when he has mastered all these points of knowledge: but by teaching him those foreign languages in which the greatest mass of information had been laid up, and thus putting all that information within his reach. The languages of Western Europe civilized Russia. I cannot doubt that they will do for the Hindoo what they have done for the Tartar.

And what are the arguments against that course which seems to be alike recommended by theory and by experience? It is said that we ought to secure the co-operation of the native public, and that we can do this only by teaching Sanscrit and Arabic.

I can by no means admit that, when a nation of high intellectual attainments undertakes to superintend the education of a nation comparatively ignorant, the learners are absolutely to prescribe the course which is to be taken by the teachers. It is not necessary, however, to say anything on this subject. For it is proved by unanswerable evidence that we are not at present securing the co-operation of the natives. It would be bad enough to consult their intellectual taste at the expense of their intellectual health. But we are consulting neither—we are withholding from them the learning for which they are craving; we are forcing on them the mock-learning which they nauseate.

This is proved by the fact that we are forced to pay our Arabic and Sanscrit students, while those who learn English are willing to pay us. All the declamations in the world about the love and reverence of the natives for their sacred dialects will never, in the mind of any impartial person, outweigh the undisputed fact, that we cannot find, in all our vast empire, a single student who will let us teach him those dialects unless we will pay him.

I have now before me the accounts of the Madrassa for one month—the month of December, 1833. The Arabic students appear to have been seventy-seven in number. All receive stipends from the public. The whole amount paid to them is above 500 rupees a month. On the other side of the account stands the following item: Deduct amount realised from the out-students of English for the months of May, June, and July last, 103 rupees.

I have been told that it is merely from want of local experience that I am surprised at these phenomena, and that it is not the fashion for students in India to study at their own charges. This only confirms me in my opinion. Nothing is more certain than that it never can in any part of the world be necessary to pay men for doing what they think pleasant and profitable. India is no exception to this rule. The people of India do not require to be paid for eating rice when they are hungry, or for wearing woollen cloth in the cold season. To come nearer to the case before us, the children who learn their letters and a little elementary Arithmetic from the village schoolmaster are not paid by him. He is paid for teaching them. Why, then, is it necessary to pay people to learn Sanscrit and Arabic? Evidently because it is universally felt that the Sanscrit and Arabic are languages the knowledge of which does not compensate for the trouble of acquiring them. On all such subjects the state of the market is the decisive test.

The fact that the Hindoo law is to be learned chiefly from Sanscrit books, and the Mahomedan law from Arabic books, has been much insisted on, but seems not to bear at all on the question. We are commanded by Parliament to ascertain and digest the laws of India. The assistance of a law commission has been given to us for that purpose. As soon as the code is promulgated, the Shasters and the Hedeya will be useless to a Moonsiff or Sudder Ameen. I hope and trust that, before the boys who are now entering at the Madrassa and the Sanscrit college have completed their studies, this great work will be finished. It would be manifestly absurd to educate the rising generation with a view to a state of things which we mean to alter before they reach manhood.

But there is yet another argument which seems even more untenable. It is said that the Sanscrit and Arabic are the languages in which the sacred books of a hundred millions of people are written, and that they are, on that account, entitled to peculiar encouragement. Assuredly it is the duty of the British Government in India to be not only tolerant, but neutral on all religious questions. But to encourage the study of a literature admitted to be of small intrinsic value only because that literature inculcates the most serious errors on the most important subjects, is a course hardly reconcilable with reason, with morality, or even with that very neutrality which ought, as we all agree, to be sacredly preserved. It is confessed that a language is barren of useful knowledge. We are told to teach it because it is fruitful of monstrous superstitions. We are to teach false history, false astronomy, false medicine, because we find them in company with a false religion. We abstain, and I trust shall always abstain, from giving any public encouragement to those who are engaged in the work of converting natives to Christianity. And, while we act thus, can we reasonably and decently bribe men out of the revenues of the state to waste their youth in learning how they are to purify themselves after touching an ass, or what text of the Vedas they are to repeat to expiate the crime of killing a goat?

It is taken for granted by the advocates of Oriental learning that no native of this country can possibly attain more than a mere smattering of English. They do not attempt to prove this; but they perpetually insinuate it. They designate the education which their opponents recommend as a mere spelling-book education. They assume it as undeniable, that the question is between a profound knowledge of Hindoo and Arabian literature and science on the one side, and a superficial knowledge of the rudiments of English on the other. This is not merely an assumption, but an assumption contrary to all reason and experience. We know that foreigners of all nations do learn our language sufficiently to have access to all the most abstruse knowledge which it contains, sufficiently to relish even the more delicate graces of our most idiomatic writers. There are in this very town natives who are quite competent to discuss political or scientific questions with fluency and precision in the English language. I have heard the very question on which I am now writing discussed by native gentlemen with a liberality and an intelligence which would do credit to any member of the Committee of Public Instruction. Indeed, it is unusual to find, even in the literary circles of the continent, any foreigner who can express himself in English with so much facility and correctness as we find in many Hindoos. Nobody, I suppose, will contend that English is so difficult to a Hindoo as Greek to an Englishman. Yet an intelligent English youth, in a much smaller number of years than our unfortunate pupils pass at the Sanscrit college, becomes able to read, to enjoy, and even to imitate, not unhappily, the composition of the best Greek authors. Less than half the time which enables an English youth to read Herodotus and Sophocles ought to enable a Hindoo to read Hume and Milton.

To sum up what I have said: I think it clear that we are not fettered by the Act of Parliament of 1813; that we are not fettered by any pledge expressed or implied; that we are free to employ our funds as we choose; that we ought to employ them in teaching what is best worth knowing; that English is better worth knowing than Sanscrit or Arabic; that the natives are desirous to be taught English, and are not desirous to be taught Sanscrit or Arabic; that neither as the languages of law, nor as the languages of religion, have the Sanscrit and Arabic any peculiar claim to our encouragement; that it is possible to make natives of this country thoroughly good English scholars, and that to this end our efforts ought to be directed.

In one point I fully agree with the gentlemen to whose general views I am opposed. I feel, with them, that it is impossible for us, with our limited means, to attempt to educate the body of the people. We must at present do our best to form a class who may be interpreters between us and the millions whom we govern; a class of persons, Indian in blood and colour, but English in taste, in opinions, in morals, and in intellect. To that class we may leave it to refine the vernacular dialects of the country, to enrich those dialects with terms of science borrowed from the Western nomenclature, and to render them by degrees fit vehicles for conveying knowledge to the great mass of the population.

The White Man's Burden

—◆—

Rudyard Kipling

Rudyard Kipling was born in India to an "Anglo-Indian" family—i.e., English people living in colonial India. He made his reputation writing about India in works such as *The Jungle Books* and *Kim*. He is, as well, perhaps the best known poet of imperialist ideology. Kipling won the Nobel Prize for Literature in 1907. The White Man's Burden first appeared in 1899.

Jaya Mehta

Take up the White Man's burden—
    Send forth the best ye breed—
Go bind your sons to exile
    To serve your captives' need;
To wait in heavy harness,
    On fluttered folk and wild—
Your new-caught, sullen peoples,
    Half-devil and half-child.

Take up the White Man's burden—
    In patience to abide.
To veil the threat of terror
    And check the show of pride;
By open speech and simple,
    An hundred times made plain,
To seek another's profit,
    And work another's gain.

Take up the White Man's burden—
    The savage wars of peace—
Fill full the mouth of Famine
    And bid the sickness cease;

And when your goal is nearest
    The end for others sought,
Watch Sloth and heathen Folly
    Bring all your hope to nought.

Take up the White Man's burden—
    No tawdry rule of kings,
But toil of serf and sweeper—
    The tale of common things.
The ports ye shall not enter,
    The roads ye shall not tread,
Go make them with your living,
    And mark them with your dead.
Take up the White Man's burden—
    And reap his old reward:
The blame of those ye better,
    The hate of those ye guard—
The cry of hosts ye humour
    (Ah, slowly!) toward the light:—
"Why brought ye us from bondage,
    "Our loved Egyptian night."

Take up the White Man's burden—
    Ye dare not stoop to less—
Nor call too loud on Freedom
    To cloak your weariness;
By all ye cry or whisper,
    By all ye leave or do,
The silent, sullen peoples
    Shall weigh your Gods and you.

Take up the White Man's burden—
    Have done with childish days—
The lightly proffered laurel,
    The easy, ungrudged praise.
Comes now, to search your manhood
    Through all the thankless years,
Cold, edged with dear-bought wisdom,
    The judgment of your peers!

From
The Subjection of Women

———◆———

John Stuart Mill [and Harriet Taylor]

John Stuart Mill (1806–1873) and Harriet Hardy Taylor were a husband and wife team prominent in philosophical and reform circles in nineteenth century England. Mill was educated by his father, a prominent Utilitarian, and early showed mastery of multiple fields from classics to science, to philosophy and law. His professional life was spent in a variety of positions with the British East India Company until its dissolution in 1858. From 1831, Mill was a close friend of Harriet Taylor, whom he married in 1851, two years after her husband's death. He claimed to have been influenced by her ideas in some of his writings. Taylor published an essay, *On the Enfranchisement of Women,* In 1851 which was one of the earliest published arguments for voting rights for women. Harriet Taylor died shortly after Mill's retirement from the British East India Company. Taylor and Mill's joint concern with women's suffrage lived on after Taylor's death when Mill played a key role in establishing the first women's suffrage society in England in 1867. Harriet's daughter, Helen Taylor continued as an active participant in the fight for women's suffrage as well as aiding her stepfather in his literary endeavors. Mill was active in advocating various other radical reform measures. Excepting one term in parliament (1865–1868), most of his life after his retirement was spent in retirement in France. His major published works were on logic, utilitarianism, political science, and women's rights. Some of these include *A System of Logic* (1843), *Principles of Political Economy,* (1849), *On Liberty* (1859), *Utilitarianism* (1863), and *On the Subjection of Women* (published in 1869 but written in 1861).

Malcolm Clark

The object of this Essay is to explain as clearly as I am able, the grounds of an opinion which I have held from the very earliest period when I had formed any opinions at all on social or political matters, and which, instead of being weakened or modified, has been constantly growing stronger by the progress of reflection and the experience of life. That the principle which regulates the

311

existing social relations between the two sexes—the legal subordination of one sex to the other—is wrong in itself, and now one of the chief hindrances to human improvement; and that it ought to be replaced by a principle of perfect equality, admitting no power or privilege on the one side, nor disability on the other.

The very words necessary to express the task I have undertaken, show how arduous it is. But it would be a mistake to suppose that the difficulty of the case must lie in the insufficiency or obscurity of the grounds of reason on which my conviction rests. The difficulty is that which exists in all cases in which there is a mass of feeling to be contended against. . . . And there are so many causes tending to make the feelings connected with this subject the most intense and most deeply-rooted of all those which gather round and protect old institutions and customs, that we need not wonder to find them as yet less undermined and loosened than any of the rest by the progress of the great modern spiritual and social transition; nor suppose that the barbarisms to which men cling longest must be less barbarisms than those which they earlier shake off. . . . In early times, the great majority of the male sex were slaves, as well as the whole of the female. And many ages elapsed, some of them ages of high cultivation, before any thinker was bold enough to question the rightfulness, and the absolute social necessity either of the one slavery or of the other. By degrees such thinkers did arise; and (the general progress of society assisting) the slavery of the male sex has, in all the countries of Christian Europe at least (though, in one of them, only within the last few years) been at length abolished, and that of the female sex has been gradually changed into a milder form of dependence. But this dependence, as it exists at present, is not an original institution, taking a fresh start from considerations of justice and social expediency—it is the primitive state of slavery lasting on, through successive mitigations and modifications occasioned by the same causes which have softened the general manners, and brought all human relations more under the control of justice and the influence of humanity. It has not lost the taint of its brutal origin. . . .

Less than forty years ago, Englishmen might still by law hold human beings in bondage as saleable property: within the present century they might kidnap them and carry them off, and work them literally to death. This absolutely extreme case of the law of force, condemned by those who can tolerate almost every other form of arbitrary power, and which, of all others presents features the most revolting to the feelings of all who look at it from an impartial position, was the law of civilised and Christian England within the memory of persons now living: and in one half of Anglo-Saxon America three or four years ago, not only did slavery exist, but the slave-trade, and the breeding of slaves expressly for it, was a general practice between slave-states. Yet not only was there a greater strength of sentiment against it, but, in England at least, a less amount either of feeling or of interest in favour of it, than of any other of the customary abuses of force: for its motive was the love of gain, unmixed and undisguised; and those who profited by it were a very small numerical fraction of the country, while the natural feeling of all who were not personally interested in it, was unmitigated abhorrence. So extreme an instance makes it almost superfluous to refer to any other: but consider the long duration of absolute monarchy. In

England at present it is the almost universal conviction that military despotism is a case of the law of force, having no other origin or justification. Yet in all the great nations of Europe except England it either still exists, or has only just ceased to exist, and has even now a strong party favourable to it in all ranks of the people, especially among persons of station and consequence. Such is the power of an established system, even when far from universal. . . . How different are these cases from that of the power of men over women! I am not now prejudging the question of its justifiableness. I am showing how vastly more permanent it could not but be, even if not justifiable, than these other dominations which have nevertheless lasted down to our own time. Whatever gratification of pride there is in the possession of power, and whatever personal interest in its exercise, is in this case not confined to a limited class, but common to the whole male sex. Instead of being, to most of its supporters, a thing desirable chiefly in the abstract, or, like the political ends usually contended for by factions, of little private importance to any but the leaders; it comes home to the person and hearth of every male head of a family, and of everyone who looks forward to being so. The clodhopper exercises, or is to exercise, his share of the power equally with the highest nobleman. And the case is that in which the desire of power is the strongest: for everyone who desires power, desires it most over those who are nearest to him, with whom his life is passed, with whom he has most concerns in common, and in whom any independence of his authority is oftenest likely to interfere with his individual preferences. If, in the other cases specified, powers manifestly grounded only on force, and having so much less to support them, are so slowly and with so much difficulty got rid of, much more must it be so with this, even if it rests on no better foundation than those. We must consider, too, that the possessors of the power have facilities in this case, greater than in any other, to prevent any uprising against it. Every one of the subjects lives under the very eye, and almost, it may be said, in the hands, of one of the masters—in closer intimacy with him than with any of her fellow-subjects; with no means of combining against him, no power of even locally overmastering him, and, on the other hand, with the strongest motives for seeking his favour and avoiding to give him offense. In struggles for political emancipation, everybody knows how often its champions are bought off by bribes, or daunted by terrors. In the case of women, each individual of the subject-class is in a chronic state of bribery and intimidation combined. In setting up the standard of resistance, a large number of the leaders, and still more of the followers, must make an almost complete sacrifice of the pleasures or the alleviations of their own individual lot. If ever any system of privilege and enforced subjection had its yoke tightly riveted on the necks of those who are kept down by it, this has. I have not yet shown that it is a wrong system: but everyone who is capable of thinking on the subject must see that even if it is, it was certain to outlast all other forms of unjust authority. And when some of the grossest of the other forms still exist in many civilised countries, and have only recently been got rid of in others, it would be strange if that which is so much the deepest rooted had yet been perceptibly shaken anywhere. There is more reason to wonder that the protests and testimonies against it should have been so numerous and so weighty as they are. . . .

But, it will be said, the rule of men over women differs from all these others in not being a rule of force: it is accepted voluntarily; women make no complaint, and are consenting parties to it. In the first place, a great number of women do not accept it. Ever since there have been women able to make their sentiments known by their writings (the only mode of publicity which society permits to them), an increasing number of them have recorded protests against their present social condition: and recently many thousands of them, headed by the most eminent women known to the public, have petitioned Parliament for their admission to the Parliamentary Suffrage. The claim of women to be educated as solidly, and in the same branches of knowledge, as men, is urged with growing intensity, and with a great prospect of success; while the demand for their admission into professions and occupations hitherto closed against them, becomes every year more urgent. Though there are not in this country, as there are in the United States, periodical conventions and an organised party to agitate for the Rights of Women, there is a numerous and active society organised and managed by women, for the more limited object of obtaining the political franchise. Nor is it only in our own country and in America that women are beginning to protest, more or less collectively, against the disabilities under which they labour. France, and Italy, and Switzerland, and Russia now afford examples of the same thing. How many more women there are who silently cherish similar aspirations, no one can possibly know; but there are abundant tokens how many *would* cherish them, were they not so strenuously taught to repress them as contrary to the proprieties of their sex. . . .

All causes, social and natural, combine to make it unlikely that women should be collectively rebellious to the power of men. They are so far in a position different from all other subject classes, that their masters require something more from them than actual service. Men do not want solely the obedience of women, they want their sentiments. All men, except the most brutish, desire to have, in the woman most nearly connected with them, not a forced slave but a willing one, not a slave merely, but a favourite. They have therefore put everything in practice to enslave their minds. The masters of all other slaves rely, for maintaining obedience, on fear; either fear of themselves, or religious fears. The masters of women wanted more than simple obedience, and they turned the whole force of education to effect their purpose. All women are brought up from the very earliest years in the belief that their ideal of character is the very opposite to that of men; not self-will, and government by self-control, but submission, and yielding to the control of others. All the moralities tell them that it is the duty of women, and all the current sentimentalities that it is their nature, to live for others; to make complete abnegation of themselves, and to have no life but in their affections. And by their affections are meant the only ones they are allowed to have—those to the men with whom they are connected, or to the children who constitute an additional and indefeasible tie between them and a man. When we put together three things—first, the natural attraction between opposite sexes; secondly, the wife's entire dependence on the husband, every privilege or pleasure she has being either his gift, or depending entirely on his will; and lastly, that the principal object of human pursuit, consideration, and all objects of social ambition, can in general be sought or obtained by her only through him, it would be a miracle if the object of being attractive to men had not become the polar star of feminine education and formation of character. And, this great means of influence over the minds of women having been acquired, an instinct of selfishness made men avail themselves of it to the utmost as a means of holding women in subjection, by representing to them meekness, submissiveness, and resignation of all individual will into the hands of a man, as an essential part of sexual attractiveness. Can it be doubted that any of the other yokes which mankind have succeeded in breaking, would have subsisted till now if the same means had existed, and had been so sedulously used, to bow down their minds to it? If it had been made the object of the life of every young plebeian to find personal favour in the eyes of some patrician, of every young serf with some seigneur; if domestication with him, and a share of his personal affections, had been held out as the prize which they all should look out for, the most gifted and aspiring being able to reckon on the most desirable prizes; and if, when this prize had been obtained, they had been shut out by a wall of brass from all interests not centring in him, all feelings and desires but those which he shared or inculcated; would not serfs and seigneurs, plebeians and patricians, have been as broadly distinguished at this day as men and women are? and would not all but a thinker here and there, have believed the distinction to be a fundamental and unalterable fact in human nature? . . .

At present, in the more improved countries, the disabilities of women are the only case, save one, in which laws and institutions take persons at their birth, and ordain that they shall never in all their lives be allowed to compete for certain things. The one exception is that of royalty. Persons still are born to the throne; no one, not of the reigning family, can ever occupy it, and no one even of that family can, by any means but the course of hereditary succession, attain it. All other dignities and social advantages are open to the whole male sex: many indeed are only attainable by wealth, but wealth may be striven for by anyone, and is actually obtained by many men of the very humblest origin. The difficulties, to the majority, are indeed insuperable without the aid of fortunate accidents; but no male human being is under any legal ban: neither law nor opinion superadd artificial obstacles to the natural ones. . . . The disabilities, therefore, to which women are subject from the mere fact of their birth, are the solitary examples of the kind in modern legislation. In no instance except this, which comprehends half the human race, are the higher social functions closed against anyone by a fatality of birth which no exertions, and no change of circumstances, can overcome . . .

Neither does it avail anything to say that the *nature* of the two sexes adapts them to their present functions and position, and renders these appropriate to them. Standing on the ground of common sense and the constitution of the human mind, I deny that anyone knows, or can know, the nature of the two sexes, as long as they have only been seen in their present relation to one another. If men had ever been found in society without women or women without men, or if there had been a society of men and women in which the women were not under the control of the men, something might have been positively known about the mental and moral differences which may be inherent in the nature of each. What is now called the nature of women is an eminently artificial thing—the result of forced repression in some directions, unnatural stimulation in others. It may be asserted without scruple, that no other class of dependents have had their character so entirely distorted from its natural proportions by their relation with their masters; for, if conquered and slave races have been, in some respects, more forcibly repressed, whatever in them has not been crushed down by an iron heel has generally been let alone, and if left with any liberty of development, it has developed itself according to its own laws; but in the case of women, a hothouse and stove cultivation has always been carried on of some of the capabilities of their nature, for the benefit and pleasure of their masters. Then, because certain products of the general vital force sprout luxuriantly and reach a great development in this heated atmosphere and under this active nurture and watering, while other shoots from the same root which are left outside in the wintry air, with ice purposely heaped all round them, have a stunted growth, and some are burnt off with fire and disappear; men, with that inability to recognize their own work which distinguishes the unanalytic mind, indolently believe that the tree grows of itself in the way they have made it grow, and that it would die if one half of it were not kept in a vapour bath and the other half in the snow. . . .

Hence, in regard to that most difficult question, what are the natural differences between the two sexes—a subject on which it is impossible in the present state of society to obtain complete and correct knowledge—while almost everybody dogmatises upon it, almost all neglect and make light of the only means by which any partial insight can be obtained into it. This is, an analytic study of the most important department of psychology, the laws of the influence of circumstances on character. . . . The profoundest knowledge of the laws of the formation of character is indispensable to entitle anyone to affirm even that there is any difference, much more what the difference is, between the two sexes considered as moral and rational beings; and since no one, as yet, has that knowledge (for there is hardly any subject which, in proportion to its importance, has been so little studied), no one is thus far entitled to any positive opinion on the subject. Conjectures are all that can at present be made . . . nothing final can be known, so long as those who alone can really know it, women themselves, have given but little testimony, and that little, mostly suborned. . . . The most favourable case which a man can generally have for studying the character of a woman, is that of his own wife: for the opportunities are greater, and the cases of complete sympathy not so unspeakably rare. And in fact, this is the source from which any knowledge worth having on the subject has, I believe, generally come. But most men have not had the opportunity of studying in this way more than a single case: accordingly one can, to an almost laughable degree, infer what a man's wife is like, from his opinions about women in general. To make even this one case yield any result, the woman must be worth knowing, and the man not only a competent judge, but of a character so sympathetic in itself, and so well adapted to hers, that he can either read her mind by sympathetic intuition, or has nothing in himself which makes her shy of disclosing it. Hardly anything, I believe, can be more rare than this conjunction. It often happens that there is the most complete unity of feeling and community of interests as to all external things, yet the one has as little admission into the internal life of the other as if they were common acquaintance. Even with true affection, authority on the one side and subordination on the other prevent perfect confidence. Though nothing may be intentionally withheld, much is not shown. In the analogous relation of parent and child, the corresponding phenomenon must have been in the observation of everyone. As between father and son, how many are the cases in which the father, in spite of real affection on both sides, obviously to all the world does not know, nor suspect, parts of the son's character familiar to his companions and equals. The truth is, that the position of looking up to another is extremely unpropitious to complete sincerity and openness with him. The fear of losing ground in his opinion or in his feelings is so strong, that even in an upright character, there is an unconscious tendency to show only the best side, or the side which, though not the best, is that which he most likes to see: and it may be confidently said that thorough knowledge of one another hardly ever exists, but between persons who, besides being intimates, are equals. How much more true, then, must all this be, when the one is not only under the authority of the other, but has it inculcated on her as a duty to reckon everything else subordinate to his comfort and pleasure, and to let him neither see nor feel anything coming from her, except what is agreeable to him. All these difficulties stand in the way of a man's obtaining any thorough knowledge even of the one woman whom alone, in general, he has sufficient opportunity of studying. When we further consider that to understand one woman is not necessarily to understand any other woman; that even if he could study many women of one rank, or of one country, he would not thereby understand women of other ranks or countries; and even if he did, they are still only the women of a single period of history; we may safely assert that the knowledge which men can acquire of women, even as they have been and are, without reference to what they might be, is wretchedly imperfect and superficial, and always will be so, until women themselves have told all that they have to tell.

And this time has not come; nor will it come otherwise than gradually. It is but of yesterday that women have either been qualified by literary accomplishments, or permitted by society, to tell anything to the general public. As yet very few of them dare tell anything, which men, on whom their literary success depends, are unwilling to hear. . . . I have dwelt so much on the difficulties which at present obstruct any real knowledge by men of the true nature of women, because . . . there is little chance of reasonable thinking on the matter, while people flatter themselves that they perfectly understand a subject of which most men know absolutely nothing, and of which it is at present impossible that any man, or all men taken together, should have knowledge which can qualify them to lay down the law to women as to what is, or is not, their vocation. Happily, no such knowledge is necessary for any practical purpose connected with the position of women in relation to society and life. For, according to all the principles involved in modern society, the question rests with women themselves—to be decided by their own experience, and by the use of their own faculties. There are no means of finding what either one person or many can do, but by trying—and no means by which anyone else can discover for them what it is for their happiness to do or leave undone. . . .

[I]f men are determined that the law of marriage shall be a law of despotism, they are quite right, in point of mere policy, in leaving to women only Hobson's choice. But, in that case, all that has been done in the modern world to relax the chain on the minds of women, has been a mistake. They never should have been allowed to receive a literary education. Women who read, much more women who write, are, in the existing constitution of things, a contradiction and a disturbing element: and it was wrong to bring women up with any acquirements but those of an odalisque, or of a domestic servant. . . .

Whether the institution to be defended is slavery, political absolutism, or the absolutism of the head of a family, we are always expected to judge of it from its best instances; and we are presented with pictures of loving exercise of authority on one side, loving submission to it on the other—superior wisdom ordering all things for the greatest good of the dependents, and surrounded by their smiles and benedictions. All this would be very much to the purpose if anyone pretended that there are no such things as good men. Who doubts that there may be great goodness, and great happiness, and great affection, under the absolute government of a good man? Meanwhile, laws and institutions require to be adapted, not to good men, but to bad. Marriage is not an institution designed for a select few. Men are not required, as a preliminary to the marriage ceremony, to prove by testimonials that they are fit to be trusted with the exercise of absolute power. . . . And how many thousands are there among the lowest classes in every country, who, without being in a legal sense malefactors in any other respect, because in every other quarter their aggressions meet with resistance, indulge the utmost habitual excesses of bodily violence towards the unhappy wife, who alone, at least of grown persons, can neither repel nor escape from their brutality; and towards whom the excess of dependence inspires their mean and savage natures, not with a generous forbearance, and a point of honour to behave well to one whose lot in life is trusted entirely to their kindness, but on the contrary with a notion that the law has delivered her to them as their thing, to be used at their pleasure, and that they are not expected to practise the consideration towards her which is required from them towards everybody else. . . .

It would be tiresome to repeat the commonplaces about the unfitness of men in general for power, which, after the political discussions of centuries, everyone knows by heart, were it not that hardly anyone thinks of applying these maxims to the case in which above all others they are applicable, that of power, not placed in the hands of a man here and there, but offered to every adult male, down to the basest and most ferocious. . . . If the family in its best forms is, as it is often said to be, a school of sympathy, tenderness, and loving forgetfulness of self, it is still oftener, as respects its chief, a school of willfulness, overbearingness, unbounded selfish indulgence, and a double-dyed and idealised selfishness, of which sacrifice itself is only a particular form: the care for the wife and children being only care for them as parts of the man's own interests and belongings, and their individual happiness being immolated in every shape to his smallest preferences. What better is to be looked for under the existing form of the institution? . . . the almost unlimited power which present social institutions give to the man over at least one human being—the one with whom he resides, and whom he has always present—this power seeks out and evokes the latent germs of selfishness in the remotest corners of his nature—fans its faintest sparks and smouldering embers—offers to him a licence for the indulgence of those points of his original character which in all other relations he would have found it necessary to repress and conceal. . . .

The family is a school of despotism, in which the virtues of despotism, but also its vices, are largely nourished. . . .

The law of servitude in marriage is a monstrous contradiction to all the principles of the modern world, and to all the experience through which those principles have been slowly and painfully worked out. It is the sole case, now that negro slavery has been abolished, in which a human being in the plenitude of every faculty is delivered up to the tender mercies of another human being, in the hope forsooth that this other will use the power solely for the good of the person subjected to it. Marriage is the only actual bondage known to our law. There remain no legal slaves, except the mistress of every house. . . .

All the selfish propensities, the self-worship, the unjust self-preference, which exist among mankind, have their source and root in, and derive their principal nourishment from, the present constitution of the relation between men and women. Think what it is to a boy, to grow up to manhood in the belief that without any merit or any exertion of his own, though he may be the most frivolous and empty or the most ignorant and stolid of mankind, by the mere fact of being born a male he is by right the superior of all and every one of an entire half of the human race: including probably some whose real superiority to himself he has daily or hourly occasion to feel. . . . What must be the effect on his character of this lesson? And men of the cultivated classes are often not aware how deeply it sinks into the immense majority of male minds. For, among right-feeling and well-bred people, the inequality is kept as much as possible out of sight; above all, out of sight of the children. As much obedience is required from boys to their mother as to their father: they are not permitted to domineer over their sisters, nor are they accustomed to see these postponed to them, but the contrary; the compensations of the chivalrous feeling being made prominent, while the servitude which requires them is kept in the background. Well brought-up youths in the higher classes thus often escape the bad influences of the situation in their early years, and only experience them when, arrived at manhood, they fall under the dominion of facts as they really exist. Such people are little aware, when a boy is differently brought up, how early the notion of his inherent superiority to a girl arises in his mind; how it grows with his growth and strengthens with his strength; how it is inoculated by one schoolboy upon another; how early the youth thinks himself superior to his mother, owing her perhaps forbearance, but no real respect; and how sublime and sultan-like a sense of superiority he feels, above all, over the woman whom he honours by admitting her to a partnership of his life. Is it imagined that all this does not pervert the whole manner of existence of the man, both as an individual and as a social being? It is an exact parallel to the feeling of a hereditary king that he is excellent above others by being born a king, or a noble by being born a noble. The relation between husband and wife is very like that between lord and vassal, except that the wife is held to more unlimited obedience than the vassal was. . . .

The example afforded, and the education given to the sentiments, by laying the foundation of domestic existence upon a relation contradictory to the first principles of social justice, must, from the very nature of man, have a perverting influence of such magnitude, that it is hardly possible with our present experience to raise our imaginations to the conception of so great a change for the better as would be made by its removal. All that education and civilisation are doing to efface the influences on character of the law of force, and replace them by those of justice, remains merely on the surface, as long as the citadel of the enemy is not attacked. The principle of the modern movement in morals and politics, is that conduct, and conduct alone, entitles to respect: that not what men are, but what they do, constitutes their claim to deference; that, above all, merit, and not birth, is the only rightful claim to power and authority. If no authority, not in its nature temporary, were allowed to one human being over another, society would not be employed in building up propensities with one hand which it has to curb with the other. . . . But so long as the right of the strong to power over the weak rules in the very heart of society, the attempt to make the equal right of the weak the principle of its outward actions will always be an uphill struggle; for the law of justice, which is also that of Christianity, will never get possession of man's inmost sentiments; they will be working against it, even when bending to it. . . .

When we consider the positive evil caused to the disqualified half of the human race by their disqualification—first in the loss of the most inspiriting and elevating kind of personal enjoyment, and next in the weariness, disappointment, and profound dissatisfaction with life, which are so often the substitute for it; one feels that among all the lessons which men require for carrying on the struggle against the inevitable imperfections of their lot on earth, there is no lesson which they more need, than not to add to the evils which nature inflicts, by their jealous and prejudiced restrictions on one another. Their vain fears only substitute other and worse evils for those which they are idly apprehensive of: while every restraint on the freedom of conduct of any of their human fellow-creatures (otherwise than by making them responsible for any evil actually caused by it), dries up *pro tanto* the principal fountain of human happiness, and leaves the species less rich . . . in all that makes life valuable to the individual human being.

Tsarist Russia

Expansion of Russian State, 1480–1794

ARCTIC OCEAN

To England

Arkangelsk (1584)

N. Dvina

URALS

Kama

St. Petersburg
(1703)

BALTIC SEA

Volga

Kazan
(1552)

Cossacks
To
Siberia
(1580–1650)

Novgorod
(1480)

W. Dvina

Moscow

Oka

Volga

Forestlands

Steppelands

Don

Kiev

(1560's–
1660's)

Dniepr

Astrakhan
(1556)

CASPIAN SEA

Odessa
(1794)

BLACK SEA

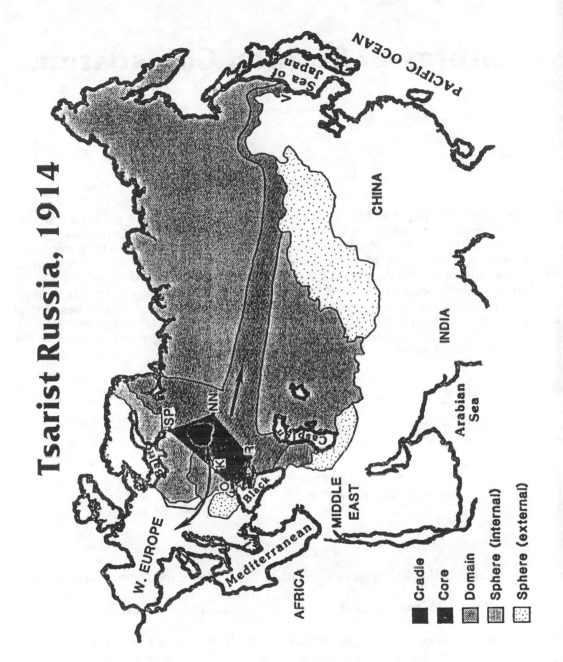

Tsarist Russia, 1914

W. EUROPE

AFRICA

Mediterranean

Baltic

SP

NN

K

O

Black

Caspian

MIDDLE EAST

Arabian Sea

INDIA

CHINA

Sea of Japan

PACIFIC OCEAN

Cradle

Core

Domain

Sphere (internal)

Sphere (external)

Liturgy of St. John Chrysostom

❖

Great Litany

The Liturgy of St. John Chrysostom is the main Sunday service in Eastern Orthodox churches, including the Russian Orthodox Church. It is the Orthodox equivalent of the Roman Catholic Mass. While the liturgy is the result of a long evolution rather than the work of a single author, it is named for a Greek bishop of Constantinople who died in 407. Bishop John, called "Chrysostomos" ("the golden-tongued") because of his eloquence as a preacher, was a vigorous critic of corruption in the Byzantine state and a defender of the poor. The Greek text of the Liturgy of St. John Chrysostom was translated into the language of the Slavs, "Slavonic," in the Middle Ages. The Great Litany is the opening portion of the liturgy. It appears below in transliterated Slavonic with English translation.

Paul Valliere

Deacon: Blagosloví, Vladko.	Bless, Father.
Priest: Blagoslovéno tsárstvo Ottsá i Syna i Sviatágo Dúkha, nyne i prísno i vo véki vekóv.	Blessed is the Kingdom of the Father and of the Son and of the Holy Spirit, now and ever and unto ages of ages.
Choir: Amin'.	Amen.
Deacon: Mírom Góspodu pomólimsia.	In peace let us pray to the Lord.
Choir: Góspodi, pomílui	Lord have mercy.
[Deacon] 1. O svyshnem míre i spasénii dush náshikh, Góspodu pomólimsia	For the peace that is from above and for the salvation of our souls, let us pray to the Lord.

[Choir] Góspodi, pomílui	Lord have mercy.

2. O mire vsegó míra, blagostoiánii sviatykh Bózhiikh tserkvéi i soedinénii vsekh, Góspodu pomólimsia.

For the peace of the whole world, for the stability of God's holy churches and for the union of all, let us pray to the Lord.

3. O sviatém khráme sem, i s véroiu, blagogovéniem i strákhom Bózhiim vkhodiáshchikh von, Góspodu pomólimsia.

For this holy temple, and for those who with faith, reverence and the fear of God enter therein, let us pray to the Lord.

4. O sviatéishem Kiríle, patriárshe bólgarskem, o sviatéishem náshem sinóde, chéstnem presvíterstve, vo Khristé diákonstve, o vsem príchte i hiúdekh, Góspodu pomólimsia.

For most holy Cyril, Patriarch of Bulgaria, for our most holy synod, honorable presbytery, diaconate in Christ, for all the clergy and people, let us pray to the Lord.

5. O blagochestívem, pravoslávnem, bólgarskem naróde, i o khristoliubívom vóinstve, Góspodu pomólimsia.

For the pious, Orthodox Bulgarian people, and for the Christ-loving army, let us pray to the Lord.

6. O posobíti i pokoríti pod nóze ikh vsiákago vragá i supostáta, Góspodu pomólimsia.

That He will aid them and subdue under their feet every foe and adversary, let us pray to the Lord.

7. O gráde sem, vsiákom gráde, strané, i véroiu zhivúshchikh v nikh, Góspodu pomólimsia.

For this city, for every city and country, and for those who with faith dwell therein, let us pray to the Lord.

8. O blagorastvorénii vózdukhov, o izobílii plodóv zemnykh i vrémenekh mímykh, Góspodu pomólimsia.

For healthful seasons, for the abundance of the fruits of the earth and for peaceful times, let us pray to the Lord.

9. O plávaiushchikh, puteshéstvuiushchikh, nedúguiushchikh, strázhdushchikh, plenénnykh, i o spasénii ikh, Góspodu pomólimsia.

For those who travel by sea, those who travel by land, the sick, the suffering, for those who are in captivity and for their salvation, let us pray to the Lord.

10. O izbávitisia nam ot viákiia skórbi, gnéva i núzhdy, Góspodu pomólimsia.

That we may be delivered from all tribulation, anger and want, let us pray to the Lord.

11. Zastupí, spasí, pomílui i sokhraní nas, Bózhe, tvoéiu blagodátiiu.

Protect us, save us, have mercy on us and keep us, O God, by Thy grace.

12. Presviatúiu, prechístuiu, preblagoslovénnuiu, slávnuiu Vladychitsu náshu Bogoróditsu i prisnodévu Maríiu so vsémi sviatymi pomianúvshe, sámi sebé i drug drúga i ves'zhivót nash Khristú Bógu predadím.

Commemorating our most holy, most pure, most blessed and glorious Lady, birth-giver of God and ever-Virgin Mary, with all the saints, let us commend ourselves and each other and all our life to Christ our God.

Choir: Tébe, Góspodi.

To Thee, O Lord.

Priest: Iáko podobáet Tebé vsiákaia sláva, chest' i poklonénie, Ottsú i Synu i Sviatómu Dúkhu, nyne i prísno i vo véki vekóv.

For unto Thee are due all glory, honor and worship, to the Father, and to the Son and to the Holy Spirit, now, and ever and unto ages of ages.

Choir: Amín'.

Amen.

Prologue to Boris Godunov

———❦———

Modest Musorgsky

Boris Godunov's story is one of passion, ambition, success, and intrigue. Musorgsky's opera premiered in 1874, a period of transition during which the Russians were examining their identity as a people.

Boris Godunov was not of noble birth, but was a valued member of the household of Tsar Ivan IV ("The Terrible"). Advanced through the Tsar's favor and his own intelligence, Boris became first an important advisor to the Tsar's successor, his dim-witted son Fyodor, then the official regent, and finally—after Fyodor's family line ended with his death—Tsar by election. Altogether as advisor, regent, and Tsar he ruled Russia from 1584–1605.

Godunov was a gifted leader. Early in his rule he ended the terrors of Ivan IV. He strengthened Russia's national identity by making the Russian Church independent of the Greek Orthodox Church, reclaiming territory lost by Ivan IV, establishing towns along the Russian borders, increasing trade, and encouraging European education.

Boris also instituted harsh limitations on the peasants and supported the middle classes at the expense of the old nobility. He was deeply suspicious and felt insecure in his position as a non-dynastic tsar. He exercised control through an ever-widening network of informants and spies and in time revived the brutalities of Ivan in order to maintain control of the state.

A severe draught, starvation, and discontent undermined Boris's position, but he remained Tsar until his sudden death in 1605. His son succeeded him for only a short time until his assassination. Russia then fell into the chaotic period remembered as the Time of Troubles.

Ellen Hodge

Scene 1

The courtyard of the Monastery of Novodievitch, near Moscow. On the right, the gate of the Monastery is seen with a tower above it. The stage is filled with people who wander about idly. A police officer enters.

POLICE OFFICER *(to the people)*
>Now then!
>Have you turned to idols?
>Quickly! On your knees!
>Come on! Quickly!
>What a lot of devils you are!

THE PEOPLE *(kneeling)*
>Why dost thou forsake us,
>O Father?
>Ah! Why dost thou forsake us,
>O Father?
>Are we not your poor defenceless orphans?
>Ah! we entreat thee,
>our tears are falling with our prayers!
>Mercy! Mercy!
>Our master and Father!
>Our Father!
>Thou art our protector!
>Boyar, have mercy!
>Mercy!

The police officer goes out
>Mitukh, say, Mitukh!
>What are we shouting for?

MITUKH (FIRST PEASANT)
>Well, how should I know?

PEOPLE
>To give our Russian land a Tsar!

FIRST PEASANT WOMAN
>Oh dear! I am quite hoarse with shouting!
>Tell me, neighbor dear,
>have you got any water left?

SECOND PEASANT WOMAN
>And who do you think you are!

WOMEN
> She shouted loudest of all.
> She should have had some with her.

SECOND PEASANT
> Now you women, stop this chatter!

WOMEN
> And who are you to give orders?
> Have you become a constable?

MITUKH (FIRST PEASANT)
> Oh, you witches! Stop this noise!

WOMEN *(amid laughter and catcalls from the men)*
> Ah! You cursed devil!
> What a pagan we have here!
> What a rascal this man is!
> Come women, let us go,
> let us flee in all haste from this ill luck!

Re-enter the police officer. Seeing him, the women quickly kneel, and all become motionless as before.

POLICE OFFICER *(to the people)*
> Now then! Why are you silent?
> Or are you saving your voices?

(He threatens them)
> Take care now!
> Have you forgotten the taste of the whip on your backs?

(He approaches them)
> I'll teach you quickly!

WOMEN
> Do not be angry, Mikitich!
> Do not be angry, my dear!

PEASANTS
> Just let us get our breath back
> and we will yell some more!

(aside)
> He won't even let us breathe, the devil!

POLICE OFFICER
Now then! Only don't spare your voices!

PEASANTS
All right.

POLICE OFFICER
Well then!

PEOPLE *(with all their might)*
Why dost thou forsake us,
O Father?
Ah! Why dost thou leave us,
O Father?
Are we not your poor defenceless orphans?
Our tears are falling with our prayers!
Mercy! Mercy!
Our boyar and Father!
Our Father! Our Father! Our Protector! Our Protector!
Ah! Ah! Ah! Ah! Ah! Ah! Ah!

Enter Shchelkalov

POLICE OFFICER *(perceives Shchelkalov and gestures to the people)*
Enough! Stand up! The clerk of the Duma speaks!

The people rise

SHCHELKALOV *(advances toward the people and salutes them, taking off his cap)*
Russian people all! The boyar will not yield!
He will not heed the appeal of the Duma and the Patriarchs,
and he will not accept the Tsar's throne.
Woe unto Russia . . . Yes, woe unto us,
ye Russian people!
Our land groans for want of a ruler.
Put your faith in the Lord,
that he may send
comfort to our troubled Russia . . .
And may He guide in His wisdom
Boris's weary soul! . . .

He goes out.

The scene is lit up by the rays of the setting sun. The singing of blind wandering pilgrims is heard in the distance.

PILGRIMS
Glory to Thee, O Lord on earth!
Glory unto the powers of Heaven,
unto all the Saints
and unto Russia!

The people whisper, "Messengers of God"
Thus spoke the Angel of the Lord:
Arise, stormy clouds,
travel through the heavens
and cover this Russian land.

The pilgrims enter, leaning upon the shoulders of their guides
Slay the cruel serpent,
the many-headed dragon,
which have brought discord to our Russian land.
Let all Christians hear this,
for they will be saved!

They distribute amulets among the people
Dress yourselves in bright vestments,
lift up the sacred icons
of all our holy Saints
and go to meet the Tsar.

As they enter the convent the song gradually dies away
Sing praises unto the Lord
and unto the holy Heaven.
Glory be to God on earth,
our heavenly Father!

Scene 2

The courtyard of the Kremlin in Moscow. Facing the spectators in the background is the Grand Staircase leading to the Tsar's apartments. On the right and near the front, the people, on their knees, occupy the space between the Cathedral of the Assumption and the Cathedral of the Archangel, the porches of which are both visible.

PRINCE SHUISKY *(from the porch of the Cathedral of the Assumption)*
Long live Tsar Boris Feodorovich!

331

THE PEOPLE
    Long life and happiness, our Tsar, our little father!

PRINCE SHUISKY
    Praise him!

THE PEOPLE
    Like unto the bright sun in the sky,
    Glory! Glory!
    is the glory of Russia's Tsar Boris!
    Glory!

*The Tsar's procession begins to come out of the Cathedral: the police make the
people fall in line*
    Long may you live and reign,
    O Tsar, our father!
    Long may you live and reign,
    O Tsar, our father!
    Long may you live, Tsar, our father, and prosper!
    Rejoice, O people!
    Rejoice and be merry, O people!
    Rejoice ye Russian people!
    Rejoice ye Russian people!
    Honor and praise Tsar Boris!

BOYARS
    All hail Tsar Boris Feodorovich!

PEOPLE
    All hail!

BOYARS
    All hail Tsar Boris Feodorovich!

PEOPLE
    Glory! Glory!
    Like unto the bright sun in the sky, glory!
    Glory! Glory!
    Thou our Tsar, our father, thou our Tsar.

BOYARS
    All hail Tsar Boris Feodorovich!

PEOPLE
    All hail!
    Like unto the bright sun in the sky,

Glory! Glory!
all hail to Boris, Russia's tsar!
Glory to the tsar, glory!
Glory, glory, glory, glory!

BORIS
My soul is sad!
Strange dark forebodings
and evil presentiments
oppress my spirit.
Oh, Holy Saint, oh my Almighty Father!
Look down from heaven on the tears of thy sinful servant,
and send down thy holy blessing
upon my reign!
May I be honest and merciful as Thou,
and reign in glory over my people.
Now let us go to kneel
before the tombs of Russia's former monarchs.
Then all the people are summoned to a feast;
all, from the boyars to the blind beggars,
all are invited, all shall be my honored guests.

The procession moves on toward the Cathedral of the Archangel.

PEOPLE
Glory, glory, glory!
Long may you live and reign, O tsar our father!

*The bells ring out, and the people rush toward the Cathedral of the Archangel.
The police try to establish order.*
Glory! Glory!
To thee, our Tsar!

BOYARS
All hail, Tsar Boris Feodorovich!

PEOPLE
All hail!
Like unto the bright sun in the sky,
Glory! Glory!
is the glory of Russia's Tsar Boris,
glory, glory and long life, glory!

*General confusion. Boris appears from the Archangel Cathedral and goes in
procession towards the Tsar's apartments*
Glory! Glory! Glory! Glory! Glory!

Newspaper Advertisements for the Sale of Serfs, 1797

⋙◆⋘

1

For sale well behaved menial craftsmen: two tailors, a shoemaker, a watchmaker, a cook, a coach maker, a wheeler, an engraver, a night workman, and two coachmen. They may be seen and the price [for them] may be ascertained from their own *pomeshchik* [landlord] in the Third Part, Fourth Quarter, No. 51. There, too, are available for sale three young racing horses, one stallion, two geldings, and a herd of hunting dogs, about fifty, which will be one year old in January or February.

2

There is for sale, in the Fifteenth Part, Second Quarter, No. 183, in the parish of Adrian and Natalia, in the Second Mashchanskaia Street near the Church, a menial man. He is twenty-five years old, a trained woman's shoemaker who knows his profession exceptionally well; in addition he performs all domestic, coachman's and footman's tasks, as well as waiting at the table. He has a pregnant wife twenty-two years old who sews, irons, starches, waits on the lady of the house, and cooks. They have a three year old daughter.

3

For sale a thirty-five year old peasant, with his wife about the same age, and three young children. Those who wish to purchase may learn the price from their owner at the Tenth Part, in Nicholas parish, on Bolvanovka, No. 529.

4

In Part Twelve, an officer has for sale a sixteen year old girl, formerly belonging to a poor house, who knows how to knit, sew, iron, starch, and dress a lady; she has a nice figure and a pretty face.

Emancipation Manifesto of Alexander II

———◆———

Succeeding to the Russian throne in 1855 as Russia was losing the Crimean War, Alexander II moved ahead quickly with basic reforms in Russian society. Of all the Great Reforms, as they were called, none was greater than the emancipation of the serfs from legal bondage to noble landowners. The proclamation of 1861, written for the tsar by Filaret, bishop of Moscow, liberated more than 22 million male "souls" and their dependents.

Paul Valliere

By the Grace of God We, Alexander II Emperor and Autocrat of All Russia, King of Poland, Grand Duke of Finland, and so forth, make known to all Our faithful subjects:

Called by Divine Providence and by the sacred right of inheritance to the throne of Our Russian ancestors, We vowed in Our heart to respond to the mission which is entrusted to Us and to surround with Our affection and Our Imperial solicitude all Our faithful subjects of every rank and condition, from the soldier who nobly defends the country to the humble artisan who works in industry; from the career official of the state to the plowman who tills the soil.

Examining the condition of classes and professions comprising the state, We became convinced that the present state legislation favors the upper and middle classes, defines their obligations, rights, and privileges, but does not equally favor the serfs, so designated because in part from old laws and in part from custom they have been hereditarily subjected to the authority of landowners, who in turn were obligated to provide for their well-being. Rights of nobles have been hitherto very broad and legally ill defined, because they stem from tradition, custom, and the good will of the noblemen. In most cases this has led to the establishment of good patriarchal relations based on the sincere, just concern and benevolence on the part of the nobles, and on affectionate submission on the part of the peasants. Because of the decline of the simplicity of morals, because of an increase in the diversity of relations, because of the weakening of the direct paternal attitude of nobles toward the peasants, and because noble rights fell sometimes into the hands of people exclusively concerned with their personal interests, good relations weakened. The way was opened for an arbitrariness burdensome for the peasants and detrimental to their welfare, causing them to be indifferent to the improvement of their own existence.

These facts had already attracted the attention of Our predecessors of glorious memory, and they had adopted measures aimed at improving the conditions of the peasants; but these measures were ineffective, partly because they depended on the free, generous action of nobles, and partly because they affected only some localities, by virtue of special circumstances or as an experiment. Thus Alexander I issued a decree on free agriculturists, and the late Emperor Nicholas, Our beloved father, promulgated one dealing with the serfs. In the Western *gubernias,* inventory regulations determine the peasant land allotments and their obligations. But decrees on free agriculturists and serfs have been carried out on a limited scale only.

We thus became convinced that the problem of improving the condition of serfs was a sacred inheritance bequeathed to Us by Our predecessors, a mission which, in the course of events, Divine Providence has called upon Us to fulfill.

We have begun this task by expressing Our confidence toward the Russian nobility, which has proven on so many occasions its devotion to the Throne, and its readiness to make sacrifices for the welfare of the country.

We have left to the nobles themselves, in accordance with their own wishes, the task of preparing proposals for the new organization of peasant life—proposals that would limit their rights over the peasants, and the realization of which would inflict on them [the nobles] some material losses. Our confidence was justified. Through members of the *gubernia* committees, who had the trust of the nobles' associations, the nobility voluntarily renounced its right to own serfs. These committees, after collecting the necessary data, have formulated proposals on a new arrangement for serfs and their relationship with the nobles.

These proposals were diverse, because of the nature of the problem. They have been compared, collated, systematized, rectified and finalized in the main committee instituted for that purpose; and these new arrangements dealing with the peasants and domestics of the nobility have been examined in the Governing Council.

Having invoked Divine assistance, We have resolved to execute this task.

On the basis of the above mentioned new arrangements, the serfs will receive in time the full rights of free rural inhabitants.

The nobles, while retaining their property rights on all the lands belonging to them, grant the peasants perpetual use of their domicile in return for a specified obligation; and, to assure their livelihood as well as to guarantee fulfillment of their obligations toward the government, [the nobles] grant them a portion of arable land fixed by the said arrangements, as well as other property.

While enjoying these land allotments, the peasants are obliged, in return, to fulfill obligations to the noblemen fixed by the same arrangements. In this state, which is temporary, the peasants are temporarily bound.

At the same time, they are granted the right to purchase their domicile, and, with the consent of the nobles, they may acquire in full ownership the arable lands and other properties which are allotted them for permanent use. Following such acquisition of full ownership of land, the peasants will be freed from their obligations to the nobles for the land thus purchased and will become free peasant landowners.

A special decree dealing with domestics will establish a temporary status for them, adapted to their occupations and their needs. At the end of two years from the day of the promulgation of this decree, they shall receive full freedom and some temporary immunities.

In accordance with the fundamental principles of these arrangements, the future organization of peasants and domestics will be determined, the order of general peasant administration will be established, and the rights given to the peasants and to the domestics will be spelled out in detail, as will the obligations imposed on them toward the government and the nobles.

Although these arrangements, general as well as local, and the special supplementary rules affecting some particular localities, estates of petty nobles, and peasants working in factories and enterprises of the nobles, have been as far as possible adapted to economic necessities and local customs; nevertheless, to preserve the existing order where it presents reciprocal advantages, we leave it to the nobles to reach a friendly understanding with the peasants and to reach agreements on the extent of the land allotment and the obligations stemming from it, observing, at the same time, the established rules to guarantee the inviolability of such agreements.

This new arrangement, because of its complexity, cannot be put into effect immediately, a time of not less than two years is necessary. During this period, to avoid all misunderstanding and to protect public and private interests, the order actually existing on the estates of nobles should be maintained until the new order shall become effective.

Towards that end, We have deemed it advisable:

1. To establish in each *gubernia* a special Office of Peasant Affairs, which will be entrusted with the affairs of the peasant communes established on the estates of the nobility.

2. To appoint in every district justices of the peace to solve all misunderstandings and disputes which may arise from the new arrangement, and to organize from these justices district assemblies.

3. To organize Peace Offices on the estates of the nobles, leaving the village communes as they are, and to open *volost* offices in the large villages and unite small village communes under one *volost* office.

4. To formulate, verify, and confirm in each village commune or estate a charter which would enumerate, on the basis of local conditions, the amount of land alloted to the peasants for permanent use, and the scope of their obligations to the nobleman for the land as well as for other advantages which are granted.

5. To put these charters into practice as they are gradually approved on each estate, and to put them into effect everywhere within two years from the date of publication of this manifesto.

6. Until that time, peasants and domestics must be obedient towards their nobles, and scrupulously fulfill their former obligations.

7. The nobles will continue to keep order on their estates, with the right of jurisdiction and of police, until the organization of *volost* and of *volost* courts.

Aware of the unavoidable difficulties of this reform, We place Our confidence above all in the graciousness of Divine Providence, which watches over Russia.

We also rely upon the zealous devotion of Our nobility, to whom We express Our gratitude and that of the entire country as well, for the unselfish support it has given to the realization of Our designs. Russia will not forget that the nobility, motivated by its respect for the dignity of man and its Christian love of its neighbor, has voluntarily renounced serfdom, and has laid the foundation of a new economic future for the peasants. We also expect that it will continue to express further concern for the realization of the new arrangement in a spirit of peace and benevolence, and that each nobleman will realize, on his estate, the great civic act of the entire group by organizing the lives of his peasants and his domestics on mutually advantageous terms, thereby setting for the rural population a good example of a punctual and conscientious execution of state regulations.

The examples of the generous concern of the nobles for the welfare of peasants, and the gratitude of the latter for that concern, give Us the hope that a mutual understanding will solve most of the difficulties, which in some cases will be inevitable during the application of general rules to the divers conditions on some estates, and that thereby the transition from the old order to the new will be facilitated, and that in the future mutual confidence will be strengthened, and a good understanding and a unanimous tendency towards the general good will evolve.

To facilitate the realization of these agreements between the nobles and the peasants, by which the latter may acquire in full ownership their domicile and their land, the government will lend assistance, under special regulations, by means of loans or transfer of debts encumbering an estate.

We rely upon the common sense of Our people. When the government advanced the idea of abolishing serfdom, there developed a partial misunderstanding among the unprepared peasants. Some were concerned about freedom and disconcerned about obligations. But, generally, the common sense of the country has not wavered, because it has realized that every individual who enjoys freely the benefits of society owes it in return certain positive obligations; according to Christian law every individual is subject to higher authority (Romans, chap. xiii., 1); everyone must fulfill his obligations, and, above all, pay tribute, dues, respect, and honor (Ibid., chap. xiii., 7). What legally belongs to nobles cannot be taken away from them without adequate compensation, or through their voluntary concession; it would be contrary to all justice to use the land of the nobles without assuming responsibility for it.

And now We confidently expect that the freed serfs, on the eve of a new future which is opening to them, will appreciate and recognize the considerable sacrifices which the nobility has made on their behalf.

They should understand that by acquiring property and greater freedom to dispose of their possessions, they have an obligation to society and to themselves to live up to the letter of the new law by a loyal and judicious use of the rights which are now granted to them. However beneficial a law may be, it cannot make people happy if they do not themselves organize their happiness under protection of the law. Abundance is acquired only through hard work, wise use of strength and resources, strict economy, and above all, through an honest God-fearing life.

The authorities who prepared the new way of life for the peasants and who will be responsible for its inauguration will have to see that this task is accomplished with calmness and regularity, taking the timing into account in order not to divert the attention of cultivators away from their agricultural work. Let them zealously work the soil and harvest its fruits so that they will have a full granary of seeds to return to the soil which will be theirs.

And now, Orthodox people, make the sign of the cross, and join with Us to invoke God's blessing upon your free labor, the sure pledge of your personal well-being and the public prosperity.

Given at St. Petersburg, March 3, the year of Grace 1861, and the seventh of Our reign.

Alexander

From the Writings of Vera Figner

<hr>

Figner appeared to be a super-revolutionary. A lot was said about her beauty, elegance, education, intelligence and ability to conduct herself properly in all social circles, aristocratic included. For us she was an ideal revolutionary, a woman with an iron will. After the fall of Perovskaia and Zheliabov [who had led the People's Will prior to their arrest], she was the only one everyone recognized as having unlimited revolutionary authority.[1]

Vera Figner was born on June 25, 1852; she was the oldest of six children in a well-to-do gentry family. Her father was a forester, and her early years were spent in the backwoods, isolated from the world. At the age of eleven, Vera was sent off to a cloistered private school for girls of the gentry, which did little to enlarge her experience. She spent six years there, cut off from contact with anyone but her fellow students as she acquired the superficial education deemed appropriate for women of her station.

In 1869, she returned to her family's estate. "After being enclosed within the four walls of my boarding school," she wrote, "I was bursting with a joyful feeling of freedom. This excess of joy, this heightened emotional state demanded action. I found it unthinkable that I might live without making some mark upon the world."[2] Influenced by a liberal uncle, she came to see the disparity between her own privileged position and the destitution of the peasantry, and she resolved to work for their benefit. "Russian journalism and the women's movement, at its height in the early seventies, provided me with a ready solution for my philanthropic aspirations: I could become a doctor."[3] Since it was impossible for women to study medicine in Russia, she made up her mind to go to Switzerland, where universities had recently begun to admit women.

But her father forbade her to go: instead he took her to Kazan, expecting that the lively social season in that city would involve her in more "feminine" pursuits. As it happened, a young lawyer, Alexei Filippov, fell in love with her and asked her to marry him. Before she agreed, Figner persuaded him to abandon his job and travel abroad with her—once married, she would no longer need her father's permission to travel. In the spring of 1872, together with her husband and her

1   I. I. Popov. *Minuvshee i perezhitoe* (Moscow, 1933), pp. 108–9.
2   Vera Figner. *Zapechatlennyi trud* (Moscow, 1964), Vol. 1, p. 100.
3   Ibid., p. 102.

sister Lydia, Vera Figner arrived in Zurich, where she was to receive the political education that led her to become a revolutionary.

A dull, steady drizzle was falling. All I could see from the window of my small hotel room on Limmatquai were the tiled roofs of the houses, nestled close to each other. That rainy day, colorless, uninviting, and dreary, was my first in a foreign land, in an unfamiliar city.

Zurich! I had yearned to go for so long: over the last two years all my thoughts and desires had been centered on Zurich. There had been so much anxiety before leaving Russia. I hadn't planned to go until the fall, but in the spring the Russian papers had carried the news that Zurich University was introducing regulations that would make admission more difficult. We had made anxious inquiries of the rector and, receiving a reassuring reply—we could still enroll without taking exams—left our home province in a hurry.

It was a clear April day in 1872, a remarkable, invigorating day, abounding with sunlight and the scent of spring, when my sister and I set out from our native village of Nikiforovo, traveling briskly on a troika with bells ringing. From the administrative center of our district we had taken a steamship, then a train, to Switzerland. Now I was in Zurich, with its ancient, narrow streets, its miserable lake, unappealing in the rain, and that ugly view of the tiled roofs from my window.

On the second day, it cleared up, and we hastily set off to request permission to enroll in the university. We walked uphill all the way from the quay, the streets growing broader, gardens becoming more frequent, until at last we were standing in front of the large building of the Polytechnical Institute, which was part of the university. I ascended the broad staircase with a feeling close to reverence, as if I were about to enter a temple of science to be accepted as one of its votaries.

As it turned out, the rector admitted us as students without any formalities: he simply shook our hands, taking this as our promise to obey university rules. Having achieved our cherished goal, we practically ran back down the stairs. Now our studies would begin. Nothing but studying and more studying. "I won't go to the theater and I won't take walks"—before leaving home I had thus assured my uncle. When he pointed out that I would be tempted by the Zurich lake, which was full of fish, I had insisted, "I won't even go fishing!" even though I loved to fish. *"No!* There'll be no fishing or boating! There'll be nothing but lectures and textbooks!"

I was enormously enthusiastic—you could almost say fanatical—about my future profession. For two whole years I had been thinking about medicine and preparing myself for the university—studying math, physics, German, and Latin. Our earlier schooling hadn't prepared us women for the university, but our desire to extract every bit of knowledge from our narrow program was enormous. Our yearning to travel abroad to study did not spring from faddishness or frivolous vanity. We were still pioneers in the struggle for women's higher education, and the journey abroad was not easy for any of us: you needed real determination and unswerving will power to overcome material difficulties, the prejudices of provincial society, parents' opposition to novelty and their fear of letting their

341

daughters travel to unknown, far-off places. The young Russians living in Zurich in 1872 were of very high caliber, indeed.

I, too, had had to overcome material difficulties. Three or four thousand rubles were needed to provide several years of a modest student life for my husband and me. To economize, I had buried myself in the backwoods, where it cost me nothing to live at my mother's estate. We set aside my husband's entire salary for our intended trip, and I sold all the things I had been given for my dowry. Relieved of all household goods—both the necessary and the superfluous—carefree, young, and happy, we were able at last to make our way to the source of knowledge.

I was nineteen when I left, and my intellectual horizons were still very narrow. In the two years I had been out of school I had read few books or journal articles of a serious nature, and I had come in contact with absolutely no one while living in the countryside. My uncle was sympathetic to my aspirations to attend the university and become a doctor, the sort of doctor who would treat only the poor, the peasants, but aside from him, there was no one in our backwoods who could have opened up the world of ideas to me. This uncle had supplied me with some basic ideas about society—and that was the extent of my knowledge.

Early in the year, at a mineralogy lecture at the university, I found myself sitting next to a young woman with a whole bush of closely cut black curls. Her eyes were like coals in their narrow slits, and the brick-red blush on her homely round face gave her a distinctive expression, half provocative, half mocking. In fact, it was her nose that really appeared mocking, and it went with her sharply etched mouth.

"Are you in medical school?" I asked.

"No, I've enrolled at the Polytechnic Institute, in agronomy."

Now, that's strange, I thought. *What's agronomy? Why is she sitting next to me, then?* I thought people went abroad only to study medicine, and that every woman student could have but one goal—that she could resolve only to serve society, that is, "the poor." I understood service to society exclusively in the sense of ministering to "the poor," by which I meant the peasants. To me, medicine was the very best way to serve them.

"Why are you going into agronomy?" I asked my neighbor. "What good is it?"

"My family are landowners in Tver province," she replied. "I'll live in the village and use my knowledge in farming the land."

Until then, I'd only seen estates run by totally uneducated stewards, and by the so-called peasant "elders," who were also stewards, but were paid less and were even less competent. The only agricultural system I knew was the one that my father and grandfather had followed, as had generations of peasants and landowners from time immemorial. I can't say, then, that I understood the intentions of Sofia Bardina any better after her reply.

On another occasion, Bardina informed me in class: "There'll be a meeting of Russian women students today."

"Why?" I asked, rather afraid that it would take time away from my studies.

"Someone suggested that we form a circle exclusively for women, in order to learn how to speak logically. At meetings with men," she continued, noting my bewildered look, "women usually keep quiet; we feel shy, and so we don't say anything. But maybe with practice we'll learn to develop our thoughts logically, and then we won't be afraid to speak in public. A women's circle would be a place where we could learn."

"Well, that sounds really good! When will the meeting be?"

"At eight, at the Palmenhof on Oberstrasse. Please come!"

That evening, after a meager student dinner, my sister Lydia and I set off for the Palmenhof. There in the hall we found a long dinner table, with a row of chairs alongside it. Plainly dressed young women were waiting around; some had broken into groups of two or three. There was a hum of conversation, and somewhere a lively argument was going on.

"Gentlemen [*sic*]! Kindly be seated!" announced a tall blond woman with closely cropped hair—Doctor Emme's wife. A bell was then rung energetically; people took their seats, and the meeting began. Emme was chosen chairwoman, and she gave the floor to the librarian whose idea it had been to call the meeting. The librarian explained the goal of the circle: to learn to speak logically. Then, as a means to this end, she proposed that we read essays and hold debates.

We proceeded to discuss whether there was really a need for such a circle, and if so, who should participate. No one took issue with the circle's goal. On the other hand, passionate arguments arose as to whether the circle should be made up exclusively of women. Many scoffed at this idea: they found it ridiculous that women should be afraid in the presence of men, and thought that it would be both more natural and more expedient to form a self-education circle jointly with men, without fear of masculine competition. But these voices were drowned out in the majority decision to begin by organizing women students exclusively. We didn't work out a set of rules for the society, which was open to all women students. Once the general question had been resolved, we immediately got down to business, proposing that those who wished choose topics for the following meeting.

As it turned out, the first paper was prepared by the librarian. Strange as it may seem, her subject turned out to be the question of suicide, which couldn't have been further from our minds at that time.[4] She argued that every suicide, without exception, was the result of psychic disorder, and proclaimed that there could be no such thing as a perfectly normal suicide.

Although none of us knew anything about the question or had the faintest notion of psychiatry, the challenge—to us it seemed a challenge to common sense—was taken up boldly. A passionate debate ensued; the chairwoman's hand got a real workout, shaking her bell to keep order. The meeting was chaotic; instead of debating in an orderly manner, everyone talked at once. It finally

---

4   Later, of those present, Kaminskaia, Bardina, Zavadskaia, Khorzhevshaia, and Grebnitskaia took their own lives.—Figner.

became clear that the majority opposed the one-sided views of the speaker, and we left for home, having exhausted ourselves over such questions as: What is a normal person? Is anyone really normal? Perhaps everyone's a little crazy, one way or another? Far into the night, loud voices resounded through the sleeping streets of Zurich: "Normal . . . abnormal . . . psychosis . . . where are the limits? . . . There are no limits!"

Varvara Alexandrova, a young, blond student who was a friend of my sister Lydia, gave the second paper. Its theme was the peasant rebellion of Stenka Razin. The paper itself was weak, but it set off a debate because it completely idealized Razin's personality—both as a mighty leader and as a destructive hero in the Bakuninist sense. At this session, the question of science and civilization was raised. Were they really necessary for mankind? Did humanity need science to be happy? Did civilization yield any benefits, or—so long as the masses were enslaved and the upper classes enjoyed lives of luxury and refined culture—did it merely harm the people?

Rousseau and that incomparable apostle of destruction, Bakunin, were invoked by ardent disputants who took the side of those adversaries of civilization and culture. Others, upset by the violent attacks on all of humanity's gains, put up an energetic defense, as if our debates could actually bring about utter barbarism by somehow destroying civilization. My devotion to science was passionate, and I yearned to dedicate my life to it, so I, too, screamed with genuine frenzy about the value it could have and about how, in order to bring justice to this earth, we must not destroy civilization but instead disseminate it among all who were deprived. One passionate woman, half-Italian, half-Russian, annihilated civilization as befit her southern temperament. The meeting degenerated into chaos; everyone was flushed and impatient, and it became impossible to hear anything over the shouting. The Italian woman got a nosebleed, while the chairwoman reproachfully paraphrased Napoleon's speech to his armies in Egypt[5]: after ringing her bell furiously, she said with deep feeling, "Mesdames— all of Europe is watching you!" This reference to a Europe which was allegedly observing Russian women students in Zurich attentively sounded so funny that everyone roared with laughter, and all the ardor of the disputing sides was extinguished immediately. The meeting ended but the agitation did not subside, and in the fresh air of the streets everyone resumed arguing the merits of civilization and science.

Ridiculous as it may seem, that was the circle's last discussion. It was as if all our passion and eagerness to learn to speak logically had been absorbed in that debate about civilization. Perhaps we realized that our cause was hopeless. In any event, after all that disorderly and overheated verbiage, the opposition to excluding men grew very powerful. There was one more meeting where the question of admitting the stronger sex arose again. The defenders of the original decision had toned down somewhat and lost strength. We argued for a while, talked a bit longer, and dispersed without reaching any decisions. It became

---

5   "Forty centuries observe us from the height of these pyramids."—Figner.

apparent that the women's circle was falling to pieces; in contrast to its former verbosity, it expired silently, to the regret of no one with the possible exception of its initiator, and was not resurrected. However, during its brief existence it had served a purpose by bringing the young Russian women of Zurich together and giving them a chance to meet and size each other up. The arguments revealed various tendencies and temperaments, making it easier for people with similar views to get together. And indeed, several new circles were soon formed in the Russian colony.

> Among these was the Fritsche circle, a radical study group composed of thirteen women, aged sixteen to nineteen, most of whom were enrolled in the medical faculty. This group played a crucial role in Figner's political development.

From my first days in Zurich, I had been confronted by a whole series of questions, the existence of which I had never even suspected and which began to shake the views I had acquired—unconsciously in childhood, actively after I left school. I was assailed by doubts and had to deal with them. Because of the moral issues that those questions raised, I eventually became a socialist and a revolutionary.

Just as I had been accustomed to viewing nature itself as something immutable, thinking about neither the past nor the future of the universe, up to this point I had accepted the existing social system and form of government without question, without examining their origins or the possibility of changing them. I knew, of course, that the world was divided into the rich and the poor—how could I have failed to see that?—but I hadn't the faintest idea of the social injustice that this division engendered. I knew that society was divided into estates—the gentry, the petty bourgeoisie, the peasantry—but I had no conception of class distinctions. The expressions "capital," "proletariat," and "social parasitism" were not in my vocabulary.

There is poverty in the world; there is ignorance and disease. People who are educated and—like me—born to well-to-do families ought to share my natural desire to assist the poor. Under the influence of my mother and my uncle, as well as of the journal articles I'd read, I made up a social program for myself before leaving for Zurich: some day I was going to help peasants in Russia buy horses, or build new huts after their old ones had burnt down; as a doctor I hoped to cure people suffering from tuberculosis and typhoid, to perform operations and give advice on medicine and hygiene; and as a *zemstvo*[6] activist I planned to set up schools, spread literacy, and provide grain elevators to help the peasants save money. As far as over-all political structures were concerned, I either failed to think of them at all, or, to the extent that I did, considered the form of government

---

6   The *zemstvo* was an organ for self-government in rural areas. Established in 1864, it had representatives from private landowners, peasant communities, and qualified urban dwellers. Its work was primarily in the realm of education and medical care.

in Switzerland or the United States to be ideal. But I never asked myself how such a system could be established in Russia—the question never even occurred to me. My uncle had once told me confidently, referring to John Stuart Mill, "Every nation gets the government it deserves." Since his words carried great weight with me, I took this as an axiom and it set my mind to rest. I could think of no exceptions to this rule—which was correct in a certain sense—and no one around me had anything else to say at the time. But if the rule was true, then Russia possessed the very government that it deserved; when Russia became a different country, it would receive a government resembling that of Switzerland or North America. And this would all work out somehow by itself.

Then I went to Zurich, and the "foundation" I had built up by the age of nineteen began to be undermined from all sides. Like a bolt from the blue it hit me that I, who was virtually fresh from school and inspired by the finest aspirations toward science and goodness, I, at the age of nineteen, was already an exploiter, and my mother and my uncle and all of my relatives were all greedy, mercenary exploiters: they belonged to a privileged minority, under whose oppression the masses, the proletariat, were born, suffered, and died. At first I failed to understand—I refused to understand—that all of us were really like that. I did become confused and morally troubled, but then I began to deny everything; I argued against and refused to accept the villainous role ascribed to me and everyone close to me.

I was obsessed by doubts and contradictions, but I was ashamed to ask anyone for explanations, afraid of appearing stupid and ignorant. Everyone else who had arrived in Zurich before me seemed so learned and intelligent. They didn't doubt: they affirmed. Bardina, my classmate from the mineralogy lectures, seemed to me the only person who would not laugh at me and could lead me out of my difficulties, and so I began to speak to her frankly.

"My father was a forester, and then a peace mediator,"[7] I said. "How could he be an exploiter? Whom did he exploit?"

And with calm certainty Bardina would point out that peasants and workers paid various taxes to the treasury, taxes that went to pay the salaries of all government bureaucrats, including those of my father and my uncle. The people worked hard to pay those taxes out of their meager earnings; they went without necessities to send their hard-earned kopecks to the state treasury. Forced in addition to pay indirect taxes on salt and other necessary items, the people bore the burden of almost the entire budget.[8] They lived in poverty, on bread and kvass[9] and worked from morning till night, wearing bark shoes and lighting their huts with splinters of wood. And this was the case everywhere: if you were a minister or a professor, a forester or a judge, a peace mediator or a zemstvo

---

7 Peace mediators—*mirovye posredniki*—were members of the gentry who helped to implement the edict of February 19, 1861, freeing the serfs. They mediated land disputes between landlords and peasants.
8 In Russia the gentry were exempt from direct taxes.
9 A sort of beer, made from fermented rye.

doctor, you lived at the people's expense, in luxury or at least in comfort. You engaged in easy, pleasant, and respectable intellectual pursuits, while the people, who fed everyone and paid for everything, bent their backs, went hungry, and lived in perpetual need and ignorance.

"But you can't do without teachers, doctors, or judges!" I would argue.

"Of course not," Bardina agreed. "But the remuneration for labor must be fair: a judge works less than a miner or a peasant, but he earns a hundred times as much as they do. The man who expends the greatest energy on his job, or performs the most difficult or unappealing tasks, should be paid the most. But now everything's just the reverse: the more a man works, the less he earns. Our whole social structure is built upon this injustice, and it's the source of everything that's evil in contemporary society. Those who benefit from such a system are exploiters and parasites, because they take what should belong to others; they live at the expense of others, stealing poor men's last morsels."

Thus, before my eyes stood, on the one hand, millions of human beings condemned to endless labor, to poverty and everything that went with it—sickness, ignorance, and crime—while on the other there was a small handful of people enjoying all the good things of life because others were laboring for them.

These ideas unexpectedly threw everything I had believed about people and life into a completely new light. My ideas and my feelings were at odds. Could a small group of people at the top be responsible for the horrors of the London slums, the shameful oppression of the factory workers, the sufferings of the laborers in industry and in workshops everywhere, as described by Flerovskii and Engels? If not for this small group, everything would be different! And I, Vera Figner, was one of those people on top; like them, I was responsible for all the misery of the vast majority.

It was difficult for me to digest such a notion—and still more difficult to accept it. All the more so because there was only one way out: if it was all true, then I would have to renounce my position, for it would be unthinkable to recognize that you are the cause of others' suffering and still retain your privileges and enjoy your advantages. But that would mean that I would have to descend into that very poverty, filth, and degradation that was the lot of the oppressed majority. It was terrible to draw such a conclusion, terrible to have to make up my mind!

I wouldn't give up. "But a person who puts money in the bank and gets interest on it—he certainly can't be living at another's expense, you can't call him an exploiter?" I asked.

Bardina demonstrated calmly and methodically that even the bank, that peaceful refuge, was a device to wring sweat from the workers, and that interest was also criminal income.

I borrowed from the library a book of statistics that every young man and woman was reading at the time. It contained cold, dry figures which demonstrated that, with only minor deviations, an inevitable number of thefts, murders, and suicides were committed year after year in every country. People lived their lives, thinking that they exercised free will, that they could choose freely whether or not to steal, whether or not to murder. But the statistics demonstrated that whatever the desires of any particular individual, out of every ten thousand people, so many people steal, kill someone, or take their own lives. Why was this fatal repetition of exactly the same figures inevitable? It must mean that there are more fundamental, more profound motivations than individual will. There could be only one answer: social conditions are such that, despite individual inclinations, temperaments, or desires, they inevitably produce crime. Hunger and deprivation of all kinds—these are the true causes of all theft and violence against human beings. Personal influences and judicial punishments are helpless against such a reality.

"Individual efforts are useless against the power of the social structure," Bardina would tell me as we paced the corridor of the upper floor of the Russian House in Zurich. "Consequently, we should direct all our resources not toward ameliorating the plight of isolated individuals, nor toward doctoring individual cases, but rather toward the struggle to subvert the social institutions that are the source of all evil. We must struggle against man's exploitation of man, against private property, against inheritance rights. All of these must be abolished," she said.

The books I was reading by Proudhon, Louis Blanc, and Bakunin told me the same thing.

It was easy enough to say, "Abolish inheritance rights," but I must confess I was sorry to part with them. I fully admit the selfishness of this feeling: I didn't want to find myself suddenly empty-handed. My father had bought some land when it was very cheap—ten or eleven rubles per *desiatina* [2.7 acres]—right after the peasants were emancipated. This land had gotten much more valuable, and in time I would inherit a part of it. How could I rebel against inheritance rights? I had a desire, a powerful instinct, to own property, even if only in the future; I certainly didn't want to stay poor. But logic led me inexorably to the conclusion that the money my father had once spent for land had been blood money. There was no avoiding it; still, I would need a great deal of time before I could rid myself of the desire to hold on to what I considered mine, or reconcile it with the new idea that labor—physical labor—is the basis of everything, that it creates all material wealth.

When people of our circle spoke of the nation's wealth, they rarely referred to the contributions of intellectual labor; the issue was discussed exclusively from the point of view of its disproportionately high compensation in comparison to that of onerous physical labor. Intellectual labor was also condemned because of its origins: it was possible only because certain conditions allowed some groups in society to liberate themselves from the burden of physical labor by shifting it to others, thus gaining the leisure to cultivate science and art. And so—we placed the highest social value on physical labor, concluding that it alone was moral and pure. Laborers alone exploit *no one*—quite the contrary, everyone exploits them, thus committing an enormous social injustice.

But how would it be possible to do away with private property, or to abolish the rights of inheritance, when everyone wanted to keep what he had? Everyone would defend his property, and those who feasted at life's table would never *voluntarily* agree to relinquish their privileges!

Both the program of the International Workingmen's Association and social-ist writings in general declared that the only way to subvert the existing order was social revolution. These two words embraced *everything;* they were com-plete and convincing unto themselves, without any further details. Social revo-lution would turn everything upside-down. The people would rise up (and we were sure that the army would at this point desert to their side) and *proclaim* the abolition of private property and inheritance rights. The land, the factories, and the mills would be declared public property. After the social revolution, every-one would have to perform physical labor. Everyone would have to labor six to eight hours per day; in their spare time, they would be able to do intellectual work or simply to enjoy themselves. Their needs would be satisfied by the product of their labor—which would be at the disposal of society as a whole. No one would need inheritance rights, because children would be raised and edu-cated at the expense of society and not their parents. Society would also care for the sick, the elderly, and the crippled.

All of this seemed clear, simple, and easy. I was captivated by the picture of Fourier's phalansteries.[10] The formula "from each according to his abilities, to each according to his needs" seemed a miraculous solution to all the complicated questions about organizing production and consumption. In the mills and facto-ries, laborers would continue their business—the business of production—natu-rally, without even the slightest disruption of routine; they would then bring the products of their labor to public stores. Meanwhile, the peasants, having made the gentry's land communal property, would till the fields as before, bringing the grain to public warehouses. Then, factory and agricultural labor cooperatives would begin to exchange their products, evaluating them according to the amount of labor expended on them. All these labor cooperatives would form a free federation of free communes—the ideal of Bakuninist anarchism.

Only people who had lived in comfort before the revolution would find life difficult after it. It would be hard on those who had worked only with their heads and were not at all accustomed to physical labor. But here, too, Fourier was helpful, pointing out that even children could perform many of the easier tasks and could be useful to society. And since work would be required from each *according to his ability,* those who were weak would be assigned the easiest kinds of work.

Everything we read about seemed easily implemented and highly practical. To us, the word "utopia" did not exist: there were simply various "plans" for social revolution. Nobody raised objections: you could say that we were unani-mous in our enthusiasms. Those who were less entranced—or not entranced at all—kept their distance, introducing no dissonance to the reigning harmony. We believed that all these new ideas of democracy and economic equality were,

---

10 Phalansteries, as described by the socialist Charles Fourier (1772–1837), were communes in which men and women would be equal and social life would be governed by the "laws" of human nature.

logically speaking, totally invulnerable, and that those who questioned them did so only out of egotism or cowardice.

If these ideas had not been subject to persecution in Russia, then it might have been possible to examine disagreements or doubts about them on their merits. However, those who defended and preached the ideas were indeed being persecuted, while all those who valued their own personal wellbeing were unable to accept them, for reasons of self-preservation—because to accept them meant to put them into practice. Those who were reluctant to forgo their privileged position, who could not find the strength to renounce it for the good of the people, would cry, "It can't be done! You're all daydreamers!"

"You go talk with the people a bit; you'll be the first to be strung up if there's a revolution!" I was told by Mrs. Shcherbatov, the wife of a justice of the peace, who seemed both old and out-of-touch to us twenty-year-olds.

Well, I thought, listening to her, *aren't you afraid that the peasants will hang you!*

In the circles I frequented most, the idea of social revolution played an enormous role. It was one of the ideas to which we'd grown accustomed, and, apparently, no one doubted that the revolution would come soon. There was no real reason for such confidence, but everyone was convinced nevertheless that the time was at hand. We looked hopefully to the Russian people. There had been great popular explosions in the past. In fact, from the outset, the entire history of serfdom had been the history of popular protest. In the most recent past, peasant riots had occurred sporadically throughout the first half of the nineteenth century. And hadn't the tsar himself said, before he emancipated the serfs, "It is better to free the serfs from above, than to wait for them to free themselves from below." In fact, the peasants had not been satisfied by the Emancipation; it had proved to be only a new form of slavery. Still dissatisfied, the people were waiting for a new emancipation, one that would give them all the land this time.

Bakunin proclaimed—and this was the predominant opinion in our circles—that their very position made workers and peasants socialists and revolutionaries. With this optimistic view, it was easy for us to face the future. "But if the people are ready, how come they're not revolting?" someone would always ask. The answer was that the people were divided; they were disorganized and weighed down by police oppression, which crushed every initiative. Therefore, it was the intelligentsia's role to bring its knowledge to the people, to organize them and to help them unite for rebellion.

Despite our absolute certainty of the masses' revolutionary mood and readiness to act, despite our belief in the proximity of a social revolution and in its ultimate victory over the entire existing order, we made a strange distinction between our own fates and the radiant prospects of the revolution. About ourselves, we were always pessimistic: we would all perish; they would persecute us, lock us up, send us into exile and hard labor (we didn't even think about capital punishment then!). I don't know how the others felt, but for me that contrast between a radiant future for the people and our own sad fate was extremely influential when I was considering how to apply my socialist beliefs in practice. That contrast was always an emotional undercurrent in the stream of ideas that flowed freely in Zurich.

If not for the persecution, I'm not at all certain that I would have become a socialist at that time.

• • •

Our circle in Zurich had arrived at the conviction that it was necessary to assume a position identical to that of the people in order to earn their trust and conduct propaganda among them successfully. You had to "take to plain living"—to engage in physical labor, to drink, eat, and dress as the people did, renouncing all the habits and needs of the cultured classes. This was the only way to become close to the people and get a response to propaganda; furthermore, only manual labor was pure and holy, only by surrendering yourself to it completely could you avoid being an exploiter. Consequently, from both the ideological and practical perspectives, you had to leave the university, which led to a doctor's diploma, renounce your privileged position, and go to work in a factory or mill in Russia.

Most of the Fritsche resolved to do precisely that. Student concerns became extraneous to them, and by 1874—within a year after they left Zurich—they had set off for Russia.

I was a renegade on this issue of manual labor. But before I could make up my mind and tell my comrades that I wouldn't join them in Russia, that I would stay at the university, I went through a period of emotional turmoil.

Was it really necessary, I asked myself, to become a factory worker, no matter what? Did I really have to renounce the position, the tastes and habits of a member of the intelligentsia? But on the other hand, could I in all honesty refuse to simplify my life completely, to don peasant dress and felt boots like a peasant, or to cover my head with a kerchief and pick through foul-smelling rags in a paper factory? Would it be honest of me to hold a position as a doctor, even if I were also conducting socialist propaganda? Finally, would it be honest of me to continue studying medicine while the women around me   also of the educated class—were abandoning their scientific studies and descending to the depths of our society for the sake of a great ideal?

I could see clearly all the beauty of my friends' consistency and sincerity, and I knew they would be doing the very best sort of work. It tormented me that I couldn't bring myself to do it, too, that I didn't want to become a worker. For so many years I had longed to go to the university; I had been studying so long, and the idea of being a doctor had become so much a part of me. Now, even after my plans for engaging in cultural activity in the *zemstvo* had been replaced by the goals of a socialist propagandist, I still wanted the trappings of a doctor's life. A worker's life was horrible, inconceivable to me! The very idea made my blood run cold. But I lacked the courage to declare outright, "I don't want to." I was ashamed to admit it, and so I said, "I can't."

I found reasons, of course: "I'm not strong enough," I said. "Why," I asked, "must everyone enter the factories? Socialists can do other things, too, even in less 'democratic' positions. A *zemstvo* doctor might seem like just another master, remote from the people—but what about a paramedic [*feldsher*]? I'm studying and I'll continue to study in order to acquire knowledge, not a diploma. Once I know enough, I won't have to become a doctor, I can serve as a paramedic in a *zemstvo*—it will still be necessary for me to bring as much knowledge as possible to the village."

The Fritsche circle was tolerant of the individual opinions of its members. It is true that many of them held the most extreme views and—as if showing off for each other—we all chose as our heroes the most irreconcilable leaders of the great French Revolution. Some were enthralled by Robespierre, while others would settle for no less than Marat, the "friend of the people" who demanded millions of heads. Nevertheless, the original decree neither compelled us to pursue a particular kind of activity nor told us when to begin, and after the rest of the Fritsche group resolved to return to Russia and begin practical work, Aptekman and I, remaining behind to complete our studies, never heard a word of reproach or saw any sign of disapproval. However, as soon as the others left Switzerland, we two were completely cut off. We heard nothing about their talks and subsequent merger with a men's circle from the Caucasus, nothing about their contact with the editors of the *Worker*.[11] I found out about all this only after I had left for Russia myself.

The inclusion of the masculine element proved very beneficial to the Fritsche: the organization's plans for action became more practical. The men were also partly responsible for the fact that the regulations of the combined organization, after being reworked in Russia, became the first ones to be based on the principles of discipline and solidarity.

The revised plan of the "Moscow Organization,"[12] as it came to be called, was this: two or three members would take turns staying in the city, to act as an administrative center for the general affairs of the organization. Everyone else was to go off to the various industrial centers—Moscow, Kiev, Odessa, Tula, Ivanovo-Voznesensk, and Orekhovo-Zuevo—where, along with some workers from Moscow who had been propagandized by earlier activists, they would enter factories and mills.[13] There were no plans to go to the villages: it was difficult for women to get positions as workers there. Besides, the circle's primary goal was clearly defined as conducting propaganda among industrial workers. When they abandoned the factories twice or three times a year for field work or to return home to their families in the villages for

---

11 The *Worker* was published by a group of Bakuninists in Geneva; it was the first attempt to found a working-class organ in the Russian language. It lasted a year ceasing publication when the Pan-Russian Social Revolutionary Organization collapsed in Russia.

12 Or the Pan-Russian Social Revolutionary Organization, as it called itself.

13 Except for the men who were already workers before they were recruited, only the women in the organization actually undertook factory work.

the holidays,[14] they would in turn influence the people—the peasantry—through oral and written propaganda. After propaganda had prepared the soil, there were to be local uprisings, which would then merge into a nationwide insurrection.

However, nothing went as planned. Everything fell apart in the very first stage.

In Moscow, Prince Tsitsianov and Vera Liubatovich served as the administration, while Bardina, Kaminskaia, and, for a while, my sister Lydia, took up factory work. Olga Liubatovich went to Tula and Alexandra Khorzhevskaia to Odessa; Anna Toporkova, Varvara Alexandrova, my sister Lydia, and two male workers were sent to Ivanovo-Voznesensk. But all these beginnings were quickly aborted. Lydia Figner and later Bardina and Kaminskaia had to slip away from the factories. It proved impossible for elegant young "ladies" dressed up as peasant girls not to attract attention in the miserable surroundings of a factory. Everything they did set them apart: their small, tender hands were unaccustomed to working, and ten or twelve hours of labor in an unsanitary workshop—Kaminskaia, for example, had to work with filthy rags in a paper factory—exhausted them beyond endurance. They couldn't even conduct propaganda, because the consciousness of their female co-workers was too low, and so, disguised in their worker's clothing, defying custom as well as the outright prohibition of the factory administration, they went to the barracks of the male workers to try to get them interested in books. They offered the material to everyone, but since very few workers were literate, they eventually resorted to reading aloud. The sight of a solitary young woman, reading in the filthy, ill-lit, stinking barracks to a circle of those workers who hadn't yet tumbled into bed, was extraordinary to behold. Since the women would permit no "fooling around," the workers couldn't figure out why they were there.

Factory routine frequently got them into trouble. For instance, when they left the factory on holidays, the "ladies" had to carry their revolutionary publications along in their knapsacks. They couldn't leave them in trunks in the barracks, where they might be found during a search or even by some accident; but on the other hand, workers' knapsacks had to be searched whenever they left the factory. Thus, as my sister was leaving the Gubner factory where she worked until she went to Ivanovo-Voznesensk, the factory guard tried to detain her and she barely managed to escape.

By 1875 the Moscow group was in jail. Nikolai Vasihev, a worker, was captured on March 29, and Daria, the woman he lived with, led the police to the group's apartment, where everyone was immediately arrested. Subsequently, between May and September 1875, the organization's members in Ivanovo-Voznesensk, Tula, and Kiev, and the "administrators" who had remained in Moscow were all arrested.

At Ivanovo-Voznesensk the entire group was arrested shortly after they had begun their work at the factory. They had rented a small apartment, the kind

---

14 Factory workers in Russia were usually seasonal.

353

usually occupied by laborers, and everyone lived together there as a work collective. It's unclear whether the police saw something suspicious about this, or whether they had somehow intercepted a letter that put them on the organization's trail; in any case, the police appeared unexpectedly and captured everyone. They found revolutionary literature in the apartment, and in order to shield her comrades, my sister Lydia immediately declared that all of it belonged to her. She was initially sentenced to five years at hard labor for this; but since all her comrades were living in Ivanovo-Voznesensk on false identity papers, they were given comparable sentences, too.

In Tula, the girlfriend of a local worker, assuming that he was cheating on her, made a denunciation to the police and led them to the apartment of Olga Liubatovich, with whom her lover was in contact. This was roughly similar to what had happened in Moscow.

After that, the "administration" of the Moscow Organization came crashing down. Prince Tsitsianov and Vera Liubatovich lived in an apartment where—just like everyone else in those days—they took no conspiratorial precautions whatsoever. Their apartment held a cache of revolutionary literature and a fully equipped "passport bureau": identity papers were cleansed with a solution that filled the rooms with a suffocating odor of chlorine, and false residency permits were concocted on the desk, in which stamps, ink, and an extensive correspondence were stored. Many people visited this place for one reason or another; the organization's sizable funds were kept there to be distributed according to need. The Subbotina sisters, who were members, had generously contributed this money, placing the whole of their large fortune at the disposal of the organization.[15] When the police raided the apartment, Prince Tsitsianov engaged in armed resistance—the first such action in the history of the revolutionary movement of the seventies.

At almost exactly the same time, Khorzhevskaia and Zhdanovich were arrested in the south, at a railway station where they were waiting to pick up a consignment of literature. They were caught with a complete text of the organization's program and statutes, and later it was all produced as evidence against them in court.

Of course, the members of the organization had established ties with various people, and the police zealously pursued all leads. Occasionally, they stumbled on the trail of people who actually had been involved in the Moscow Organization's work; in other instances, however, they contrived to tie in people who were not implicated at all. That's how the "Trial of the Fifty" came about. It included eleven of the women who had studied in Zurich; a twelfth, Kaminskaia, was not brought to trial, ostensibly because she became mentally disturbed during her preliminary detention. There was a rumor that the quiet melancholia from which she suffered would not have saved her from trial if her father hadn't given the

---

15 When he was arrested in Tsitsianov's apartment, Kardashev was caught with 10,000 rubles, which he had been given for one assignment—an indication of how much money the organization possessed.—Figner.

police 5,000 rubles. After her comrades were sentenced, Kaminskaia's thwarted desire to share their fate led her to poison herself by swallowing matches.

By the fall of 1875 I was in my seventh semester of medical school in Bern. Since there were only nine semesters in the program, I was to start work on my dissertation within a year. But my life had reached a critical juncture.

Mark Natanson came to Europe that November, seeking to bring back to Russia the revolutionaries who had migrated west. He spent time in London and Paris, and when he got to Switzerland, he sought out Aptekman and me to tell us about the wretched state of the socialist cause in Russia. The Moscow Organization, including the original Fritsche group, had been destroyed, he told us; all of its members had been arrested and no one was left to continue their work. Nevertheless, wherever they had been active, they had established connections, and these had to be maintained. And so, in the name of the revolutionary cause and for the sake of comradely solidarity, he was inviting us to leave the university and come to the aid of our perishing comrades. These comrades, behind prison walls, were calling out to us, he said, to become their reinforcements in the emptying ranks of propagandists and agitators.[16]

Natanson's proposal took me totally by surprise. I had received no letters from my friends since they left; it had never even occurred to me that I might in general be needed in Russia, or that they in particular might need me. I had been moving toward my goal calmly and confidently, intending to begin my practical activity only after I'd finished my studies. Natanson's invitation came as a real catastrophe.

Once again I was forced to ask: What should I do with my life?

For the third time since I'd left the provinces and forsaken the peaceful country fields, I was plunged into painful introspection, faced with the sort of choices that decide the direction of one's life.

I had first been tormented by hesitation and doubt when I was passing from the secure camp of liberalism and complacent philanthropy to the uneasy sphere of revolution and socialism. I suffered torments for a second time when my sister and our friends were leaving for Russia. And now, after all that had finally passed and I had regained sufficient confidence to devote myself to what I was doing, now, for a third time, I was confronted with those disturbing moral questions, questions that demanded immediate answers. My soul was divided, my feelings were at war.

The Fritsche group had themselves demonstrated all the difficulties facing a woman of the intelligentsia who tried to become a laborer. Their experience showed how brief such unaccustomed activity would be—activity that put you in an illegal position from the very start, since you had to use false identity papers. The results of their noble attempt to become ordinary laborers did not

---

16 When she returned to Russia, Figner discovered that this was untrue, that her comrades had never asked Natanson to convey a message to her, nor to request her to return to Russia.

encourage others to choose that method of approaching the people; henceforth, moderately "democratic" positions, such as I had chosen—that of a paramedic— were seen as providing opportunities for enduring work.

But if I was going to serve as a paramedic in a *zemstvo,* why did I need a doctor's diploma? If I had no intention of becoming a doctor, why did I have to finish school? All I needed was enough knowledge to carry out my duties and help the people and I had that much already: surely three and one-half years of study were sufficient time for that. If I wasn't seeking the piece of paper that would publicly attest to my knowledge, why shouldn't I leave the university at once and rush to the aid of the revolution and my friends who were serving it?

And . . . suddenly I realized that the diploma, that piece of paper of which I'd been so scornful, was in fact precious to me: it enticed me and bound me. It would signify official recognition of my knowledge, evidence that I'd finished what I'd started, achieved the single, absolutely fixed goal I had pursued for so many years with such energy, constancy, and self-discipline. How could I retreat now, how could I abandon the program without finishing? I was ashamed to abandon it—ashamed in my own eyes and in relation to others. What would be the reaction of all the people who knew about my efforts, which had no precedent in our provincial backwoods? What about the friends and relatives who had sympathized with me, encouraged me, and sent me off to Zurich with their best wishes for my success in a pursuit that was still so new to women?

Yet, on the other hand, there was the revolutionary cause, which, I was told, also needed my energies! Locked in cells, bound hand and foot, my friends were calling out to me for help! Now that they had communicated their needs to me, could I ignore them and give preference to my pride, my vanity, and—alas!—my ambition? I had never admired these qualities in others and had tried never to let them rule me either, but now I realized how strong my vanity and ambition really were! Would I actually succumb to them? My self-esteem, my faith in myself demanded that I answer "No!" Nevertheless, it was painful; I regretted having to leave the university, regretted that I, Vera Figner, would never have the right to sign my name "Doctor of Medicine and Surgery."

I asked myself, did they really need me in Russia—for the revolutionary cause in general, and to maintain the contacts of the Moscow Organization in particular? This was the first time I'd met Natanson; I had never heard anything about him before, and he brought no letters of introduction—all he told me was that Varvara Shatilova, a relative of the Subbotina sisters, was the only one left in Moscow after the arrest of my friends, and despite her best efforts, she couldn't cope with all the problems facing her. The people she had managed to enlist to do some work had also been quickly arrested, and there was no one to replace them.

Rationally, I knew that either Aptekman or I ought to check things out personally to make sure that we were really needed in Moscow. Only one of us would have to leave Bern to do this, and if temperament counted for anything, Aptekman ought to be the one: she was calm and judicious, and would make a thorough examination of the existing conditions. If she found that the two of us weren't really needed, she would return and keep me from going. On the other hand, if I left the university to go to Russia, it could safely be predicted that I would never return.

But Aptekman remained silent; I could see that she didn't want to go.

Why couldn't I say to her: "There's no need for both of us to leave right now. You're cautious and level-headed—you go first and then write me to come, if it's necessary. If I go first myself, I'll never come back"?

But I couldn't say it. I was incapable of asking another person to do something I wouldn't do myself.

And so, with these feelings, I approached Aptekman and said: "You stay! I'll go alone and write whether it's worthwhile for you to come, too." That's how I made the decision that determined the course of my life.

The spiritual crisis I underwent in order to make this decision was my last. My personality had been formed and tempered during those years of struggle with myself. After the decision was made, my mind was finally at rest, and I vacillated no longer; I set to work without a backward glance. Social concerns had gained ascendance over personal ones for good. It was the victory of a principle that had been imprinted long ago on my thirteen-year-old mind, when I read in the Bible "Leave thy father and thy mother and follow me. . . ."

I left the university without earning my diploma; I abandoned Switzerland, where I had found a new world of generous, all-embracing ideas, and, still feeling the effects of my recent emotional turmoil, set off for Russia. I was twenty-three years old.

> When Figner arrived in Russia, she found that there was nothing she could do to help her comrades of the Moscow Organization. She got her license as a paramedic (concealing her studies in Zurich, which were politically suspect), obtained a divorce from her husband, and set out to establish herself among the peasantry. Henceforward, her life was totally bound up with the revolutionary movement.
>
> In the following pages, drawn from Figner's statement at her trial in 1884, she describes the stages in her political development.

When I returned to Russia and found that the movement had already suffered defeat, I underwent an initial crisis, but before long I was able to find a good number of people whose ideas were similar to my own, and whom I liked and trusted; together, we worked to develop what came to be known as the populist program. I then left for the countryside.

As the court knows, the goal defined by the populist program was the transfer of all lands to the peasant collective—a goal that was, of course, against the law. However, the revolutionaries who went to live among the people were to begin by playing a different kind of role: we were to engage in what is known in all other countries as "cultural activity." I, for example, became a paramedical worker in a *zemstvo*. Thus, although I went to the countryside as a committed revolutionary, my behavior would never have been subject to persecution anywhere but in Russia—indeed, elsewhere I would have been considered a rather useful member of society.

In short order, I found that a whole league had formed against me. It was headed by the marshal of the gentry[17] and the district police officer, and included, among others, the village policeman and the clerk. They spread all sorts of false rumors: that I had no identity card, that my diploma was false, and so forth. When peasants were unwilling to make an unprofitable deal with the landlord, it was said that Figner was to blame; when the district assembly lowered the clerk's salary, it was alleged that the paramedic was responsible. Inquiries about me were made in public and in private; the district police officer came by to see me; some peasants were arrested and my name was raised when they were questioned; there were two denunciations to the governor, and only the fact that the chairman of the *zemstvo* administration interceded on my behalf spared me further trouble. I lived in an atmosphere of suspicion. People began to be afraid of me: peasants made detours through back yards when they visited my house. Finally, I was forced to ask myself: What can I do under these circumstances?

I'll tell you frankly: when I settled in the countryside, I was old enough to avoid making crude mistakes with people simply out of tactlessness, old enough to be more tolerant of the views of others. My goal was to explore the terrain, to learn what the peasant himself was thinking and what it was he wanted. The authorities had no evidence against me: they were just incapable of imagining that a person with some education would settle in the countryside unless she had the most dreadful aims. What I was actually being persecuted for was my spirit, my attitudes.

Thus, even physical proximity to the people had become an impossibility for, me; not only was I unable to accomplish anything, I couldn't even have the most ordinary kind of contact with them. I began to wonder: *Perhaps I'm making mistakes that could be avoided if I move to another place and try again?* But as I reflected upon my own experience and gathered information about that of other people, I became completely convinced that the problem wasn't my personality, or the conditions of my particular village—the problem was the absence of political freedom in Russia. Hitherto, I had been concerned strictly for the peasantry and its economic oppression; but now, for the first time, I was experiencing for myself the drawbacks of Russia's form of government.

I had two options at this time: I could either take a step backward—go abroad and become a doctor, but a doctor for rich people, and not for peasants; or—and this was my preference—I could use my strength and energy to break through the obstacle that had dashed my hopes. Somewhat earlier, Land and Liberty had invited me to join up and work among the intelligentsia. I hadn't accepted at that time, because I'd already decided to work among the peasantry, and when I made decisions, I stuck to them. Now, out of bitter necessity and not through any lack of serious consideration, I was finally relinquishing my original views and embarking on another path. When I was ready to leave the countryside, I announced to Land and Liberty that I considered myself free of any obligations and wanted to join the party. I was invited to the Voronezh Congress [June 1879].

---

17 The highest official elected by the gentry.

At this time, various people were beginning to suggest that the element of political struggle had to play a role in the tasks of the revolutionary movement. Two factions, drawn in different directions, had emerged in Land and Liberty. Although the party didn't split at the Voronezh Congress, everyone's position became more or less clear: some people said that we had to continue working as before—i.e., that we must live in the countryside and organize peasant uprisings in particular localities; others asserted that we should live in the cities and direct our activities against the central government itself.

Shortly thereafter, when the party finally broke up, I was invited to become an agent of the Executive Committee of the People's Will. I agreed. My past experience had convinced me that the only way to change the existing order was by force. If any group in our society had shown me a path other than violence, perhaps I would have followed it; at the very least, I would have tried it out. But, as you know, we don't have a free press in our country, and so ideas cannot be spread by the written word. I saw no signs of protest—neither in the *zemstvos,* nor in the courts, nor in any of the other organized groups of our society; nor was literature producing changes in our social life. And so I concluded that violence was the only solution. I could not follow the peaceful path.

Once I had accepted this proposition, I remained committed to it until the end. I had always demanded that a person—myself as well others—be consistent, that she harmonize word and deed. Thus, once I had accepted violence in theory, I felt a moral obligation to participate directly in the violent actions undertaken by the organization I had joined. In fact, the organization preferred to use me for other purposes, for propaganda among the intelligentsia, but I desired and demanded another role for myself. I knew I would be judged, both in court and by public opinion, according to whether I had participated directly in acts of violence. That is why I did the things I did. My deeds—deeds that some people might call "bloodthirsty" and might regard as terrible and incomprehensible, deeds that, if they were simply enumerated, might seem callous to the court— were prompted by motives that, to me in any event, have an honorable basis.

The destruction of the absolutist form of government was the most vital aspect of our program, the part that had the greatest importance to me. I really didn't care whether the regime was replaced by a republic or a constitutional monarchy: the crucial thing was that conditions be created under which people could develop their capacities and apply them to the benefit of society. It seems to me that under our present system, such conditions do not exist.

After the congress in Voronezh, I went underground, going through all the metamorphoses involved in that process, such as adopting a pseudonym. I settled in Kviatkovskii's apartment in Lesnoi for a while, but after the division in the party was finalized, we moved to the city. Under the name of Likhareva, I lived with Kviatkovskii in the apartment where he was arrested that November.

After completing its theoretical and organizational work, the Committee announced to the members its decision to organize attempts on the tsar's life at three different points as he was en route to the capital from the Crimea. Designated individuals were instructed to go to Moscow, Kharkov, and Odessa, respectively. Although all the attempts were to involve blowing up railroad track with dynamite prepared in advance, each team of agents was left free to determine precisely where and how it would act. The various plans they devised were to go to the Committee for confirmation. Agents could choose assistants from among the local people. Each agent was to be kept in the dark about the personnel and methods used at the other points.

In addition to all these operations, the Committee was preparing an explosion at the Winter Palace in St. Petersburg. None of us agents[18] were privy to this secret.

I was not among those assigned to carry out the assassination. However, the prospect of bearing only moral responsibility for an act that I had endorsed, of having no material role in a crime that threatened my confederates with the gravest punishment, was intolerable to me, and so I made every effort to get the organization to give me a role in implementing the plan. After being reprimanded for seeking personal satisfaction instead of placing my resources at the disposal of the organization, to use as it thought best, I was sent to Odessa, where a woman was needed.

Early in September I left for Odessa with the supply of dynamite needed for the operation there. Nikolai Kibalchich and I found a suitable apartment within a few days, and moved in as the Ivanitskiis. Soon Kolodkevich and Frolenko arrived; Tatiana Lebedeva followed. All meetings and conferences were held in our apartment; the dynamite was stored there, the gun cotton dried there, the fuses prepared, induction apparatus tested—in short, all our work was carried out there, under the direction of Kibalchich, but with the aid—sometimes the very vital aid—of others, myself included.

We decided that the best plan would be for one of our people to get a job as a railroad watchman and lay the mine from out of his cabin. I volunteered my services in obtaining the job. I went as an anonymous petitioner to see Baron Ungern Sternberg, an influential person in the administration of the Southwestern Railroad, and asked him to place a man I knew, representing this request as an act of philanthropy.[19] Sternberg couldn't help me, but he wrote a note to the engineer who was actually in charge of the post. I noticed that the reception given me by the baron was not the sort usually accorded to society people, and so I hastened to correct the mistakes I had made in my outfit before my next interview. I appeared in velvet, dressed as befitted a lady petitioner. This time, my reception was courteous in the extreme, and they asked me to send "my man" over the very next day. I went home and made up a passport for Frolenko in the name of Semyon Alexandrov, the name I had given to his future superiors. The next day, he went to the administrator of the railroad division and was assigned to a place eleven to thirteen kilometers from Odessa, near Gniliakov.

Frolenko was given his own cabin, and he brought Tatiana Lebedeva there as his "wife." We transferred the dynamite to him so that he could plant it under the tracks, but then Grigorii Goldenberg arrived unexpectedly and demanded that

---

18 Members of the Executive Committee referred to themselves as agents in order to conceal their importance from the police.

19 This was a common practice at the time.

we send some of the explosives back to Moscow, since they didn't have enough there and the Moscow-Kursk railroad was the line that the tsar was most likely to use. We had to submit.[20]

> A second operation was established in the vicinity of Kharkov. Here a group of seven spent weeks channeling under the tracks. By the time the two trains carrying the imperial party approached, the dynamite was in place, but it failed to explode when the detonating circuit was closed—apparently there had been a technical error. A day later, as the trains approached Moscow, a third attempt was carried out. The People's Will had purchased a small house adjacent to the railroad and had dug a tunnel from its cellar. The tsar's trains reached the ambush at about 10 p.m. on November 19. Sofia Perovskaia, who lay waiting in the bushes alongside the railroad tracks, allowed the first train to go by, assuming that it was testing the way; she gave the signal as the second train passed, and the resulting explosion derailed and destroyed it. As it turned out, the tsar had been traveling on the first train after all, and so he escaped unharmed. A fourth attempt took place in the tsar's residence itself. In September 1879, Stepan Khalturin, a skilled carpenter and member of the People's Will, had gotten a job on a renovation project in the Winter Palace. Along with the other workmen, he started living in the basement of the Palace. Despite the tight security surrounding the tsar, over a period of months Khalturin gradually smuggled in a substantial quantity of dynamite, which he stored among his personal belongings. He was able to determine the tsar's routine, and at dinnertime on the evening of February 5, when none of the other workmen were around, Khalturin lit a slow fuse and left the Palace. Moments later, the explosion resounded. A first-floor room was destroyed, and a number of soldiers were killed or wounded, but the royal dining room on the second floor was only slightly damaged.

> Figner remained in Odessa after the operation there was abandoned.

Frolenko and Lebedeva soon gave up the cabin near Gniliakov, then left Odessa altogether. Kibalchich left the city in mid-December, Kolodkevich in January. The remainder of the more influential people went with them, and the party's work was turned over to me and a few little-known local people who proved so unsuitable that I had to get rid of them later on. But in any case, after Kibalchich's departure I rapidly established an extensive circle of acquaintances among all classes of society—professors and generals, landlords and students, doctors, civil servants, workers, and seamstresses. I advanced revolutionary ideas and defended the methods of the People's Will wherever possible, but my favorite sphere was the youth, among whom feeling was so strong and enthusiasm so sincere. Unfortunately, I knew few students personally, and those I did

---

20 Goldenberg left Odessa for Moscow, but at Elizavetgrad he was arrested and proceeded to betray the party. Nevertheless, the party carried out the bombing on November 19 as planned.—Figner.

know were generally pessimistic about the rest, resolutely refusing to believe that there were good people among them.

In March or April 1880, Nikolai Sablin and Sofia Perovskaia arrived in Odessa. They announced to me that they'd been sent by the Executive Committee to prepare mines in Odessa, in the event that the tsar passed through the city en route to the Crimea. Meanwhile, I had been busy preparing another terrorist action—the assassination of Paniutin, right-hand man of the governor-general. Everything was practically ready, but Perovskaia's arrival with the Committee's instructions forced me to abandon this project.

Sablin and Perovskaia had come with a plan for the attempt: they were to choose the street most likely to be used by the sovereign in getting from the station to the steamship pier; to rent a store on this street and carry on a business as man and wife; and from this store, lay a mine under the pavement of the street.[21]

We found a shop on Italianskaia Street and began work immediately. We had to hurry; the sovereign was expected in May, and it was already April. Moreover, we could work only at night, since the shaft had to be laid from the store itself, rather than the attached living quarters, and of course customers were around during the day. Instead of digging, we proposed to use a drill. The work turned out to be very difficult: the ground was clay, and it choked the drill, which required enormous physical effort and even then advanced exceedingly slowly. At long last, we found ourselves beneath the paving stones: the drill bit moved upward and emerged into the light of day.

Shortly thereafter, Grigorii Isaev lost three fingers in an explosion caused by careless handling of mercury fulminate. He bore it like a stoic, but we were terribly upset—he should have stayed in the hospital.[22] After this incident, everything that we had been keeping at Isaev's—the dynamite, mercury fulminate, wire, and so forth—was brought over to my house, since we were afraid that the roar of the explosion in his apartment might have aroused the curiosity of all his neighbors.

So we had one less worker. I offered to bring some local people I knew into the operation, but everyone was opposed to this. We decided to stop using the drill temporarily, make a tunnel a few yards long, and then resume drilling. It was imperative to remove all the dirt as soon as possible, in the event that the houses along the tsar's route were checked. We got rid of some of it, and the rest was brought over to my apartment in baskets, packages, and bundles. After sending the maid off on errands, I would empty them in a place I'd found there.

---

21 In short, this was the very project that was later carried out on Malaia Sadovaia Street in St. Petersburg—Figner. [That is, the successful attempt of March 1, 1881.]

22 Anna Iakimova, who was present during the explosion, acted promptly. She bound Isaev's hand, cleaned up the blood and pieces of flesh, and brought him to a *zemstvo* hosptial. She even managed to be present during the operation, for fear he would talk under the anesthetic.

But meanwhile, rumors of the tsar's trip died down, and the Committee instructed us to stop our preparations. We proposed taking advantage of the work we had done to blow up Count Totleben: at the time, we envisioned destroying the entire institution of governors-general[23] by systematically exterminating its individual representatives, but the Committee turned us down. It did give us permission, however, to make an attempt on the count's life by some other method, and so Sablin, I, and a few people I enlisted began following the governor-general around. We intended to use some kind of projectile, and if we had had the devices Isaev and Kibalchich invented somewhat later, the count certainly would have lost his life.[24] But all we had was dynamite and some unperfected fuses: any projectile we made would have been of awkward size and might not have been accurate. Even so, we would have carried out our plans if Count Totleben hadn't been transferred out of Odessa. After he left, all our preparations had to be liquidated. First we covered the tunnel with the earth we had extracted. I helped with this work, which wasn't very difficult: at night I would drag sacks of dirt from the living quarters and lower them into the basement, where the men trampled down the loose earth. We closed up the shop on Italianskaia Street. When everything was in order, Sablin and Perovskaia left. Isaev and Iakimova followed.

Through them I transmitted a request to the Committee, asking that they recall me from Odessa and designate a person to whom I could transfer local party business and contacts. However, I left for St. Petersburg—it was July, I think—without a successor's having arrived. I was greeted with a reprimand for my absence without leave, which had destroyed the possibility of effecting a personal transfer of contacts to the new agent.

In February 1880, in response to the bombing of the Winter Palace, Alexander II had created the Supreme Administrative Commission, headed by General Loris-Melikov. Until then, repression had been relatively indiscriminate; the most timid criticism of the regime could bring harsh penalties, and as a result much of liberal society had become sympathetic to the revolutionaries. Melikov's regime—the "dictatorship of the heart," as it became known—made repression more selective and rational, focusing its full force on known revolutionaries and on them alone, while offering limited concessions to the liberals: a greater voice in public life at the local level, less stringent censorship, and certain positive measures in the area of education.

The People's Will did not accept Loris-Melikov's policies as evidence of the regime's commitment to fundamental reform. However, as indiscriminate police repression was curtailed, the possibilities for

---

23 In the spring of 1879, the government attempted to subdue the revolutionary movement by establishing six special regional commands, each headed by a governor-general who was given far-reaching powers over civilian life.

24 These bombs were used for the first time on March 1, 1881.

propaganda and organizing increased significantly, and the party moved to take advantage of them.

The period from the fall of 1880 through the beginning of 1881 was one of intensified propaganda and organizational work for the People's Will. The absence of police harassment and gendarme searches during this period made work among the students and factory workers a lot easier: in St. Petersburg itself, propaganda, agitation, and organizing were being conducted on a massive scale. Everyone was animated and hopeful. The depression that had appeared as a result of the failures of the early 1870's and the ensuing reaction was gone without a trace. The demand for regicide still resounded loudly, because the policies of Count Loris-Melikov deceived no one: the essence of the government's attitude toward society, the people, and the party hadn't changed a bit—the count had merely substituted milder forms of repression for crude, harsh ones. And so the Executive Committee devised another assassination: a shop would be rented on one of the streets in St. Petersburg most frequently used by the tsar, and from there, a mine would be laid for an explosion. I proposed to the Committee that my friend and comrade Iurii Bogdanovich serve as the store's proprietor, and he was accepted for this role [Anna Iakimova posed as his wife]. Meanwhile, the Committee's technicians were working to perfect explosive projectiles: these were to play an auxiliary role in landmining operations, which had hitherto proved inadequate.

As for me, I didn't know the location of the shop, or Bogdanovich's alias— "Kobozev"—until the end of February, when I had to make up duplicate identity papers for him. My role during this period was propaganda and organizing. I participated as an agent of the Committee in two organizational groups that operated in two different spheres; I also went with Zheliabov from time to time to speak to military men—his special area of involvement. In addition, the Committee designated me secretary for foreign communications in the fall of 1880. The bombings of 1879 and 1880 had stimulated tremendous interest among all strata of Western European society, and in view of the importance that European public opinion could have for the party, the Committee decided to publicize our goals and aspirations abroad and acquaint Europe with the Russian government's domestic policy. I sent party reports, biographies and photographs of revolutionaries who'd been executed or imprisoned, revolutionary publications, and Russian journals and newspapers to Lev Hartman;[25] later, after March 1, I sent him a copy of the Executive Committee's letter to Alexander III[26] and a drawing showing the inside of the Kobozev store, done by Kobozev—that is, Bogdanovich—himself.

---

25 Hartman, a participant in the November 19 train bombing in Moscow, was forced to flee abroad because the police were on his trail.

26 In mid-March 1881 the Executive Committee set forth its political demands in a letter to Alexander III, son and successor of Alexander II.

In January 1881 the Executive Committee suggested that Isaev and I establish an apartment exclusively for its members. We found a place, and lived there together as the Kokhanovskiis. During February, a series of important meetings were held on alternate days at this apartment. The Executive Committee had called together its agents in the provinces, Moscow, and St. Petersburg and asked them for detailed accounts of the state of party affairs in all localities and spheres of activity. These, in turn, were summarized in one general account and presented by the Committee to the assembly of agents, who were invited to express their opinions on certain internal organizational questions, as well as on the party's over-all policy. In particular, the Committee wanted to know whether the agents considered the party organization sufficiently strong and extensive, and the public mood sufficiently favorable, for the question of insurrection to be placed on the agenda immediately—that is, should all subsequent party work be aimed at fomenting an insurrection in the immediate future, and should the central group devote itself to elaborating a serious, detailed plan for that insurrection? By a huge majority, the agents responded that a practical formulation of the question of an insurrection was indeed warranted. At the conclusion of the meetings, the agents were dispersed by the Committee to begin work pending new, detailed instructions.

Several months earlier, in November 1880, Alexander Mikhailov had been arrested. This was an irreparable loss, one we remembered whenever misfortune struck us. Mikhailov had guarded party security from within: he was the organization's all-seeing eye, the guardian of the discipline so essential to the revolutionary cause. Now, around the time of the February meetings, we lost the one remaining person most valuable to the organization, the external guardian of its security: Alexander Kletochnikov, who had made his way into the government's Third Section,[27] and, for the past two years, had helped to ward off the government's attacks against the party by warning us in advance.

By this time, the tunnel in the Kobozev store had been completed. One Sunday in mid February, the tsar passed by the Kobozev shop on Malaia Sadovaya on one of his weekly visits to the riding hall. There was general dismay in the party that we had missed this opportunity because the mine wasn't ready yet: we might have to wait a whole month before he passed by again. The Committee ordered that all work both on the mine and on the projectiles be completed by March 1. By that date our agents had been familiarized with the plans: there would be an underground explosion as the ruler was passing, and in case the explosion didn't coincide with the tsar's passage, or proved too weak to achieve its intended goal, people stationed on opposite sides of the street would throw explosive shells. We also knew that the personnel involved in the attack had already been chosen. Beginning March 1, we were to expect the attempt on each and every Sunday.

I don't remember the twenty-seventh of February at all, but the twenty-eighth is clear in my memory—I think because Andrei Zheliabov was arrested on the

_____

27 The political police.

365

evening of the twenty-seventh, and on the morning of the twenty-eighth, Suk-hanov brought us the news at our apartment.

On the twenty-eighth, the Committee sent Tsaev to the Kobozev store in order to lay the mine. That same day, we learned that not one of the projectiles was ready yet; furthermore, the people responsible for the apartment where all the technical operations were to be carried out had announced the evening before that they thought their apartment was being watched. At the same time, a rumor was spreading through the city that the police believed they were on the trail of an extraordinary discovery in the very precinct where the Kobozev store was located. Some young people had conveyed to us a conversation overheard between the concierge of the Kobozev apartment house and the police concerning a search in the building; then Bogdanovich-Kobozev himself stopped by our place to tell us that the shop had been inspected by an alleged health commission that was obviously acting under instructions from the police. Although Kobozev told us the inspectors had turned up nothing—indeed, they had fully legalized him—his story left us thunderstruck. It was clear that our mission—conceived long ago and brought nearly to conclusion through all the difficulties and dangers, the mission that was to climax the struggle that had bound our hands for two years—was hanging by a thread and might be thwarted on the eve of its execution.

We could have borne anything but that! It wasn't that we were worried about the personal safety of individual members of our organization—the party's entire past, our whole future, was at stake on the eve of March 1. There was no nervous system that could have tolerated such intense strain for long. Thus, when Sofia Perovskaia asked the Executive Committee how to proceed if the tsar did not go down Malaia Sadova on March 1, whether in that situation we should act with only the shells, the Committee responded, "Act in any case," and drew up a contingency plan. Sukhanov alone expressed some reservations, because the shells had never been used in action.

The Committee's decision was made on February 28. I was informed that three people would arrive at our apartment at 5 p.m.—Sukhanov, Kibalchich, and Grachevskii—and work on the shells all night.

During the early evening, agents stopped in at the apartment continually, some with news, others with routine requests, but this hindered the work, and so around eight o'clock they all dispersed. Five people were left in the apartment, including Perovskaia and myself. I persuaded the exhausted Perovskaia to lie down in order to marshal her strength for the following day; then I began helping the workers wherever an inexperienced hand could be of use—pouring metal with Kibalchich or, along with Sukhanov, trimming the tin kerosene cans I'd bought to serve as molds for the shells. I left them at 2 a.m., when my services were no longer needed. When Perovskaia and I got up five hours later, the men were still working. Two shells were all finished, and Perovskaia took them away; Sukhanov left shortly thereafter. I helped Kibalchich and Grachevskii fill the other two cans with detonating jelly, and Kibalchich took those away. And so, at 8 a.m. on the morning of March 1, four shells were ready, after fifteen hours of work by three people.

The Committee had instructed me to remain at my apartment until 2 a.m. on March 1, in order to receive the Kobozevs, who were supposed to abandon the store—he an hour before the sovereign passed, she after a signal that the sovereign had appeared on Nevskii Prospect. A third person was to activate the electric current; should he survive the explosion produced by his own hand, he was to leave the store, pretending to be an outsider. But the Kobozevs never showed up at my place. Instead, Isaev appeared, with the news that His Majesty hadn't passed by the store, and that he had proceeded home after finishing at the riding hall. I left the apartment, thinking that, for some unforeseen reason, the attempt hadn't been carried out. I totally forgot that the Kobozevs hadn't been notified of the Committee's final decision: to use bombs at a particular point on his return trip.

Everything was peaceful as I walked through the streets. But half an hour after I reached the apartment of some friends, a man appeared with the news that two crashes like cannon shots had rung out, that people were saying the sovereign had been killed, and that the oath was already being administered to the heir. I rushed outside. The streets were in turmoil: people were talking about the sovereign, about wounds, death, blood.

On March 3, Kibalchich came to our apartment with the news that Gesia Gelfman's apartment had been discovered, that she'd been arrested and Sablin had shot himself. Within two weeks, we lost Perovskaia, who was arrested on the street. Kibalchich and Frolenko were the next to go. Because of these heavy losses, the Committee proposed that most of us leave St. Petersburg, myself included. I wanted to remain, however, and so I argued with the Committee until it gave me permission. Unfortunately, my stay turned out to be a brief one.

On April 1, Isaev failed to come home. He was arrested on the street, like several other agents who'd been caught during March. To avoid worry and misunderstandings, we had previously agreed that the people responsible for the party's apartments were not to spend the night away from home without prior arrangement; consequently, by 12 midnight of April 1 I was certain that Isaev had been arrested.

For various reasons, our apartment had gradually become a warehouse for all sort of things: type and other printing equipment, all the utensils and a large supply of dynamite from the chemistry lab, half of our passport department, party literature, and so forth. Such resources could not be allowed to fall into the hands of the police: I decided to save everything and leave the apartment absolutely empty. During the afternoon of April 4 Sukhanov appeared, and with his usual efficiency, removed everything of value from the apartment in the space of two hours. He insisted that I leave the house immediately, but I saw no need to go before morning; I was sure Isaev wouldn't give the police our address. I stayed till morning, then, finding a suitable pretext to get rid of the woman who came to clean, I left, locking up the ravaged apartment. I've heard that the authorities arrived before the samovar I used to make tea that morning had cooled.

In the period after March 1,1881, Vera Figner became the acting leader of the People's Will. She tried to restore the party to its former strength, securing funds, recruiting new members, and working to expand its organization among military units. But most of the other experienced leaders were in jail, and the party had been infiltrated by the police; on February 1 0, 1883, Figner was arrested.

In September 1884, at the Trial of the "Fourteen"—members of the People's Will who continued to be active after the assassination of the tsar—"Vera Figner alone succeeded in getting herself heard out. Both the judges and the public listened with uncommon attention, and the chairman of the tribunal did not stop her once," recalled a co-defendant, A. A. Spandoni.[28] She received the death penalty, but her sentence was subsequently commuted to life imprisonment. She spent the next two decades in the Shlisselburg fortress.

After the revolution of 1917 Vera Figner wrote extensively of her experiences as a revolutionary. She died in the Soviet Union in 1943.

---

28 A. A. Spandoni. "Stranitsa iz vospominanii." *Byloe*, No. 5, May, 1906.

The New Democracy

―――――❖―――――

Constantine P. Pobedonostsev

The emancipation of the serfs in 1861 profoundly affected all aspects of Russian life. It contributed to the decline of the power of the nobility, discontent among the peasantry, restlessness among the workers, dissatisfaction among the intelligentsia, and increasing reaction among the advocates of autocracy. The principal spokesman of the latter from 1880 to 1905 was Constantine P. Pobedonostsev (1827–1907). A constitutional lawyer by training, Pobedonostsev taught civil law at Moscow University from 1860 to 1865. He left teaching to become first a member of the Senate (Russia's Supreme Court), then a member of the Council of State (a consultative body that advised the tsar in legislative matters), and from 1880 to 1905 he acted as Procurator of the Holy Synod (lay administrator of the Orthodox Church). Since Pobedonostsev was also a tutor in law of Alexander III and Nicholas II, he was, between 1881 and 1905, the most influential member of the government and the prime inspirer of its reactionary policies. [In the following piece, written in the early 1880s, Pobedonostev expresses his criticism of the westernization and liberalization of Russia.]

Basil Dmytryshyn

What is this freedom by which so many minds are agitated, which inspires so many insensate actions, so many wild speeches, which leads the people so often to misfortune? In the democratic sense of the word, freedom is the right of political power, or, to express it otherwise, the right to participate in the government of the State. This universal aspiration for a share in the government has no constant limitations, and seeks no definite issue, but incessantly extends, so that we might apply to it the words of the ancient poet about dropsy: *crescit indulgens sibi.*[1] Forever extending its base, the new Democracy now aspires to universal suffrage—a fatal error, and one of the most remarkable in the history

1   Horace: "nursed by self-indulgence"

of mankind. By this means, the political power so passionately demanded by Democracy would be shattered into a number of infinitesimal bits, of which each citizen acquires a single one. What will he do with it, then? How will he employ it? In the result it has undoubtedly been shown that in the attainment of this aim Democracy violates its sacred formula of "Freedom indissolubly joined with Equality." It is shown that this apparently equal distribution of "freedom" among all involves the total destruction of equality. Each vote, representing an inconsiderable fragment of power, by itself signifies nothing; an aggregation of votes alone has a relative value. The result may be likened to the general meetings of shareholders in public companies. By themselves individuals are ineffective, but he who controls a number of these fragmentary forces is master of all power, and directs all decisions and dispositions. We may well ask in what consists the superiority of Democracy. Everywhere the strongest man becomes master of the State; sometimes a fortunate and resolute general, sometimes a monarch or administrator with knowledge, dexterity, a clear plan of action, and a determined will, in a Democracy, the real rulers are the dexterous manipulators of votes, with their place—men, the mechanics who so skillfully operate the hidden springs which move the puppets in the arena of democratic elections. Men of this kind are ever ready with loud speeches lauding equality; in reality, they rule the people as any despot or military dictator might rule it. The extension of the right to participate in elections is regarded as progress and as the conquest of freedom by democratic theorists, who hold that the more numerous the participants in political rights, the greater is the probability that all will employ this right in the interests of the public welfare, and for the increase of the freedom of the people. Experience proves a very different thing. The history of mankind bears witness that the most necessary and fruitful reforms—the most durable measures—emanated from the supreme will of statesmen, or from a minority enlightened by lofty ideas and deep knowledge, and that, on the contrary, the extension of the representative principle is accompanied by an abasement of political ideas and the vulgarization of opinions in the mass of the electors. It shows also that this extension—in great States—was inspired by secret aims to the centralization of power, or led directly to dictatorship. In France, universal suffrage was suppressed with the end of the Terror and was reestablished twice merely to affirm the autocracy of the two Napoleons. In Germany, the establishment of universal suffrage served merely to strengthen the high authority of a famous statesman who had acquired popularity by the success of his policy. What its ultimate consequences will be, Heaven only knows!

The manipulation of votes in the game of Democracy is of the commonest occurrence in most European states, and its falsehood, it would seem, has been exposed to all; yet few dare openly to rebel against it. The unhappy people must bear the burden, while the Press, herald of a supposititious public opinion, stifles the cry of the people with its shibboleth, "Great is Diana of the Ephesians." But to an impartial mind, all this is nothing better than a struggle of parties, and a shuffling with numbers and names. The voters, by themselves inconsiderable unities, acquire a value in the hands of dexterous agents. This value is realised by many means—mainly, by bribery in innumerable forms, from gifts of money and trifling articles, to the distribution of places in the services, the financial departments, and the administration. Little by little, a class of electors has been formed which lives by the sale of votes to one or another of the political organizations. So far has this gone in France, for instance, that serious, intelligent, and industrious citizens in immense numbers abstain from voting, through the difficulty of contending with the cliques of political agents. With bribery go violence and threats, and reigns of terror are organised at elections by the help of which the respective cliques advance their candidates; hence the stormy scenes at electoral demonstrations, in which have been used, and the field of battle strewn with the bodies of the killed and wounded.

Organization and bribery—these are the two mighty instruments which are employed with such success for the manipulation of the mass of electors. Such methods are in no way new. Thucydides depicts in vivid colors their employment in the ancient republics of Greece. The history of the Roman Republic presents monstrous examples of corruption as the chief instrument of factions at elections. But in our times a new means has been found of working the masses for political aims, and joining them in adventitious alliances by provoking a fictitious community of views. This is the art of rapid and dexterous generalization of ideas, the composition of phrase and formulas, disseminated with the confidence of burning conviction as the last word of science, as dogmas of politicology, as infallible appreciations of events, of men, and of institutions. At one time it was believed that the faculty of analyzing facts, and deducing general principles, was the privilege of a few enlightened minds and deep thinkers; now it is considered an universal attainment, and, under the name of convictions, the generalities of political science have become a sort of current money, coined by newspapers and rhetoricians. . . .

The October Manifesto of Nicholas II

The "Bloody Sunday" massacre had an electrifying effect on all segments of Russian society. It intensified radicalism, increased agitation, and brought on clashes with authorities; it precipitated strikes and demands for a constitutional government, equal rights, and autonomy for minorities; and even led to mutiny. Under the mounting nationwide radicalism, which was accompanied by critical military reverses in the war with Japan, Nicholas II was forced to yield. On October 30, 1905, he issued a manifesto (drafted by Sergei J. Witte) which granted the people of the Empire "personal inviolability, freedom of conscience, speech, assembly and association," and promised to allow the disenfranchised elements of society to participate in the election to the Duma. Finally, it established as an "unbreakable rule" that no law should be promulgated without the sanction of the Parliament. The October Manifesto marked the end of absolute monarchy in Russia.

. . . The . . . concessions [of the tsar], while failing to satisfy the extreme radicals, pacified the liberals and the majority of the people, thus enabling the authorities to restore order and direct Russia to a period of "constitutional experiment."

By the Grace of God, We, Nicholas II, Emperor and Autocrat of All Russia, Tsar of Poland, Grand Duke of Finland, etc.,

Make known to all Our loyal subjects: Rioting and disturbances in the capitals and in many localities of Our Empire fill Our heart with great and heavy grief. The well-being of the Russian Sovereign is inseparable from the national well-being; and the national sorrow is His sorrow. The disturbances which have appeared may cause a grave national tension that may endanger the integrity and unity of Our state.

By the great vow of Tsarist service We are obligated to use every resource of wisdom and Our authority to bring a speedy end to an unrest dangerous to Our state. We have [already] ordered the responsible authorities to take measures to terminate direct manifestations of disorder, lawlessness, and violence, and to protect peaceful people who quietly seek to fulfill the duties incumbent upon them. To successfully fulfill general measures which We have designed for the pacification of state life, We feel it essential to coordinate the activity of the higher government.

We impose upon the government the duty to execute Our inflexible will:

1. To grant the population the inviolable foundations of civic freedom based on the principles of genuine personal inviolability, freedom of conscience, speech, assemblies, and associations;

2. Without postponing the scheduled elections to the State Duma, to admit in the participation of the Duma insofar as possible in the short time that remains before its scheduled meeting all those classes of the population which presently are completely deprived of voting rights, and to leave further development of general elective law to the future legislative order;

3. To establish as an unbreakable rule that no law shall become effective without the confirmation by the State Duma, and that the elected representatives of the people shall be guaranteed an opportunity of real participation in the supervision of the legality of the acts by authorities whom We shall appoint.

We summon all loyal sons of Russia to remember their duties towards their country, to assist in terminating this unprecedented unrest, and together with Us to make every effort to restore peace and tranquility in Our native land.

Given in Peterhof, October 30, the year of Our Lord 1905, and eleventh of Our reign.

Nicholas

Colonial Nigeria

From The Interesting Narrative of the Life of Olaudah Equiano

———◆———

Born Olaudah Equiano and given the slave name Gustavus Vassa, Equiano published his *Interesting Narrative* in 1789. The text went into nine editions in the next five years and was translated into various European languages.

Born in the kingdom of Benin in what is now southeastern Nigeria, on the border between the Igbo [Eboe] and Edo, Equiano was captured and sold to British slavers at age ten, around 1755. He was in the service of a British naval officer during the Seven Years War; while enslaved he also learned to read and, by his own request, became a Christian. When Equiano challenged his master's right, under British law, to own him, his vengeful master sold him to a captain bound for the New World. Equiano endured slavery in the West Indies and Virginia, and finally managed to save enough money to buy his freedom in 1766. After attaining his freedom, Equiano became a traveller and adventurer: a sailor, a merchant, a plantation overseer on the Mosquito Coast in Central America, a visitor to Europe and the Near East, and even a polar explorer. Equiano was also an important witness, public speaker, and leader in the British abolition movement which, led by Granville Sharp, took off around 1765. He became a Methodist minister and was involved in the missionary movement for the repatriation of British freed slaves in Sierra Leone. In 1792 Equiano married an Englishwoman and was able to leave a considerable estate to his two daughters on his death in 1797.

Equiano's narrative is more than a tale of high adventure—it is at once a "conversion narrative" in the tradition of St. Augustine, an ethnographic source on pre-colonial Nigeria, and a powerful argument for the abolition of slavery and the recognition of the equality of all human beings.

Jaya Mehta

Chapter 1

I believe it is difficult for those who publish their own memoirs to escape the imputation of vanity; nor is this the only disadvantage under which they labour; it is also their misfortune, that whatever is uncommon is rarely, if ever, believed; and what is obvious we are apt to turn from with disgust, and to charge the writer with impertinence. People generally think those memoirs only worthy to be read or remembered which abound in great or striking events; those, in short, which in a high degree excite either admiration or pity: all others they consign to contempt and oblivion. It is, therefore, I confess, not a little hazardous, in a private and obscure individual, and a stranger too, thus to solicit the indulgent attention of the public; especially when I own I offer here the history of neither a saint, a hero, nor a tyrant. I believe there are a few events in my life which have not happened to many; it is true the incidents of it are numerous; and, did I consider myself an European, I might say my sufferings were great; but, when I compare my lot with that of most of my countrymen,[1] I regard myself as a *particular favourite of Heaven,* and acknowledge the mercies of Providence in every occurrence of my life. If, then, the following narrative does not appear sufficiently interesting to engage general attention, let my motive be some excuse for its publication. I am not so foolishly vain as to expect from it either immortality or literary reputation. If it affords any satisfaction to my numerous friends, at whose request it has been written, or in the smallest degree promotes the interest of humanity, the ends for which it was undertaken will be fully attained, and every wish of my heart gratified. Let it therefore be remembered that, in wishing to avoid censure, I do not aspire to praise.

That part of Africa, known by the name of Guinea, to which the trade for slaves is carried on, extends along the coast above 3400 miles, from Senegal to Angola, and includes a variety of kingdoms. Of these the most considerable is the kingdom of Benin, both as to extent and wealth, the richness and cultivation of the soil, the power of its king, and the number and warlike disposition of the inhabitants. It is situated nearly under the line[2] and extends along the coast about 170 miles, but runs back into the interior part of Africa to a distance hitherto I believe unexplored by any traveller; and seems only terminated at length by the empire of Abyssinia[3] near 1500 miles from its beginning. This kingdom is divided into many provinces or districts: in one of the most remote and fertile of which [called Eboe], I was born, in the year 1745, in a charming fruitful vale, named Essaka.[4] The distance of this province from the capital of Benin and the sea coast must be very considerable; for I had never heard of white men or Europeans, nor of the sea; and our subjection to the king of Benin was little more than nominal; for every transaction of the government, as far as my slender observation extended, was conducted by the chiefs or elders of the place. The manners and government of a people who have little commerce with other countries are generally very simple; and the history of what passes in one family or village may serve as a specimen of the whole nation.

My father was one of those elders or chiefs I have spoken of, and was styled Embrenché; a term, as I remember, importing the highest distinction, and signi-

---

1 Countrymen: used here to mean those born in the same geographical area, in the widest sense, Africa.
2 That is, nearly on the equator.
3 Abyssinia: the ancient name for modern Ethiopia.
4 Equiano's homeland was that of the present Ibo people of modern Nigeria; scholars' attempts to locate Essaka have been so far unsuccessful.

fying in our language a mark of grandeur. This mark is conferred on the person entitled to it, by cutting the skin across at the top of the forehead, and drawing it down to the eye-brows; and, while it is in this situation, applying a warm hand, and rubbing it until it shrinks up into a thick *weal* across the lower part of the forehead. Most of the judges and senators were thus marked; my father had long borne it: I had seen it conferred on one of my brothers, and I was also *destined* to receive it by my parents. Those Embrenché, or chief men, decided disputes and punished crimes; for which purpose they always assembled together. The proceedings were generally short; and in most cases the law of retaliation prevailed.

I remember a man was brought before my father, and the other judges, for kidnapping a boy; and, although he was the son of a chief or senator, he was condemned to make recompense by a man or woman slave. Adultery, however, was sometimes punished with slavery or death; a punishment which I believe is inflicted on it throughout most of the nations of Africa:[5] so sacred among them is the honour of the marriage bed, and so jealous are they of the fidelity of their wives. Of this I recollect an instance. A woman was convicted before the judges of adultery, and delivered over, as the custom was, to her husband to be punished. Accordingly he determined to put her to death: but it being found, just before her execution, that she had an infant at her breast; and no woman being prevailed on to perform the part of a nurse, she was spared on account of the child. The men, however, do not preserve the same constancy to their wives, which they expect from them; for they indulge in a plurality, though seldom in more than two.

Their mode of marriage is thus—both parties are usually betrothed when young by their parents (though I have known the males to betroth themselves). On this occasion a feast is prepared, and the bride and bridegroom stand up in the midst of all their friends, who are assembled for the purpose, while he declares she is thenceforth to be looked upon as his wife, and that no other person is to pay any addresses to her. This is also immediately proclaimed in the vicinity, on which the bride retires from the assembly. Some time after, she is brought home to her husband, and then another feast is made, to which the relations of both parties are invited: her parents then deliver her to the bridegroom, accompanied with a number of blessings, and at the same time they tie round her waist a cotton string of the thickness of a goose-quill, which none but married women are permitted to wear: she is now considered as completely his wife; and at this time the dowry is given to the new married pair, which generally consists of portions of land, slaves, and cattle, household goods, and implements of husbandry. These are offered by the friends of both parties; besides which the

---

5   Equiano's emphasis on the sanctity of marriage and the consequent severe punishment for adultery contrasts sharply with the common pro-slavery assertions of African sexual promiscuity, which, the apologists for slavery claimed, accounted for the low birthrate among slaves that required the constant resupply provided by the slave trade.

parents of the bridegroom present gifts to those of the bride, whose property she is looked upon before marriage; but after it she is esteemed the sole property of her husband. The ceremony being now ended, the festival begins, which is celebrated with bonfires, and loud acclamations of joy, accompanied with music and dancing.

We are almost a nation of dancers, musicians, and poets. Thus every great event, such as a triumphant return from battle, or other cause of public rejoicing, is celebrated in public dances, which are accompanied with songs and music suited to the occasion. The assembly is separated into four divisions, which dance either apart or in succession, and each with a character peculiar to itself. The first division contains the married men, who in their dances frequently exhibit feats of arms, and the representation of a battle. To these succeed the married women, who dance in the second division. The young men occupy the third; and the maidens the fourth. Each represents some interesting scene of real life, such as a great achievement, domestic employment, a pathetic story, or some rural sport; and as the subject is generally founded on some recent event, it is therefore ever new. This gives our dances a spirit and variety which I have scarcely seen elsewhere. We have many musical instruments, particularly drums of different kinds, a piece of music which resembles a guitar, and another much like a stickado. These last are chiefly used by betrothed virgins, who play on them on all grand festivals.

As our manners are simple, our luxuries are few. The dress of both sexes is nearly the same. It generally consists of a long piece of calico, or muslin, wrapped loosely round the body, somewhat in the form of a Highland plaid. This is usually dyed blue, which is our favourite colour. It is extracted from a berry, and is brighter and richer than any I have seen in Europe. Besides this, our women of distinction wear golden ornaments, which they dispose with some profusion on their arms and legs. When our women are not employed with the men in tillage, their usual occupation is spinning and weaving cotton, which they afterwards dye, and make into garments. They also manufacture earthen vessels, of which we have many kinds. Among the rest, tobacco pipes, made after the same fashion, and used in the same manner, as those in Turkey.

Our manner of living is entirely plain; for as yet the natives are unacquainted with those refinements in cookery which debauch the taste: bullocks, goats, and poultry supply the greatest part of their food. These constitute likewise the principal wealth of the country, and the chief articles of its commerce. The flesh is usually stewed in a pan. To make it savory, we sometimes use also pepper, and other spices, and we have salt made of wood ashes. Our vegetables are mostly plantains,[6] eadas, yams, beans, and Indian corn. The head of the family usually eats alone; his wives and slaves have also their separate tables. Before we taste food, we always wash our hands: indeed our cleanliness on all occasions is extreme; but on this it is an indispensable ceremony. After washing, libation is made, by pouring out a small portion of the drink on the floor, and tossing a small

---

6 Plantain: a type of banana that must be cooked before being eaten.

quantity of the food in a certain place, for the spirits of departed relations, which the natives suppose to preside over their conduct, and guard them from evil. They are totally unacquainted with strong or spiritous liquours; and their principal beverage is palm wine. This is got from a tree of that name, by tapping it at the top, and fastening a large gourd to it; and sometimes one tree will yield three or four gallons in a night. When just drawn it is of a most delicious sweetness; but in a few days it acquires a tartish and more spirituous flavour: though I never saw any one intoxicated by it. The same tree also produces nuts and oil. Our principal luxury is in perfumes; one sort of these is an odoriferous wood of delicious fragrance: the other a kind of earth; a small portion of which thrown into the fire diffuses a most powerful odour. We beat this wood into powder, and mix it with palm-oil; with which both men and women perfume themselves.

In our buildings we study convenience rather than ornament. Each master of a family has a large square piece of ground, surrounded with a moat or fence, or enclosed with a wall made of red earth tempered, which, when dry, is as hard as brick. Within this are his houses to accommodate his family and slaves; which, if numerous, frequently present the appearance of a village. In the middle stands the principal building, appropriated to the sole use of the master, and consisting of two apartments; in one of which he sits in the day with his family, the other is left apart for the reception of his friends. He has besides these a distinct apartment in which he sleeps, together with his male children. On each side are the apartments of his wives, who have also their separate day and night houses. The habitations of the slaves and their families are distributed throughout the rest of the enclosure. These houses never exceed one story in height; they are always built of wood, or stakes driven into the ground, crossed with wattles, and neatly plastered within, and without. The roof is thatched with reeds. Our dayhouses are left open at the sides; but those in which we sleep are always covered, and plastered in the inside, with a composition mixed with cow-dung, to keep off the different insects which annoy us during the night. The walls and floors also of these are generally covered with mats. Our beds consist of a platform, raised three or four feet from the ground, on which are laid skins, and different parts of a spungy tree called plaintain. Our covering is calico or muslin, the same as our dress. The usual seats are a few logs of wood; but we have benches, which are generally perfumed, to accommodate strangers; these compose the greater part of our household furniture. Houses so constructed and furnished require but little skill to erect them. Every man is a sufficient architect for the purpose. The whole neighbourhood afford their unanimous assistance in building them, and, in return, receive and expect no other recompense than a feast.

As we live in a country where nature is prodigal of her favours, our wants are few and easily supplied; of course we have few manufactures. They consist for the most part of calicoes, earthen ware, ornaments, and instruments of war and husbandry. But these make no part of our commerce, the principal articles of which, as I have observed, are provisions. In such a state money is of little use; however we have some small pieces of coin, if I may call them such. They are made something like an anchor; but I do not remember either their value or denomination. We have also markets, at which I have been frequently with my mother. These are sometimes visited by stout, mahogany-coloured men from the south west of us: we call them *Oye-Eboe,* which term signifies red men living at a distance. They generally bring us firearms, gun-powder, hats, beads, and dried fish. The last we esteemed a great rarity, as our waters were only brooks and springs. These articles they barter with us for odoriferous woods and earth, and our salt of wood-ashes. They always carry slaves through our land; but the strictest account is exacted of their manner of procuring them before they are suffered to pass. Sometimes indeed we sold slaves to them, but they were only prisoners of war, or such among us as had been convicted of kidnapping, or adultery, and some other crimes which we esteemed heinous. This practice of kidnapping induces me to think, that, notwithstanding all our strictness, their principal business among us was to trepan our people. I remember too they carried great sacks along with them, which, not long after, I had an opportunity of fatally seeing applied to that infamous purpose.

Our land is uncommonly rich and fruitful, and produces all kinds of vegetables in great abundance. We have plenty of Indian corn, and vast quantities of cotton and tobacco. Our pineapples grow without culture; they are about the size of the largest sugar-loaf, and finely flavoured. We have also spices of different kinds, particularly pepper; and a variety of delicious fruits which I have never seen in Europe; together with gums of various kinds, and honey in abundance. All our industry is exerted to improve those blessings of nature. Agriculture is our chief employment; and everyone, even the children and women, are engaged in it. Thus we are all habituated to labour from our earliest years. Everyone contributes something to the common stock; and as we are unacquainted with idleness, we have no beggars. The benefits of such a mode of living are obvious. The West-India planters prefer the slaves of Benin or Eboe to those of any other part of Guinea, for their hardiness, intelligence, integrity, and zeal. Those benefits are felt by us in the general healthiness of the people, and in their vigour and activity; I might have added too in their comeliness. Deformity is indeed unknown amongst us, I mean that of shape. Numbers of the natives of Eboe now in London might be brought in support of this assertion; for, in regard to complexion, ideas of beauty are wholly relative. I remember while in Africa to have seen three negro children, who were tawny, and another quite white, who were universally regarded by myself and the natives in general, as far as related to their complexions, as deformed. Our women too were, in my eyes at least, uncommonly graceful, alert, and modest to a degree of bashfulness; nor do I remember to have ever heard of an instance of incontinence amongst them before marriage. They are also remarkably cheerful. Indeed cheerfulness and affability are two of the leading characteristics of our nation.

Our tillage is exercised in a large plain or common, some hours walk from our dwellings, and all the neighbours resort thither in a body. They use no beasts of husbandry; and their only instruments are hoes, axes, shovels, and beaks, or pointed iron to dig with. Sometimes we are visited by locusts, which come in large clouds, so as to darken the air, and destroy our harvest. This however happens rarely, but when it does, a famine is produced by it. I remember an instance or two wherein this happened. This common is oftimes the theatre of war; and therefore when our people go out to till their land, they not only go in a body, but generally take their arms with them, for fear of a surprise; and when they apprehend an invasion they guard the avenues to their dwellings, by driving sticks into the ground, which are so sharp at one end as to pierce the foot, and are generally dipt in poison. From what I can recollect of these battles, they appear to have been irruptions of one little state or district on the other, to obtain prisoners or booty. Perhaps they were incited to this by those traders who brought the European goods I mentioned amongst us. Such mode of obtaining slaves in Africa is common; and I believe more are procured this way, and by kidnapping, than any other. When a trader wants slaves, he applies to a chief for them, and tempts him with his wares. It is not extraordinary, if on this occasion he yields to the temptation with as little firmness, and accepts the price of his fellow creature's liberty with as little reluctance, as the enlightened merchant. Accordingly, he falls on his neighbours, and a desperate battle ensues. If he prevails, and takes prisoners, he gratifies his avarice by selling them; but, if his party be vanquished, and he falls into the hands of the enemy, he is put to death: for, as he has been known to foment their quarrels, it is thought dangerous to let him survive, and no ransom can save him, though all other prisoners may be redeemed. We have firearms, bows and arrows, broad two-edged swords and javelins; we have shields also, which cover a man from head to foot. All are taught the use of the weapons. Even our women are warriors, and march boldly out to fight along with the men. Our whole district is a kind of militia: on a certain signal given, such as the firing of a gun at night, they all rise in arms and rush upon their enemy. It is perhaps something remarkable, that when our people march to the field, a red flag or banner is borne before them.

I was once a witness to a battle in our common. We had been all at work in it one day as usual when our people were suddenly attacked. I climbed a tree at some distance, from which I beheld the fight. There were many women as well as men on both sides; among others my mother was there and armed with a broad sword. After fighting for a considerable time with great fury, and many had been killed, our people obtained the victory, and took their enemy's Chief prisoner. He was carried off in great triumph, and, though he offered a large ransom for his life, he was put to death. A virgin of note among our enemies had been slain in the battle, and her arm was exposed in our market-place, where our trophies were always exhibited. The spoils were divided according to the merit of the warriors. Those prisoners which were not sold or redeemed we kept as slaves: but how different was their condition from that of the slaves in the West-Indies! With us they do no more work than other members of the community, even their master. Their food, clothing, and lodging were nearly the same as theirs, except that they were not permitted to eat with those who were free born and there was scarce any other difference between them, than a superior degree of importance which the head of a family possesses in our state, and that authority which, as such, he exercises over every part of his household. Some of these slaves have even slaves under them, as their own property, and for their own use.

As to religion, the natives believe that there is one Creator of all things, and that he lives in the sun, and is girded round with a belt, that he may never eat or drink; but, according to some, he smokes a pipe, which is our own favourite luxury. They believe he governs events, especially our deaths or captivity; but, as for the doctrine of eternity, I do not remember to have ever heard of it: some however believe in the transmigration of souls in a certain degree. Those spirits, which are not transmigrated, such as our dear friends or relations, they believe always attend them, and guard them from the bad spirits of their foes. For this reason, they always, before eating, as I have observed, put some small portion of the meat, and pour some of their drink, on the ground for them; and they often make oblations of the blood of beasts or fowls at their graves. I was very fond of my mother, and almost constantly with her. When she went to make these oblations at her mother's tomb, which was a kind of small solitary thatched house, I sometimes attended her. There she made her libations, and spent most of the night in cries and lamentations. I have been often extremely terrified on these occasions. The loneliness of the place, the darkness of the night, and the ceremony of libation, naturally awful and gloomy, were heightened by my mother's lamentations; and these, concurring with the doleful cries of birds, by which these places were frequented, gave an inexpressible terror to the scene.

We compute the year from the day on which the sun crosses the line, and, on its setting that evening, there is a general shout throughout the land; at least I can speak from my own knowledge throughout our vicinity. The people at the same time make a great noise with rattles, not unlike the basket rattles used by children here, though much larger, and hold up their hands to heaven for a blessing. It is then the greatest offerings are made; and those children whom our wise men foretell will be fortunate are then presented to different people. I remember many used to come to see me, and I was carried about to others for that purpose. They have many offerings, particularly at full moons; generally two at harvest, before the fruits are taken out of the ground: and, when any young animals are killed, sometimes they offer up part of them as a sacrifice. These offerings, when made by one of the heads of a family, serve for the whole. I remember we often had them at my father's and my uncle's, and their families have been present. Some of our offerings are eaten with bitter herbs. We had a saying among us to any one of a cross temper, "That if they were to be eaten, they should be eaten with bitter herbs."

We practised circumcision like the Jews, and made offerings and feasts on that occasion in the same manner as they did. Like them also, our children were named from some event, some circumstance, or fancied foreboding at the time of their birth. I was named *Olaudah,* which, in our language, signifies vicissitude, or fortunate also; one favoured, and having a loud voice and well spoken. I remember we never polluted the name of the object of our adoration; on the contrary, it was always mentioned with the greatest reverence; and we were totally unacquainted with swearing, and all those terms of abuse and reproach which find the way so readily and copiously into the languages of more civilized people. The only expressions of that kind I remember were "May you rot, or may you swell, or may a beast take you."

I have before remarked, that the natives of this part of Africa are extremely cleanly. This necessary habit of decency was with us a part of religion, and therefore we had many purifications and washings; indeed almost as many, and used on the same occasions, if my recollection does not fail me, as the Jews. Those that touched the dead at any time were obliged to wash and purify themselves before they could enter a dwelling-house. Every woman too, at certain times, was forbidden to come into a dwelling-house, or touch any person, or any thing we ate. I was so fond of my mother I could not keep from her, or avoid touching her at some of those periods, in consequence of which I was obliged to be kept out with her, in a little house made for that purpose, till offering was made, and then we were purified.

Though we had no places of public worship, we had priests and magicians, or wise men. I do not remember whether they had different offices, or whether they were united in the same persons but they were held in great reverence by the people. They calculated our time, and foretold events, as their name imported, for we called them Ah-affoe-way-cah, which signifies calculators, or yearly men, our year being called Ah-affoe. They wore their beards; and, when they died, they were succeeded by their sons. Most of their implements and things of value were interred along with them. Pipes and tobacco were also put into the grave with the corpse, which was always perfumed and ornamented; and animals were offered in sacrifice to them. None accompanied their funerals but those of the same profession or tribe. These buried them after sunset, and always returned from the grave by a different way from that which they went.

These magicians were also our doctors or physicians. They practised bleeding by cupping, and were very successful in healing wounds and expelling poisons. They had likewise some extraordinary method of discovering jealousy, theft, and poisoning; the success of which no doubt they derived from their unbounded influence over the credulity and superstition of the people. I do not remember what those methods were, except that as to poisoning. I recollect an instance or two, which I hope it will not be deemed impertinent here to insert, as it may serve as a kind of specimen of the rest, and is still used by the negroes in the West Indies. A young woman had been poisoned, but it was not known by whom; the doctors ordered the corpse to be taken up by some persons, and carried to the grave. As soon as the bearers had raised it on their shoulders, they seemed seized with some sudden impulse, and ran to and fro', unable to stop themselves. At last, after having passed through a number of thorns and prickly bushes unhurt, the corpse fell from them close to a house, and defaced it in the fall: and the owner being taken up, he immediately confessed the poisoning.

The natives are extremely cautious about poison. When they buy any eatable the seller kisses it all round before the buyer, to shew him it is not poisoned; and the same is done when any meat or drink is presented, particularly to a stranger. We have serpents of different kinds, some of which are esteemed ominous when they appear in our houses, and these we never molest. I remember two of those ominous snakes, each of which was as thick as the calf of a man's leg, and in colour resembling a dolphin in the water, crept at different times into my mother's night-house, where I always lay with her, and coiled themselves into folds, and each time they crowed like a cock. I was desired by some of our wise men to touch these, that I might be interested in the good omens, which I did, for they were quite harmless, and would tamely suffer themselves to be handled; and then they were put into a large, open earthen pan, and set on one side of the highway. Some of our snakes, however, were poisonous: one of them crossed the road one day when I was standing on it, and passed between my feet, without offering to touch me, to the great surprise of many who saw it; and these incidents were accounted by the wise men, and likewise by my mother and the rest of the people, as remarkable omens in my favour. . . .

These instances, and a great many more which might be adduced, while they shew how the complexions of the same persons vary in different climates, it is hoped may tend also to remove the prejudice that some conceive against the natives of Africa on account of their colour. Surely the minds of the Spaniards did not change with their complexions! Are there not causes enough to which the apparent inferiority of an African may be ascribed, without limiting the goodness of God, and supposing he forbore to stamp understanding on certainly his own image, because "carved in ebony?" Might it not naturally be ascribed to their situation? When they come among Europeans, they are ignorant of their language, religion, manners, and customs. Are any pains taken to teach them these? Are they treated as men? Does not slavery itself depress the mind, and extinguish all its fire, and every noble sentiment? But, above all, what advantages do not a refined people possess over those who are rude and uncultivated? Let the polished and haughty European recollect that *his* ancestors were once, like the Africans, uncivilized, and even barbarous. Did Nature make *them* inferior to their sons? and should *they too* have been made slaves? Every rational mind answers, No. Let such reflections as these melt the pride of their superiority into sympathy for the wants and miseries of their sable brethren, and compel them to acknowledge, that understanding is not confined to feature or colour. If, when they look round the world, they feel exultation, let it be tempered with benevolence to others, and gratitude to God, "who hath made of one blood all nations of men for to dwell on all the face of the earth; and whose wisdom is not our wisdom, neither are our ways his ways."

Chapter 2

I hope the reader will not think I have trespassed on his patience in introducing myself to him with some account of the manners and customs of my country. They had been implanted in me with great care, and made an impression on my mind, which time could not erase, and which all the adversity and variety of fortune I have since experienced served only to rivet and record: for, whether the love of one's country be real or imaginary, or a lesson of reason, or an instinct of nature, I still look back with pleasure on the first scenes of my life, though that pleasure has been for the most part mingled with sorrow.

I have already acquainted the reader with the time and place of my birth. My father, besides many slaves, had a numerous family, of which seven lived to grow up, including myself and a sister, who was the only daughter. As I was the youngest of the sons, I became, of course, the greatest favourite with my mother, and was always with her; and she used to take particular pains to form my mind. I was trained up from my earliest years in the arts of agriculture and war: my daily exercise was shooting and throwing javelins; and my mother adorned me with emblems, after the manner of our greatest warriors. In this way I grew up till I was turned the age of eleven, when an end was put to my happiness in the following manner:—Generally, when the grown people in the neighbourhood were gone far in the fields to labour, the children assembled together in some of the neighbours' premises to play; and commonly some of us used to get up a tree to look out for any assailant, or kidnapper, that might come upon us; for they sometimes took those opportunities of our parents' absence, to attack and carry off as many as they could seize. One day, as I was watching at the top of a tree in our yard, I saw one of those people come into the yard of our next neighbour but one, to kidnap, there being many stout young people in it. Immediately, on this, I gave the alarm of the rogue, and he was surrounded by the stoutest of them, who entangled him with cords, so that he could not escape till some of the grown people came and secured him. But, alas! ere long it was my fate to be thus attacked, and to be carried off, when none of the grown people were nigh.

One day, when all our people were gone out to their works as usual, and only I and my dear sister were left to mind the house, two men and a woman got over our walls, and in a moment seized us both; and, without giving us time to cry out, or make resistance, they stopped our mouths, tied our hands, and ran off with us into the nearest wood: and continued to carry us as far as they could, till night came on, when we reached a small house, where the robbers halted for refreshment, and spent the night. We were then unbound, but were unable to take any food; and, being quite overpowered by fatigue and grief, our only relief was some sleep, which allayed our misfortune for a short time. The next morning we left the house, and continued travelling all the day. For a long time we had kept the woods, but at last we came into a road which I believed I knew. I had now some hopes of being delivered;[7] for we had advanced but a little way before I discovered some people at a distance on which I began to cry out for their assistance; but my cries had no other effect than to make them tie me faster, and stop my mouth, and then they put me into a large sack. They also stopped my sister's mouth, and tied her hands; and in this manner we proceeded till we were out of the sight of these people. When we went to rest the following night they offered us some victuals; but we refused them; and the only comfort we had was in being in one another's arms all that night, and bathing each other with our tears. But, alas! we were soon deprived of even the smallest comfort of weeping together.

---

7   Equiano's use of *deliverance* here to mean only physical salvation, as opposed to its later meaning in the *Narrative* of spiritual salvation, parallels the dual use of the term in spiritual biographies, including fictional ones, like *Robinson Crusoe* (1719), by Daniel Defoe (1660–1731). During the stage of his life before being exposed to Christianity, Equano fails to yet recognize that, from a theological perspective, release from the slavery of sin is far more important than release from bodily bondage.

The next day proved a day of greater sorrow than I had yet experienced; for my sister and I were then separated, while we lay clasped in each other's arms. It was in vain that we besought them not to part us: she was torn from me, and immediately carried away, while I was left in a state of distraction not to be described. I cried and grieved continually; and for several days did not eat any thing but what they forced into my mouth. At length, after many days travelling, during which I had often changed masters, I got into the hands of a chieftain, in a very pleasant country. This man had two wives and some children, and, they all used me extremely well, and did all they could to comfort me; particularly the first wife, who was something like my mother. Although I was a great many days journey from my father's house, yet these people spoke exactly the same language with us. This first master of mine, as I may call him, was a smith, and my principal employment was working his bellows, which were the same kind as I had seen in my vicinity. They were in some respects not unlike the stoves here in gentlemen's kitchens; and were covered over with leather; and in the middle of that leather a stick was fixed, and a person stood up, and worked it, in the same manner as is done to pump water out of a cask with a hand-pump. I believe it was gold he worked, for it was of a lovely bright yellow colour, and was worn by the women on their wrists and ankles.

I was there I suppose about a month, and they at last used to trust me some little distance from the house. . . .

Soon after this my master's only daughter and child by his first wife sickened and died, which affected him so much that for some time he was almost frantic, and really would have killed himself had he not been watched and prevented. However, in a small time afterwards he recovered, and I was again sold. I was now carried to the left of the sun's rising, through many dreary wastes and dismal woods, amidst the hideous roarings of wild beasts. The people I was sold to used to carry me very often, when I was tired, either on their shoulders or on their backs. I saw many convenient well-built sheds along the roads, at proper distances, to accommodate the merchants and travellers, who lay in those buildings along with their wives, who often accompany them; and they always go well armed.

From the time I left my own nation I always found somebody that understood me till I came to the sea coast. The languages of different nations did not totally differ, nor were they so copious as those of the Europeans, particularly the English. They were therefore easily learned; and, while I was journeying thus through Africa, I acquired two or three different tongues. In this manner I had been travelling for a considerable time, when one evening, to my great surprise, whom should I see brought to the house where I was but my dear sister. As soon as she saw me she gave a loud shriek, and ran into my arms—I was quite overpowered; neither of us could speak, but, for a considerable time, clung to each other in mutual embraces, unable to do any thing but weep. Our meeting affected all who saw us; and indeed I must acknowledge, in honour of those sable destroyers of human rights, that I never met with any ill treatment, or saw any offered to their slaves, except tying them, when necessary, to keep them from running away.

When these people knew we were brother and sister they indulged us to be together; and the man, to whom I supposed we belonged, lay with us, he in the middle, while she and I held one another by the hands across his breast all night; and thus for a while we forgot our misfortunes in the joy of being together: but even this small comfort was soon to have an end; for scarcely had the fatal morning appeared, when she was again torn from me for ever! I was now more miserable, if possible, than before. The small relief which her presence gave me from pain was gone, and the wretchedness of my situation was redoubled by my anxiety after her fate, and my apprehensions lest her sufferings should be greater than mine, when I could not be with her to alleviate them. Yes, thou dear partner of all my childish sports! thou sharer of my joys and sorrows! happy should I have ever esteemed myself to encounter every misery for you, and to procure your freedom by the sacrifice of my own. Though you were early forced from my arms, your image has been always rivetted in my heart, from which neither *time nor fortune* have been able to remove it: so that, while the thoughts of your sufferings have damped my prosperity, they have mingled with adversity, and increased its bitterness. To that heaven which protects the weak from the strong, I commit the care of your innocence and virtues, if they have not already received their full reward; and if your youth and delicacy have not long since fallen victims to the violence of the African trader, the pestilential stench of a Guinea ship, the seasoning in the European colonies, or the lash and lust of a brutal and unrelenting overseer.[8]

I did not long remain after my sister. I was again sold, and carried through a number of places, till, after travelling a considerable time, I came to a town called Tinmah, in the most beautiful country I had yet seen in Africa. It was extremely rich, and there were many rivulets which flowed through it; and supplied a large pond in the center of the town, where the people washed. Here I first saw and tasted cocoa nuts, which I thought superior to any nuts I had ever tasted before; and the trees, which were loaded, were also interspersed amongst the houses, which had commodious shades adjoining, and were in the same manner as ours, the insides being neatly plastered and whitewashed. Here I also saw and tasted for the first time sugar-cane.[9] Their money consisted of little white shells, the size of the finger nail: they are known in this country by the name of *core*.[10] I

---

8   Equiano refers to the four stages of the African slave trade: the original capture by other Africans and transportation to the coast, during which many died from hunger, thirst, and exhaustion; the middle passage across the Atlantic, when disease and despair posed the most lethal threats; the seasoning, or period between arrival in the West Indies and full-time employment on the plantations, when the Africans, were somewhat gradually introduced to the life of forced labor and when they were suddenly introduced to a new and therefore deadly disease environment; and the final stage of enslavement.

9   Equiano may be sublty reminding his readers of the common abolitionist argument that sugar could be profitably cultivated in Africa by free native labor.

10 Core: cowry, a shell used as currency in West Africa.

was sold here for one hundred and seventy-two of them by a merchant who lived and brought me there.[11]

I had been about two or three days at his house, when a wealthy widow, a neighbour of his, came there one evening, and brought with her an only son, a young gentleman about my own age and size. Here they saw me; and, having taken a fancy to me, I was bought of the merchant, and went home with them. Her house and premises were situated close to one of those rivulets I have mentioned, and were the finest I ever saw in Africa: they were very extensive, and she had a number of slaves to attend her. The next day I was washed and perfumed, and when meal-time came, I was led into the presence of my mistress, and ate and drank before her with her son. This filled me with astonishment: and I could scarce help expressing my surprise that the young gentleman should suffer me, who was bound,[12] to eat with him who was free; and not only so, but that he would not at any time either eat or drink till I had taken first, because I was the eldest, which was agreeable to our custom. Indeed every thing here, and all their treatment of me, made me forget that I was a slave. The language of these people resembled ours so nearly, that we understood each other perfectly. They had also the very same customs as we. There were likewise slaves daily to attend us, while my young master and I, with other boys, sported with our darts and bows and arrows, as I had been used to do at home. In this resemblance to my former happy state I passed about two months, and I now began to think I was to be adopted into the family, and was beginning to be reconciled to my situation, and to forget by degrees my misfortunes, when all at once the delusion vanished; for, without the least previous knowledge, one morning early, while my dear master and companion was still asleep, I was awakened out of my reverie to fresh sorrow, and hurried away even among the uncircumcised.

Thus, at the very moment I dreamed of the greatest happiness, I found myself most miserable: and it seemed as if fortune wished to give me this taste of joy only to render the reverse more poignant.[13] The change I now experienced was as painful as it was sudden and unexpected. It was a change indeed from a state of bliss to a scene which is inexpressible by me, as it discovered to me an element I had never before beheld, and till then had no idea of, and wherein such instances of hardship and cruelty continually occurred as I can never reflect on but with horror. . . .

The first object which saluted my eyes when I arrived on the coast was the sea, and a slave-ship, which was then riding at anchor, and waiting for its cargo. These filled me with astonishment, which was soon converted into terror, which I am yet at a loss to describe, nor the then feelings of my mind. When I was carried on board I was immediately handled, and tossed up, to see if I were sound,

---

11 Equiano must mean 172 pounds of cowry shells, because the price of slaves during the the century ranged between 100 and 300 pounds apiece.

12 Bound: enslaved.

13 Equiano refers to fortune here because, as a pagan, he still saw life as a matter of chance, rather than as a working out of providential design and order.

by some of the crew; and I was now persuaded that I had gotten into a world of bad spirits, and that they were going to kill me. Their complexions too differing so much from ours, their long hair, and the language they spoke, which was very different from any I had ever heard, united to confirm me in this belief. Indeed, such were the horrors of my views and fears at the moment, that, if ten thousand worlds had been my own, I would have freely parted with them all to have exchanged my condition with that of the meanest slave in my own country. When I looked round the ship too, and saw a large furnace of copper boiling, and a multitude of black people of every description chained together, every one of their countenances expressing dejection and sorrow, I no longer doubted of my fate, and, quite overpowered with horror and anguish, I fell motionless on the deck and fainted. When I recovered a little, I found some black people about me, who I believed were some of those who brought me on board, and had been receiving their pay; they talked to me in order to cheer me, but all in vain. I asked them if we were not to be eaten by those white men with horrible looks, red faces, and long hair? They told me I was not; and one of the crew brought me a small portion of spirituous liquor in a wine glass; but, being afraid of him, I would not take it out of his hand. One of the blacks therefore took it from him and gave it to me, and I took a little down my palate, which, instead of reviving me, as they thought it would, threw me into the greatest consternation at the strange feeling it produced, having never tasted any such liquor before. Soon after this, the blacks who brought me on board went off and left me abandoned to despair.

I now saw myself deprived of all chance of returning to my native country, or even the least glimpse of hope of gaining the shore, which I now considered as friendly: and I even wished for my former slavery in preference to my present situation, which was filled with horrors of every kind, still heightened by my ignorance of what I was to undergo. I was not long suffered to indulge my grief; I was soon put down under the decks, and there I received such a salutation in my nostrils as I had never experienced in my life; so that with the loathsomeness of the stench, and crying together, I became so sick and low that I was not able to eat, nor had I the least desire to taste any thing. I now wished for the last friend, Death, to relieve me; but soon, to my grief, two of the white men offered me eatables; and, on my refusing to eat, one of them held me fast by the hands, and laid me across, I think, the windlass, and tied my feet, while the other flogged me severely. I had never experienced any thing of this kind before; and although, not being used to the water, I naturally feared that element the first time I saw it; yet, nevertheless, could I have got over the nettings, I would have jumped over the side, but I could not; and, besides, the crew used to watch us very closely who were not chained down to the decks, lest we should leap into the water; and I have seen some of these poor African prisoners most severely cut for attempting to do so, and hourly whipped for not eating. This indeed was often the case with myself.

In a little time after, amongst the poor chained men, I found some of my own nation, which in a small degree gave ease to my mind. I inquired of these what was to be done with us? they gave me to understand we were to be carried to these white people's country to work for them. I then was a little revived, and thought, if it were no worse than working, my situation was not so desperate: but still I feared I should be put to death, the white people looked and acted, as I thought, in so savage a manner; for I had never seen among any people such instances of brutal cruelty. . . .

At last, when the ship we were in had got in all her cargo, they made ready with many fearful noises, and we were all put under deck, so that we could not see how they managed the vessel. But this disappointment was the least of my sorrow. The stench of the hold while we were on the coast was so intolerably loathsome, that it was dangerous to remain there for any time, and some of us had been permitted to stay on the deck for the fresh air; but now that the whole ship's cargo were confined together, it became absolutely pestilential. The closeness of the place, and the heat of the climate, added to the number in the ship, which was so crowded that each had scarcely room to turn himself, almost suffocated us. This produced copious perspirations, so that the air soon became unfit for respiration, from a variety of loathsome smells, and brought on a sickness among the slaves, of which many died, thus falling victims to the improvident avarice, as I may call it, of their purchasers. This wretched situation was again aggravated by the galling of the chains, now become insupportable; and the filth of the necessary tubs, into which the children often fell, and were almost suffocated.[14] The shrieks of the women, and the groans of the dying, rendered the whole a scene of horror almost inconceiveable. Happily perhaps for myself I was soon reduced so low here that it was thought necessary to keep me almost always on deck; and from my extreme youth I was not put in fetters. In this situation I expected every hour to share the fate of my companions, some of whom were almost daily brought upon deck at the point of death, which I began to hope would soon put an end to my miseries. Often did I think many of the inhabitants of the deep much more happy than myself; I envied them the freedom they enjoyed, and as often wished I could change my condition for theirs. Every circumstance I met with served only to render my state more painful, and heighten my apprehensions, and my opinion of the cruelty of the whites.

One day they had taken a number of fishes; and when they had killed and satisfied themselves with as many as they thought fit, to our astonishment who were on the deck, rather than give any of them to us to eat, as we expected, they tossed the remaining fish into the sea again, although we begged and prayed for some as well as we could, but in vain; and some of my countrymen, being pressed by hunger, took an opportunity, when they thought no one saw them, of trying to get a little privately; but they were discovered, and the attempt procured them some very severe floggings.

One day, when we had a smooth sea, and moderate wind, two of my wearied countrymen, who were chained together (I was near them at the time), preferring death to such a life of misery, somehow made through the nettings, and jumped into the sea: immediately another quite dejected fellow, who, on account of his illness, was suffered to be out of irons, also followed their example; and I believe

---

14 Necessary tubs: latrines.

many more would very soon have done the same, if they had not been prevented by the ship's crew, who were instantly alarmed. Those of us that were the most active were, in a moment, put down under the deck; and there was such a noise and confusion amongst the people of the ship as I never heard before, to stop her, and get the boat out to go after the slaves. However, two of the wretches were drowned, but they got the other, and afterwards flogged him unmercifully, for thus attempting to prefer death to slavery. In this manner we continued to undergo more hardships than I can now relate; hardships which are inseparable from this accursed trade.—Many a time we were near suffocation, from the want of fresh air, which we were often without for whole days together. This, and the stench of the necessary tubs, carried off many.

From Through African Doors

—◆—

Janheinz Jahn

Life history or biography is a valuable tool that we can use to understand the lives of people from other cultures, where individual experience is a reflection of the larger social whole. The story of a young Yoruba woman named Ewumi is no exception. First, historically we can locate her in the center of the colonial period: she was born in 1933 and the narrative which follows brings us to the brink of Nigeria's independence in 1960. Through Ewumi we learn, for example, of the interplay between European and Yoruba religions; the introduction of cash cropping; and the effects of European schooling. In turn, however, these histori- cally-rooted themes provide the backdrop to a larger picture: the daily experi- ences of girls and women who live in rural village settings of a territory we now call Nigeria. Through Ewumi's story we can explore Yoruba attitudes towards such issues as kinship, child rearing practices, polygynous marriage, pregnancy, and romantic love. As daughter, spouse, mother, co-wife, and market woman, Ewumi's life epitomizes those of other successful Yoruba—and even, more gen- erally, many West African women.

Lesley Sharp

. . . [A] woman whom I will call Ewumi [was] born twenty-seven years ago in the town of Ede, which may be regarded as fairly typical of Nigeria. It is in Yoruba country, 150 miles from the coast and thus not directly exposed to the commercial influences of the ports. It is not too deep in the bush either, but on the main railway line from Lagos to Kano; and it has a good asphalt road leading to it. It is of medium size, with about 70,000 inhabitants; much of my information on "Ewumi" comes from European friends who live there.

Ewumi, then, was born in 1933. Her father, a respectable citizen of Ede, was like most other citizens a farmer, his land being a day's walk away from the town. He would be away from home for days, planting the yams, hoeing the round

---

hillocks, weeding his land, tying up the beans, harvesting the maize, digging up the yams, and so on. With uncles, cousins and neighbours he marched out into the bush, where amidst much singing and also encouragement from the drummers they would lend each other a hand in tilling their fields. Sometimes, but not often, baby Ewumi was there too, on the back of her mother, who might be helping to hoe, should there ever be a shortage of hands. But Ewumi's mother had her own field between her family's estates, which was usually looked after by her brothers.

In her first years Ewumi seldom saw her father, and he played no part in her life. Only the mother was ever present: Ewumi was strapped to her back, and it was from there that by degrees the girl came to take in her own little world. This included her brother, three years old, and her sister, six years older, who was already helping mother and was sometimes allowed to carry her little sister on her own back. Then there were the grandmother and aunts and their children. Ever since she could think, Ewumi's family provided a solid framework within which she could feel secure; but she was never away from her mother.

Her mother slept near Ewumi. She took Ewumi to market on her back (with the purchases stacked on her head) and to the seasonal dances of town or clan. Ewumi would go to sleep there whenever she felt like it, whether her mother was going out to the fields, sitting at the market or dancing through the night at one of the religious festivals: practically before she could stand, Ewumi learnt the rhythms of the music for these. She sucked at her mother's breasts whenever she wanted, she never had to cry in hunger or lie alone in the dark. "Timetable-feeding is unheard of and self-regulation of the child is the absolute rule," writes Beier. Moreover the child can get as much erotic pleasure from its mother's breast as it likes, as it will be allowed to play with the breast at any time. Weaning too is done most gently and carefully. In some cases, where a child is extremely difficult, it may even be allowed to come to its mother's breast (very occasionally) after the new child is born.

When Ewumi was three, her mother gave birth again, and this time it was a boy. By now Ewumi had grasped something of life, she was weaned and no longer so completely dependent on her mother. But so that she should not feel neglected, she was now treated by her mother with extra tenderness, a cock was sacrificed for her, and she was bathed in the same water as her baby brother to develop feelings of kinship with him. Three years later, when Ewumi was six, her mother had another baby, and now it was the three-year-old brother who was bathed with the baby.

It is no matter of chance that the mother has a child every three years, and there would be great disapproval in her family if things were any different. For as soon as a woman finds herself pregnant, she may not have any more intercourse with her husband until the child is weaned. Most mothers leave their husbands for quite a long time and return to their own mothers, so as to devote themselves wholly to the children. "All this is only possible," Beier remarks, "in a society where men have many wives, because otherwise they would have to remain celibate for stretches of nearly three years."

The three-year rhythm of births has many advantages for the child. In a European family the father may often feel the accidentally-born child as an intruder robbing him of his wife's attention, and conversely the child may feel neglected because of his father, which sometimes leads to an Oedipus complex; whereas here the father does not figure in the small child's existence at all. Moreover the baby's feeding is ensured in a country where the protective bodies contained in the mother's milk are essential defences against a whole series of dangerous diseases; cow's milk would provide no adequate substitute, even if cattle-breeding were possible in these areas infested by the tsetse fly. But there is of course no cow's milk, except for European tinned milk or milk powder, which is both far too expensive and also very hard to obtain, especially in the quantities that would be necessary if the native population were to depart from the three-year rhythm of births. Finally this also stops an elder child feeling too jealous on the birth of the next baby. It is natural for a child of less than two to feel neglected when the new baby arrives; a three-year-old is already more sensible and beginning to discover a world of his own. "All these things may account for the balance and harmony we find in Yoruba children."

While her brother came under his father's care at seven, Ewumi, being a girl, stayed on with her mother, learning housework and having her own household duties, going to fetch water from the well in a calabash, which she had learnt to carry on her head, helping look after her small brother, now four, and minding him when her mother went to market; for her mother had grown older too and did not find it so easy now to have the four-year-old strapped to her hips, as well as the market goods on her head and the baby on her back. Yet Ewumi was by no means alone with her little brother, she was in the midst of her elder sisters and cousins, a whole troop of children going about their games and duties under the surveillance of relatives and neighbours.

She learnt to cook, and wash clothes, to grind pepper, and pound maize and dried yam slices in the mortar. On Sundays she went with her mother and sisters and brothers to the Baptist Mission church, and eagerly joined in the hymns she had learnt there. That did not stop her taking part in the town's old religious festivals, especially in the four-day festival of the new yams in July in honour of the *Orishas* (the gods) and the seven-day festival in honour of the god Shango at the end of the rainy season. Ewumi was an intelligent girl, and the Baptist minister thought she ought to go to the mission school; but since her parents couldn't afford to pay school fees for all the children, they decided to send only the two boys, who might thereby get an office job later on.

Ewumi grew up into a fine girl. At fifteen she was going to market on her own, her wares being matches, razor-blades and cigarettes; and this gave her a chance to talk to and flirt with young men while selling. When her mother had reached marriageable age, *her* parents had long chosen their daughter a mate, who had as little choice in the matter as the girl. Ewumi, however, could herself choose—of course within limits. She was shrewd enough to consider only the young men of whom her clan would approve; it would have been foolish for a young woman to throw away lightheartedly the support she needed from her family when married. Partly with her knowledge and partly without, contacts were made between families: a few young men were tipped off by their relatives to buy razor-blades or cigarettes from her, and between the three or four proposed candidates she could exercise a free choice.

The one she liked best was Dele from the Olabisi family, a merry fellow and a hard-working farmer, who besides the traditional crops grew cocoa on his land—the fashionable new crop from which you were supposed to get rich quick. When both were sure that their families approved the connection, Ewumi received expensive bridal gifts from her suitor, worth the equivalent of about £25. These belonged to her, they were the basic capital for her subsequent trading, and had nothing to do with the bride-price, which at Ede is fixed at £12. Dele found no difficulty in paying this price, for a marriage here is not so much a contract between two individuals as the symbol of two families being joined together. Every member of Dele's family contributed something to the sum needed, and Ewumi's father, who received the bride-price, had to distribute it among all the members of the family.

So the day came when amidst the customary ceremonies and festivities she entered her husband's household. The young couple lived in an annexe, a mud hut with a corrugated-iron roof and room for further expansion. At first she had much to order and arrange before she could settle down in the new clan. Being a true Yoruba woman, she could not let her husband keep her, and with the price of her bridal gifts she bought wares for sale; she set them out on a rough-hewn table outside the hut at a corner of the road, where there would be a lot of people passing. She offered sugar, tinned milk, tinned sardines, soap, matches, kerosene for lamps and refrigerators—all European articles which did not spoil.

When she became pregnant, the marriage had so far fulfilled its purpose, for marriage is not consummated by two people living together but by the begetting of children. Ewumi was proud of her fertility, and as she loved her husband, she brought him her friend Toro, who with Ewumi had for years excelled in the Baptist Church choir, as second wife—after thorough consultation with all the families concerned. Dele's hut got an extension, and Ewumi carried out her duties at the wedding of Dele and Toro, thereby showing herself a true *"iyali"*—mother of the house—as she could now call herself. Having welcomed her husband's guests in the prescribed way, and initiated Toro into her duties, she now returned with all her belongings into her parents' family.

She was now free to concentrate on her business. She got rid of the European wares, which were likely to bring only a small profit, and transferred her activity to the market. She was very good at making *ogi,* a maize-meal dish. Since both her own family and her husband's grew maize, she bought the raw material cheap direct from the producer. She had only to take the maize to the miller to be ground into meal, and then make *ogi* with it. So her profit came from the difference between the retail and wholesale price as well as from the work she put in. These profits were "ploughed back" into wares that would not spoil.

Her confinement was properly celebrated: Dele was proud of Ewumi and buried the after-birth, the ceremony required to make him the legal father, the "owner" of the child. It was a girl, and was given the name of Gbemi after a dead great-grandmother. Ewumi carried her baby daughter on her back, went to the market every day with fresh *ogi,* and increased her prosperity. The only snag was the miller's price for grinding, which was gradually going up.

Communication with her husband and Toro was confined to periodical friendly visits, going to church with them on Sundays, and taking part in the festivals of town and clan. Little Gbemi on her back grew bigger, and when she was beginning to wean her daughter, many a man at the market made her friendly offers—for she was beautiful, had shown she could bear healthy children and had enough milk for them. She was now nineteen.

But she only laughed at her suitors' advances; as soon as Gbemi was weaned, she returned to her husband's house. Toro had still not become pregnant, and Ewumi told her of all sorts of effective "medicines" (charms), recommended prayers and sacrifices to Shango, the *Orisha* embodying reproduction powers, and to *Egungun* (the ancestors). As "mother of the house" she organized communal living according to the prevailing custom: for five days she cooked the food for her husband and slept with him; then Toro cooked for him and slept with him for the next five days. Ewumi as *"iyale"* had to welcome guests when they came, but this is the only privilege she had. For a few months the two wives looked after their husband in turn, till Ewumi was sure she was pregnant again and returned once more to her family's farm.

At the market she had long had her fixed place among other women who also sold *ogi;* her two neighbours were old, and their *ogi* was not so good, but their clans saw to it that they also had their turnover. Their children were already grown up, so they no longer needed to earn such large amounts.

When Ewumi was delivered again, it was a boy, and they called him Adebayo. But great as was their joy, it was mixed with anxiety, for Adebayo was rather delicate, and also prone to fits. And when the worried parents brought him to the *Ifa* oracle, it transpired that he was an *abiku,* a spirit-child, who only comes on earth to leave it again soon. Ewumi would have to make all possible efforts to see the child stayed on the earth and did not go back again to his spirit companions. An *abiku* has wonderful dreams, he has visions of his spirit companions and plays wonderful imaginary games with them. And when his time comes, some time between the ages of four and ten, the spirits demand that the child returns to them. However attached he may be to his mother, if he is not strong enough, he must obey them. The mother will then pray that the child be restored to her, and there are women who maintain that they have given birth to the same child seven times. If the child is reborn, it can easily be recognized by a small mark which is scratched on a dead child's face or body; the scar will then appear on the new-born baby in the same place. Many grown-ups show such "identification marks"; in one confirmed case, Beier notes, "the parents expected a certain mark to appear, and described it before the baby was born. The mark appeared as expected, and I saw it myself."

Ewumi would treat Adebayo with the greatest care, would never let him out of her sight, would satisfy his every want, put up with all his moods. If he was called away even so, she could be sure he would be born to her again and again, until one day he would stay alive and with her. But if her care for him never let up for a moment, the *abiku* might even stay with her the first time, and she would be able to have more children than if she had to give birth to the same one several times.

"The *abiku* is often a problem child," says Beier. "Many of those I have known are very temperamental and make great demands on their parents. If a wish is not fulfilled at once, they will threaten to die. The terrified parents will then all too often put up no resistance to the child and suffer its tyranny in the hope that it may be persuaded to live. The *abiku* is nearly always the unusual one, the out-of-the-ordinary child, in many cases it is the exceptionally brilliant child. Therefore the *abiku* is given exceptional treatment. But this does not offend the other children, who are treated much more sternly. Because after all, they know that these are not ordinary children like themselves. Thus Yoruba society has solved the educational problem of how to give the exceptional child the freedom it requires to develop its personality, while at the same time supplying the more rigid discipline which the average child must have to feel secure."

So Ewumi had given birth to a spirit-child, a problem child; but soon other worries were added. The price the miller demanded for grinding the maize had gone up so much that the women who sold *ogi* found their earnings seriously reduced. Ewumi discussed the matter with the other women at the main market, and they all agreed not to accept the price any longer; so Ewumi appealed to the *iyalode,* the woman chief of the town, who looked after the women's interests in their dealings with the men and the king: every town in Yoruba country has such a woman chief.

Ewumi was one of the delegation which conducted negotiations with the millers for the *iyalode.* But millers are men: they were adamant and refused to lower the grinding price. The *iyalode* began to threaten, and after a few days the millers said they were ready to come to terms; yet the negotiations trailed on, and the *iyalode* had the impression that the millers were dragging them out till the *ogi*-sellers' stores were used up and one or other of them would be forced to have more maize ground and pay the price demanded. Then the *iyalode* called all the *ogi*-sellers out on strike. She sent her messengers—and on the same day all the *ogi*-sellers began to grind their maize by hand. After a week the millers yielded and accepted unconditionally the price fixed by the *iyalode* according to the women's wishes.

The *iyalode* and the *ogi*-sellers would scarcely have heard of such a thing as a trade union. Their strike was no imitation of European methods, no transference of modem European processes into Yoruba life; it was simply the way such conflicts were traditionally settled. As every clan has its chief and every professional group its spokesman, so the women too have their independence and their own organizations, which owe their impact above all to the traditional religious cults. In the Shango cult, which is the most important one at Ede, the high priest is a woman, the *Iya Shango* (Mother of Shango), and it gives her tremendous influence. There are two male secret societies, the *egungun* (ancestors) society, which makes the bond between the living and the dead, and the *oro* society, which has a secret executive power. But the *ogboni* society, which controls both these and is a check on the king's power—it consists of all important tribal chiefs and priests—contains women members as well as men. Unlike Christian social life, that of the Yorubas has never been patriarchal; so the women have long been able to secure special economic monopolies for themselves. Pottery, dyeing, spinning and the batik process are exclusively women's business; no man may practise these trades. At the market women have a monopoly in most of the goods for sale. Men may sell meat and leather goods there, but almost everything else is in the hands of the women: yams and cassava, tomatoes and other vegetables, cola nuts, palm oil, cooked dishes, mats, baskets, skins, necklaces, jewelry, native "medicines," and materials.

Ewumi was now earning well again at the market. Her attention to customers was often distracted, of course, by Adebayo, her spirit-child, but the customers were patient and understanding, for they knew the duties of a mother to an *abiku*. Dele often came to visit her either in the market or in her house, not only to see how Adebayo was going on. He was worried about Toro, who had still not conceived, was unhappy over it and moody, now imploring Ewumi and Dele for new counsels and "medicines," now accusing people of making her barren by witchcraft. Ewumi advised Dele to take a third wife, particularly as she herself had given birth to an *abiku,* did not know if he would stay in this world and how often she might have to bring him into it again. Dele had for some time been toying with the idea, and had already picked out a woman called Efuncye, a blacksmith's second wife, who had already born her husband two healthy children and who sold cola nuts a few market alleys away. Dele had now and then bought cola nuts from her for years, but in the last weeks his need for them seemed to have increased enormously, and Efuneye had shown that she did not object to his wooing—Dele being ten years younger than her husband. So a meeting was arranged between Efuneye and Ewumi, the two women liked each other, and the rest was only a financial matter.

Since Efuneye had lived with her husband for over five years, she had to return only half the bride-price on divorce, and could keep the bridal gifts. Dele readily gave her further bridal gifts, and his family readily found the bride-price. The blacksmith was not exactly pleased, but had to admit that he sometimes beat Efuneye, so that grounds had been given for the divorce. After the usual formalities Efuneye entered Dele's household with her two children, a six-year-old boy and a three-year-old girl.

The coming of a new wife already blessed with children made Toro even more painfully aware of her failure. Her depressions alternated with fits of temper, and Dele's aunts and grandmother had to intervene to see that order was kept in his house. Efuneye, however, was very popular with all, which incensed Toro all the more. Ewumi watched the situation with distress; Efuneye often came and asked her to come home soon, as with two of them Toro's tempers would be more easily controlled. Dele would have been glad to get rid of Toro, he beat her to give her grounds for divorce, dropped hints to friends about her beauty—she was certainly the most beautiful and also the youngest of his wives—yet no suitor would turn up. Dele had even got his family's permission to do without the return of the bride-price if need be, but Toro wanted to stay, so he just had to put up with her.

The nearer the time came when Ewumi had to wean her problem child, the more worried she became. She went on feeding him longer than usual, which in itself was good for an *abiku,* but because of this child she was afraid of going back into her husband's house. With a directness that was almost unseemly she pointed out to the men who flirted with her at the market that there was a fine shapely girl to be had in Dele's house; but they only laughed, they knew the situation and paid all the more compliments to Ewumi herself. She entreated Dele either to bring Toro somehow to her senses or else get rid of her. But neither the sacrifices to Shango and other *Orishas* nor prayers in the churches seemed to help. Even Toro's mother couldn't cope with her.

Ewumi began to listen more attentively to the friendly things said to her, and in particular she could not help thinking about the advances of a rich elderly merchant. He already had eight wives and a lot of children, all of whom lived together in harmony and comfort; and he offered most attractive bridal gifts.

When Dele learnt that the merchant's hopes were well founded, Ewumi and he had a long discussion. Dele would like to have kept her, but for the sake of her little *abiku* she refused to return into a house of strife. The air the child breathed there was poison, she said: a spirit-child had to have happiness round him and peace; if he saw Toro in one of her rages, he would die. Dele admitted she was right. He loved Ewumi, and she loved him, yet the child's welfare was decisive as ever. "The child is the cornerstone of African society."

She gave him and his family half the bride-money back, neglect on the part of the husband was given as grounds for the divorce, and both wept on parting. The merchant was received formally but very politely by Ewumi's family; his gifts to the bride were in keeping with his wealth, but Ewumi did not seem particularly impressed and kept them with her own savings.

The *iyale* of her new home was an elderly, wise and kindly woman, who took great care over household arrangements and saw to it that the rota of wifely duties did not get out of hand. Some of the wives were already quite old, and only two were suckling children. Ewumi had to prepare her husband's food only five days every month. In such a well-off household there was no lack of assistance or space; she found the peace she had longed for in order to devote herself entirely to her little *abiku.* After she had carried out her wifely duties three times—she had to be passed over at her first turn because of menstruation—it transpired that she was again pregnant. But as she had learnt to appreciate the household's cheerful and harmonious atmosphere, she did not go back to her own family. Adebayo was thriving, and it really seemed as if he meant to stay with her; while Gbemi, now five, romped about with the other children as if they were her brothers and sisters.

With Dele, meanwhile, things were much less peaceful. When Efuneye became pregnant, Toro almost went out of her mind, and the two women came to blows. The relatives had to intervene, and Toro was sternly rebuked, but she only worked everybody up the more with her poisonous talk, and when Dele came home from his fields two days later, he beat her harder than ever. She cried the whole night, but next morning immediately started a new row. Dele's clan conferred, after which a delegation was sent off to Toro's clan, earnestly requesting them to take the misguided creature back. But she would not even listen to the remonstrances of her own relatives, and abused the clan elder so violently that they formally renounced her: the elder said that never in human memory had such a thing occurred in his clan. So Dele had to take her back home again. Divorce is easy for a woman, almost impossible for a man. For morals in Yoruba society, and the rules derived therefrom, are based on a simple but good principle: any arrangement which tends to ensure the production of many children and which guarantees that no women will be left to die as spinsters, is moral in this society. Since nobody now wanted to have Toro, Dele was obliged to go to the last resort.

Having donned his ceremonial robes and taken some money, he seized Toro's hand, pulled her crying out of the house, and went with her into the palace of the king, the Timi of Ede. There he threw himself down before the king, gave him the money, and pointing to Toro said: "Timi, I present her to you." Then he told the king how things had come to this pass. The king could not refuse the present, but had to take her.

A "town king" among the Yorubas has some privileges, of course, in the choice of wives: for instance, if a woman kneels on his carpet by mistake, he may claim her as his wife. But he has more duties than rights, he must marry the crippled and sick girls, all those who normally would have no chance of finding a husband, and must take the women nobody wants.

When she heard what Dele had done, Ewumi did not stay much longer in the merchant's house. She discussed things with Dele and her family, gave the merchant the full bride-money back and all the rich personal gifts, for she had been with him less than a year. In order to marry her again, Dele had to make good half the bride-money which she returned. It was his right to hold it back three months, to make sure of her faithfulness and constancy; but he paid it at once, being sure of his Ewumi.

The celebrations for her re-entry into his house coincided with a farewell party; for Efuneye's eldest son was now seven and returned to his real father, the blacksmith, according to custom. Since both wives, Ewumi and Efuneye, were now pregnant again, they together looked for a third wife for Dele; their choice fell on Ewumi's youngest sister, with whom Ewumi had always got on extremely well.

Since then another three years have passed, Ewumi and Efuneye have had their babies, and their entire offspring, including the "problem child," Adebayo, have stayed alive. Ewumi's sister has also had a baby, but it died soon after it was born—infant mortality is still high. Ewumi and Efuneye have remained close friends, they mind the children alternately and also swap stalls at the market. Efuneye too now sells *ogi,* but Ewumi has spent her savings on hardware: lamps, bicycle-chains, clothes-hangers, alarm-clocks, aluminum pots and buckets. Her youngest brother, a lanky lad of seventeen, still single, who lives with a great-uncle, looks after her stall in the covered market at Onitsha. He is a reliable boy and hands over his profits every month, which she puts back into goods. If her businesses go on flourishing like this, she will soon have her own lorry (as her aunt has), will engage a good driver, and earn still more with haulage deals, which bring in good money. Adebayo will then one day be able to study in Europe.

"Sitting on a Man":
Colonialism and the
Lost Political Institutions of
Igbo Women[1]

———◆———

Judith Van Allen

"Sifting on a Man" has become a classic in both African and gender studies since it shatters the false assumption that colonized people remain passive in the face of injustice. As this essay reveals, Igbo culture was characterized by several institutions which enabled women to exert effective collective social and political pressure, forcing men to reform their behavior. When faced with the threat of unfair policies imposed by the British, Igbo women responded creatively, drawing on tactics used previously only in village settings. As Van Allen shows, it is not the social structural weakness of women in Igbo culture that insured their protests went unheeded; rather, failure was rooted in the ethnocentric attitudes of their colonizers.

Lesley Sharp

In the conventional wisdom, Western influence has "emancipated" African women—through the weakening of kinship bonds and the provision of "free choice" in Christian monogamous marriage, the suppression of "barbarous" practices, the opening of schools, the introduction of modern medicine and hygiene, and, sometimes, of female suffrage.

From *Canadian Journal of African Studies*, 6, pp. 165–182. Copyright © 1972 by the *Canadian Journal of African Studies*. Reprinted by permission.

1 An earlier version of this paper was presented at the Annual Meeting of the African Studies Association, Denver, Colorado, November, 1971.

But Westernization is not an unmixed blessing. The experience of Igbo women under British colonialism shows that Western influence can sometimes weaken or destroy women's traditional autonomy and power without providing modern forms of autonomy of power in exchange. Igbo women had a significant role in traditional political life. As individuals, they participated in village meetings with men. But their real political power was based on the solidarity of women, as expressed in their own political institutions—their "meetings" (*mikiri* or *mitiri*), their market networks, their kinship groups, and their right to use strikes, boycotts and force to effect their decisions.

British colonial officers and missionaries, both men and women, generally failed to see the political roles and the political power of Igbo women. The actions of administrators weakened and in some cases destroyed women's bases of strength. Since they did not appreciate women's political institutions, they made no efforts to ensure women's participation in the modern institutions they were trying to foster.

Igbo women haven't taken leadership roles in modern local government, nationalist movements and national government and what roles they *have* played have not been investigated by scholars. The purpose in describing their *traditional* political institutions and source of power is to raise the question of *why* these women have been "invisible" historically, even though they forced the colonial authorities to pay attention to them briefly. We suggest that the dominant view among British Colonial officers and missionaries was that politics was a man's concern. Socialized in Victorian England, they had internalized a set of values and attitudes about what they considered to be the natural and proper role of women that supported this belief. We suggest further that this assumption about men and politics has had a great deal to do with the fact that no one has even asked, "Whatever happened to Igbo women's organizations?" even though all the evidence needed to justify this question has been available for 30 years.

Igbo Tradtional Political Institutions[2]

Political power in Igbo society was *diffuse*. There were no specialized bodies or offices in which legitimate power was vested and no person, regardless of his

---

2　The Igbo-speaking peoples are heterogeneous and can only be termed a "tribe" on the basis of a common language and a contiguous territory. They were the dominant group in southeastern Nigeria, during the colonial period numbering more than three million according to the 1931 census. The Igbo in Owerri and Calabar Provinces, the two southernmost provinces, were relatively homogeneous politically and it is their political institutions which are discussed here. Studies in depth were done of the Igbo only in the 1930s, but traditional political institutions survived "underneath" the native administration, although weakened more in some areas than in others. There were also many informants who

status or ritual position, had the authority to issue *commands* which others had an obligation to obey. In line with this diffusion of authority, the right to enforce decisions was also diffuse: there was no "state" that held a monopoly of legitimate force, and the use of force to protect one's interests or to see that a group decision was carried out was considered legitimate for individuals and groups. In the simplest terms, the British tried to create specialized political institutions which commanded authority and monopolized force. In doing so they took into account, eventually, Igbo political institutions dominated by men but ignored those of the women. Thus, women were shut out from political power.

The Igbo lived traditionally in semi-autonomous villages, which consisted of the scattered compounds of 75 or so patri-kinsmen; related villages formed "village-groups" which came together for limited ritual and jural purposes. Villages commonly contained several hundred people; but size varied, and in the more densely populated areas there were "village-groups" with more than 5,000 members.[3] Disputes at all the levels above the compound were settled by group discussion until mutual agreement was reached.[4]

The main Igbo political institution seems to have been the village assembly, a gathering of all adults in the village who chose to attend. Any adult who had something to say on the matter under discussion was entitled to speak—as long as he *or she* had something the others considered worth listening to; as the Igbo say, "a case forbids no one."[5]

Matters dealt with in the village assembly were those of concern to all— either common problems for which collective action was appropriate ("How can

---

remembered life in the pre-colonial days. The picture of Igbo society drawn here is based on reports by two Englishwomen, Leith-Ross and Green, who had a particular interest in Igbo women; the work of a government anthropological officer, Meek; a brief report by Harris; and the work of educated Igbo describing their own society, Uchendu and Onwuteaka. See M. M. Green, *Igbo Village Affairs* (London: Frank Cass & Co., Ltd., 1947: page citations to paperback edition, New York: Frederick A. Praeger, 1964); J. S. Harris, "The Position of Women in Nigerian Society," *Transactions of the New York Academy of Sciences,* Series II, Vol. 2, No. 5, 1940; Sylvia Leith-Ross, *African Women* (London: Faber and Faber, 1939); C. K. Meek, *Law and Authority in a Nigerian Tribe* (Oxford University Press, 1957, orig. published 1937); J. C. Onwuteaka, "The Aba Riot of 1929 and its Relation to the System of Indirect Rule," *The Nigerian Journal of Economical and Social Studies,* November 1965; Victor C. Uchendu, *The Igbo of Southeast Nigeria,* (New York: Holt, Rinehard and Winston, 1965).

3 Daryll Forde and G. I. Jones, *The Ibo- and Ibibio-Speaking Peoples of South-Eastern Nigeria* (London: International African Institute, 1950), p. 39; J. S. Harris, *op. cit.,* p. 141.

4 Victor C. Uchendu, *op. cit.,* pp. 41–44.

5 *Ibid.,* p. 41; M. M. Green, *op. cit.,* pp. 78–79.

we make our markets 'bigger' than the other villages' markets?") or conflicts which threatened the unity of the village.[6]

Decisions agreed upon by the village assembly did not have the force of law in our terms, however. Even after decisions had been reached, social pressure based on consensus and the ability of individuals and groups to enforce decisions in their favour played a major part in giving the force of law to decisions. As Green[7] put it:

> (O)ne had the impression . . . that laws only establish themselves by degrees and then only in so far as they gain general acceptance. A law does not either exist or not exist: rather it goes through a process of establishing itself by common consent or of being shelved by a series of quiet evasions.

Persuasion about the rightness of a particular course of action in terms of tradition was of primary importance in assuring its acceptance and the leaders were people who had the ability to persuade.

The mode of political discourse was that of proverb, parable and metaphor drawn from the body of Igbo tradition.[8] The needed political knowledge was accessible to the average man or woman, since all Igbo were reared with these proverbs and parables. Influential speech was the creative and skillful use of tradition to assure others that a certain course of action was both a wise and right thing to do. The accessibility of this knowledge is indicated by an Igbo proverb: "If you tell a proverb to a fool, he will ask you its meaning."

The leaders of Igbo society were men and women who combined wealth and generosity with "mouth"—the ability to speak well. Age combined with wisdom brought respect but age alone carried little influence. The senior elders who were ritual heads of their lineages were very likely to have considerable influence, but they would not have achieved these positions in the first place if they had not been considered to have good sense and good character.[9] Wealth in itself was no guarantee of influence: a "big man" or "big woman" was not necessarily a wealthy person, but one who had shown skill and generosity in helping other individuals and, especially, the community.[10]

Men owned the most profitable crops such as palm oil, received the bulk of the money from bride wealth, and, if compound heads, presents from the members. Through the patrilineage, they controlled the land, which they could lease

---

6   J. S. Harris, *op. cit.*, pp. 142–43; Victor C. Uchendu, *op. cit.*, pp. 34, 42–43.

7   M. M. Green, *op. cit.*, p. 137.

8   The sources for this description are Uchendu and personal conversations with an Igbo born in Umu-Domi village of Onicha clan in Afikpo division who, however, went to mission schools from the age of seven and speaks Union Igbo rather than his village dialect.

9   Victor C. Uchendu, *op. cit.*, p. 41.

10 *Ibid.*, p. 34; C. K. Meek, *op. cit.*, p. 111.

to non-kinsmen or to women for a good profit. Men also did most of the long-distance trading which gave higher profit than local and regional trading which was almost entirely in women's hands.[11]

Women were entitled to sell the surplus of their own crops and the palm kernels which were their share of the palm produce. They might also sell prepared foods or the products of special skills, for instance, processed salt, pots and baskets. They pocketed the entire profit, but their relatively lower profit levels kept them disadvantaged relative to the men in acquiring titles and prestige.[12]

For women as well as for men, status was largely achieved, not ascribed. A woman's status was determined more *by her own achievements* than by the achievements of her husband. The resources available to men were greater, however; so that while a woman might rank higher among women than her husband did among men, very few women could acquire the highest titles, a major source of prestige.[13]

At village assemblies men were more likely to speak than were women; women more often spoke only on matters of direct concern to them.[14] Title-holders took leading parts in discussion, and were more likely to take part in "consultation." After a case had been thoroughly discussed, a few men retired in order to come to a decision. A spokesman then announced the decision, which could be accepted or rejected by the assembly.[15]

Apparently no rule forbade women to participate in consultations but they were invited to do so only rarely. The invited women were the older women, for while younger men might have the wealth to acquire the higher titles and thus make up in talent what they lacked in age, younger women could not acquire the needed wealth quickly enough to be eligible.[16]

Women, therefore, came second to men in power and influence. While status and the political influence it could bring were achieved and there were no formal limits to women's political power, men through their ascriptive status (members of the patrilineage) acquired wealth which gave them a head start and a life long advantage over women. The Igbo say that "a child who washes his hands clean deserves to eat with his elders."[17] But at birth some children were given water and some were not.

---

11 M. M. Green, *op. cit.*, pp. 32–42.

12 Sylvia Leith-Ross, *op. cit.*, pp. 90–92, 138–39, 143.

13 C. C. Meek, *op. cit.*, p. 203; Victor C. Udiendu, *op. cit.*, p. 86.

14 M. M. Green, *op. cit.*, p. 169.

15 Victor C. Uchendu, *op. cit.*, p. 41.

16 C. K. Meek, *op. cit.*, p. 203.

17 Victor Uchendu, *op. cit.*, p. 19.

Since political authority was diffuse, the settling of disputes, discussions about how to improve the village or its market, or any other problems of general concern were brought up at various gatherings such as funerals, meetings of kinsmen to discuss burial rituals, and the marketplace, gatherings whose ostensible purpose was not political discussion.[18]

The women's base of political power lay in their own gatherings. Since Igbo society was patrilocal and villages were exogamous, adult women resident in a village would almost all be wives, and others were divorced or widowed "daughters of the village" who had returned home to live. Women generally attended age-set gatherings (*ogbo*) in their natal villages, performed various ritual functions, and helped to settle disputes among their "brothers."[19] But the gatherings which performed the major role in self-rule among women and which articulated women's interests *as opposed to* those of men were the village-wide gatherings of all adult women resident in a village which under colonialism came to be called *mikiri* or *mitiri* (from "meeting").[20]

Mikiri were held whenever there was a need.[21] In *mikiri* the same processes of discussion and consultation were used as in the village assembly. There were no official leaders; as in the village women of wealth and generosity who could speak well took leading roles. Decisions appear often to have been announced informally by wives telling their husbands. If the need arose, spokeswomen—to contact the men, or women in other villages—were chosen through general discussion. If the announcement of decisions and persuasion were not sufficient for their implementation, women could take direct action to enforce their decisions and protect their interests.[22]

Mikiri provided women with a forum in which to develop their political talents among a more egalitarian group than the village assembly. In *mikiri,* women could discuss their particular interests as traders, farmers, wives and mothers. These interests often were opposed to those of the men, and where individually women couldn't compete with men, collectively they could often hold their own.

One of the *mikiri's* most important functions was that of a market association, to promote and regulate the major activity of women: trading. At these discussions prices were set, rules established about market attendance, and fines fixed for those who violated the rules or who didn't contribute to market rituals. Rules were also made which applied to men. For instance, rowdy behavior on the part of young men was forbidden. Husbands and elders were asked to control the young men. If their requests were ignored, the women would handle the matter

---

18 C. K. Meek, *op. cit.,* p. 125; M. M. Green, *op. cit.,* pp. 132–38.
19 M. M. Green. *op. cit.,* pp. 217–32.
20 Sylvia Leith-Ross, *op. cit.,* pp. 106–08.
21 M. M. Green, *op. cit.,* pp. 178–216.
22 *Ibid.,* p. 180; Sylvia Leith-Ross, *op. cit.,* pp. 106–107.

by launching a boycott or a strike to force the men to police themselves or they might decide to "sit on" the individual offender.[23]

"Sitting on a man" or a woman, boycotts and strikes were the women's main weapons. To "sit on" or "make war on" a man involved gathering at his compound, sometimes late at night, dancing, singing scurrilous songs which detailed the women's grievances against him and often called his manhood into question, banging on his hut with the pestles women used for pounding yams, and perhaps demolishing his hut or plastering it with mud and roughing him up a bit. A man might be sanctioned in this way for mistreating his wife, for violating the women's market rules, or for letting his cows eat the women's crops. The women would stay at his hut throughout the day, and late into the night, if necessary, until he repented and promised to mend his ways.[24] Although this could hardly have been a pleasant experience for the offending man, it was considered legitimate and no man would consider intervening.

In tackling men as a group, women used boycotts and strikes. Harris describes a case in which, after repeated requests by the women for the paths to the market to be cleared (a male responsibility), all the women refused to cook for their husbands until the request was carried out.[25] For this boycott to be effective, all women had to cooperate so that men could not go and eat with their brothers. Another time the men of a village decided that the women should stop trading at the more distant markets from which they did not return until late at night because the men feared that the women were having sexual relations with men in those towns. The women, however, refused to comply since opportunity to buy in one market and sell in another was basic to profit-making. Threats of collective retaliation were enough to make the men capitulate.

As farmers, women's interests conflicted with those of the men as owners of much of the larger livestock—cows, pigs, goats and sheep. The men's crop, yams, had a short season and was then dug up and stored, after which the men tended to be careless about keeping their livestock out of the women's crops. Green reports a case in which the women of the village swore an oath that if any woman killed a cow or other domestic animal on her farm the others would stand by her.[26]

A woman could also bring complaints about her husband to the *mikiri*. If most of the women agreed that the husband was at fault, they would collectively support her. They might send spokeswomen to tell the husband to apologize and to give her a present, and, if he was recalcitrant they might "sit on" him. They might also act to protect a right of wives. Harris describes a case of women's solidarity to maintain sexual freedom:

---

23 J. S. Harris, *op. cit.*, pp. 146–47.
24 *Ibid.*, pp. 146–48; M. M. Green, *op. cit.*, pp. 196–97; Sylvia Leith Ross, *op. cit.*, p. 109.
25 J. S. Harris, *op. cit.*, pp. 146–147.
26 M. M. Green, *op. cit.*, pp. 210–11.

The men . . . were very angry because their wives were openly having relations with their lovers. The men . . . met and passed a law to the effect that every woman . . . should renounce her lover and present a goat to her husband as a token of repentance. . . . The women held. . . . secret meetings and a few mornings later they went to a neighboring [village], leaving all but suckling children behind them. . . . The men endured it for a day and a half and then they went to the women and begged their return . . . [T]he men gave [the women] one goat and apologized informally and formally.[27]

Thus through *mikiri* women acted to force a resolution of their individual and collective grievances.

Colonial Penetration

Into this system of diffuse authority, fluid and informal leadership, shared rights of enforcement, and a more or less stable balance of male and female power, the British tried to introduce ideas of native administration derived from colonial experience with chiefs and emirs in northern Nigeria. Southern Nigeria was declared a protectorate in 1900 but it was ten years before the conquest was effective. As colonial power was established in what the British perceived as a situation of "ordered anarchy," Igboland was divided into Native Court Areas which violated the autonomy of villages by lumping many unrelated villages into each court area. British District Officers were to preside over the courts but were not always present as there were more courts than officers. The Igbo membership was formed by choosing from each village a "representative" who was given a warrant of office. These Warrant Chiefs also constituted the Native Authority. They were required to see that the orders of the District Officers were executed in their own villages and were the only link between the colonial power and the people.[28]

It was a violation of Igbo concepts to have one man represent the village in the first place and more of a violation that he should give orders to everyone else. The people obeyed the Warrant Chief when they had to, since British power backed him up. In some places Warrant Chiefs were lineage heads or wealthy men who were already leaders in the village. But in many places they were simply ambitious, opportunistic young men who put themselves forward as friends of

---

27 J. S. Harris, *op. cit.*, pp. 146–47.

28 Daryll Forde, "Justice and Judgment among the Southern Ibo under Colonial Rule" unpublished paper prepared for Interdisciplinary Colloquium in African Studies, University of Califorifia, Los Angeles, pp. 9–13.

the conquerors. Even the relatively less corrupt Warrant Chief was still more than anything else an agent of the British.[29]

The people avoided using Native Courts when they could do so. But Warrant Chiefs could force cases into the Native Courts and could fine people for infractions of rules. By having the ear of the British, the Warrant Chief could himself violate traditions and even British rules and get away with it since his version would be believed.[30]

Women suffered particularly under the arbitrary rule of Warrant Chiefs, who were reported as having taken women to marry without conforming to the customary process which included the woman's right to refuse a particular suitor. They also helped themselves to the women's agricultural produce and to their domestic animals.[31]

Recommendations for reform of the system were made almost from its inception both by junior officers in the field and by senior officers sent out from headquarters to investigate. But no real improvements were made.[32]

Aba and the Women's War

The Native Administration in the years before 1929 took little account of either men's or women's political institutions. In 1929, women in southern Igboland became convinced that they were to be taxed by the British. This fear on top of their resentment of the Warrant Chiefs led to what the British called the Aba Riots and the Igbo Women's War. The rebellion provides perhaps the most striking example of British blindness to the political institutions of Igbo women. The women, "invisible" to the British as they laid their plans, for Native Administration, suddenly became highly visible for a few months, but as soon as they quieted down, they were once again ignored and the reforms made in Native Administration took no account of them politically.[33]

---

29 *Ibid.*, pp. 9–13; J. C. Anene, *Southern Nigeria in Transition, 1885–1906* (New York: The Cambridge, University Press, 1967), p. 259; C. K. Meek, *op. cit.*, pp. 328–30.

30 Daryll Forde, *op. cit.*, p. 12.

31 J. C. Onwuteaka, *op. cit.*, p. 274.

32 C. K. Meek, *op. cit.*, pp. 329–30; Harry A. Gailey, *The Road to Aba* (New York: New York University Press, 1970), pp. 66–74.

33 Information on the Women's War is derived mainly from Gailey and Perham, who based their descriptions on the reports of the two Commissions of Enquiry, issued as Sessional Papers of the Nigerian Legislative Council, Nos. 12 and 28 of 1930, and the Minutes of Evidence issued with the latter. Gailey also used the early 1930's Intelligence Reports of political officers. Meek and Afigbo also provided quotations from the reports, which were not, unfortunately, available to me in full. See Margery Perman, *Native Administration in Nigeria* (London: Oxford University Press, 1937); Idem, *Lugard: The Years of Adventure, 1858–1898* (London: Collins, 1960); A. E. Afigbo, "Igbo Village Affairs," *Journal of the Historical Society Nigeria*, 4: December 1967.

In 1925 Igbo men paid taxes, although during the census count on which the tax was based the British had denied that there was to be any taxation. Taxes were collected without too much trouble. By 1929, the prices for palm products had fallen, however, and the taxes, set at 1925 levels, were an increasingly resented burden.[34] In the midst of this resentment, an overzealous Assistant District Officer in Owerri Province decided to update the census registers by recounting households and household property, which belonged to women. Understandably, the women did not believe his assurances that new taxes were not to be invoked. They sent messages through the market and kinship networks to other villages and called a *mikiri* to decide what to do.

In the Oloko Native Court area of Owerri Province, the women decided that as long as only men were approached in a compound and asked for information, the women would do nothing. They wanted clear evidence that they were to be taxed before they acted.[35] If any woman was approached, she was to raise the alarm and they would meet to discuss retaliation.

On November 23, the agent of the Oloko Warrant Chief, Okugo, entered a compound and told a married woman, Nwanyeruwa, to count her goats and sheep. She retorted angrily "Was your mother counted?" Thereupon "they closed, seizing each other by the throat."[36] Nwanyeruwa's report to the Oloko women convinced them that they were to be taxed. Messengers were sent to neighboring areas. Women streamed into Oloko from all over Owerri Province. They massed in protest at the district office and after several days of protest meetings succeeded in obtaining written assurances that they were not to be taxed, and in getting Okugo arrested. Subsequently he was tried and convicted of physically assaulting women and of spreading news likely to cause alarm. He was sentenced to two years' imprisonment.[37]

News of this victory spread rapidly through the market *mikiri* network, and women in 16 Native Court areas attempted to get rid of their Warrant Chiefs as well as the Native Administration itself. Tens of thousands of women became involved, generally using the same traditional tactics, though not with the same results as in Oloko. In each Native Court area, the women marched on Native Administration centers and demanded the Warrant Chiefs' caps of office and assurances that they would not be taxed. In some areas the District Officers assured the women to their satisfaction that they were not to be taxed and the women dispersed without further incident. But the British in general stood behind the Warrant Chiefs; at that point they interpreted the women's rebellion as motivated solely by fear of taxation, and Oloko was the only area in which a Warrant Chief had directly provoked the women's fears of taxation by counting their property.

---

34   Harry A. Gailey, *op. cit.*, pp. 94–95; C. K. Meek, *op. cit.*, pp. 330–31.
35   Harry A. Gailey, *op. cit.*, pp. 107–08.
36   Margery Perham, *Native Administration in Nigeria, op. cit.*, p. 207.
37   Harry A. Gailey, *op. cit.*, pp. 108–13.

Women in most areas did not get full satisfaction from the British, and, further, some British district officers simply panicked when faced by masses of angry women and acted in ways which made negotiation impossible.

In most of the Native Court areas affected, women took matters into their own hands—they "sat on" Warrant Chiefs and burned Native Court buildings, and, in some cases, released prisoners from jail. Among the buildings burned were those at Aba, a major administrative center from which the British name for the rebellion is derived. Large numbers of police and soldiers, and on one occasion Boy Scouts, were called in to quell the "disturbances." On two occasions, clashes between the women and the troops left more than 50 women dead and 50 wounded from gunfire. The lives taken were those of women only—no men, Igbo or British, were even seriously injured. The cost of property damage—estimated at more than £60,000, was paid for by the Igbo, who were heavily taxed to pay for rebuilding the Native Administration centers.[38]

The rebellion lasted about a month. By late December, "order" was somewhat restored but sporadic disturbances and occupation by government troops continued into 1930. In all, the rebellion extended over an area of six thousand square miles, all of Owerri and Calabar Provinces, containing about two million people.[39]

The British generally saw the rebellion as "irrational" and called it a series of "riots." They discovered that the market network had been used to spread the rumors of taxation, but they did not inquire further into the concerted action of the women, the grassroots leadership, the agreement on demands, or even into the fact that thousands of women showed up at native administration centers dressed in the same unusual way: wearing short loincloths, their faces smeared with charcoal or ashes, their heads bound with young ferns, and in their hands carrying sticks wreathed with young palms.[40]

In exonerating the soldiers who fired on the women, a Commission of Enquiry spoke of the "savage passions" of the "mobs," and one military officer told the Commission that "he had never seen crowds in such a state of frenzy." Yet these "frenzied mobs" injured no one seriously, which the British found "surprising."[41]

It is not surprising if the Women's War is seen as the traditional practice of "sitting on a man," only on a larger scale. Decisions were made in *mikiri* to respond to a situation in which women were acutely wronged by the Warrant Chiefs' corruption and by the taxes they believed to be forthcoming. Spokes-

38 S. O. Eskie, "The Aba Riots of 1929," *African Historian,* Vol. 1. No. 3 (1965): 13; J. S. Harris, *op. cit.,* p. 143; Margery Perham, *Native Administration in Nigeria, op. cit.,* pp. 209–12.

39 Harry A. Gailey, *op. cit.,* p. 137; Margery Perham, *Native Administration in Nigeria, op. cit.,* pp. 209–12.

40 J. S. Harris, *op. cit.,* pp. 147–48; Margery Perham, *Native Administration in Nigeria, op. cit.,* pp. 107ff.; C. K. Meek, *op. cit.,* p. IX.

41 Margery Perham, *Native Administration in Nigeria, op. cit.,* pp. 212–19.

and women followed their leadership, on several occasions sitting down to wait for negotiations or agreeing to disperse or to turn in Warrant Chiefs' caps.[42] Traditional dress rituals and "weapons" for "sitting on" were used: the head wreathed with young ferns symbolized war, and sticks, bound with ferns or young palms, were used to involve the powers of the female ancestors.[43] The women's behavior also followed traditional patterns: much noise, stamping, preposterous threats and a general raucous atmosphere were all part of the institution of "sitting on a man." Destroying an offender's hut—in this case the Native Court buildings—was clearly within the bounds of this sanctioning process.

The Women's War was coordinated throughout the two provinces by information sent through the market *mikiri* network. Delegates travelled from one area to another and the costs were paid by donations from the women's market profits.[44] Traditional rules were followed in that the participants were women— only a few men were involved in the demonstrations—and leadership was clearly in the hands of women.

The absence of men from the riots does not indicate lack of support. Men generally approved, and only a few older men criticized the women for not being more respectful toward the government. It is reported that both men and women shared the mistaken belief that the women, having observed certain rituals, would not be fired upon. The men had no illusions of immunity for themselves, having vivid memories of the slaughter of Igbo men during the conquest.[45] Finally the name given the rebellion by the Igbo—the Women's War—indicates that the women saw themselves following their traditional sanctioning methods of "sitting on" or "making war on" a man.

Since the British failed to recognized the Women's War as a collective response to the abrogation of rights, they did not inquire into the kinds of structures the women had that prepared them for such action. They failed to ask, "How do the women make group decisions? How do they choose their leaders?" Since they saw only a "riot," they explained the fact that the women injured no one seriously as "luck," never even contemplating that perhaps the women's actions had traditional limits.

Because the women—and the men—regarded the inquiries as attempts to discover whom to punish, they did not volunteer any information about the women's organizations. But there is at least some question as to whether the British would have understood them if they had. The market network was discovered, but sug-

---

42 *Ibid.*, pp. 212ff.

43 Harris reports a curse sworn by the women on the pestles: "It is I who gave birth to you. It is I who cook for you to eat. This is the pestle I use to pound yams and coco yams for you to eat. May you soon die!" See J. S. Harris, op. cit., pp. 143–45.

44 Harry A. Gailey, *op. cit.,* p. 112.

45 Margery Perham, *Native Administration in Nigeria, op. cit.,* 212ff; J. C. Anene, *op. cit.,* pp. 207–24; S. O. Esike, *op. cit., p.* 11; C. K. Meek, *op. cit.,* p. x.

gested no further lines of inquiry to the British. The majority of District Officers thought that the men organized the women's actions and were secretly directing them. The Bende District Officer and the Secretary of the Southern Province believed that there was a secret "Ogbo Society" which exercised control over women and was responsible for fomenting the rebellion.[46] *The women's demands that they did not want the Native Court to hear cases any longer and that all white men should go to their own country, or, at least, that women should serve on the Native Courts and one be appointed District Officer—demands in line with the power of women in traditional society—were ignored.[47]*

All these responses fell into a pattern: *not* of purposeful discrimination against women with the intent of keeping them from playing their traditional political roles, but of a prevailing blindness to the possibility that women had *had* a significant role in traditional politics and should participate in the new system of local government. A few political officers were "of the opinion that, if the balance of society is to be kept, the women's organizations should be encouraged alongside those of the men."[48] Some commissioners even recognized "the remarkable character of organization and leadership which some of the women displayed" and recommended that more attention be paid to the political influence of women.[49] But these men were the exception: their views did not prevail. Even in the late 1930's when the investigations of Leith-Ross and Green revealed the decreasing vitality of women's organizations under colonialism, the British still did not include women in the reformed Native Administration. When political officers warned that *young men* were being excluded, however, steps were taken to return their traditional political status.[50]

"Reforms" and Women's Loss of Power

In 1933 reforms were enacted to redress many Igbo grievances against the Native Administration. The number of Native Court Areas was greatly increased and their boundaries arranged to conform roughly to traditional divisions. Warrant Chiefs were replaced by "massed benches" allowing large numbers of judges to sit at one time. In most cases it was left up to the village to decide whom and how many to send.[51] This benefitted the women by eliminating the corruption of the Warrant Chiefs, and it made their persons and property more secure. But it provided no outlet for collective action, their real base of power.

---

46 Harry A. Gailey, *op. cit., pp. 130ff.*

47 Sylvia Leith-Ross, op. cit., p. 165; Margery Perham, *Native Administration in Nigeria, op. cit.,* pp. 165ff.

48 Margery Perham, *Native Administration in Nigeria, op. cit.,* p. 246.

49 A. E. Afigbo, *op. cit.,* p. 187.

50 C. K. Meek, *op. cit.,* p. 336.

51 Margery Perham, *Native Administration in Nigeria, op. cit.,* pp. 365ff.

As in the village assembly, the women could not compete with the men for leadership in the reformed Native Administration because as individuals they lacked the resources of the men.[52] In the various studies done on the Igbo in the 1930's, there is only one report of a woman being sent to the Native Court and her patrilineage had put up the money for her to take her titles.[53]

Since the reformed Native Administration usually took over many functions of the village assemblies, women's political participation was seriously affected. Discussions on policy no longer included any adult who wished to take part but only members of the native courts. Men who were not members were also excluded, but men's interests and point of view were represented, and, at one time or another, many men had some chance to become members; very few women ever did.[54]

The political participation and power of women had depended on the diffuseness of political power and authority within Igbo society. In attempting to create specialized political institutions on the Western model with participation on the basis of individual achievement, the British created a system in which there was no place for group solidarity, no place for what thereby became "extra-legal" or simply illegal forms of group coercion, and thus very little place for women.

The British reforms undermined and weakened the power of the women by removing many political functions from *mikiri* and from village assemblies. In 1901 the British had declared all jural institutions except the Native Courts illegitimate, but it was only in the years following the 1933 reforms that Native Administration local government became effective enough to make that declaration meaningful. When this happened, the *mikiri* lost vitality,[55] although what has happened to them since has not been reported in detail. The reports that do exist mention the functioning of market women's organizations but only as pressure groups for narrow economic interest[56] and women's participation in Igbo unions as very low in two towns.[57]

The British also weakened women's power by outlawing "self-help"—the use of force by individuals or groups to protect their own interests by punishing

---

52 C. K. Meek, *op. cit.*, p. 203.

53 *Ibid.*, pp. 158–159. She was divorced and had to remain unmarried as a condition of her family's paying for her title as they wanted to be sure to get their investment back when future initiates paid their fees to the established members. If she remarried, her husband's family, and not her own, would inherit her property.

54 Sylvia Leith-Ross, *op. cit.*, pp. 171–72; Lord Hailey, *Native Administration in the British African Territories, Part III, West Africa* (London: H. M. Stationary Office, 1951), pp. 160–65.

55 Sylvia Leith-Ross, *op. cit.*, pp. 110, 163, 214.

56 Henry L. Bretton, "Political Influence in Southern Nigeria," in Herbert J. Spiro (ed.), *Africa: The Primacy of Politics* (New York: Random House, 1966), p. 61.

57 Audrey C. Smock, *Ibo Politics: The Role of Ethnic Unions in Eastern Nigeria* (Cambridge: The Harvard University Press, 1971), pp. 65,137.

wrongdoers. This action—in accord with the idea that only the state may legitimately use force—made "sitting on" anyone illegal, thereby depriving women of one of their best weapons to protect wives from husbands, markets from rowdies, or coco yams from cows.[58]

The British didn't know, of course, that they were banning "sitting on a man"; they were simply banning the "illegitimate" use of force. In theory, this didn't hurt the women, as wife-beaters, rowdies and owners of marauding cows could be taken to court. But courts were expensive, and the men who sat in them were likely to have different views from the women's on wife-beating, market "fun" and men's cows. By interfering with the traditional balance of power, the British effectively eliminated the women's ability to protect their own interests and made them dependent upon men for protection against men.

Since the British did not understand this, they did nothing to help women develop new ways of protecting their interests within the political system. (What the women *did* do to try to protect their interests in this situation should be a fruitful subject for study.) What women did *not* do was to participate to any significant extent in local government or, much later, in national government, and a large part of the responsibility must rest on the British, who removed legitimacy from women's traditional political institutions and did nothing to help women move into modern political institutions.

Missionary Influence

The effect of the colonial administration was reinforced by the missionaries and mission schools. Christian missions were established in Igboland in the late 19th century. They had few converts at first, but their influence by the 1930's was considered significant, generally among the young.[59] A majority of Igbo eventually "became Christians"—they had to profess Christianity in order to attend mission schools, and education was highly valued. But regardless of how nominal their membership was, they had to obey the rules to remain in good standing, and one rule was to avoid "pagan" rituals. Women were discouraged from attending *mikiri* where traditional rituals were performed or money collected for the rituals, which in effect meant all *mikiri*.[60]

---

58 Sylvia Leith-Ross, *op. cit.*, p. 109.

59 *Ibid.*, pp. 109–18; C. K. Meek, *op. cit.*, p. xv. Maxwell states that by 1925 there were 26 mission stations and 63 missionaries (twelve of them missionary wives) in Igboland. The earliest station was established in 1857, but all but three were founded after 1900. Fifteen mission stations and 30 missionaries were among Igbo in Owerri and Calabar Provinces. See J. Lowry Maxwell, *Nigeria: The Land, the People and Christian Progress* (London: World Dominion Press, 1926), pp. 150–52.

60 Sylvia Leith-Ross, *op. cit.*, p. 110; J. F. Ade Ajayi, *Christian Missions in Nigeria, 1841–1891: The Making of a New Elite* (Evanston, Ill.: The Northwestern

Probably more significant, since *mikiri* were in the process of losing some of their political functions anyway, was mission education. English and Western education came to be seen as increasingly necessary for political leadership—needed to deal with the British and their law—and women had less access to this new knowledge than men. Boys were more often sent to school, for a variety of reasons generally related to their favored position in the patrilineage.[61] But even when girls did go, they tended not to receive the same type of education. In mission schools, and increasingly in special "training homes" which dispensed with most academic courses, the girls were taught European domestic skills and the Bible, often in the vernacular. The missionaries' avowed purpose in educating girls was to train them to be Christian wives and mothers, not for jobs or for citizenship.[62] Missionaries were not necessarily against women's participation in politics—clergy in England, as in America, could be found supporting women's suffrage. But in Africa their concern was the church, and for the church they needed Christian families. Therefore, Christian wives and mothers, not female political leaders, was the missions' aim. As Mary Slessor, the influential Calabar missionary, said: "God-like motherhood is the finest sphere for women, and the way to the redemption of the world."[63]

Victorianism and Women's Invisibility

The missionaries' beliefs about woman's natural and proper role being that of a Christian helpmate, and the administration's refusal to take the Igbo women seriously when they demanded political participation, are understandable in light of the colonialists having been socialized in a society dominated by Victorian values. It was during Queen Victoria's reign that the woman's-place-is-in-the-home ideology hardened into its most recent highly rigid form.[64] Although attacked by feminists, it remained the dominant mode of thought through that

University Press, 1965), pp. 108–09.

61 Sylvia Leith-Ross, *op. cit.*, pp. 133, 196–97, 316.

62 *Ibid.*, pp. 189–90. According to Leith-Ross, in the "girls' training homes . . . the scholastic education given was limited, in some of the smaller homes opened at a later date almost negligible, but the domestic training and the general civilizing effect were good." Evidence of these views among missionaries can be found in J. F. Ade Ajayi, *op. cit.*, pp. 67, 142–44; G. T. Basden, *Edith Sarner of the Niger* (London: Seeley, Service and Co., Ltd., 1927), pp. 13, 16, 33, 55, 77, 86; Josephine C. Bulifant, *Forty Years in the African Bush* (Grand Rapids, Mich.: Zondervan Publishing House, 1950), pp. 163 and *passim;* W. P. Livingstone, *Mary Slessor of Calabar* (New York: George H. Doran Co., n.d.), pp. iii–vi; J. Lowry Maswell, *op. cit.*, pp. 55,118.

63 W. P. Livingstone, *op. cit.*, p. 328.

64 Page Smith, *Daughters of the Promised Land* (Boston: Little, Brown and Co. 1970).

part of the colonial period discussed here; and it is, in fact, far from dead today, when a woman's primary identity is most often seen as that of wife and mother even when she works 40 hours a week outside the home.[65]

We are concerned here primarily with the Victorian view of women and politics which produced the expectation that men would be active in politics, but women would not. The ideal of Victorian womanhood-attainable, of course, by only the middle class, but widely believed in throughout society-was of a sensitive, morally superior being who was the hearthside guardian of Christian virtues and sentiments absent in the outside world. Her mind was not strong enough for the appropriately masculine subjects: science, business, and politics.[66] A woman who showed talent in these areas did not challenge any ideas about typical women: the exceptional woman simply "had the brain of a man," as Sir George Goldie said of Mary Kingsley.[67]

A thorough investigation of the diaries, journals, reports, and letters of colonial officers and missionaries would be needed to prove that most of them held these Victorian values. But preliminary reading of biographies, autobiographies, journals and "reminiscences," and the evidence of their own statements about Igbo women at the time of the Women's War, strongly suggest the plausibility of the hypothesis that they were deflected from any attempt to discover and protect Igbo women's political role by their assumption that politics isn't a proper, normal place for women.[68]

---

65 Eva Figes, *Patriarchal Attitudes* (New York: Stein and Day, 1970); Ruth E. Hartley, "Children's Concepts of Male and Female Roles', *Merrill-Palmer Quarterly,* January 1960.

66 Walter E. Houghton, *The Victorian Frame of Mind, 1830-1870* (New Haven: The Yale University Press, 1957), pp. 349-53. Numerous studies of Victorian and post-Victorian ideas about women and politics describe these patterns. In addition to Houghton, Smith and Stenton, see, for example, Kirsten Amundsen, *The Silenced Majority* (Prentice-Hall, 1970); and Harriet Taylor Mill, *Essays on Sex Equality* (University of Chicago Press, 1970); Martha Vicinus (ed.), Suffer *and Be Still: Women in the Victorian Age* (Indiana University Press, 1972); *Cecil* Woodham-Smith, *Florence Nightingale, 1820-1910* (McGraw-Hill, 1951). It was not until 1929 that all English women could vote; women over 30 who met restrictive property qualifications got the vote in 1918.

67 Stephen Gwynn, *The Life of Mary Kingsley* (London: Macmillan and Co., Ltd., 1932), p. 252. Mary Kingley, along with other elite female "exceptions" like Flora Shaw Lugard and Pargery, all of whom influenced African colonial policy, held the same values as men, at least in regard to women's roles. They did not expect ordinary women to have political power any more than the men did, and they showed no particular concern for African women.

68 See, for non-missionary examples, J. C. Anene, *op. cit.,* pp. 222–34; W. R. Crocker, *Nigeria: a Critique of British Colonial Administration* (London: George Allen and Unwin, Ltd., 1936); C. K. Meek, *op. cit.;* Mary H. Kingsley, *Travels in*

When Igbo women with their Women's War forced the colonial administrators to recognize their presence, their brief "visibility" was insufficient to shake these assumptions. Their behavior was simply seen as aberrant. When they returned to "normal," they were once again invisible. Although there was a feminist movement in England during that time, it had not successfully challenged basic ideas about women nor made the absence of women from public life seem to be a problem which required remedy. The movement had not succeeded in creating a "feminist" consciousness in any but a few "deviants," and such a consciousness is far from widespread today; for to have a "feminist" consciousness means that one *notices* the "invisibility" of women.

Understanding the assumptions about women's roles prevalent in Victorian society—and still common today—helps to explain how the introduction of supposedly modern political structures and values could reduce rather than expand the political lives of Igbo women. As long as politics is presumed to be a male realm, no one wonders where the women went. The loss of Igbo women's political institutions—in life and in print—shows the need for more Western scholars to develop enough of a feminist consciousness to start wondering.

West Aftica (London: Macmillan and Co., Ltd., 1897); Idem, *West African Studies* (London: Macmillan and Co;, Ltd., 1899); Margery Perham, *op. cit.;* A. H. St. John Wood, "Nigeria: Fifty Years of Political Development among the Ibos," in Raymond Apthorpe (ed.), *From Tribal Rule to Modern Government* (Lusaka, Northern Rhodesia: Rhodes-Livingstone Institute for Social Research, 1960).

Hausa Dilemma Tales

The traditional dilemma tales belong to the Hausa of Northern Nigeria. Instrumental in the ethical upbringing of the youth, the stories are part of the oral culture, and they illustrate how Islam as well as older traditions inform ethical conduct among the Hausa. Typically told during evening gatherings, each tale develops a complicated human situation and ends with an irresolute dilemma for both the protagonist and the young listeners. In "Who Should He Kill?" for instance, a son is asked to kill either his natural father or his adoptive father. The purpose of the dilemma tales is not so much to "teach" correct ethical behavior as it is to engage youngsters in a lively discussion about ethical values among themselves so that they seek and understand the right and the wrong through collective reasoning. More specifically, the tales demonstrate two crucial aspects of ethical decision-making: that it takes place in a public context, and that understanding the subtle difficulties of a human situation is, at the least, as important as passing judgment on its ethical correctness.

Aron Aji

Who Should He Kill?

There was once a man who did no other job but digging out pesky ground squirrels. Taking his son to work with him one day, he said, "You stop up the back entrances, and I'll dig." But when the father set about digging in the ground squirrel's hole, the ground squirrel came out where the son was, and made off. Then the father hit his son and with the handle of his hoe and knocked him senseless.

A little later in the evening, up came an Arab taking a stroll, and he saw the son of the squirrel digger, who was just coming to his senses. Now this Arab had never had any children, so he picked up the boy and took him home. His nose was dirty and full of ants, and the Arab wiped them away and had him bathed in hot water. When the boy recovered completely, the Arab dressed him in a black

---

and white gown, embroidered trousers, and a heavily indigoed gown, as well, with a turban twenty cubits long and twenty strips wide.

Now in this area, the rich merchants' sons used to ride and compete at the racetrack. The Arab brought out a saddle ornamented in gold and silver, with brass stirrups from Tripoli, and all the other trappings for a horse. Then he told the boy to mount up, and said to him, "When you get to the track, whatever you see the other riders do—you do it, too!" So the boy joined the rich merchants' sons and went along with them. Some great arguments arose among the people over whose son he was, but no one knew the truth.

When the merchants' sons got home, each one said to his father, "There's an Arab who has a son who has more finery than we have." And their fathers answered, "No, it's not really his son. That's false." But they added, "All the same, we will test him. Tomorrow when you go riding with him, let each one give away his horse and equipment before he comes home. Then we'll see! For generosity is the way to demonstrate true wealth."

So the sons went out the next day, and afterwards they gave away their horses. And watching carefully, the Arab's boy, too, gave away his horse.

After this, the merchants gave their sons other horses, each worth a million cowries, and told them, "When you go riding, before you come home, cut down your horses!" And the Arab's boy was given a horse worth ten million. When they had had their gallop, each one took his sword and cut down his horse. Then the Arab's boy, without even troubling to take the saddle off, cut down his horse and went off home. And they said, "Did you see? He cut down his horse," and again, "Well! The Arab's boy didn't even take off the horse's equipment; he left it there." Then people said, "So it seems he is his son after all!"

Time passed and the Muslim festival was at hand. In the morning, the usual mounted procession took place, and in all the town, there wasn't a youth whose horse was fitted out to touch the Arab's. And as they were coming back from the mosque, they passed among the common people who had come from the country into the town for prayers.

Well, it happened that the squirrel digger, the real father of the boy, had come to town for the festival and had joined the crowd. When he saw his son, he exclaimed, "Hey! Get down from that horse—you know it's not your own father's, you rascal! Look at your brothers there—one of them has killed nine ground squirrels, one of them ten, and you—here are you in dissipation and idleness!" And the Arab said to him, "Please, please keep it to yourself! Here—take your son!"

And in the evening, the Arab chose two horses and saddled them up, picked out two gowns, a black one and a white one, and gave them to the boy's father. And the Arab gave him twenty thousand cowry shells and provisions for the journey. Then all three mounted up and rode out.

They left the town and came into the bush. Suddenly, the Arab produced a sword and gave it to the boy, saying, "Now! Either me or your father——cut down one of us!"

Well that's the question—the Arab, who had given him so many things? Or his own father, who had struck him unconscious because of the ground squirrel? Which should he kill?

An Eye for an Eye?

The son of a chief once heard tell of the beautiful daughter of another chief and set off to visit her. And as he traveled, he met a young fellow. He said, "Young man, I'd like you to come with me, for I'm off to seek a wife." "Oh, no," said the other, "for I have a father who has nothing, neither gown nor trousers nor loincloth; and this leather loincloth that you see me wearing is all that we have between us, my father and I. If my father is going out from our hole in the baobab tree, then he takes it and puts it on; and I do the same when I'm going out." "Where is your father?" asked the chief's son. "Over there, in the hole in the baobab tree." And the chief's son asked to be taken to him.

And off they went. When the boy got to the hole in the baobab tree, he said "Daddy, look! I was out walking, I met the son of a chief who said he wanted me to go with him to seek a wife. But I answered that I must come and tell you first and hear whatever you had to say about it." "By all means go along with him," answered his father. And the chief's son said, "Take the leather loincloth off and give it to your father." And the chief's son had a traveling bag opened and a gown taken out, and trousers, and a turban, and a cap, and a sword, and sword sling, and all these together were given to the other. And he had him shaved and bathed, too.

And so they took the road and traveled till they reached the other town. When word was brought to the chief's daughter that she had visitors, they were taken to lodgings. She had food prepared for them—three rams were slaughtered, and chickens, too.

Soon the chief's daughter rose and came to them. But when she got there, her heart went out to the servant of the chief's son, he whose father lived in the hole of the tree. And she spoke and said that he was the one she loved. "No, no!" he said, "I wouldn't dare. See, here's my master." "No," she answered, "You're the one I love." But again he protested that he and his father had nothing, but lived in a hole in baobab tree, and added, "Even the clothes that I'm wearing were given me by the chief's son here." "Oh," she replied, "is that all?"

She sent home to her father's compound, asking for two carrying bags, one with a gown, and one with trousers; and she sent for a turban, as well. All her wishes were conveyed to her father, who got together everything she had asked for, and handed it over to her. Then she said, "Take those things off, and return them to him. Take these and put them on." "Very well," he answered, and did as she had said. He collected the chief's son's clothes, and returned them to him.

So the chief's son set off home alone, leaving the son of the man with the leather loincloth. For the chief's daughter had decided it was he that she loved.

Then she went and told her father, saying, "Father, today I want to be married." "Very well," he said, and so they were married.

Time passed and her father died. His large estate was duly divided and she inherited it all as he had no sons or other daughters. Her mother left the chief's compound and had a separate compound built for herself. Then the girl said to her husband, "Where is your father? Let someone go and fetch him, and let him and my mother be married." And he answered, "He's back there in the hole in the baobab tree."

They went and fetched him, and when they returned, the marriage duly took place and so they lived for some time.

But after a while there came a time when the elder couple had a quarrel and the father of the girl's husband knocked his wife down, striking out one of her eyes. The girl then said, angrily, "Your father has quarreled with my mother and knocked her eye out. If you value our marriage, you'll go and put out one of your father's eyes. If you don't, take your leather loincloth, and you and your father can go back to your hole in the baobab tree. But if you do, then let our marriage continue." Well, here was a nice problem! He had been quite destitute. If he put out his own father's eye, he might continue to live with his wife; but if he didn't, then he must go back with his father to the hole in the baobab tree, whence they had come!

The Devil Comes between Them

A youth once saw a maiden and told her that he loved her; she saw him and told him the same. So the young fellow went and picked up his sleeping mat, took the girl by the hand, and went off with her into the bush. There the boy spread out the mat and invited the girl to sit. The two sat and chatted. *Iblis* the devil came by that way, seized the boy, killed him, and then cut off his head. The girl could do nothing but sit on the mat and lament.

Meanwhile both mothers and both fathers were searching for their son and daughter. An old woman told them where they should look for them. Thanking her, they went quickly off down the road, where, the boy's parents found their son killed, with his head taken off. At this, they began to lament, as well.

Suddenly, up came *Iblis* again. He made a river of fire, and a river of water, and a river of black-hooded cobras, and in this last he placed a land monitor. Then he went up to the group—the girl's mother and her father, and the boy's mother and his father, and the girl herself—and said to them, "Would you like me to help you recover your son and bring him back to life?" "Of course!" they answered. "Very well," he said, "You, the boy's mother, must go into the river of fire, and then into the river of water, and then into the river of cobras, where you must seize the land monitor and bring it out." But the boy's mother answered, "No! I'm not going into a river of fire to be burnt up, nor am I going into the river of cobras, to be thoroughly bitten." *Iblis* said, "Had you gone and captured the land monitor, I'd have helped you with your son."

Whereupon the girl said, "Is that so? If that land monitor is captured and brought here, will the boy come to life?" "Yes," said *Iblis*. Up jumped the girl and swam across the river of fire. Then she plunged into the river of water and swam till she was through it. Then into the river of cobras, where pushing aside the slithering snakes, she seized the land monitor. Back she came through the rivers, and handed the lizard to *Iblis*.

Then, said *Iblis*, "So! So you've got the land monitor for me?" And the boy came to life and stood up. Then *Iblis* spoke again, saying, "Now, if this land monitor is slaughtered, the boy's mother will die, but if it isn't slaughtered, the girl's mother will die."

Well then—is the boy going to slaughter the land monitor, so that his own mother dies or will he spare it, so that the girl's mother dies? Which of the two will he choose do you think?

A Spirited Contending

There were once two young men who were courting the same girl, and each man had two spears. One day, on their way home with her, they passed through the bush, and a lion waylaid them. The girl fell down saying that her stomach was paining her. The lion leapt at them, and the first youth threw his spear, but the lion dodged and the spear fell to the ground. The youth threw his second spear also, and that, too, fell to the ground.

In his turn, the other young fellow. stepped forward and he, too, threw a spear, but like the rest it just fell to the ground. Then he threw his second spear, but again he missed the lion. So all their spears were used up and still the beast hadn't been hit.

Then one of the two youths said to the other, "Hurry, and run home. In my mother's hut, at the head of the bed, you'll find some spears. Bring them, and some water in a calabash, and some potash, too." At once, the boy ran off to do these things.

Meanwhile, the other young fellow leapt at the lion, and after a struggle, threw him, and taking his knife cut his throat. Then he lifted the lion into a squatting position, and the girl came over and lay down beside the lion. The youth got behind the mane and hid.

Soon the one who had left returned with the spears, the water, and the potash, but he couldn't find the other youth and the girl. A little further on, he bumped into the lion crouching there, with the girl lying in front of him, but he didn't recognize her. He said to himself, "So that was the trick was it? The two went off and ran away, and left the lion to kill someone else's child! Well, then, I can't let the lion live to do that again." And tossing away his spears and his little calabash of water and the potash, he threw himself at the lion. He grappled with it, and the lion, of course, fell right over. The girl and the other boy got up laughing.

Well then—which of the two, the boy who killed the lion, or the other boy who went and fetched the spears and the little calabash of water and the potash—which of the two of them showed greater spirit?